DIRTY OLD LONDON

THE VICTORIAN FIGHT AGAINST FILTH

LEE JACKSON

YALE UNIVERSITY PRESS
NEW HAVEN AND LONDON

For information about this and other Yale University Press publications, please contact:

U.S. Office: sales.press@yale.edu   www.yalebooks.com
Europe Office: sales@yaleup.co.uk   www.yalebooks.co.uk

Typeset in Adobe Garamond Pro by IDSUK (DataConnection) Ltd
Printed in Great Britain by Hobbs the Printers Ltd, Totton, Hampshire

Library of Congress Cataloging-in-Publication Data

Jackson, Lee, 1971–
    Dirty old London: the Victorian fight against filth/Lee Jackson.
        pages cm
    ISBN 978-0-300-19205-6 (cl: alk. paper)
1. London (England)—History—19th century.   2. Sanitation—England—
London—History—19th century.   3. London (England)—Social conditions—
19th century.   I. Title.
    DA683.J17 2014
    363.7009421'09034—dc23

                                                            2014014234

A catalogue record for this book is available from the British Library.

ISBN 978-0-300-21611-0 (pbk)

10 9 8 7 6 5 4 3 2 1

CONTENTS

INTRODUCTION

IN 1899, THE Chinese ambassador was asked his opinion of Victorian London at the zenith of its imperial grandeur. He replied, laconically, 'too dirty'.[1] He was only stating the obvious. Thoroughfares were swamped with black mud, composed principally of horse dung, forming a tenacious, glutinous paste; the air was peppered with soot, flakes of filth tumbling to the ground 'in black Plutonian show'rs'.[2] The distinctive smell of the city was equally unappealing. Winter fogs brought mephitic sulphurous stinks. The summer months, on the other hand, created their own obnoxious cocktail, 'that combined odour of stale fruit and vegetables, rotten eggs, foul tobacco, spilt beer, rank cart-grease, dried soot, smoke, triturated road-dust and damp straw'.[3] London was the heart of the greatest empire ever known; a financial and mercantile hub for the world; but it was also infamously filthy. The American journalist Mary H. Krout, visiting London for the Diamond Jubilee of 1897, found Londoners' response to the dirt strangely apathetic. She felt sure that, if the same conditions were visited upon Washington or New York, some solution would have been found.[4]

This was a peculiar state of affairs. The Victorians, after all, had invented 'sanitary science' – the study of public health, dirt and disease – and considered cleanliness the hallmark of civilisation. Moreover, they had not been idle. London had seen millions of pounds invested in a vast network of modern sewers. This was a gargantuan project, planned and managed by Joseph Bazalgette of the Metropolitan Board of Works, and brought to fruition in the

1860s – a concrete testament to the importance accorded 'sanitary reform'. Indeed, mile upon mile of meticulously executed brickwork still survives beneath modern streets, and popular histories regularly credit Bazalgette as 'the man who cleaned up London' – which only makes the filthy condition of the late-Victorian metropolis all the more baffling.

In fact, the Victorian passion for sewerage – and latter-day awe at Bazalgette's engineering genius – has obscured the true history of metropolitan dirt. The fight against filth was waged throughout Victoria's reign on many fronts, with numerous battles ending in stalemate or defeat. Reforming zeal was frequently met with plain indifference. The stench of overflowing dustbins, dung-filled thoroughfares, the choking soot-filled atmosphere – even the peculiar history of the public toilet – these are as much part of the (in)sanitary history of Victorian London as the more familiar story of its sewers. The aim of this book is to give these overlooked aspects of 'dirty old London' their due; and to explain why, far from cleansing the great metropolis, the Victorians left it thoroughly begrimed.

The capital's century-long struggle with filth was intimately connected with its unprecedented growth. Between 1801 and 1901, the population of London soared from one million to over six million. Suburbia replaced green fields, 'crushing up the country in its concrete grasp'.[5] Waste products multiplied in due proportion, whether smoke from household fires or mud from ever-increasing horse traffic. Some types of dirt posed a challenge in terms of the sheer volume of unwanted matter; others contained a real or perceived danger to public health. Nuisance and discomfort abounded. Some saw metropolitan dirt as the harbinger of moral decay. Filth implied social and domestic disorder; and, when discovered in the home, inculcated immoral habits – for it was widely agreed that working men, faced with poor housekeeping, sought refuge in the glittering comforts of the gin palace.

The worst types of filth, solely in terms of volume, were human excrement; mud on the streets; and 'dust' (cinders and ash from coal fires). In the eighteenth century, their disposal had been less problematic. Human waste was stored in household cesspools, emptied occasionally by 'night soil men', who sold it to farmers as manure. Mud was swept up by parish contractors, and, likewise, sold as fertiliser. Ashes and cinders were collected by dustmen and sold to brickmakers, who added the ash to their bricks, and used cinders as fuel. These tried-and-tested recycling arrangements, however, were not suited to the expanding nineteenth-century metropolis. The brickfields, market gardens and farms grew ever more distant; the country more separate from the town. Transport costs mushroomed; and the sheer volume of refuse produced by Londoners began to outstrip any possible demand – 'such a vast amount of sheer useless rubbish'.[6] Simply finding somewhere to put the mess became a problem.

Nineteenth-century Londoners also grew increasingly apprehensive about the health risks associated with dirt. This heightened awareness is generally associated with the 'sanitary movement' of the 1840s – when public health reform became the subject of intense national debate – but its roots go further back. Doctors at the London Fever Hospital were attempting to organise systematic cleansing of the slums, to eradicate typhus, as early as 1801. The smoke from factories and furnaces was damned in parliament as 'prejudicial to public health and public comfort' in 1819. Fears about water pollution were first raised in the 1820s, when wealthier households began to connect more and more water closets to the main drainage, which ultimately fed into the Thames. In 1827, a pamphlet was issued which pointed out that a west London water company was drawing its domestic supply from the river at Chelsea, within a few yards of a sewer outfall. When a doctor examined the resultant murky-looking tap water, 'the very sight of the turbid fluid seemed to occasion a turmoil in his stomach'.[7] The gentlefolk of Westminster, although accustomed to a degree of mud and sediment, were shocked to discover they had actually been imbibing a solution composed of their own 'ejectamenta'.

The important link between drinking-water and disease would, admittedly, not be fully recognised for several decades; and even Bazalgette's sewers would be built on the widely held, mistaken assumption that 'miasma' (foul air, generated by decaying matter) was the cause of cholera and typhoid. Indeed, the connection between dirt, *smell* and disease was a source of ongoing anxiety, not limited to sewers. The refusal of dustmen to remove household waste from slums (largely because slum inhabitants could not provide tips) generated its own worrying stench. Many a backstreet contained 'a sort of pigstye' accommodating the refuse of dozens of households: 'cinders, bones, oyster-shells, broken bottles and rag, flavoured by a sprinkling of decaying vegetable matter, or a remnant of putrefying fish, or a dead and decomposing kitten'.[8] The repellent odour from overcrowded, poorly maintained metropolitan burial grounds was the catalyst for a lengthy campaign in favour of the introduction of out-of-town cemeteries.

The sheer public nuisance occasioned by dirt should not be under-estimated. Again, foreigners marvelled at locals' toleration of filthy streets ('An American town-bred lady would as soon think of swimming up the Thames against tide as walking far in such ankle-deep mud').[9] Added to mud was general litter, varying from the relatively harmless – 'old newspapers, cast-off shoes, and crownless hats'[10] – to broken glass and mouldering food. Lady F.W. Harberton, inveighing against the fashionable 'train' in female dress (i.e. a trailing skirt), presented the following gruesome inventory to her readers, of relics recovered from a train allowed to drag along the Piccadilly pavement: '2 cigar ends; 9 cigarette ditto; A portion of pork pie; 4 toothpicks; 2 hairpins; 1 stem of a clay pipe; 3 fragments of orange peel; 1 slice of cat's meat; Half a sole of a boot; 1 plug of tobacco (chewed); Straw, mud, scraps of paper, and miscellaneous street refuse, *ad.lib*'.[11]

The air, meanwhile, was vitiated by smoke. Ladies of refinement were advised to wash the face repeatedly, to remove the fine patina of soot that accompanied every sojourn outdoors ('if one lives in dear, dirty old London, or in any smoky city, three times a day is none too often').[12] Clothing was continually sullied by cascades of 'blacks', i.e. soot-flakes. Public buildings, parks, gardens, statuary – everything outdoors acquired a dull, dirty coating, making London 'a city in which no beautiful thing, on which art and trouble has been bestowed, can long keep its beauty'.[13] When winter came, there was the additional danger of soot-drenched fogs. Tourists marvelled at a popula-tion that could accustom itself to days spent in complete darkness; doctors noted the rising mortality from bronchitis and other pulmonary complaints. The capital ended the century with the nickname of 'The Smoke' – a city named after its most enduring pollutant.

There were various bodies responsible for clearing up this mess, some more serviceable than others.

Managing dust and mud fell to London's vestries – the backbone of local government – parish committees composed of eminent ratepayers. Vestries, in turn, usually employed private contractors to remove refuse, largely because contractors were often willing to work for free. The potential profits from selling on dust to the brick trade were such that entrepreneurs vied for exclusive rights to empty household bins. Many even paid for the privilege, or cleaned the streets at a discount. Unfortunately, whilst vestrymen congratulated themselves on the economy of this arrangement, the public often suffered. When demand for bricks dropped – e.g. when the stock market bubble of the mid-1820s burst, and the building trade slumped – the demand for dust plummeted. Contractors went bankrupt; dustmen and street cleaners disappeared; complaints about unemptied bins were legion ('Bribes offered to the dustmen, complaints lodged at the Court-house, and appeal to Hobbs, the dust contractor, have all alike been utterly futile').[14] Construction booms – e.g. during the railway mania of the 1840s – which encouraged brickmakers to over-produce and stockpile, with the inevitable drop in prices, had a similar knock-on effect.

The vestry system was reformed in the mid-century, amalgamating smaller authorities into 'district boards', and abolishing various antiquated arrangements. Some of the new vestries began to take over cleansing work from contractors. Ratepayers, however, were sceptical that officialdom could provide a better service. Lord Shaftesbury damned local government as full of 'obstinate and parsimonious wretches'; others preferred the Dickensian catch-all of 'Bumbledom', with its overtones of pomposity and self-interest. In truth, sanitary enthusiasm and activity varied from district to district. Some local authorities were better organised than others; some were wealthier. Revenue from the rates would not be put into a collective metropolitan pot until the 1890s. For most of the century, therefore, West End parishes had considerably more money to spend on sanitary matters than their pauper-ridden counterparts in the east.

London's sewerage, unlike dust and mud, was not parish business. At the start of the century, sewers were mainly the responsibility of eight ancient Sewer Commissions, each with its own portion of the capital. Londoners, however, had no more respect for these officials than for vestrydom. Their work would be derided in the 1840s as 'a vast monument of defective administration, lavish expenditure and extremely defective execution'.[15] They would ultimately be replaced by the Metropolitan Board of Works, which would commission Bazalgette's masterwork, incorporating 82 miles of tunnels, ornate pumping stations and the Thames Embankment. Yet even this much vaunted improvement was imperfect. The new sewer system removed filth and stink from central London, only to shift it upstream to Beckton and Crossness. When sewage was discharged, twice a day, the river seemed to revolt against the imposition, 'hissing like soda-water with baneful gases, so black that the water is stained for miles, and discharging a corrupt charnel-house odour'.[16] In the

1850s, this was not terribly troublesome – the new sewage outfalls were several miles beyond London's boundaries. By the 1880s, the volume of sewage had grown and the spread of the East End had outpaced Bazalgette's 'out of sight, out of mind' solution. The inhabitants of new working-class suburbs like East Ham found their lives blighted by the same stench of decomposing excrement which had once troubled the inhabitants of Westminster. Worse still, more and more filth was swept back on the estuarine tide towards central London.

Smoke proved an equally intractable problem. Legislation was introduced in 1853 to reduce factory emissions, with some success; and the police were deputised to watch factory chimneys for infractions. Yet the voluminous filth poured into the atmosphere by tens of thousands of domestic coal fires went completely unchallenged by parliament. Prolonged, black winter fogs prompted reformers to try to persuade householders to invest in 'smoke consuming' grates. The English, however, were too fond of the cheery, blazing hearth, the symbol of cosy domesticity, and content to take the consequences, even as the soot filled their lungs. The overwhelming public response to agitation on the 'smoke nuisance' was the grim resignation which Miss Krout found so mystifying on the eve of the Jubilee.

There were, of course, some worthwhile reforms. The introduction of extra-mural cemeteries put a definitive end to noxious, overcrowded burial grounds, and the gruesome churn of bodies by gravediggers ('I have severed heads, arms, legs, or whatever came in my way, with a crowbar, pickaxe, chopper and saw').[17] The London County Council, established in 1889, took an interest in all things 'sanitary' and would prosecute local authorities for failure to carry out regular collections of rubbish. There were also magnificent new facilities for communal cleansing, including public baths and public toilets (although the latter were a long time coming). The improvement of slum housing, prin-cipally through social housing schemes established by various 'model housing' charities, also had a modest but measurable impact on the filth-ridden lives of some working-class families.

Nonetheless, at the very end of the Victorian era, it was remarkably diffi-cult to gainsay the damning, undiplomatic remark of the Chinese ambas-sador. London was, without question, 'too dirty'. This book will examine the nature of that dirt; tally both the successes and failures of reformers; and consider why filth emerged triumphant.

1

THE GOLDEN DUSTMAN

THE HUMBLE DUSTMAN, the collector of household refuse, was a familiar figure on London's streets. In the early 1800s, he wore 'a fan-tailed hat, loose flannel jacket, velveteen red breeches, worsted stockings, short gaiters'.[1] This traditional get-up was protective clothing and its key elements would not change during the century. The hat with a long reversed brim of canvas material, trailing over the back of the neck, prevented filth from shouldered baskets of rubbish entering clothes. Gaiters and/or straps and buckles offered similar protection to the legs and feet. It was a distinctive outfit which also served as the unofficial uniform of the trade, albeit supplied by the dustman himself, not his employer. The distributors of coal wore a similar working costume, including the fantail hat, but they were easily distinguished. Coalmen and their clothes were always black with coal dust; dustmen were uniformly grey, covered in cinders and ash, which formed the vast bulk of household waste.

Dustmen began their rounds early in the morning, working in pairs, driving a high-sided horse-drawn cart, announcing their presence with the loud toll of a handbell or a hearty shout of 'dust ho!'[2] Collection was very much an 'on request' service. Householders or servants, if they wanted rubbish to be removed, were expected to catch the dustman's attention. This was partly a matter of age-old custom, and partly because domestic bins were not portable. They were typically fixed brick or wooden bunkers (known variously as the 'dust-bin', 'dust-hole' or 'ashpit'),[3] situated unobtrusively in the basement area, backyard or back garden. Someone from the house, therefore, needed to be present, to provide access to the bin and generally supervise proceedings. This was particularly important when a property lacked a basement or side-entrance and the dustman had to walk, back and forth, through the main hallway, to bring out several loads of filth. This troublesome progress was rarely accomplished 'without leaving some trace of his visit on the wall-paper or floor'.[4]

There were some cases of street collection. In the crowded, central areas of London, especially in areas like Soho where shops and houses had no basement area at the front of the house, and little in the way of gardens or yards, rubbish would be left outside the front door in 'wooden boxes, tin pails, zinc bins and every conceivable vessel'.[5] Nonetheless, most London homes retained an old-fashioned static bin until the turn of the twentieth century, emptied on a rather ad hoc basis. The practicalities of emptying such bins did not change. At the dust-hole itself, one dustman would act as the 'filler', shovelling the dust into a large wicker basket. His workmate would act as the 'carrier', shouldering the basket and carrying it out to the open cart. Some bins had a sliding panel, allowing the contents to spill out on to the ground, to facilitate shovelling; and the dustcart was usually equipped with a ladder so that the carrier could climb up high enough to deposit his load. When their cart was full, the dustmen would go to 'shoot' the rubbish at their employer's 'dust-yard' – essentially a recycling centre, where refuse was stored by the contractor, to be sorted and sold on. A pair of dustmen could usually manage to fill four or five cartloads in a day.

In theory, this process was straightforward enough. There were, however, several recurring, long-standing sources of friction between householder (or servant) and refuse collector.

First, getting the dustman's attention could prove difficult. The onus was on the household to avail itself of the dustman's services. Arguments over houses being missed out were commonplace, particularly as dustcarts often came at unexpected hours, no more than once a week (often considerably less frequently). To avoid confusion about calling, some areas introduced 'cards of request' – nothing more complicated than a large 'D' neatly printed on a piece of card. These were to be placed in windows, to let the dustman know that his services were required. Residents, however, complained that these were ignored. Vice versa, dustmen grumbled that, if they called too regularly at a house – particularly when large bins could hold a month's worth of refuse – they would be rudely dismissed and told that their visit was 'not convenient'.

The use of open carts, which persisted well into the twentieth century, was another source of complaint. Ashes were constantly being blown out of the carts, peppering the road, neighbouring houses, passing vehicles and unwary pedestrians. This was a perennial problem. A contract between the Commissioners of the Clink Pavements and a contractor, made in 1799, specifies (one suspects more in hope than expectation) 'fitting carriages with covers, ledges, or other conveniences to prevent the dust ashes and filth and soil from blowing shaking or falling out'. In practice, few contractors went to such trouble. A hundred years later, the London County Council was still attempting to enforce the use of covers.[6]

By far the greatest bugbear for the householder, however, was the dustman's insistence on tips. Providing 'beer money' for labourers was an old tradition, which dustmen exploited to the full. Before taking his leave of a premises, the dustman would request either beer or a tip for his trouble, quaintly known in the trade as 'sparrows'. To ignore this demand – even if it was only a hint, a cough, or an open palm – was a dangerous business. At best, it was likely to result in the house being conveniently 'forgotten' during the next collection; at worst 'clumsiness' or 'accidents' as the dust was conveyed through the kitchen or hallway. The customary gratuity was two or three pence. Anything less was not taken kindly. Occasionally matters came to a head, and individual cases went to court:

> Mrs. Elizabeth Pierce, a lady who keeps a haberdasher's shop, deposed that . . . the defendant called at her house to take away the dust, and when taking away the last basket he opened the shop door and asked her for the price of some beer, or something to drink. This she refused on account of his general inactivity, upon which he jerked the basket off his shoulder on to the floor, scattering the dust all over the place and seriously injuring many of the articles in her shop and window.[7]

Tips were not seen as an optional extra by the dustmen, but their right. There was some justification for this attitude. If we look at figures from the 1850s, quoted by the journalist Henry Mayhew, dustmen would be paid by the cartload at eightpence per load; or, alternatively, they might receive a flat salary, on condition they fill a certain number of loads per day. In either case, this could amount to as little as ten shillings a week, a low wage for a manual labourer. Tips could add another several shillings to the weekly income. Small wonder, then, that dustmen were quite zealous in demanding their 'sparrows'; not least because many dust contractors systematically underpaid their workers, on the grounds that tips would inevitably boost their earnings.

This insistence on gratuities, however, was not merely an irritation for the middle class. It had wider unintended consequences for where and how often rubbish was collected, particularly in poor districts. If the bin of a disgruntled middle-class householder was not emptied, he might make peace with the dustmen with renewed 'sparrows'; or he might attempt to obtain some redress from the vestry or the magistrate. Those living in poverty had nowhere to turn. The poor were unlikely to tip or to complain, and suffered as a result. Slums and poor areas were referred to as 'dead pieces' by dustmen, and treated accordingly. It was not unknown for the tenements and crowded courtyards in East End districts not to see the dustcart for weeks on end, conveniently overlooked in favour of more remunerative portions of the parish. Such wilful negligence created a vicious circle as miscellaneous rubbish accumulated, making collection even less appealing.

Contractors regularly promised to stem the practice of taking tips. The London County Council would make it an offence in the Public Health (London) Act of 1891. Whitechapel had 'No Gratuity Allowed' painted on the side of dustcarts.[8] None of these measures seems to have made much difference. Charles Booth, the late-Victorian social investigator, was one of many who noted the dustmen's implacable determination to retain their time-honoured perquisites: 'though gratuities are almost in every case forbidden, she is a bold woman who risks the cleanliness of her house by neglecting to tip the dustman, and it is of course notorious that the rule is systematically broken'.[9]

The underlying thread running through all this discord was the dustman's healthy disregard for authority and the general public. Dustmen would be somewhat harshly characterised by Henry Mayhew in the 1850s as part of 'the plodding class of labourers, mere labourers, who require only bodily power and possess little or no mental development',[10] but they did possess a certain rough-hewn independence and solidarity, which enabled them, amongst other things, to demand gratuities and, if thwarted, to exact their messy revenge with some degree of impunity. The *Builder* would damn them for this conduct, as coming from 'a class of men so brutal and degraded that their very presence in a decent household is an offence'.[11] Yet their lack of anxiety about 'customer satisfaction' reflected the nature of the work. Dustmen, employed by private contractors, were in no sense public servants, or part of a 'public sector' – a concept which barely belongs to the Victorian era. Collecting dust was a profit-making enterprise and the individual dustman's wage depended on how many loads he could shift in a day. The convenience of the public was of little concern.

The profits for contractors lay in recycling. Our ancestors were adept at converting all sorts of refuse into cash. Numerous articles from contemporary periodicals describe with relish the thrift and ingenuity of the dust trade. Food, offal and bones could be sold for manure; linen rags to manufacturers of paper; 'hard-ware' or 'hard-core', consisting of broken pots, crockery and oyster shells, could be crushed and used as a foundation for roads; old shoes could help 'making the fiercest of fires for colouring fine steel' or, more commonly, be used by bootmakers as stuffing; bread scraps might serve as pig food; old iron utensils, empty meat and biscuit tins could be melted down and used by trunk-makers for clamping the corners of their trunks. Even dead cats were a valuable commodity, once sold to furriers ('sixpence for a white cat, fourpence for a coloured cat, and for a black one according to her quality').[12]

All the above, however, played second fiddle to ashes and cinders – the great bulk of household refuse – which could make the recycling of rubbish a potential gold mine. Ashes had always had some value to farmers as fertiliser, and could be profitably mixed with the dung of road sweepings, but the great market in the early nineteenth century was amongst the brickmakers, whose works ringed the ever-expanding capital. Fine ash was mixed with clay in the manufacture of bricks, and the larger cinders or 'breeze' – coal that was incompletely burnt in household fires – were used as fuel. These cinders were placed between layers of clay bricks in the great open-air 'clamps' of the brickfields. Once fired, the cinders both kept the bricks separate from each other and provided the slow combustion necessary for brick-making. As London grew at an unprecedented rate, the construction industry's demand for bricks – and breeze – was insatiable. The profits for the dust contractor were commensurate. Wags joked that London was a phoenix, rising again from its own ashes. In fact, this was doubly true. It was common to use hard-core as a foundation not only for roads but for new houses.

There were large sums to be made – and the wealth of certain contractors would become notorious. Mr Boffin of Dickens's *Our Mutual Friend* (1865) is Victorian literature's famous dust contractor (the 'Golden Dustman') having inherited Mr Harmon's King's Cross dust heap, together with £100,000 (earned from the dust business). Dickens's portrayal of Boffin's new-found wealth – he can suddenly afford a West End mansion and all the trappings, although it does not suit him – would not have struck his readers as an exaggeration. Boffin was most likely based on Henry Dodd, a successful contractor from Islington, whom the great author met while both were involved in an attempt to set up a charity for retired actors. Dodd reputedly began his working life as a farmhand. When he died in 1881, he left a thriving business in London and a renovated Jacobean manor house in Essex, with his personal estate worth an astonishing £111,000 (in comparison, Dickens's estate, in 1870, was worth £93,000 – both men would have been millionaires by modern standards).

The sheer scale of Dodd's wealth was, in fairness, exceptional; but his background was typical. Contractors were, as a rule, working-men-made-good – with the 'plain-speaking' typical of the type. Thomas Rook of Gibraltar Walk, Bethnal Green, for example, was brought before the local magistrate by his neighbours in July 1859, in the heat of the summer. They complained of the stench from rotting material in his dust-yard. Rook merely turned to the judge and replied insouciantly: 'It only smells when it's stirred.'[13] The verbatim minutes of an interview between the Chairman and Directors of the Southwark and Vauxhall Water Company and a certain Mr Covington (a contractor whose dust was blowing into the company's reservoirs), preserved in the London Metropolitan Archives, reveal a similar native truculence. During the entire meeting, Mr Covington repeatedly and doggedly demands £200 to help him to amend his working practices, whilst the company's chairman grows increasingly exasperated by this unwarranted insistence on compensation: 'It is all very well to laugh over it, but there will be another summons taken out against you . . . But you see the sentiment of the thing? Dust!! And we drink the water and must stop it!'[14]

Not only were contractors intransigent, but they jealously guarded their privileges. In 1793, the Contractor for Cleansing for Holborn, a certain Mr Haygarth, expended £200 – a sum which might have paid the annual wages of half a dozen of his dustmen – on various court cases, trying to obtain redress from other scavengers who had infringed his exclusive contract to remove household refuse within the parish.[15] Contractors would distribute handbills informing inhabitants of their right to collect dust and ashes 'in preference to any other Dustman'. [16] The great object was to defeat 'flying dustmen' – for the value of dust was such that it was even worth stealing (i.e. removing before the official parish contractor could acquire it). In 1822, two men were caught, having been 'in the constant habit of creeping down into the area, and removing by stealth ashes from the dirt-hole', from a house in Downing Street. They confessed that they 'sold the cinders for 4d. or 5d. a bushel, and disposed of the small dust to the brick-makers'.[17]

Fictionalised versions of Dodd and his bluff contemporaries remained of interest to the public throughout the Victorian era, appearing repeatedly on the stage, both in adaptations of *Our Mutual Friend* and in plays like *The Dustman's Belle* (1846) and *Our Party* (1896). The former play is particularly interesting, prefiguring several aspects of Dickens's plot. A simple dustman is left a fortune by 'Thomas Windfall' a wealthy contractor; predatory 'friends' attempt to covertly rob him of the money; and the audience learns the moral, 'people aint always happier because they're richer, specially people that haven't been used to it like'. *Our Party,* on the other hand, a 'musical absurdity' written by and featuring the music-hall star Arthur Lloyd, revolves around a retired dust contractor named Marmaduke Mugg – again, the archetype of a 'self-made man'. Keen for his heiress daughter to marry an aristocrat, he cannot quite shake off his working-class roots and his belief in the power of hard cash. Talking of his daughter's happiness, he opines:

'Nothing as it were – squelches her.'
  'Squelches her?'
  'I mean nothing puts the kybosh on her.'
  'Don't talk like that, dear. I've often begged you to drop those slang phrases, I think you might oblige me. You know how people stare at you when you make use of such language.'
  'Let 'em stare. I ham as I ham and – as the song says – I can't be any hammer. Never mind, old girl; I've got the coin, the dinari. That's wot licks 'em. They may say wot they like. Money makes the man.'

Yet, although dust contracting was lucrative, not every 'golden dustman' retired as complacent and content as the fictional Mr Mugg. There were risks as well as opportunities. In particular, contractors were extremely vulnerable to changes in the demand for ashes and cinders. The price paid by brick-makers for ashes was volatile, mirroring fluctuations in the building trade. Contractors' finances, in turn, could swiftly become very precarious. Records from the 'Day Book' of a contractor in the early 1800s show prices dropping from 16s. per chaldron (wagon-load) to 9s. within the space of two months, and down to 6s. within a year. [18] The annual accounts of individual parishes, likewise, show how prices rose and fell. In St Clement Danes, Westminster, the dust contractor paid £1,100 for the privilege of collecting dust in 1824/25 but only £900 guineas in the following year. In 1826/27, when it was clear the metropolitan economy had fallen into a spectacular slump, 'he would give nothing, nor would he have it at all'.

Less prudent contractors, gambling on how much they might get for dust in any given year, were constantly dodging bankruptcy. William Hearn of Stangate Wharf, Lambeth, finally bankrupted in 1854, owed the magnificent sum of over £5,000 to his creditors, with £2,000 worth of assets, in 'brick field horses and carts'. Hearn had moved into brick-making in conjunction with refuse removal, making the most of the circular trade between brickfields and the metropolis – i.e. taking dust out to the kilns, and using the same horses, carts and drivers to return with finished bricks. Others invested in their own fleets of barges, used for shipping London dust ever further afield. The stubborn Mr Covington owned his own fleet of sixty boats, taking breeze from his Thames-side wharf at Battersea. Henry Dodd, whose dust yard was on the banks of the Regent's Canal, left in his will £19 9s. to 'each of the Captains of my two Canal Boats, whose names I do not recollect' and, more impressively, £5,000 to provide annuities for 'the support and comfort of poor Bargemen and Lightermen'. Not everyone, however, had Dodd's business acumen; and what seemed like a canny investment in carts or barges, reducing transport costs, could soon turn into a costly liability when the market for dust collapsed. Some dustmen were golden; others had feet of clay.

Bankruptcies pointed to the weakness inherent in the contracting system – the reliance on the brick trade. As the century progressed, dramatically rising costs, and an increasingly poor service to the public, threatened to undermine the whole lucrative enterprise.

There had, of course, always been some complaints about failure to collect rubbish. Some parishes actually had very effectual remedies. The detailed logs of activity preserved by the paving committee for the parish of St James in Mayfair, for instance, show that 'dust complaints' were frequently resolved by dustmen returning on the same day to make good their mistake.[19] St James's, however, was wealthy, central and compact; sprawling suburbia and the slums tended to receive a poorer response. Contractors themselves were generally reluctant to shoulder the blame for their omissions, with excuses ranging from the personal ('he had been ill and obliged to trust the business to the care of his Brother') to the whims of householders ('That on account of the late extreme cold weather and winds the Inhabitants did not like to have their Dust removed') [20] and the financial ('he had given a very high premium for the contract and is obliged to wait until he can turn the Bills taken by him for the Breeze into Money').[21]

Some better organised parishes, aware of the problem, provided their own 'quality control'. St Andrew and St George, Holborn, possessed an active and enthusiastic 'paving, cleansing and lighting committee' (which heard the above excuses) and had its own Inspector of Nuisances, patrolling the streets and giving notice of any neglect, as early as the 1790s. Other parishes simply waited for complaints from the public and responded as best they were able. Contracts did include penalty clauses for negligence but, as a rule, fines and the threat of legal action were employed sparingly. Few cases went to court and most parishes 'shewed a disposition to relieve their Contractors' when they fell into financial difficulty.[22] Charitably, they preferred to avoid legal costs and keep the machinery of refuse collection working, however imperfectly. Less charitably, contractors had undue influence on their employers – accusations of corruption in awarding contracts were frequently levelled.

For better or worse, this tolerance of failure was predicated on the assumption that contractors would return to paying for the privilege of collecting refuse – perhaps not this year, but the next year, or the one after that. In the second half of the century, this model became increasingly unsustainable; rubbish did not yield profits; and the contracting system began to buckle under the strain.

In essence, there came a tipping point, where the outward expansion of the metropolis became a negative rather than a positive for contractors. There was some irony in this. The growth of London had created enormous wealth in the dust trade, because of the synergy with brickmaking, but then London grew *too* big. There were inklings of this change in the 1850s, and the trend became clear over the next two decades. The supply of cinders and ashes from the ever larger metropolis began to exceed the demand. Likewise, the transport costs involved in shipping breeze to ever more distant brickfields increased proportionately. The price paid for dust by brickmakers dropped and – unlike in the past – did not always recover. The railways also brought more and more factory-made bricks from the provinces, not cut from London clay. The Chelsea vestry, newly constituted after the reformation of London's local government in 1855, would summarise the consequences for the general public in its second annual report:

> When building operations are brisk, the parish receives large payments for the privilege of collecting the ashes &c., and the accumulations are rapidly removed; when, on the other hand, it is of little or no value, notwithstanding that the parish pays for its removal, the complaints are numerous.

In other words, the contractors, with their traditional profits from the sale of dust squeezed, tried to reduce costs in the most obvious way possible – by cutting corners, missing out places where it was difficult or unremunerative to collect waste. Complaints from the public grew more numerous. Dozens of neglected homes became hundreds, and even thousands.[23] Rich and poor alike found themselves with overflowing bins.

Local authorities did attempt to address the growing problem, taking various measures to supervise their existing contractors. Suburban Chelsea, from the beginning, prided itself on the stringent nature of its contract and the regular imposition of fines for failing to remove rubbish. The district of Bethnal Green, replete with slums, terribly ill served by its contractors for much of the century, grew better organised in the 1880s and divided its territory into eighteen 'blocks' which were to be 'cleared daily in rotation in accordance with a printed list and block plan, copies of which are supplied to the contractor', such that 'the dustmen are thus restrained from wandering all over the Parish at irregular intervals as heretofore'.[24] St Giles District Board appointed an 'Inspector of Dustbins' in 1883, who reported that he had carried out 41,168 inspections in his first year in office.[25] Similar supervisory measures were adopted throughout the capital, the Victorian aptitude for organisation and order belatedly applied to the collection of rubbish.

But this improved supervision came at a price. The contractors, forced to stick to the terms of their contracts, were obliged to charge for their services to make any kind of profit. Contractors became unwilling to pay for the rights to collect refuse; vestries, in turn, faced a growing administrative and financial burden. Sprawling St Pancras received £1,525 from its dust contractor as late as 1867 and yet, by the end of the century, was paying out over £16,000 for the service. The result was that some vestries began to question whether contracting out remained value for money – and reluctantly concluded it did not.

Faced with rising costs, local authorities began to take on responsibility for 'dusting', employing their own men, hiring vehicles, investing in plant, arranging for disposal of rubbish. This did not happen overnight – nor, by any means, did every vestry choose to abandon the contracting system – but a growing number of authorities elected to do without 'the golden dustman'.[26]

Revised sanitary priorities in the capital were also a factor. With Bazalgette's great sewers completed in the 1870s, public health reformers had begun to look afresh at sanitary problems, and focus more on the minutiae of daily life. The International Health Exhibition, held in Kensington in 1884, provided fresh stimulus and ideas for sanitary improvement – and this also encouraged local authorities to think again about dust.[27]

The exhibition contained a typically Victorian mixture of the quirky and the educational: a recreation of an insanitary medieval London street ('London in the Olden Times'); the 'largest display of electric lighting in the World'; 'Laundries in operation'; 'A Chicken Hatching Establishment'; and a selection of 'English and Foreign Restaurants' (including the capital's first Japanese eaterie).[28] Amongst the more down-to-earth exhibits were two full-sized model houses, one 'sanitary' and one 'insanitary', through which visitors could parade, moving from 'insanitary' to 'sanitary' establishment via a bridge between the upper floors – as if following the march of progress. The insanitary house displayed poor heating and plumbing, arsenical wallpaper and, in the basement area at the front of the house, 'a large wooden dustbin, placed as is frequently the case, where its malodorous and often dangerous contents must be a constant nuisance on the premises'. Worse still, visitors could observe, 'there is no lining, and as will be seen inside, the damp has struck through the wall of the house'. The humorous magazine *Punch* did its best to mock the whole 'Insane-itary Exhibition' but struggled to find much fault with the two houses and their object lesson. Rival magazine *Fun* pictured depressed home-owners going home and dynamiting their own universally defective residences, leaving the capital a derelict ruin, containing only remnants of 'slack-baked bricks, defective drains, poisonous cisterns, malarious dustbins'.[29]

Dustbins and rubbish began to feature more prominently in discussions about overcrowding and slum clearance, particularly amongst the local officials responsible for public health. Medical Officers of Health, Surveyors, Sanitary Inspectors et al., issuing annual reports to their respective vestries, drew atten-tion to long-standing public health problems with the disposal of domestic rubbish.[30] Vestries, in turn, having abandoned contractors (or held them to better account) began to reframe refuse collection: not as a failed profit-making enterprise but a civic good; an overlooked sanitary necessity that now demanded the full attention of local government. Others had argued for reform in the past – the Metropolitan Sanitary Association, founded in 1850, had listed 'non-removal of refuse' amongst the evils it hoped to address – but this was a change of heart *within* local government. Vestries would also be supported and encouraged by the newly created London County Council (LCC), formed in 1889, which made rubbish collection one of its first priorities, both in the Public Health (London) Act of 1891 and subsequent by-laws.

One sign of this change was that dustbins themselves were finally given due consideration as a potential public health problem. Suggestions for improvement were put forward. A lengthy correspondence appeared in *The Times* during 1885. The *British Medical Journal* ran an article, summarising the discussion, entitled 'A Domestic Problem in Public Health'.[31] The lady vice-president of the National Health Society proposed the removal of bins and the introduction of re-usable sacks, which could be hung up outside houses, ready for swift collection.[32] Others looked at sanitising existing bins. The dustmen of St Giles – servicing one of the poorest and most disease-ridden districts in the capital – were obliged to sprinkle carbolic powder in emptied dust-holes from the early 1880s. The Metropolitan Board of Works (the overarching administrative body for London, from 1855 until 1889, before the LCC) took a belated interest in rubbish and canvassed support for 'an amendment of the law, so as to provide for the abolition of dustbins', both in 1884 and 1888,[33] keen to replace bins with the 'moveable receptacles' used elsewhere in the country.[34]

One possibility, widely adopted in the East End, was the galvanised pail, a small and transportable open bucket – '18 inches deep, 15 inches diameter at top, 12 inches diameter at bottom weighing 16 pounds'[35] – that could be left outside the house and collected at fixed times – even daily. Pails were particularly suited to those living in social housing and tenements, where communal bins often became foul and fell into disuse. Bethnal Green had introduced a thousand pails for the use of some of its poorer inhabitants in 1883, and had 18,000 in use by 1889. Although their size prevented large accumulations of rubbish, pails could still cause difficulties. The frequency of collection – the level of attention which innumerable small pails required – was a challenge in itself. The Chief Inspector of Bethnal Green's sanitary department, evaluating the system in the following decade, found pails left too long in the street, and workers emptying them in a slipshod and neglectful manner ('Whatever energy our Pail-men may lack in other respect, is more than made up for in explaining away complaints to their own entire satisfaction').[36] Whitechapel, adopting the same system, found fault with the general public, who put pails in the street 'with very little regard in many cases to the time at which the dust cart is due'.[37] Hackney complained of 'pails used for other purposes, such as coals and in one instance a corn-bin for a pony'.[38]

In the end, all London would be legally obliged to follow London County Council by-laws and use portable bins, 'constructed of metal . . . with one or more suitable handles and cover . . . capacity no more than 2 cubic feet'.[39] It would be several decades before a standard metal bin actually became universal; nonetheless the principle was established in the final years of the nineteenth century.[40]

Frequency of collection also now came under fierce scrutiny – much discussed in the 1880s and addressed by the London County Council in the 1890s. The LCC, having produced a detailed report on rubbish collection in 1894, mandated once-a-week removal[41] and decided to interpret 'once-a-week' as 'irrespective of whether occupier indicates by placing a card in the window or [asks] in any other way for a call to be made'.[42] This irked several local authorities that relied on the 'D' card. Some pointed out that residents themselves were liable to refuse dustmen access. There was some truth in this. After complaints about non-collection of waste in Kensal Green in the 1880s, the vestry demanded that their contractor call on *every* house in the district during the following week. A total of 3,092 houses were visited; 359 had dust removed; 2,549 refused access; and 184 houses were vacant at the time of the dustman's call. The vestry concluded that, as these houses possessed traditional capacious bins, which were capable of holding a month's worth of rubbish, few householders saw the point in weekly refuse collection disrupting their routine. But a test case challenging the LCC rules, in which a member of the public refused dustmen entry to his home ('it was an unnecessary annoyance to collect his refuse once a week') was lost.[43] Obstructing weekly removal of domestic waste, actively or passively, henceforth meant a fine for the householder.

Meanwhile, the LCC employed its own specially appointed sanitary inspector to covertly observe the worst-managed areas of the metropolis over a period of several months. This proceeding, naturally enough, caused some resentment. But in Marylebone and Camberwell, the inspector found very familiar problems – failure to collect; complaints unanswered; 'a very large number of accumulations of refuse due to non-removal for periods of from two to twelve weeks' – and threatened to prosecute the vestries involved. This threat proved remarkably effective, coming from a body with the power and resources of the new County Council. The LCC would proceed to do a thorough job of enforcing a weekly standard across the capital. Full of sanitary enthusiasm, the LCC also organised two London-wide conferences on rubbish collection, and a competition for an improved design for dustcarts.

The LCC would end the century justifiably proud of its intervention in refuse collection; and the general public undoubtedly benefited. But it did not take a comprehensive approach to the subject. There was a wider issue emerging, which both vestries and the LCC struggled to address – or perhaps did not want to address: the final destination for metropolitan rubbish. When contractors held universal sway, there was an element of 'out of sight, out of mind', i.e. once rubbish left the home, it was no longer a concern. Whenever local authorities took back control from dust contractors, they were faced with the fundamental problem of disposing of their own dust – and it proved something of a challenge.

Vestries, of course, had a template to follow. Historically, once removed from the dust-hole, London's rubbish proceeded to the contractor's dust yard, for sifting and sorting, ready to be sold and shipped on to likely buyers. Most of these yards were located near the capital's network of canals – sites such as Paddington Basin, home to several contractors – or along the bank of the Thames. This was so that ashes and cinders could be swiftly removed by barge to the countryside and the waiting brickfields. The dust yards themselves were more than just vacant lots containing heaps of filth. They were, in effect, recycling centres, with not only dust and sundry labourers, but related plant – including a furnace for material that was not recyclable, and some machinery.[44] The actual process of sorting and sifting, however, remained primitive, performed by female dust-sifters using large metal sieves to separate out the valuable fine ashes and cinders and find other small objects. Dust-sifters themselves were somewhat weary, bedraggled figures – '[wearing] stout aprons of leather or sackcloth, often with men's jackets over their shoulders . . . [they] sometimes indulge themselves in a pipe of tobacco'[45] – usually the wives of dustmen, toiling, knee-deep in the towering heaps.[46] Contemporary journalistic accounts mock their appearance and rude, plebeian habits – yet the enormous wealth of the mid-Victorian dust contractor relied upon the back-breaking labour of these hard-pressed females.[47]

Vestries that took over refuse collection began to build or let their own yards, and hire their own employees. They soon found it was an expensive business. Bethnal Green, investigating the possibility of abandoning contractors in the early 1880s, concluded that it would cost them too much money.[48] Mile End, a growing industrial district further east, having taken the opposite decision, noted despondently in its annual report that the expense of sifting was greater than their receipts. Another predictably heavy expense was transportation: not so much purchasing dustcarts as the care and feeding of horses.[49]

Not only were costs high, but finding ways to dispose of rubbish proved increasingly vexing. Although most districts still sent some of their dust to brickmakers, much was left behind – there was simply insufficient demand.[50] Burning refuse, unsorted, produced foul stinks and public protest.[51] The alternative was the use of 'shoots' where rubbish could be dumped, or dumping at sea. 'Shooting', however, brought its own problems. Shoots within the metropolis and its immediate vicinity were constantly under threat of being closed.[52] Magistrates had acquired greater powers to deal with 'nuisances' under legislation passed in the 1840s and 1850s; and local residents were themselves less tolerant of foul stenches from dust yards and their ilk. Mile End, for example, having obtained an interest in a shoot at Carpenter's Road, Stratford (now buried deep under London's Olympic Park), found itself subjected to the close scrutiny of the local West Ham District Board, who prohibited the dumping of organic matter in their district. LCC inspectors also weighed in when shoots were sited too close to nearby residential areas.[53] Disposing of rubbish began to give local officials nightmares: 'One morning you will find that it [dust] will have to be left in the houses, attended with all the serious results which must arise from such a catastrophe, or you will be in the ignominious position of having to accede to any terms contractors may dictate.'[54]

By the mid-1890s, local authorities found themselves between a rock and a hard place. Contractors were inordinately expensive; performing the work 'in-house' involved high start-up costs, was more challenging and often resulted in no savings. The increasing use of gas fires did mean that household refuse came in slightly smaller quantities, but that greater proportions were useless and unsaleable. Without the high-value recycling of cinders, the remainder of household rubbish was barely worth sorting. East London vestries, like Mile End, began buying up land in Essex, transporting their rubbish ever further afield, dumping at Rainham or Gravesend, with all the increased transport costs that entailed ('Barges, steam-tugs and cranes are used for this purpose, the cost of which is serious to contemplate').[55] An LCC official would note ruefully that, in the absence of any other answer, 'the natural solution is to shoot it in some sparsely inhabited district where public opinion is not strong enough to effectually resent it being deposited'.[56]

The picture did vary a little across the capital. Some local authorities found ingenious ways to make their refuse yield a return. In the 1870s St Mary Newington developed an extensive business selling 'Newington Mixture', an artificial manure conjured up from street sweepings and dust,[57] shipped by rail from its dust depot to purpose-built storage facilities at Meopham and Long-field in Kent, whence it was sold to farmers. It was claimed that Newington had invented 'the only system hitherto adopted in London that completely covers the entire annual outlay for scavenging'.[58] But Newington's business was an exception – and it did little more than break even.[59] Most of the vestries that had ditched contractors found themselves faced with rising costs, growing heaps of rubbish and few options, apart from the expense of shooting rubbish in ever more distant locations. In 1889, Kensington was obliged to send its rubbish to Purfleet in Essex, 16 miles below London Bridge, the nearest wharf ...ver that would accept it.

Then a ray of hope shone through the gloom – the great answer to the rubbish problem – the white heat of technology.

Vestries, scrabbling around for a solution to their difficulties, were drawn to a new machine, first developed in the mid-1870s, already used in industrial cities like Manchester, Liverpool and Leeds – the dust destructor. Destructors were essentially giant incinerators. Some London authorities and contractors already burnt rubbish – but usually only in modestly sized furnaces at the dust yard, or sometimes torched piles of refuse in the open air.[60] Destructors, on the other hand, could burn 24 tons of refuse in a day and reduce the weight to 4 tons of inert 'clinker',[61] which could then be used as ballast in road-making or similar work. Depending on the design, they could even accommodate street sweepings and 'sewer residuum', i.e. not merely household rubbish. An LCC survey from 1892 reveals the local authorities that made early experiments in incineration: Whitechapel was the pioneer, purchasing a 'Fryer's' destructor in 1876 (Albert Fryer was the original patentee of the technology, in 1874), then Mile End in 1881, followed by the City of London in 1884. Battersea and Hampstead followed suit in 1888, the first districts to put the entirety of their rubbish through the process; then Woolwich in 1892. The great advantage of incineration was the reduction of the bulk of refuse and consequent reduction in transport costs. The disadvantage was the heavy investment in plant – which also had to be centrally located. The chimneys of destructors emitted bad smells and smoke, which annoyed local inhabitants. It seemed perverse for any sanitary activity to be adding to the foul atmosphere of the metropolis. A resident in Lambeth, writing to *The Times* in 1892, complained of the Battersea destructor: 'All last week, the smell was perceptible in Whitehall and Parliament-street. The dust permeates everywhere, as witness the silk hats of our parish.'

Despite these problems, the destructor appeared to be the future of refuse disposal. The reason was another new technology: electricity. This was the period when the commercial generation and supply of electricity became a realistic possibility throughout the capital (although it was far from clear whether this would be largely by private companies, local authorities or a mixture of the two). In 1893, Shoreditch Vestry saw the opportunity to kill two birds with one stone – it commissioned a feasibility study for the creation of a destructor integrated with an electric lighting station (using heat from

the destructor to power a steam engine to generate the current).[62] The dream
was – in effect – to make rubbish pay for itself once more, by generating
electricity. There was also a secondary agenda. The complexities of Board of
Trade regulation of the nascent electric industry meant that the vestry had to
put down a marker, promising to create its own electricity supply, or see the
district controlled by private firms.[63]

In one leap, local authorities went from taking on refuse collection to
generating power for the people.

Before the 1890s, few local authorities would have considered undertaking
such a demanding new role – but the political landscape of local government
was changing, in favour of more civic-minded, less parochial, less penny-
pinching authorities. Two crucial pieces of legislation in 1894 would accel-
erate this change and put 'progressives' in charge: the Rate Equalisation Act
shared funds for local government across the metropolis, effectively distributing money from wealthy corners of the capital to the poorer, heavily populated districts (like Shoreditch); and the Local Government Act removed
rating qualifications and opened up membership of vestries to all local residents, including women. Vestries, once dominated by 'tradesmen, publicans,
builders and solicitors',[64] with a smattering of aristocrats and MPs adding their
names to the list, were now wide open to political activists from every background and social group. Fabian pamphlets began to appear, urging socialists
to stand for the vestry, citing the parsimony of previous administrations:

> In many a narrow court, where the poorest people dwell, the dustbins
> are not emptied for months at a time, the water-closets are allowed to
> remain out of order, the drains smell, and all manner of filth pollutes the
> air. This is because the Vestrymen are not doing their duty. Many of the
> smaller streets are badly paved, dark and often very dirty. When the snow
> comes, little or no attempt is made to sweep it away. All this neglect by
> the Vestry may save money, but it means discomfort and misery and
> disease to the poor.[65]

Socialist candidates did stand. Furthermore, in Shoreditch, the success of
'municipal socialism' became bound up with the proposed dust destructor
project. Progressive electoral candidates felt obliged to make the creation of a

destructor their key electoral pledge – so vast was the proposed expenditure, it was essential to have public backing. The progressives won, and Shoreditch embarked on a groundbreaking project which would cost the ratepayer £70,000, borrowed at low interest from the LCC.[66]

The opening of the new plant, in Coronet Street, Hoxton, in 1897 was marked by the issue of a souvenir brochure with full details and photographs. The building was emblazoned with the motto 'E PULVERE LUX ET VIS' ('From dust, light and power'). Electricity was made available to 'artizan and small users of motive power in the parish' (i.e. local workshops, particularly in the furniture trade which dominated the area) via penny-in-the-slot meters; [67] electric street lighting was introduced on major thoroughfares (although the district would not be completely lit by electricity until the 1920s); surplus heat was used to warm the adjoining public baths. The project attracted national and international attention and others would follow Shoreditch's example, most notably Bermondsey (which likewise wished to see off the private interests that threatened to dominate the local electricity supply). By the time the Bermondsey destructor opened in 1902, London's vestries had been reorganised into new metropolitan boroughs. The Bermondsey site, containing not only the destructor but 'town hall, library, baths and wash-houses, mortuary, disinfecting station, electric light works', remained a grand memorial to the late-Victorian vestry's vaulting ambition.

The Shoreditch model, however, was a false dawn. It swiftly became clear that the demand for electricity in the metropolis was such that dust could only provide the smallest fraction, even after burning refuse from industry. Most districts decided it was more economical to rely entirely on the most obvious source of power. Coal would drive the capital's electricity stations and, ultimately, only a handful of authorities would doggedly persist in the attempt to turn dust into light.[68]

Ultimately, this was the lesson for London's local authorities: there was no simple economical solution to the disposal of refuse. Certainly, in the following decades, no single method of disposal would come to dominate: some dust would still go to brickmakers; some would be dumped in the Home Counties, some at sea; incinerators would continue to be used, to reduce the bulk of material, as well as new processes like mechanical crushing. Metropolitan boroughs of the twentieth century employed a variety of these methods, according to local topography and previous custom and practice.[69] Dust-sifters would be gradually replaced by mechanical sorting – a process already being tried in the 1890s.[70] The collection of rubbish, on the other hand, changed very little, except for the gradual introduction of portable bins. Contractors, although out of favour in the early 1900s, did not disappear from the scene. Full of enthusiasm for destructors and reform, the officials of metropolitan boroughs were happy to resolve, at an LCC-organised conference in 1903, that 'dust collection should be carried out by the responsible officers of the sanitary authority, without the intervention of a contractor'.[71] In fact, private firms would return to dominate refuse collection in the capital.[72]

The hope of making a profit from dust finally died away. Indeed, the last decades of the nineteenth century, through to the end of the Edwardian era, can be viewed as a long and tortuous period of readjustment, in which vestries reluctantly accepted the inevitable – that the days of the 'golden dustman' and his bounty were no more.

The lasting influence of the Victorians – or, at least, the late-Victorian vestries and the LCC – is still visible today in London's regular and systematic collection of rubbish. Victorian solutions to disposal have not been improved upon. The dust destructor actually had a future, albeit not generating profits. London currently disposes of a fifth of its waste by incineration; and this is expected to continue. Landfill, likewise, still accounts for almost 50 per cent of London's rubbish, although here the clock is ticking. Waste is still despatched to the Home Counties but 'These regions are increasingly reluctant to accept London's waste and this landfill capacity is due to expire by 2025.' It is hoped that recycling, composting and anaerobic digestion will take up the slack. There is another Victorian survival – or perhaps a phoenix from the ashes. The latest strategy document from the Mayor of London notes that 'Many waste authorities have not yet capitalised on the growing markets for recycled materials or on the demand for the energy that can be produced from waste', blaming 'long-term, inflexible contracts' with private firms and a 'preference to outsource risk'. The report concludes that 'waste authorities have not actively pursued the opportunity to generate income from their waste management activities'.[73] The nineteenth century's alchemical dream of extracting gold from dust is alive and well, and living in City Hall.

2

Inglorious Mud

IT IS PERFECTLY possible to find contemporary paeans to the streets of Victorian London. Some hymned 'the rapid current of human life'; others praised grand architectural statements, like Nash's Regent Street; or monumental feats of engineering, like Holborn Viaduct. Nonetheless, throughout the nineteenth century, London was routinely damned by visitors for having 'the dirtiest streets of any city in the civilised world'.[1]

Mud was the great culprit, covering the road, bespattering the pavement. This was not the mud of the field or the stable-yard. For a start, although largely composed of horse dung, it was black. The capital's sooty atmosphere tainted everything it touched, even the dirt on the streets. London mud was also terribly sticky, 'enough to suck off your boots',[2] because it contained a large proportion of macadam, the granite used to surface the majority of carriageways.[3] Macadam had many advantages – a relatively cheap road surface, composed of layers of small pieces of stone, compacted together – but it was prone to becoming pocked and rutted. Thus, ground-down particles of stone combined with moist dung to create an adhesive paste. The amount of grit 'in solution' was astonishing. A twelvemonth survey by Dr Letheby, the City of London's Medical Officer, found the average blend of London mud, once moisture was evaporated: 'Horsedung, 57 parts; abraded stone, 30 parts; and abraded iron, 13 parts' (with the last of these coming from iron-shod wheels and horseshoes).[4] The water, of course, was crucial in determining the mud's overall consistency, making roads 'greasy when there was fog, sloppy when there was mist, and liquid when there was drizzle'.[5] Yet even the driest summer months were not free of vexation, producing a 'coffee-coloured sirocco' of desiccated filth, which besmirched clothing and stung the eyes and throat.

The sheer volume of London traffic, drawn by the humble, long-suffering horse, was the principal source of all this dirt. By the 1890s, it took 300,000 horses to keep London moving, generating 1,000 tons of dung daily, not to mention a large volume of urine.[6] Livestock being driven to market also contributed. Smithfield market, which traded in live animals until 1855, could house 4,000 cattle and 30,000 sheep – all of which were driven weekly into the very heart of the city.

The mud was not only foul but dangerous. Streets could be rendered so greasy that horses might 'flounder about upon it as they would upon ice'.[7] Tests showed that traction on granite blocks was actually improved by a smattering of dung, but there was rarely the correct amount or consistency of filth. Newer, smoother road surfaces, particularly wood paving and asphalt, once muddied, became hazardous with only a light fall of rain. These dangers were patent and some local authorities did grit major roads. Still, the spectacle of a 'downed' horse, flailing in the mud, remained a common sight ('I have myself frequently seen three or four omnibuses standing in a line in London, each with its fallen horse').[8] Most falls were relatively minor but, without fail, curious crowds gathered to offer advice.[9] In the worst cases, when the animal was judged beyond help, the more morbid stayed to witness the work of the slaughterer. By end of the century, the firm of Harrison Barber had seven depots in strategic positions round London, with carts and men 'on call' by telephone, just for this purpose. They stood by, 'in readiness, tools and all, like fire engines, ready to be turned out', a grim sort of emergency breakdown service.[10]

Humans, too, had their share of spills in the mud – 'many a sprained ankle, "jarred" spine and "shocked" nervous system'[11] – and finding somewhere safe to cross the street could be a risky undertaking. The greatest impact, however, was on clothing. Women required a good deal of skill and judgement, if they were to modestly raise the mass of underclothes beneath their skirts, such that filth did not ruin their petticoats. Even the most dainty and careful pedestrian could be splashed with filth by passing vehicles. Removing mud from shoes and clothing was a daily chore. Guidance on brushing down material, proper treatment of fabrics and useful chemicals abounded in women's magazine advice columns. More delicate fabrics were, ideally, not to be exposed to the streets at all. The aristocratic ladies who remained in their carriages on Regent Street or Bond Street, letting milliners and shop-girls bring out samples to their coaches, were not merely declaring their social status but protecting their outfits, avoiding the hazards of the pavement. For those who had to step out, one answer was goloshes, rubber overshoes, which allowed one 'to enter a friend's drawing-room in the smartest of patent foot-gear, instead of with the mud-bespattered boots resulting from even a short walk in London streets in the winter-time'.[12]

Men, naturally, suffered less damage to their sparser attire, but still had to make their own accommodation with the mire. It was said that an Englishman abroad could always be recognised by his turned-up trousers, a practice which became second nature.[13] From 1851 onwards, gentlemen could, at least, resort to the Shoe-Black Brigade – a charity initially founded to give boys from the Ragged School movement employment during the Great Exhibition. The Brigade, under the patronage of Lord Shaftesbury, provided uniforms and cleaning equipment, and placed its boys at fixed locations, ready to scrub and polish footwear for a penny. A previous attempt to introduce shoeblacks, commonplace in some Continental cities, had failed due to Londoners' innate modesty – 'foot passengers evinced great reluctance to have their boots or shoes cleaned in the open streets'[14] – but the Exhibition brought more unabashed foreign customers, and made the work acceptable.[15] Yet, even if the discerning gentleman took every precaution, there was also the possibility of collateral damage. For example, in the cramped conditions of the London omnibus crinolined skirts of females spread mud and dust over the knees of fellow passengers.[16]

Shoes and clothing were not the only casualties. Mud splashed deliveries of food and goods, house fronts and shop windows, and personal possessions were lost or damaged in the muck. The *Lady's Newspaper* advice column was obliged to concede in 1850, to one inquirer, 'there is nothing we know of to remove mud stains from a book'.[17]

The responsibility for cleaning the streets lay with vestries and their contractors, with one important caveat. Historically, cleansing the 'footway' (or 'foot pavement' or 'side walk' – i.e. what we would now call 'the pavement') was considered the responsibility of each individual householder. In some districts this was merely customary. Other local authorities, however, actually required residents to sweep the pavement outside their home at regular intervals or face a fine.[18] Under the Metropolitan Paving Act of 1817, regardless of local statutes, the removal of snow from pavements was also made obligatory for all the London householders. Unfortunately, by the early 1800s the tradition of exercising personal responsibility had already begun to die out. The capital had grown too large and anonymous for such a cosy arrangement.

The pavements, therefore, were often treated as nobody's problem; and grew filthy. In many districts, slipshod parish contractors, sweeping the road, splashed and splattered dirt on to the footway with impunity. There were also many 'blank walls', unoccupied houses and public buildings where the adjoining footway was never cleansed – but pedestrians still had to pick their way through the mire. The police did remind householders of their responsibility in the case of heavy snowfall but there seem to have been few prosecutions.[19] Snow, in fact, was largely cleared from the footway by bands of men carrying brooms and shovels, 'usually far from prepossessing in appearance, or in language, who offered to do the statutory work of a householder for a remuneration perhaps ten times in excess of the proper value of their labour'.[20] This was clearly a poor way of proceeding – described by *The Times* as 'a grotesque survival of village organization in metropolitan conditions'[21] – but survived until the 1890s, when the new London County Council intervened. Londoners, however, did not rejoice. The LCC, naturally enough, placed pavements in the charge of the vestries. The public had little confidence that the work would be performed adequately. These were the same local authorities, after all, that patently struggled to clear mud off the road.

Much of the blame undoubtedly lay with the vestries' contractors. The *Spectator* joked that the word contractor derived from 'the contracted interpretation which men of the class commonly give to their duties'.[22] Not that street cleaning was inherently complex. Street cleaners worked in gangs, from two or three men to a dozen at a time, brushing the mud into heaps by the side of the road, from where it could be shovelled into a cart and thence removed to a dust yard or wharf. There was some additional technology available. From the 1840s, 'sweeping machines' – horse-drawn carts with rotating brushes at the rear – swept up mud into containers, or to the side of the street. Hoses, too, could be used to loosen up mud or sluice it into the sewers, providing an ample water supply was available, which was not always a given. But both these methods were expensive to operate and rather blunt instruments, liable to damage macadam; and risked choking up gullies and drains. For the most part, therefore, street scavenging remained manual labour of the most straightforward type (although hosing was increasingly used as more durable smooth surfaces, like asphalt, were introduced).

The fundamental problem with the contractors' work was essentially that cleaning was not done thoroughly or systematically – and, as with dust, money was at the root of the neglect. For a start, street sweeping was often bundled together with refuse removal into a single contract for 'scavenging', and so suffered whenever the dust trade felt any economic pinch. Contractors who undertook street sweeping in order to win the lucrative dust contract let it slide when times were hard. Mud itself, meanwhile, although it could be resold as fertiliser, was never as lucrative a proposition as dust. There was little incentive to meticulously cleanse any given street, as long as a couple of token cartloads were cleared. Alleys and courts were mostly neglected.[23] Swept heaps of mud were allowed to grow higher and higher before mud carts arrived – left overnight or even longer, risking being churned up again by traffic – all to keep transport costs to a minimum. Collection of mud also became infrequent whenever the weather made the work difficult. Contractors were particularly chary of dealing with the consequence of heavy snowfalls, even if mandated by their contracts, because such work created massive extra costs, both in cartage and manpower, and generated little or no extra income.[24]

In short, contractors, once again, tended to place profit above the interests of the public. They also faced a growing problem disposing of mud economically – just as with cinders and ashes. Transport costs increased as the city grew, making the sale of mud less and less profitable; competition in the form of guano and chemical fertilisers undermined sales further. Less scrupulous operators tried to keep down their costs by doing the absolute minimum of work. The practice of sweeping dirt down gutters into the sewers became widespread – the street equivalent of the housemaid sweeping dust under the rug.

Such failings were not universal – the multiplicity of local authorities and contractors allowed for great variation – but they were very common sources of complaint. Vestries themselves, meanwhile, were widely seen as negligent and/or corrupt, hand-in-glove with failing contractors. Many contemporary commentators saw muck on the streets as symbolic of a greater malaise. Throughout the nineteenth century, poor and parsimonious administration, 'jobbery', factionalism, and the unaccountability of local bodies tarnished the collective reputation of vestrydom. The state of the streets seemed emblematic of everything that was wrong – as one writer put it, with heavy irony, 'an object lesson in the blessings of local government'.[25] After St George's, Hanover Square seemed to abnegate its responsibility for clearing away snow (and the mud beneath it), *The Times* ran a lengthy editorial, summing up the public mood, fulminating, 'The great duty of their officials is to raise difficulties and their own great delight is to see them and succumb to them.'[26]

Certain local authorities would despair of the contracting system and choose to do their own scavenging. But they, too, would struggle with the question of how to clean the streets effectively and economically. Some looked to cheap labour. Holborn, for example, experimented in 1848 with '12 able-bodied Paupers taken out of the Workhouse for the purpose'.[27] Even paupers considered the work degrading – a previous trial in St Pancras in 1839 had been abandoned due to 'the insubordination and insult of most of the paupers (in spite of all encouragement to industry)'[28] – and there was some debate as to whether pauper labour drove down the wages of the regular workforce. Ultimately, it was agreed that unmotivated paupers did an even worse job than the contractors.

Other authorities would attempt to shed contractors and replace them with their own employees, but the expense of maintaining carts and horses, as well as a workforce of street sweepers, made poorer vestries very nervous. Bethnal Green tried various combinations of employing its own staff *and* contractors during the 1860s, before finally abandoning the idea and reverting entirely to contractors in 1869. Nearby Whitechapel was more decisive, establishing its own scavenging department in the mid 1870s – but at a cost of over £7,000 a year. Others would follow suit. Many districts, however, were not prepared to make a long-term investment and, of necessity, kept faith with the contracting system.

The public despaired of ever walking on clean streets. But there was help at hand. The filthy swamp on London's carriageways created an opening for a lowly class of entrepreneurs.

Crossing-sweepers tried to scratch a living from the superabundant mud. They were beggars of a sort, demanding alms in return for a useful, almost essential public service: clearing and maintaining paths from one side of the road to the other.

It is often mistakenly assumed that the 'crossings' in question were simply gaps in the mud, created by sweepers' brooms. Sweepers did brush anywhere they might turn a penny (including preceding likely benefactors along the pavement) and impromptu crossings did exist; but their traditional 'pitches' were 'paved crossings' which were part of the built environment. These were special sections of road made of stronger material than the main carriageway, 'so as to form a regular continuation of the foot paving for the convenience of foot passengers'[29] – a primitive predecessor of the modern pedestrian crossing. Some were even lit accordingly, 'illuminated at either end by a somewhat dim street lamp'.[30] They were often, but not exclusively, located at the junctions between side roads and main thoroughfares (junctions were themselves, confusingly, also referred to as 'crossings'). Local residents had crossings constructed;[31] some petitioned paving boards to do the work for them;[32] or local authorities and their surveyors simply had them built for the benefit of the public, without any special prompting.[33] Crossings seem to have varied in size (minutes of the Kensington paving board include arguments over whether their suburban crossings should be 6 feet or 9 feet wide)[34] but hard-wearing granite was the commonest material. They were used as clean, relatively safe places to cross over. A judge in 1862, for example, controversially ruled that compensation for a traffic accident was not possible, 'unless the child was walking on a paved crossing'.[35] These, then, were the principal haunts of London's self-employed crossing-sweepers.

Once installed on a crossing, the only equipment a would-be sweeper required was a handmade besom, with twigs bound together for a brush.[36] The art was finding a suitable pitch to claim as one's own – a spot that was not regularly swept by another sweeper, where plenty of people crossed the road and the local constable was amenable to a sweeper's presence. The most lucrative pitches were in the wealthy West End, particularly outside the gentlemen's clubs of Pall Mall and St James's, but sweepers could also be found in the City and the suburbs, even if only outside churches on a Sunday. Work literally 'dried up' during the summer, so the trade was very much a seasonal one.

The sweepers themselves, poor and ragged, were often children, the disabled or the elderly, since they were more likely to elicit sympathy than an able-bodied male. Adult sweepers, however, did exist. They might be accompanied by their own children (or those of friends and acquaintances, posing as their own) with men 'bull-nursing' babies or even having pets with them, to suggest 'good nature'.[37] 'Exotic' sweepers were also of great interest to the public. St Paul's Churchyard had an individual variously described as a 'Hindoo' or Sikh, who won brief fame by being adopted as a translator by the Nepalese ambassador, and then reputedly retired to run an East End opium den.[38] Wounded and crippled soldiers turned to sweeping to supplement small army pensions, many wearing their old uniform or medals. A court case of 1859, for example, records a drunken sweeper in Bayswater Road, accused of assaulting a young girl – 'a man with two wooden legs . . . who receives a pension as an old soldier at the rate of 10s. 6d. per week . . . repeatedly convicted at this court for ruffianly attacks upon the police and others'.[39]

The few able-bodied men who worked at sweeping were generally in rather a 'degraded' state. The inquest into the accidental death of one Thomas Kenning in 1891, aged fifty-one, records a typical downward spiral – the man in question went from owning a prosperous boot-making business to becoming a commercial traveller, an alcoholic, being deserted by his wife, and finally 'reduced to the position of a crossing-sweeper, lodging in the vicinity of Leather-lane, Holborn'. The work of crossing-sweeper was very much the last rung of the employment and social ladder. A combination of begging and their intimate connection to the filth of the streets made sweepers the lowest of the low. To remove the taint of mendicity, attempts were made by charities to form 'crossing sweeper brigades' in the same vein as the Shoe-Black Brigade, but none seems to have gathered much momentum.[40]

It is undeniable that sweepers were beggarly. It is not difficult to find contemporary complaints against individuals accused of pursuing pedestrians with unwanted cries of 'tip us a copper!' or 'pitch us a brown!'; or, conversely, not appearing on their crossing in bad weather, when their services were most needed. One letter-writer, walking from Kensington to St James's, counted seventeen sweepers, 'nine or ten . . . troublesomely importunate, sufficiently so as to make the walk a nuisance', and testified that his wife and daughters positively avoided swept crossings, 'in order to escape the worry and occasional abuse that they habitually encounter'.[41] It was claimed, only half in jest, that sweepers finished the day by sweeping dirt back on to their crossings, dubbing it 'shutting up shop for the night'.[42] The most frequently levelled accusation was that sweepers, as beggars, could earn astonishing amounts of money. There was a persistent urban myth that a canny sweeper might earn enough from a 'good' crossing by day to live in luxury by night, and pass as a gentleman. This appeared in the Victorian press as a 'true story' in various forms throughout the nineteenth century, and was given a literary incarnation by Thackeray in his short story 'Miss Shum's Husband'.[43] Another myth was that good pitches were sold on for hundreds of pounds. Unsurprisingly, actual examples are hard to track down. A case reported in *Reynolds's Newspaper* in 1885 with the marvellous headline of 'Wealthy Pauper Choked to Death' records a crossing-sweeper 'of sober habits' with a pitch outside Rectory Road Station in Stoke Newington, 'in receipt of parish relief up to the time of his death' but found with the magnificent sum of £27 6s. 9d. at his lodgings. That a supposed pauper should possess such savings was certainly notable; but, equally, this was not great riches. Certainly, in interviews and court reports, where actual sweepers mention their takings, they rarely amount to more than 1s. 6d. a day, often considerably less.

Yet, if crossing-sweepers were beggars, they were also rather useful. It is significant that there were several attempts by West End vestries to license sweepers – largely to ensure they were suitably respectful to pedestrians – rather than simply abolish them.[44] Partly this was charitable impulse; but partly it was because the value of a swept crossing was heartily appreciated. Many crossing-sweepers seem to have forged strong bonds with the respectable classes. Trusted sweepers were used by householders to run errands, hold horses and carry parcels, as well as being employed by the timid, elderly and infirm to help them cross the street – no easy feat in the busy metropolis. Some households were on surprisingly intimate terms with their 'local' sweeper. In larger houses, servants would employ a sweeper to do small jobs in the kitchen or pantry, in return for small helpings of food and drink. A court case of 1895 even mentions a crossing-sweeper 'engaged to make an inspection of all the doors and fastenings every evening' while the family took its annual holiday.[45] Charles Dickens himself took an interest in a boy-sweep who industriously kept the pavement clean near his house in Tavistock Square, and 'saw to it that the little chap got his meals in the kitchen of Tavistock House, and sent him to school at night'. When the youth turned seventeen, he helped him emigrate to Australia – a more positive ending than the one the great author subsequently contrived for 'Jo' of *Bleak House*.[46] One can even find a few cases where sweepers were left small bequests, reflecting gratitude for long service.[47]

Crossing-sweepers spied one sort of opportunity in the mud. There were others thinking on a grander scale. Charles Cochrane, radical, public health reformer and general busybody, is now almost entirely forgotten. Yet he developed his own grand scheme to rid London of mud – the only sanitary agitator to really address the problem – and spent the best part of a decade trying to bring his scheme to fruition.

Cochrane was the illegitimate offspring of an aristocratic father, who died and left him a substantial fortune. He first came to public notice, after a fashion, as the anonymous author of *Journal of a Tour*, published in 1830. The *Tour* was a record of Cochrane's teenage perambulation around Great Britain and Ireland whilst, bizarrely enough, disguised as a Spanish troubadour, 'Don Juan de Vega'. This unlikely spree gained modest notoriety – not least for the anonymous young author's gauche chronicling of feminine charms, and hints of amorous adventures. Restless for adventure, Cochrane then proceeded to lead a troop of volunteers into the Portuguese Civil War, albeit no longer masquerading as a Spanish nobleman. Both these episodes reveal something of his charisma, determination and eccentricity. By the end of the 1830s, however, he had settled down in highly respectable Devonshire Place in the parish of Marylebone, and found a new all-consuming passion – reforming the streets of London.

The catalyst for Cochrane's interest was a specific local dispute: choosing the best carriageway paving for Oxford Street. In 1837 Marylebone vestry threatened to replace the existing macadam road surface – which cost an appalling £4,000 per annum to maintain – with more durable granite blocks – which would cost £20,000 to install. Neither of these expensive alternatives was terribly agreeable (and both figures were disputed) and the proposed change angered many local shopkeepers. They feared losing trade during the roadworks and were concerned about the noise of granite blocks (the racket of iron-shod wheels rattling over hard stone deterred casual shoppers). With livelihoods seemingly at risk, it was not long before the argument became rancorous. Existing vestry factions of 'moderates' and more plebeian 'democrats' claimed to represent the best interests of the neighbourhood. Some dubbed it 'the Oxford Street job',[48] asserting that one of the chief 'repavers' on the vestry, a Mr Kensett, was taking money from the parish's stone contractor. Interminable, argumentative meetings occupied months of parish time. There was even the real threat of a new 'paving board' being established by Act of Parliament, to wrench the street from vestry control – such was local politics. Finally, experimental sections of asphalt, bitumen and wood were laid down and, after much delay, the parish's paving committee recommended wood paving.[49] This, at least, satisfied many of the shopkeepers: wood was smooth and noiseless. The debate, however, was far from over. The following years were spent arguing retrospectively about the decision – not least whether wood was proving too slippery for horses when wet – and whether wood paving should be extended even further. It was amidst this endless wrangling that Charles Cochrane first entered public life, as a Marylebone vestryman. It is tempting to speculate that Marylebone's fevered debates over paving – in which both parties were accustomed to bring noisy 'deputations' into the vestry room – set the pattern for Cochrane's own heated exchanges with local authorities in the following decade.

At first, Cochrane's interests revolved solely around a single issue: promoting the case for wood paving in Marylebone. In 1842, unhappy with the vestry's progress, he founded the Marylebone Practical and Scientific Association for the Promotion of Improved Street Paving. The stated aim of the body was to lobby for better paving and support innovation by offering prizes for inventions and ideas.[50] The Association had a 'Museum of Paving' at its offices in Vere Street, and held meetings of engineers, scientists and omnibus proprietors to assess the latest technology, such as the 'concave horse shoe' (which purportedly gave better traction on wood) and the street-sweeping machine of Joseph Whitworth.

The following year, however, Cochrane's focus widened from paving to mud. The great argument against wood was that it became too slippery with mud – so why not abolish mud itself? Cochrane came up with a simple idea which he thought could revolutionise the state of the roads throughout London: that the able-bodied poor should be mobilised as a workforce to cleanse the streets, and scavenging should be constant, so as to prevent the streets ever becoming dirty. Under his scheme, workers would be allocated a stretch of road and remain on duty, continually busy, sweeping away dung as soon as it appeared. The work was not meant to be degrading. Cochrane would give his workers uniforms, and enjoin them to act as a 'ready, though unpaid, auxiliary to the police constable'. He envisaged them assisting in everything from arresting pickpockets to helping old ladies across the street.

Cochrane's proposal was different from the parishes' existing occasional use of paupers in that he advocated paying his workers a wage, albeit a low one, and stressed the prevention of the accretion of filth, rather than its periodic removal. His stated aims included providing worthwhile labour for the struggling poor, saving them from the workhouse. A brief trial of the system, in Regent Street and Oxford Street on wooden paving in January 1844, received universal acclaim, particularly from the shopkeepers, with roads 'so clean that a lady's shoe would not be soiled in crossing at any part of them'.[51] Buoyed by this success, never one to hide his light under a bushel, Cochrane began an endless round of public meetings, explaining his revolutionary idea to the masses, and trying to persuade – or shame – vestries into adopting something similar.

These meetings would also mark the beginning of a greater project, which would address wider problems relating to public health and poverty. Cochrane was drawn to Chartism and radical politics, and reform of the streets became linked in his mind to social reform. In 1846 he renamed the association the National Philanthropic Association and created a sister organisation, the Poor Man's Guardian Society, which would fight the harshness and iniquities of the 1834 Poor Law (highlighting complaints of physical cruelty to workhouse inmates, poor diet, overcrowded, verminous buildings etc.). Cochrane, with his trademark manic energy, began to write letters and hold meetings on a range of issues, not just paving. He now tackled the failings of workhouse authorities; demanded vestries build public baths and washhouses; promoted model housing schemes for the poor; investigated the notorious problem of the city's full-to-the-brim burial grounds; and explored and documented 'low lodgings' in the slums. Nor did he limit his activity to social investigation and propaganda. In January 1847, he set up a soup kitchen in Ham Yard, Windmill Street, with its own washing and bathing facilities for the general public, as well as public lavatories – including, most likely, the first public lavatory for women in the capital. At the close of 1847, he published a radical magazine, the *Poor Man's Guardian*, which ran for only eight issues but encouraged the poor to write in with accounts of their oppression. And, throughout all this, Cochrane still pushed his notion of systematic, constant street cleaning using workers whom he now called 'street orderlies'.

It was a novel idea and there was considerable interest. Several vestries in the West End trialled the system between 1845 and 1852, as did the City of London, and it was universally agreed that the results were a remarkable improvement in cleanliness. It could hardly be otherwise. Never had London streets received such detailed attention. The only difficulty was that not a single West End authority decided to continue the experiment. After all the energy Cochrane had expended on the street orderly project, this must have been terribly frustrating.

One factor, regrettably, was Cochrane himself. With even the merest hint of diplomacy and tact, he might have done much better. Instead, he was proud, arrogant and made a point of lambasting those who disagreed with him, actively seeking out confrontation. For example, when St Martin's churchwardens advised him – quite reasonably – to address his scheme to the parish's paving committee rather than the vestry, he publicly accused them of being 'underhand', damned the committee in print as 'corrupt or ignorant' and advised parishioners to 'look to it themselves if they hoped for attention to their wishes'.[52] Such rabble-rousing did little to endear him to local authorities. *Lloyd's Weekly London Newspaper*, a keen supporter of his work, still described him as 'a gentleman possessed with a greater share of personal vanity than any man ought to exhibit whose beard has imposed upon him a familiar knowledge of a razor'.[53]

Cochrane's enthusiasm for grandstanding would also fatally undermine his wider ambitions. In 1848, when the ruling classes feared Chartism and revolution, he twice attempted to set up public meetings: both descended into violence, with slightly farcical overtones. The first, in Trafalgar Square, was declared illegal by the police. On this basis, Cochrane himself decided not to attend and felt obliged to advertise his absence on billboards – a peculiar sort of advertisement, intended to dissuade others from attending. Nonetheless, fellow Chartists spoke to a crowd of more than ten thousand, who finished the day in violent scuffles with the constabulary, spilling out into a general riot in St James's.[54] Fearing that he had appeared cowardly, Cochrane foolishly attempted to set in motion a new demonstration a month later, protesting against the Poor Law. Circling Leicester Square in an advertising van, showing enlarged lithographs of workhouse atrocities from the *Poor Man's Guardian*, he succeeded in attracting no more than a couple of hundred malcontents. The mob, although not large in number, swiftly engaged in pitched battles with a waiting contingent of police. The day ended with Cochrane meekly delivering a petition to a petty official in the Home Office, jeered by locals and ashamed of his own supporters.

The Times, wholly unimpressed by Cochrane's politics and methods, put the following in the mouth of a policeman at the scene: 'You want to get notoriety at the expense of the country, and honest tradesmen are to be put to all this inconvenience to tickle the vanity of a strolling adventurer.'[55] An unlikely editorialising sentiment in the middle of a riot, but the perception of Cochrane as a self-aggrandising rabble-rouser was one that stuck, and impacted on his credibility. It was an unfortunate fall from grace – only two months earlier his soup kitchen had been visited by Prince Albert, who 'tasted the soup and pronounced it to be excellent'.[56] Any prospect of increased donations to the National Philanthropic Association disappeared. *Punch* repeated the accusations of self-promotion, timidity and cowardice, gleefully dubbing him 'COCKROACH'.

It was not, however, Cochrane's aggression and bombastic rhetoric – which one opponent described as 'intended to be irritating and offensive'[57] – or his political radicalism, which ultimately decided vestries against adoption of the 'street orderly'. The riots did him much harm, but Cochrane retained some supporters in the press, and vestries continued to trial the street orderly system for several years. Those authorities that did try Cochrane's system were very happy with street orderlies' work, which seems to have been exemplary. In fact, vestries were generally very interested in street orderlies – until they realised how much they cost.

The cost was initially opaque because virtually every trial of Cochrane's system was managed at the National Philanthropic Association's own expense. This was a rash policy, given that Cochrane had no intention of managing parish scavenging on a long-term basis and merely wished to display a 'model'. True, the Association possessed some notable patrons but it continually struggled to raise cash.[58] By 1850 its balance sheet showed it was heavily in debt to its presiding genius,[59] and Cochrane frequently adverted to spending thousands from his personal fortune on the project. He doggedly argued that street orderlies would, ultimately, save parishes money – or, at worst, be no more expensive than the existing scavenging arrangements. He claimed parishes could offset the increased cost in manpower against decreased costs for maintaining paupers; proper street cleansing would remove the need to water down dust in the summer; less would be spent on road repairs; fresh dung could be sold at a greater profit. Such arguments, however, ignored the great expense of wages and cartage.

It was, therefore, presumably with some relief that Cochrane discovered that the City of London authorities were willing to attempt and, crucially, *pay for* a third trial of street orderlies in 1852.[60] He had spent several months lobbying at 'wardmotes' (local meetings of each ward of the City) and generated sufficient interest and enthusiasm for one last effort.

In fact, this trial would prove the death knell of the National Philanthropic Association. First, there were questions about the quality of the work, with insufficient numbers of men, shoddy cleansing and 'an utter want of organisation'.[61] In retrospect, this was unsurprising, since the City paid its regular contractor, Mr Sinnott, to make all the arrangements. It is unlikely Sinnott harboured much enthusiasm for the plan, not least since the system demanded supervision of a minimum of 265 men, working in shifts in multiple locations. Things seem to have got better as the months passed and the weather improved – but the condition of the streets was not the only problem. Cochrane had, as always, profoundly underestimated the money required. By the time the trial finished, the bill for cleaning proved to be nearly £12,000, more than double the contractor's usual figure.[62] The City's General Purposes Committee met in May 1852 and 'much as they admired the clean state in which the city streets were now kept, they thought that it would be best to submit the whole matter to an open tender, so that, if they pleased the advocates of the orderly system might become contractors'.[63] Whole wards of City residents who had supported the project decided that it was 'not only an inefficient but a most expensive method, entailing on the over-taxed citizens an enormous increase to their burthens'.[64] Sinnott reluctantly worked with orderlies until the summer of 1853; but he was then permitted to return to the old system of cleansing.

Cochrane's private funds and the charities' coffers were all but exhausted. On the verge of bankruptcy, he fled to France and, seeking a new cause, became an ardent proponent of Sabbatarianism. He died two years later, 'alone and with his affairs in hopeless confusion'.[65]

Cochrane's story reveals a good deal about the problems of vestry government, when it came to management of the streets. Choosing the paving material for a single road could cause several years' worth of rancorous debate; and the result could still differ markedly from the paving in the next road, let alone parish. Factionalism and rowdyism dominated many a vestry meeting; and it was necessary to win the same arguments time and again, in countless different locations, in order to make any impact on the metropolis as a whole. Cochrane had the energy and enthusiasm of a dozen men – and still failed. Tellingly, his lithograph in the National Portrait Gallery's collection is captioned simply 'Travelling player and diarist', as if the creation of 'Don Juan de Vega' were his greatest achievement.

The street orderly scheme would, however, have a second life in the City of London, a decade after Cochrane's demise. This final twist was rather ironic, as it was the City's rejection that had put the last nail in the coffin of the National Philanthropic Association.

It is not entirely surprising that City officials eventually revisited the idea of the street orderly. The City was the financial and mercantile heart of London and, consequently, its crowded, narrow medieval streets suffered most from heavy traffic and mud. Part of the congestion problem lay in the character of the vehicles. The City was not merely a centre for commuters – full of clerks, bankers and stockbrokers, making it a hub for omnibus traffic – but packed with riverside wharves and warehouses. Large and sluggish four-wheelers, such as railway vans, drays and coal carts, dominated the road, causing lengthy 'stoppages' (traffic jams) simply by going about their business.[66] The roads took a heavy pounding, and mud exacerbated the problem. Every fall and accident meant damage to the City's economy – and hence street improvement was taken seriously. The City had, for example, ordered its principal thoroughfares to be swept daily as early as 1839, and this was extended to every street, alley and court in 1845; few other parts of London had such a regime.[67] Whether contractors fully lived up to these exacting demands was another matter, but their contracts spelt out the obligation in full.

The revival of the street orderly idea came after the officials took the momentous step of doing away with contractors in 1867. As in the rest of the metropolis, contractors' bills for refuse removal and street cleaning had been rising and service seemed increasingly poor.[68] Contractors blamed not only the fall in the price of dust but the 'nuisance removal' legislation of the 1850s which had forced them to remove several of their centrally located dust yards on grounds of public health, massively increasing their costs.[69] This was undoubtedly true, but their complaints received short shrift. Instead, it was decided to set up an entire City scavenging department from scratch, with men, carts, horses and wharf – and street orderlies would form part of this new model regime.

The high costs of Cochrane's plan were not forgotten; but the City would surmount the difficulty with a very Victorian strategy – the use of child labour. Cochrane had been happy to employ some boys; but the new workforce of street orderlies would be almost entirely comprised of teenagers, with a starting salary of merely five shillings per week and 'the right to a dip in the copper every morning – the dip being a gratuitous pint of hot cocoa'. This was a neat arrangement, in which large numbers of hands could be employed with low wages, under the eye of a few senior men and inspectors. In fairness, it may be a little harsh to talk of child labour in this context. It was the norm for teenage boys to make their own way in the world, particularly on the streets, with low-paid jobs ranging from selling newspapers to delivering messages. Boys were also more willing to do the work; grown men considered it had a 'workhousey, parish relief air about it'.[70] Likewise, boys were perhaps better suited to the military discipline which was Cochrane's legacy, wearing numbered badges, and a work uniform of 'frock, leggings, stout boots, and shiny hat', supplied at wholesale price from money taken out of their salaries.

The work itself was arduous, beginning in darkness in the early morning, and the hours long; but there were prospects in the new scavenging department for a boy 'by turns handling scraper and broom, and sorting in the yard, and driving a van, and making himself useful about the wharf'.[71] Meanwhile, William Haywood, the City's energetic and hard-working surveyor constantly looked for ways to improve the orderly system. The squeegee – a rubber scraper, formerly used to clean ships' decks – was introduced to the orderly's arsenal of brushes and shovels and was found to be ideal for removing 'slop' from the newer road surfaces of wood and asphalt. The problem of heaps of mud awaiting collection by the kerbside was resolved by the introduction of 'street orderly bins'. It was a running joke in the 1870s that these bins, lidded metal containers to be filled with dung, were frequently mistaken for post-boxes by visitors from the country – much to their consternation. Other ideas were trialled but abandoned as impractical or too expensive – such as the use of a sprinkler system, built into kerbstones, to periodically sluice mud from the street.[72]

Within a few years, the sight of uniformed 'boy scavengers', darting between the traffic, risking life and limb to scoop up horse muck, was as familiar and commonplace in the City as that of the humble crossing-sweeper. Indeed, a combination of new smoother street surfaces[73] and the work of street orderlies began to put City crossing-sweepers out of business; or, at least, render them simply beggars and nothing more.[74] The overall results were very positive: 'It deserves to be recognised with gratitude that in the vast expanse of London mud the City offers an oasis where the streets are always clean and the roadway always in good order.'[75] By the 1890s, orderlies' wages had increased; and two hundred boys were employed.

In many ways, therefore, Cochrane was posthumously vindicated. St Giles District Board would also adopt a street orderly system in the 1870s, although still contracting out for the removal of the accumulated filth.[76] Likewise the small Strand District Board, which was employing forty boys by the 1890s.[77]

London as a whole, however, remained plagued by mud. The scale of the problem at the end of century is, admittedly, rather hard to assess. Statistics are little help. Vestries tallied loads of mud collected; but we have no way of knowing how much went uncollected. Interestingly, at a meeting of surveyors and sanitary experts in 1899, William Weaver, the surveyor for Kensington, looked back at the 1850s and claimed that 'if a little mud was left in the streets now, there was more grumbling than formerly, when the mud was inches deep everywhere'. In his own territory, he stated that 'once upon a time he had taken 100 loads off the Brompton-road in one day, but he would have a job to get 100 loads in a month now'.[78] The leading speaker at the meeting, on the other hand, Thomas Blashill, inventor of the street orderly bin, was happy to describe London as, in his experience, the dirtiest city in Europe, and affirm that the dirt continued to increase. Such disagreements reflected the confused condition of the capital's roads. 'The State of London Streets' (the title of Blashill's speech) still differed dramatically according to the district and the whims of particular local authorities. No one was sure, in 1899, whether matters would improve; but there was one casual utterance at the meeting that would prove highly prophetic. Dr Smith of St Pancras noted in passing, regarding horse dung, that 'a great improvement would be noticed as motors became general'.

The 'horse-less carriage' first made its appearance in London in 1896. Some deplored the cold, lifeless machine – 'you can't give it a carrot or lump of sugar' – and the 'bloodless satisfaction' of a car journey. Others made rash predictions: 'The railways also were to have wiped out the horses, but have they? There are more horses now than there ever were.'[79]

True, horses would remain on the London streets for decades, but their numbers began to diminish soon after Victoria's reign ended. The motor bus, in particular, would gain rapid popularity, instantly preferred to its flesh-and-blood rival ('almost invariably you see the passenger for choice mount the speedier conveyance').[80] There was no surer augury of the future than the London General Omnibus Company's decision in 1905 to take its existing buses and mount them on motor chassis – it became obvious that horses would become obsolete: it was merely a question of when.

The sanitary benefits, although incidental, were equally plain: the streets would gradually become cleaner. The car, of course, brought new forms of pollution, and some unexpected consequences. One writer to *The Times* in 1910 noted that automotives' fast, unpredictable movements meant the dogs were no longer trained to defecate in the gutter, leaving a new menace for pedestrians on the pavement.[81] Traditional street filth was being replaced by new forms of rubbish, tokens of the new 'consumer society' of the period – more paper litter from discarded newspapers, bus and train tickets, wrapping and packaging.[82] Nonetheless, the twentieth century promised one great improvement – the internal combustion engine would make both street orderlies and crossing-sweepers a relic of the Victorian age, and finally rid London of mud.

3

NIGHT SOIL

Drains and sewers famously became something of a national obsession in the mid-nineteenth century. The stink of decomposing human excrement was posited as the main source of epidemic disease; improved sewerage demanded as the essential public health reform. Yet, at the start of the century, it was far from obvious that sewers would come to be viewed as a sanitary panacea. Removing human waste seemed no more or less important than abolishing mud or clearing away dust.

Indeed, in 1800, London did not rely on sewers *at all* to remove excrement. They existed merely to carry off surface water, to prevent flooding. Admittedly, they often served as a convenient receptacle for filth. Mud from the streets ended up in 'gullies' (drains from street to sewer) by accident or design. Rubbish, too, was pushed through larger gully grates by those unwilling or unable to make proper arrangements with the dustman. Sewer workers were often sent to unblock tunnels clogged with everything from 'coals, cinders, bottles, broken pots' to 'old hats, dead cats, scrubbing brushes'; and they frequently suffered cuts from broken glass.[1] Most respectable householders, however, disposed of human waste in the proper place – their own self-contained amenity, the humble cesspool.

These were brick-lined underground chambers, directly beneath the wooden seat of a privy, or connected via a brick-built drain. They, too, could be abused, 'receptacles for all sorts of rubbish . . . especially in the poorer districts, where, for want of proper receptacles they often serve the purpose of dust-bins'.[2] Cesspools were cylindrical or cuboid, according to the whim of their creator, and their size varied, although they were rarely less than six feet deep, and about four or five feet wide. Once filled up with excrement, they were emptied by 'night soil men' who would scoop out the contents with a bucket, before clambering inside the chamber to shovel out the last dregs of 'soil' – all to be carted away for sale to farmers as manure. The term '*night* soil' was used because emptying was legally restricted to the hours of darkness, when Londoners would least object to nightmen's foul-smelling carts passing through the streets.[3] By the nineteenth century, some cesspools were also connected to brick-built drainage pipes coming from sinks in the house (to take additional wet filth from cooking and laundering). In some cases, these connecting drains were 'trapped' – i.e. had a kink containing water, to capture any foul smells. The cesspool itself was usually covered in some fashion, typically domed over with bricks, topped with a flagstone. It is difficult, however, to give a full and accurate description of 'cesspoolage' because arrangements varied considerably from house to house. There were no building regulations regarding the internal drainage of a property. Plumbers and bricklayers could, therefore, devise any system that seemed workable.

Hence, although the ideal location for the privy was the backyard or garden, allowing any smell to disperse, it was not unusual for smaller, cramped tenement houses to have both privy and cesspool in the cellar.[4] Builders sometimes cut corners by connecting multiple houses to a single pit. One ancient cesspool, unearthed in Long Acre, was discovered to be running beneath the foundations of twelve houses and providing significant structural support for one of the properties. So vast was the chamber in question that 'when last opened carts were employed constantly for a week to remove the soil'.[5] The better class of house, on the other hand, might have multiple cesspools, serving different parts of the property, not least so that servants would have their own separate privy and pit.[6] In grander houses, when one cesspool became full, it was also customary to arch it over and dig another, 'to avoid the expense and trouble of removing the soil'. Some of the best homes in the West End were 'literally honeycombed' in their foundations, with chambers full of ancient ordure.[7]

Such arrangements were undoubtedly a little improvised and chaotic – but, at the start of the nineteenth century, they were not considered a danger to public health. Indeed, the cesspool's real sanitary failings went unrecognised.

Some pits were built watertight with 'clay puddling outside the walls and cement rendering inside' and an overflow drain to a smaller adjoining chamber for the liquid, which could be regularly pumped out.[8] Many London cesspools, however, were designed to be permeable, so that liquid could percolate from the chamber into the ground below, leaving a more solid sludge behind. In other words, they were *designed to leak*, with either no proper base whatsoever, or 'with open joints, so as to economise the labour of emptying them'.[9] The potential for pollution, in an era when many Londoners still relied on local wells and pumps for water, was considerable – and largely overlooked. Potable water was judged on its clarity and odour. Recognising the subtle invisible peril of bacterial contamination was beyond the science of the day.

Of course, no one thought that cesspools, porous or otherwise, were terribly fragrant or conducive to health – rather that, properly maintained, they were not especially dangerous. Whenever dysfunctional cesspools appear in vestry records of the early 1800s, they are generally treated as tokens of individual neglect, not some wider malaise ('Mrs. Beverstock of Great Guildford Street is continuously suffering her Necessary to be overflowing and thereby committing a great nuisance to the Street').[10] There were vociferous complaints against nightmen accumulating soil in their yards, since it was common to leave great heaps of excrement to dry out before being sold. Similar complaints were made against the smell and nuisance of dust yards.[11] The problem, however, was the sheer volume of foul material collected in one spot – not the manner of domestic storage.

The cesspool, therefore, began the nineteenth century as the unchallenged mainstay of metropolitan sanitation, an unpleasant necessity, nothing more nor less. Yet the great catalyst for change – the reason why the cesspool would begin to acquire an unhealthy reputation – had already made inroads into the more fashionable parts of the great city: the water closet.

Water closets were not an eighteenth-century invention. Famously, Sir John Harrington devised an impressive WC in 1596, which would be installed for his godmother, Elizabeth I, in Richmond Palace. Whilst the first patented water closet appeared in 1775 (by Alexander Cummings, a watchmaker in Bond Street),[12] writers who claim the idea was 'forgotten' in England between 1596 and 1775 are mistaken. The 1747 sale catalogue for the Duke of Chandos's mansion near Edgware, for example, describes an exquisite bathroom containing, amidst black and white marble, 'leaden pipes down from the cistern to the water closet and then to the drains'.

Nonetheless, it is true that water closets only began to be widely adopted by wealthy Londoners in the late 1700s. By all accounts, this growth in numbers was largely due to the popularity of an improved model built by the firm of locksmith and inventor Joseph Bramah. One only has to look at press advertisements of the period for evidence of the WC's growing popularity. Advertisements for the better class of rental property – 'spacious houses', 'capital family dwellings', 'substantial family homes' – increasingly mention water closets from the 1790s onwards. The Lincoln's Inn Fields houses of the renowned architect John Soane (now the Soane Museum) offer some corroboration. All three houses had water closets installed when they were built, commencing with the first house, No.12, finished in 1794.[13] This is not to say that demand for the WC was universal, even amongst those who could easily afford the amenity. An 1831 memo from Lord Chamberlain's Office, planning the private suites of rooms for the monarch in Buckingham Palace, specifies a 'Dressing Room, Bath Room, Water Closet, Wardrobe' for King William. There is an identical list for Queen Adelaide – with the notable exception of a WC.[14] As late as 1847, a third of properties in the wealthy, aristocratic parish of St James's still lacked a modern convenience; in poverty-stricken areas like Southwark the figure was more like 90 per cent.

The adoption of the flush toilet, therefore, was a gradual process. There was no sudden overturning of existing arrangements. In fact, the first toilets were connected to the existing infrastructure – to cesspools, not sewers – and often supplemented rather than replaced existing facilities. John Soane paid one Mrs Sarah Yandall to remove '36 tuns of Nt Soil' in 1808, some fourteen years after the introduction of the first water closet at No.12.[15] Many of London's sewer authorities – concerned with flooding and street drainage, not excrement – actually forbade householders from connecting water closets to their main drainage. In the early 1800s, the water closet and cesspool were not competing models of sanitation – they were conjoined.

This happy union, however, could not be long maintained. The increase in flushing toilets – combined with growing availability of piped water generally – meant that cesspools began to fall out of favour.

The problem was the greater volume of water entering the cesspool chamber once the WC was installed. Impermeable pits filled up more quickly;

sullied liquid had to be pumped out with greater frequency. Porous cesspools, on the other hand, either could not drain away quickly enough or turned the surrounding ground into a damp, foul-smelling bog. The result, in either case, was increased smell and nuisance. The combination of water closet and cesspool began to generate a literal and metaphorical stink amongst the selfsame 'early adopters' who had looked to the WC for convenience, comfort and hygiene. The familiar pit in the back garden became an object of increasing anxiety, particularly in an era when the ancient notion of dangerous 'miasma' – vitiated air engendering disease – was gaining renewed currency. A latter-day commentator in the *British Medical Journal* would write:

> Bramah's water-closets, in fact, wafted a hidden incense to our noses, and made us acquainted for the first time with the fact that our houses were little better than inverted bell-glasses, so constructed as to receive without possibility of escape, the noxious vapours reposing manufactured on the premises.[16]

Notably, few blamed the WC itself for this trouble – its introduction 'revealed' the foul-smelling vapours of the cesspool, even though the miasma only arose after the connection of the WC. The luxury of the flush toilet was simply too appealing. The cesspool, meanwhile, was increasingly despised for wafting the foul, dangerous odours of the slum into the home.

Respectable householders sought release from this miasma. They took advice from their plumbers, who recommended redirecting filth down into the sewers. Not every house was close enough to an existing sewer for a cesspool or WC to be conveniently connected to the main drainage; but large numbers made the change – even though sewer authorities forbade it. Tower Hamlets, for example, reportedly had thousands of drains, 'made by stealth . . . imperfectly constructed and scarcely ever trapped'.[17]

The sewer authorities eventually yielded to the inevitable and allowed household connection. Again, this was an evolutionary process. William Haywood, the City of London's chief engineer and surveyor, identified three stages: householders being allowed to connect sinks directly to the sewers (i.e. to drain liquids only); then plumbers cannily building or adapting cesspools, to include overflow sewer-drains just beneath their doming 'by which means the solid matters deposited, and the supernatent liquid ran off' (i.e. using the permission to drain liquids to empty over-burdened cesspools); then, finally, straightforward direct connection.[18] The latter promised to put nightmen out of a job – but no one mourned the 'infinite annoyance of the senses' occasioned by the process of shovelling out the soil.

This, then, was the first step towards a universal system of waterborne sewerage in the metropolis, replacing cesspoolage. Haywood's chronology is vague and the restrictions on making connections varied from district to district, but, broadly speaking, the change seems to have happened between 1800 and 1830.[19] Homes gradually began to be connected to the main drainage. It was not the result of any particular sanitary agitation or government intervention. Rather, it came from the middle and upper classes' enthusiasm for the comforts of the water closet; and the discovery of the awkward fit between WC and cesspool.

But it would not be long before householders were given cause to wonder whether this was altogether a good idea.

The first great public health scandal relating to sewerage occurred in 1827. It was triggered by an incendiary pamphlet, running to more than a hundred pages, written by the journalist John Wright, editor of *Hansard*. The pamphlet was entitled *The Dolphin, or Grand Junction Nuisance; proving that Seven Thousand Families in Westminster and its Suburbs are supplied with Water in a state offensive to the sight, disgusting to the imagination, and destructive to health*. Wright showed that the Grand Junction Water Works Company was drawing water from the Thames, pumping it out by steam engine – and that the company's pipe lay within yards of the outfall of a major sewer. The pipe's location was patently obvious, marked by a 'dolphin', a protective wooden buoy. The company's water was neither allowed to settle in a reservoir (which might remove some impurities through subsidence) nor filtered, before being distributed to about seven thousand customers, many of them in the fashionable, aristocratic West End. The elite of the metropolis were receiving diluted excrement for drinking, cooking and laundering – and paying handsomely for the privilege.

Strangely enough, Wright's motivation in exposing this scandalous arrangement was not primarily public health. In fact, he was opening up a new front in a long-running but somewhat dormant campaign to regulate London's water companies. In 1817, five north London companies had agreed on precise boundaries to define where each could deliver their water, ending competition and hiking up prices.[20] An 1821 parliamentary select committee had suggested a cap on future water rates, but ultimately nothing was done.[21] Wright realised that the foul state of the Grand Junction's water was a very convenient stick with which to beat the triumphant 'monopolists'. The Grand Junction Company had issued marketing material promising water that was 'always pure' and 'constantly fresh', 'fed by the streams of the vale of Ruislip'. In truth, it had first drawn water from the rather more dubious Grand Junction Canal (owned by the company's original investors) and then, finding the canal increasingly polluted and inadequate, switched to the Thames supply in 1820.

Customers already knew their water was, to some degree, filthy. A letter to the *Morning Chronicle* in 1824 by 'An Inhabitant of St George's Parish' provides ample description of the capital's supply at its worst: black liquid, swarming with 'vermin of the most disgusting description', including leeches and tadpoles.[22] A stock market speculation in the same year, the Thames New Water Company, promised the public 'pure and wholesome filtrated water, divested of the earthy and destructive particles with which most water abounds'.[23] Nonetheless, the significant detail in *The Dolphin* – i.e. the close proximity of *water* and *sewer* pipes – generated an unprecedented public outcry. Wright also used very emotive language, describing water customers under the monopoly 'counted out and handed over . . . like so many negroes on a West Indian estate, or so many herd of cattle at a fair'. He gave the testimony of numerous West End doctors – all of whom preferred to rely on sending their servants out for groundwater rather than use their own taps. Here is Wright describing how he showed a sample of tap water to the eminent surgeon John Abernethy, in terms worthy of a cheap melodrama:

> Never shall I forget the countenance of this eminent man at that moment! The very sight of the turbid fluid seemed to occasion a turmoil in his stomach. He began pacing the room backwards and forward, and the only words I could extract from him were 'How can you ask me such a question? There is such a thing as Common Sense! There is such a thing as Common Sense!'

Wright even dragged in the question of temperance ('the very sight of a jug of Grand Dolphin water serves as an excuse for a glass of spirits, to qualify the effects it may have on the stomach').

The pamphlet was despatched to the great and the good – many of whom were Grand Junction Company's customers – and immediately found favour. A public meeting demanding 'pure and wholesome water' was held at Willis's Rooms in St James's, *the* gathering place for the beau monde, 'crowded to excess by persons of respectability'.[24] Opponents would later claim that Wright was funded by a disgruntled director of the Grand Junction Company, and had an interest in establishing a commercial rival – but there was no doubting the instant popularity of the cause. After sundry meetings and petitions, a parliamentary commission was convened 'to inquire into the State of the Supply of Water in The Metropolis'. The Commissioners duly gathered further evidence during the summer of 1828, producing a lengthy report.

Those who had hoped for new regulation to cleanse the river, or legislation to control the water companies, were disappointed by the report's conclusions – or, rather, the lack of them. There would be a government-sponsored survey of alternative water sources by the leading civil engineer Thomas Telford – nothing more of any substance. There were, however, some positive outcomes. Several of the companies took steps to allay public concerns: promising to build new reservoirs; move their 'dolphins' further upstream; and trial filtration schemes. This limited commitment to 'self-regulation', combined with the guarantee of Telford's survey, calmed public opinion. In turn, Wright's supporters proclaimed themselves, if not satisfied, 'deeply impressed with a conviction of the value of Mr Wright's zealous and successful exertions'.[25]

In retrospect, however, it is hard to see Wright's campaign as anything but a lost opportunity. This was an early chance to prevent wholesale pollution of the Thames, which would only grow worse as the century progressed. Why was there no prohibition on excrement entering the sewers? Or – if that seemed impracticable – no outright ban on drawing water from the river?

The answer lay in the fact that there was no real consensus on the scientific and medical evidence. No one disputed that the sewers were now pouring out 'no small portion of undivided floating filth from privies'[26] into the river, or that the Grand Junction's water was often objectionable to the senses – but what were the actual consequences? Medical men might shun the Grand Junction Company's product; but they could only rely on Abernethy's 'Common Sense!' as justification. There was no contemporary science linking foul water to particular illnesses; nor did the constitutional medicine of the period, which conceived illness as imbalance in the body's natural equilibrium, encourage physicians to think in such terms. The Grand Junction Company, meanwhile, made counterclaims, not least that its water, settling in household cisterns, 'very speedily becomes bright in repose, and is then the finest water in the world'.[27] Once the water became 'bright' – i.e. once floating matter settled – it was considered pure. Opposition to Wright was not confined to the boardrooms of the water companies. The *Westminster Review* condemned him as a rabble-rouser, a novice in matters chemical and scientific, ignorantly stirring up 'hydrophobia'. The great volume of water in the Thames, and its continual movement, surely diluted and destroyed all harmful substances. The Grand Junction was merely a little foolish in placing its pipe quite so close to the sewer outfall.[28]

Even when there seemed to be quantifiable facts, it was hard to reach firm conclusions about cause and effect. The parliamentary commission heard evidence that the Thames, only twenty-five years previously, had supported '400 fishermen, each having a boat and a boy' with a plentiful supply of 'roach, plaice, smelts, flounders, salmon, eels, shads, gudgeon, dace, dabs'.[29] But no doctor or scientist could say whether their disappearance was the consequence of increasing volumes of excrement, steamboats churning up the mud, overcrowding on the river, industrial effluent released by the gas industry and others – or all the above. The proponents of the 'common sense' argument were left frustrated. All they could do was make the most generalised dire prognostications. Thus, Dr John Paris, future president of the Royal College of Physicians, suggested, rather vaguely, that, unless the river was cleansed, 'the ravages of some fatal epidemic may be fairly anticipated'.[30]

Four years later, as it happened, Dr Paris would be proved quite correct. The scourge in question was *cholera morbus*.

The Asiatic cholera epidemic which loomed in 1831, having already decimated cities in Eastern Europe and the Baltic ports – threatening to arrive in England via merchant shipping – should have vindicated John Wright. For cholera is a bacterial infection of the intestine, largely transmitted in water polluted by the faeces of its victims. There could be no better proof of the risks involved in mixing drinking water and excrement.

Wright himself actually wrote to *The Times* in November 1831, warning that water companies in south London were still drawing water from between

Southwark and Lambeth Bridge, 'at which the great common sewers of London discharge their disgusting and noxious contents'.[31] A scathing broadside, entitled 'Salus Populi Suprema Lex', was also produced, making the same point in rather earthier terms. The accompanying illustration by Cruikshank features sickly residents of Southwark pleading for clean water from the chief of the Southwark Water Company. The water company supremo, meanwhile, poses in the middle of the Thames like a foul Britannia, crowned with a chamber pot. His honorifics include: 'Autocrat of all the Slushes, Raining Prince of the Golden Showers, Protector of the Confederation of the (U) Rhine'. Unfortunately, John Wright cut a Cassandra-like figure in 1831. Everyone was dreading the prospect of cholera appearing in London. Its symptoms were alarming: violent vomiting, diarrhoea and cramps; the skin turning blue, the face haggard. Victims were afflicted with little warning; many of them died, and did so very quickly, within 24 to 48 hours. Yet the scourge's origins and transmission were a complete mystery.[32] A link between cholera and polluted water – between disease and sewage – seemed no more likely than any other explanation. Wright's voice was just one amongst many, utterly lost amidst a confusing hubbub of medical and scientific claims.

There was, in fact, rather a hysterical atmosphere in the capital. Since the beginning of the summer of 1831, daily reports in the press had tracked cholera's seemingly inexorable progress across the Continent, together with the rising toll of dead. Government warnings, bearing the ominous legend CHOLERA MORBUS, containing graphic descriptions of symptoms, had begun to be pasted up on walls. The insistence of certain medical men that nervous anxiety rendered one more vulnerable to cholera had done little to calm matters. Meanwhile, the medical profession was in disarray, split between 'contagionists' and 'anti-contagionists', who could not agree whether transmission was the result of intimate contact with victims or exposure to 'miasma' (air somehow rendered poisonous). Londoners, their nerves quite frayed, veered between 'fatuous contempt' and 'extravagant terror'.[33] Gallows humour was the order of the day. George Cruikshank's publishers sold his latest collection of cartoons as 'A New and Certain Antidote to the Cholera Morbus', parodying the sales pitch of purveyors of quack nostrums, already much in evidence.

The government tried to calm the panic. Maritime quarantine, a contentious restriction on trade, was already in force. On 14 November 1831, as rumours abounded that the disease had already appeared in Sunderland – which would prove true – the Privy Council took a further step and reconstituted its medical advisory body, the Central Board of Health. This was an important reshuffle. Senior members of the Royal College of Physicians, cruelly mocked by *The Lancet* as 'titled courtiers', allegedly more used to attending royal nose-bleeds, were replaced with men possessing practical experience of epidemics. These included William Russell and David Barry. Dr Russell and Dr Barry had been sent during the summer to St Petersburg, to watch the progress of the disease in Russia. They confirmed that there was no cure for cholera – they knew nothing about the significance of polluted water – but they had suggestions to arrest cholera's progress, which were immediately put into effect.

The new government plan was to establish a network of 'local boards of health', at parish level, reporting back to the Central Board. These volunteer groups would consist of 'substantial householders', a clergyman and at least one medical professional. They would employ inspectors to monitor outbreaks, and organise whatever 'precautionary measures' seemed appropriate. The Central Board also told their subordinates that they had a particular duty:

> To endeavour to remedy, by every means which individual and public
> charitable exertion can supply, such deficiency as may be found to exist in
> their respective districts, in the following primary elements of public
> health, viz.: the food of the poor, clothing, bedding, ventilation, space,
> cleanliness, outlets for domestic filth, habits of temperance, prevention of
> panic.[34]

This was a startling and rather radical injunction. For it implied that the poor required a minimum standard of food, clothing, accommodation and sanitation; and that maintaining the health of the poor was essential in order to prevent the spread of disease to the middle and upper classes. Admittedly, the call was for 'individual and charitable exertion' – i.e. the government would not provide financial assistance. But the Central Board was itself an agency of government; and the local boards were inevitably composed largely of the same worthies who ran local vestries. The doctors' implication was quite clear: existing parochial assistance afforded to the destitute was inade-quate. For the greater good, from whatever source, the poor urgently needed a programme of comprehensive help and support.

Some found this recommendation politically unpalatable – particularly if one generalised beyond the present emergency. The existing welfare system, the Poor Laws which provided some food, income and shelter, varying from parish to parish, was already criticised for creating a culture of dependency. The *London Medical and Surgical Journal* denied the doctors' basic premise – that dire living conditions fostered disease – blustering, 'What an abuse of language! According to this phraseology the rich can never be sick!'[35] Nevertheless, many paid heed to the doctors' call. Following Russell and Barry's advice, slum improvement suddenly became the order of the day. As one contemporary writer memorably put it: 'Awake ye sluggards and idle, arise and clean; lest ye sleep the sleep of death.'[36]

Parish officials were encouraged to visit crowded tenements, to clear 'filth of every description'; cleanse drains and privies; and preach 'extreme cleanliness and free ventilation'. Soup kitchens were established. Water companies committed to providing water from their 'fire-plugs' every night for flushing clean the streets. The Ladies' Committee of the City of London raised £1,000 to purchase warm clothing for the poor. Doctors, parish beadles, overseers of the poor were, in effect, employed as health inspectors, despatched to neglected courts and alleys to discover the worst public nuisances and remedy them (whether by supplying inhabitants with cleaning materials, employing labourers or paupers to do the work, or forcing scavengers to fulfil their contracts to the letter). Likewise, 'to go through the Parishes and ascertain the state of health of the occupiers of houses in these confined places and to take particular notice of any disorders of a contagious character'.[37]

And they found people living in filth.

The most detailed surviving records of these cholera investigations come from the City of London. The commonest problem identified in the City was actually the refusal of dustmen to clear refuse from slums. The authorities hastily published posters listing the terms of scavengers' contracts, and the requirement that they operate 'without any charge or expense to the inhabitants or occupiers'. A close second to dust, however, came a disgusting revelation: the appalling state of the poor man's privy.

The problem was neglect: slum properties with either no toilet facilities whatsoever, or privies and cesspools shared between dozens of tenants, completely ignored by landlords, never emptied. Water closets were all but unknown. The worst places were abominably foul: '12 inches deep in soil on the floor and seat and flowing through the gutters'.[38] As the metropolis expanded, landlords had packed more tenants into old, decrepit housing; and tenants themselves sublet their rooms. Filthy conditions had become the norm in numerous gloomy courts and alleys. Emptying cesspools cost money; slum landlords were loath to pay for the service; residents could not or would not pay. The result was a horrible accumulation of dirt in and around privies, cellars, down neglected alleyways – wherever needs must. Passengers on the Thames infamously had to avert their eyes from the riverside slums built over tidal creeks: 'so little regard is paid to decency that women may be seen entering and leaving these projecting privies, and the filth dropping into the water, by any passer by'.[39]

The City's investigating officials received so many complaints of full cesspools that the City Board of Health distributed a separate printed circular on the subject.[40] Officials also uncovered the ad hoc nature of London's plumbing. Porous cesspools were often dug too deep, making a connection with the groundwater – which meant rising surges of filth whenever there was heavy rainfall. Along London Wall, there was a stretch of sewer built slightly higher than the drains of the houses, with predictable consequences. Investigation of a foul-smelling house on Old Fish Street revealed not only an overflowing privy, but 'a sort of open drain in the cellar to contain what would otherwise overrun the place', built by an enterprising tenant.[41] The idiosyncratic efforts of some builders and plumbers were no better than those of hapless tenants. *The Times* reported on a resident of Long Acre who discovered he had three other houses draining into the cesspool directly below his property, and repaid his neighbours in kind:

> To relieve himself as much as possible from the nuisance – indeed, to prevent being inundated with putrid wash – he has a pump on the outside of his house by means of which a great many hogsheads are poured into the kennel in the night time, twice a week, diffusing over the whole neighbourhood the most suffocating effluvia imaginable. And this is not a solitary instance, for there are many pumps used for the same purpose.[42]

Such nuisances were not exclusive to slums. Builders of new streets were not obliged to connect them to existing sewers or construct new ones; and it was not unknown for respectable inhabitants of fashionable suburbs to relieve their overburdened cesspools by nightly pumping raw sewage into the road.[43]

The overall picture was far from rosy. A few optimists ventured to hope that local boards' investigations would kick-start a revolution: a grand project to improve the lives of the 'lower orders'. But nothing of the sort happened, even after cholera arrived in London in January 1832. Those who took comfort that the cholera was 'awakening the attention of the rich and luxurious to the condition of the poor'[44] would find themselves sorely disappointed. Shamefaced landlords emptied their cesspools; dustmen were persuaded to venture into unfamiliar backstreets; but the cholera epidemic vanished by the autumn, and the enthusiasm for public cleansing vanished with it. Once the emergency had passed, local boards of health and their programmes of cleansing were abruptly dissolved, with grateful thanks from the parish vestry.

This sudden switch from frenzied activity to inactivity now seems strange and inexcusable – another lost opportunity. The dreadful state of the slums and their impact on public health had been forcibly brought to the attention of the general public, local officials and national government. Indeed, the Central Board of Health's focus on poverty and slumdom was not misguided – quite the reverse. Within the first couple of weeks of cholera appearing in London, it was clear that poor districts would bear the brunt of sickness. By the end of March 1832, half the cases were in the crowded tenements of Southwark, Bermondsey and Lambeth – the very districts that Wright had identified in his letter to *The Times*. Wealthy St James's, on the other hand, built a temporary hospital, employing physicians, nurses and stretcher bearers, which reportedly only treated a single patient.[45]

The reasons for inaction were manifold – and provide us with an insight into how 'public health' was not yet a welcome or fully formed ideal.

First, the local boards created by the Central Board of Health (itself dissolved in December 1832) were very much envisaged as temporary affairs. Unelected, composed of vestrymen, medical men and sundry volunteers, they had no mandate beyond the immediate crisis. By the summer of 1832, they had acquired unprecedented powers, not least to enter any dwelling to 'wash, scour, cleanse, whitewash and fumigate'.[46] Such emergency powers, however, required a degree of compliance from existing local authorities and the general public, which was often unforthcoming. The problem posed by cholera victims among Irish immigrants provides a prime example of such difficulties. Irish families, living in slum districts, insisted on holding lengthy wakes for their dead, during which infected corpses remained in the home. Boards of health, on the other hand, were understandably keen on swift burial. This created tensions that led to near riots whenever the authorities attempted to remove bodies by force – a clash in which few were keen to become involved.

A typical incident occurred in August 1832, when a family refused to yield up their dead relative in the slum of St Giles. The local board of health resorted to the local magistrate. The magistrate, in turn, appealed to the police, only to be told that they had instructions not to interfere in burials (even though the Central Board's regulations demanded burial within twenty-four hours). There were sound pragmatic reasons for this reticence amongst the constabulary: the district was notoriously riotous; the Metropolitan Police, established in 1829, were still finding their feet. The magistrate then offered to empower twenty special constables himself; but the parish beadle found 'a great unwillingness on the part of the inhabitants'. Finally, watermen were offered five shillings each to do the work – i.e. a cohort of mercenary roughs, hired at an extortionately extravagant rate.[47] Such ad hoc dealings were typical of how local boards of health were obliged to operate; they could not form the basis of a permanent organisation. Nor was there political appetite for such permanence. The 'medical policing' of 1832 – especially the interjection of the state between landlord and tenant – was an emergency measure. Most politicians considered such interference fundamentally incompatible with the much vaunted liberties and freedoms of the English nation.

The fear of rising costs also played a part. Parliament remained wary of writing local authorities a blank cheque to support the work of local boards of health, even in the midst of the epidemic. MPs declared themselves, rather conveniently, fearful of stifling the admirable outpouring of local charity which surged forward to greet the outbreak; and it was finally agreed that any costs could be defrayed from the parish poor rate. This, in turn, terrified the vestries of poorer local authorities, districts blighted by poverty and unemployment, struggling to support growing numbers of paupers. Bethnal Green, for instance, had doubled its population between 1811 and 1831, but more than tripled the amount it spent on the relief of the poor.[48] No one was keen to add permanent, additional burdens to the rates. The Lambeth Vestry effectively dissolved its local board of health when the board demanded £200 to set up a cholera hospital; the good citizens of neighbouring St Mary Newington, likewise, revolted at the prospect of a penny rate towards the same end.

There was also some scepticism about the medical profession and its motives. Under the local board system, doctors were suddenly finding copious employment in the slums – which could be charged to the rates. To cynics, this seemed like something of a gold rush. Doctors from the Central Board of Health were also found to be claiming exorbitant salaries. A Cruikshank cartoon of February 1832 depicts the Central Board as fat, gout-ridden and complacent, dining on roast beef, raising a glass to the toast 'May we preserve our health by bleeding the Country.'[49]

Finally, there was outright scepticism about the practical need for any further action. The long wait for cholera to arrive in the metropolis, the fears stoked by the press, meant that its ravages did not quite match the expectation. It was clear that only a relatively small percentage of the population had succumbed.[50] More importantly, it was plain that the disease was clustered in the most wretched parts of the city (in Southwark, almost one in a hundred died; in leafy, suburban Islington, on the other hand, the figure was closer to one in a thousand). Cholera was a dreadful contagion, but one that mainly haunted the dens of Irish immigrants; and lingered in the narrow courts and alleys that bred filth and depravity – *it was a disease of the poor*. It claimed few famous casualties in the metropolis: Adam Clarke, an eminent Wesleyan preacher; 'Dando the Notorious Oyster Eater', whose party trick consisted of devouring thirty dozen oysters at a sitting 'with a proportionate quantity of bread, porter and brandy and water'. The bulk of the population merely gave thanks that they had avoided the scourge; and hoped that enough had already been done. And – if cholera was to return – they knew which parts of the city to avoid.

Remarkably, the ravages of cholera engendered no lasting sanitary improvements. Neglected cesspools and dustbins returned to being private matters. It was exactly as if nothing had happened; a bad dream. But one aspect of metropolitan sanitation remained under a degree of scrutiny: the capital's sewers.

In theory, sewers now served two useful functions: clearing surface water and removing excrement. Unfortunately, the epidemic of 1832 revealed that many of London's sewers were not up to the job.

In some districts they simply did not exist. The local board of St Margaret and St John the Evangelist, Westminster, produced a report concluding that 'the want of a proper sewerage appears to the Committee one of the greatest and most lamentable obstacles to the ultimate improvement of the comfort of the poor'.[51] Efforts at removing filth from blocked tunnels highlighted the fact that many drains had an inadequate incline, were prone to becoming clogged, and odoriferous until 'scoured' by heavy rainfall, having been 'built by speculative builders on irregular levels of inferior materials and insufficient size'.[52] Elsewhere, open drainage ditches – a familiar sight in low-lying districts south of the river and semi-rural suburbs[53] – were denounced as the source of miasma likely to cause future disease. An anonymous broadside, printed in August 1832 in Lambeth, blamed the sewers for the 'frightful mortality' in the district, and threatened 'salutary Vengeance' upon the local sewer authorities.[54]

The relevant authorities were not parish vestries – which only had control over a small number of local drains – but eight ancient Sewer Commissions, whose purlieus and privileges had first been established in the reign of Henry VIII.[55] They were managed by committees of unpaid Crown appointees (Commissioners), supported by a small professional staff, typically composed of a few clerks, inspectors and surveyors. An 1820s' select committee had already conducted hearings into the Commissions' powers, competence and governance – a matter of some public interest, since they levied a sewer rate.[56] In 1832, the Commissions' critics suggested that the cholera epidemic revealed the baneful consequences of a long-standing failure to invest in appropriate drainage. The Commissioners of Sewers, in turn, responded with a ready-made, plausible defence for any inactivity and omission. With some justification, they blamed the notorious reluctance of Londoners to pay for their drains.

This peculiar reluctance was a genuine problem, diffused amongst all social classes. In lower-class areas, residents traditionally considered sewer rates a burdensome and unnecessary expense. The Commissions accepted, with due fatalism, that 'the parties generally wait for a summons before they pay'.[57] The middle and upper classes, surprisingly, were little better. It was an established legal principle that rates for sewers could only be raised on properties that 'derived a benefit or avoided damage' from local sewerage. Many respectable citizens vigorously protested that *their* house had no connection to the main drainage; or that they would not pay for sewers in distant parishes ('But in the name of common sense, what had the inhabitants of the northern part of the Parish of Hackney to do with a covered drain from the Commercial-road to the Thames?').[58] The residents of Hampstead flatly refused to be rated – since they lived on high ground, surface water swiftly dissipated – and won a test case in 1815, which effectively exempted the whole district.[59] Likewise, when Tower Hamlets Commission proactively built a new sewer mains in the bustling Ratcliffe Highway, locals launched indignant protests that there was 'no public necessity' for such an amenity – i.e. they had no wish to pay the additional rates levied for the work. There was a widespread culture of complaint and non-payment.

Householders were also expected to pay to make their own connection to any new sewer; and many baulked at the cost. In poor districts, neglectful landlords were reluctant to pay for such improvements and their tenants too penurious ('there are instances where sewers have been laid down to the extent of 5,000 feet in length, and there had not been 50 applicants to communicate, though they have come opposite the house').[60] The middle classes were equally loath to commit themselves. Home ownership was not the norm. Most middle-class Victorians were on short-term lets, and resented paying to improve their landlord's property.

Admittedly the Commissions were also at fault. The fixation on the 'benefit' afforded by sewers – rather than sewers as a communal good – created bodies which did not see themselves as public servants. The clerk of the Surrey and Kent Commission, asked whether they ever spontaneously built sewers to improve streets (i.e. without a request and financial contribution from inter-ested parties), replied '[the Commissioners] think it would not be right for them, with public money, to improve the property of private individuals'.[61] In other words, whilst the Commissions were not parish vestries, they often possessed a similar mindset, revolving around keeping down the rates and respecting private interests – they were not about performing public works, for the public good. Indeed, throughout the capital, most new sewers were private projects: not part of some carefully planned civic scheme, but the ad hoc work of speculative builders, accompanying new housing developments and handed over to the local Commission on their completion.

This had always been a chaotic, fragmentary way to manage the sewerage of the metropolis, even when sewers only contained rainwater. Few, however, had worried about the long-term consequences before 1832. After the cholera epidemic, anti-contagionists began to wonder if the source of the catastrophe lay under their very noses. Poor drainage produced miasma; and miasma produced cholera. Noisome drains in any part of the metropolis might harbour the seeds of future disease.

In 1834, therefore, 'thirty of the most eminent gentlemen of the medical profession' petitioned parliament for an end to the 'noxious exhalations' emanating from sewers, which they deemed 'injurious to the health and prejudicial to the comforts of inhabitants'. They had first brought their concerns to the Westminster Sewer Commission, with little result. The Commissioners believed that 'trapping' gullies with flaps or other devices, to block the rising miasma, would only lead to dangerous build-up of sewer gas; the existing system was the lesser of two evils. Parliament obliged the petitioners with a select committee. The committee would address these new public health concerns and take a fresh look at the role and responsibilities of the Sewer Commissions.

In the event, much of what took place in the 1834 committee was a pointless rehash of the earlier hearings held in 1823. But the medical claims – that the stench from badly maintained sewers now posed a danger to the public – were relatively novel. Dr Peter Fuller, who had instigated the petition to parliament, stated his belief that 80 per cent of typhus cases came from houses with untrapped drains, 'a very curious coincidence'. Timothy Bramah, civil engineer (son of the famous manufacturer of water closets), testified to the ubiquity of foul-smelling drains: 'I find it every day in walking, as I daresay we all do' (sadly he made no comment about the role of his father's business in generating the stink). George Watkins, a builder, claimed that open sewers were depreciating the value of his property in Pimlico, and that he had a petition signed by 'a hundred medical men of the first respectability' which testified to the need for covering them. Most of the witnesses made some allusion to their experience of cholera, hinting that failure to act on the stink from bad drains might encourage its return. Yet, strikingly, no one would go further. Fuller believed that 'effluvia from the sewers must be prejudicial to health' but would not commit to saying it was the *cause* of any given disease. This was exactly the same uncertainty about cause and effect that had hampered John Wright's campaign. The committee itself, meanwhile, retained a degree of scepticism, noting that, during the recent epidemic, none of the men employed to clean sewers had caught the disease.

The committee members reached some predictable and rather lukewarm conclusions: Sewer Commissioners ought to attend properly to their work; their financial accounts should be made available to the public; tenders should be free and fair. Their report acknowledged the problem of public hostility to sewer rates, and suggested that communication with new sewers should be made compulsory. More radically, the prospect of a 'Central Board' to manage London's sewerage was briefly considered – and hastily dismissed as 'unpalatable to the inhabitants of the respective districts' (i.e. there would be local hostility to any 'centralising' measure). The committee offered no conclusions whatsoever on the medical question (rather peculiar, since the fear of miasma had been the initial impetus for an inquiry). Overall, the tenor of the report was diffident and noncommittal. Unsurprisingly, it was ignored by the government of the day.

There was, however, one witness at the committee hearings who refused to take 'no' for an answer: a gentleman by the name of John Martin.

Martin was a successful painter and engraver. He had come to London as a young man, virtually penniless, and made his fortune through his skill as an artist. He painted large biblical and classical scenes, in which people were dwarfed by apocalyptic disasters (subjects for his early work included the fall of Babylon, the destruction of Pompeii and the plagues of Egypt). Latter-day critics have not always been kind to Martin's *oeuvre* ('vast architectural designs, populated with myriads of hacking soldiers and fleeing women in Regency dresses, and lit simultaneously by moonlight or red sunsets').[62] Nonetheless, Martin's canvases were extremely popular in their day. Even those contemporary critics like Charles Lamb, who derided the 'squalling, contorted little antics' of Martin's human figures, nonetheless praised his rendering of vast, awe-inspiring classical buildings as a distinctive architectural vision.[63] And it was this visionary conception of urban landscape that spurred Martin to draw up his own personal plan for remaking London's water and sewer network.

Martin's initial scheme was actually inspired by the agitation surrounding *The Dolphin*. The painter first published 'A Plan for Supplying the Cities of London and Westminster with pure water from the River Colne' in 1828, then swiftly produced a somewhat revised edition in the same year. His ambitious suggestion was to build an aqueduct from the River Colne, in Hertfordshire, to a reservoir in west London. The cost of the scheme would be immense; but the core idea was simple enough – a pure source of water for west London, to provide for the 'health and comfort of millions, present and future'. Martin, however, did not believe in simplicity when he could 'superadd beauty'. He anticipated that there would be considerable surplus water, so he conceived various novel artistic touches, beautifying the city in his imagination. There would be a vast public bath at Paddington, 500 by 150 feet, capable of holding one thousand bathers; a powerful stream of water to cleanse the Serpentine (which was notoriously befouled, connected to the drainage of a common sewer); various new fountains, grottos and water features in the Royal Parks. More prosaically, he also included 'a proposition for separating the soil of the sewers from the water previous to its entering the Thames' – allowing filth to settle in large vats by the river – with a view to selling the collected night soil as manure.

Martin's original plan was submitted to the 1828 Commission on water supply, but given short shrift.[64] Martin, undeterred, published it again the following year, removing the costly aqueduct and suggesting a weir across the Thames, which would power a waterwheel/pumping system (the location for the weir varied from London Bridge to Teddington, as the plan went through various further iterations). By the time Martin came before the 1834 select committee, there were other amendments and improvements. Most importantly, two 'intercepting sewers' on either side of the river which would trap all London sewage before it entered the river, and deliver it to storage tanks by the Regent's and Surrey Canal (whence filth could be separated out, then shipped by barge to eager farmers). The intercepting sewers would be hidden beneath two great embankments, topped within tiered classical colonnades – lovingly sketched by the artist – replacing the traditional higgledy-piggledy shoreline of wharves and warehouses. Martin was now so taken with the possibility of recycling sewage for profit that he declared it the 'principal merit' of the plan.

Just as in 1828, the committee of 1834 did not share the artist's vision. Likewise, the Select Committee on Metropolis Water, of the same year.[65] Martin presented the next version of his plan to yet another select committee in 1836 (a committee on 'Metropolis Improvements', considering both new roads and related sewerage) stressing that cesspools should be abolished in order to perfect the scheme ('no cesspools being allowed, the disgusting and offensive work of the nightmen would cease to contaminate the air').[66] There were, in addition, public lectures and meetings at the Royal Institution, the Institute of British Architects and the Institute of Civil Engineers. Yet, despite all his best efforts, nothing came of Martin's exertions. By his own account, Martin published six different editions of his plan between 1828 and 1836 – with no tangible result. Meanwhile, his finances suffered. Lavish hospitality, lending money unwisely to friends, family and acquaintances, led the once prosperous artist to declare in 1837, 'I have earned £20,000 in a few years and I am now not with a penny.'[67] Martin, however, would not relinquish his obsession with improved water supply and sewerage. His closest friend noted ruefully: 'his time is absolutely lost upon those subjects; but to oppose or dissent is to anger and offend him, so I am obliged to be a listener in torture'.[68]

It is tempting to suggest that John Martin was unfairly ignored – that this was yet another lost opportunity. For his scheme would, in effect, be realised some three decades after its conception. Joseph Bazalgette, as chief engineer of the Metropolitan Boards of Works, would construct both a Thames embankment and intercepting sewers in the 1860s – a decade after the painter's death. Martin's son, writing in the 1880s, had no hesitation in considering his father 'the original projector' of Bazalgette's great work, and demanded public recognition.[69] Yet Martin himself lacked the technical expertise and experience that might have convinced the authorities of the merits of his plan. He was, after all, an artist, not a civil engineer. He may also have seemed a little quixotic in his relentless pursuit of 'Thames improvement'. There was a well-known history of eccentricity and madness in the family: his brother William, an inventor, claimed to have discovered perpetual motion in a dream; his brother Jonathan infamously set fire to York Minister in 1829, citing divine inspiration, and was confined to Bedlam. This unfortunate family association may have coloured perceptions. Martin had *some* well-placed friends and acquaintances – he was, for example, on good terms with the eminent scientist Michael Faraday – but he came from a humble background and possessed no political influence. Nor could his work on Thames improvement, however visually appealing, produce a popular outcry like Wright's *Dolphin*. A pamphlet offering support to Martin in 1836 – a so-called 'Report' under the patronage of the Earl of Euston – provides us with a clear hint of his limitations. Such documents usually conclude with a list of supporters or subscribers. This one has a list of 'Gentlemen . . . willing to concur in consideration of Mr. Martin's Plan'. The list is impressive, packed with contingents of aristocrats, members of parliament, doctors, scientists and artists – but 'willing to concur in consideration' is a most dismal phrase, a mealy-mouthed pseudo-endorsement, tinged with desperation.[70]

Martin would, at least, recover his fortune with a striking painting of the Coronation of Queen Victoria – but his plans for the Thames remained unrealised in his lifetime.

At the end of the 1830s, few anticipated imminent improvement in the sanitary state of the metropolis. John Wright had drawn attention to the foul state of the Thames; cholera had revealed the dire conditions in Lambeth, Southwark and elsewhere; John Martin had laid out his positive vision of clean water and classical colonnades. None of this had stirred the authorities into action. The cesspools of the slums were still brimming over; the sewers inadequate; the river polluted. Again and again, select committees and commissions skirted around the problems of metropolitan water and sewerage, and failed to bring forth any practical measures. A 'Metropolis Sewers Bill', laid before the House of Commons in 1838 – by the same MP who had brought forward the 1834 petition – proposed to create new reformed sewer commissions with the power to enforce connection to the mains, overseen by a central 'Metropolitan Court'. It did not proceed beyond the committee stage.[71] London seemed cursed by the indifference and inactivity of those in power.

One man would change all this: Edwin Chadwick, progenitor of the 'sanitary movement' that swept the country in the mid-century. Under his influence, most *bien pensant* Victorians would come to believe that improved sanitation – particularly replacing the cesspool with waterborne sewerage – was essential for the future well-being of the nation. Throughout the 1840s and 1850s, the cry of 'public health' echoed far and wide; charities lobbied for improvement; parliamentarians promised action. This was a remarkable sea change. A useful parallel, perhaps, is our modern concern for 'the environment'. We may argue about the details, but the importance of green issues has become axiomatic within the space of a generation. The same sort of orthodoxy emerged around the need for improved sanitation – with far-reaching consequences for the capital.

The story of how this change came about – how London moved from the uncertainty and indifference of the 1820s and 1830s to Joseph Bazalgette's renowned multimillion-pound sewer project – is essentially the story of Edwin Chadwick's rise and fall.

4

Removable Causes

Edwin chadwick was born in Longsight, near Manchester, in 1800. His family moved to London a decade later. His father was a radical journalist with no great wealth or influence. Chadwick, therefore, had to rely upon his own wits. He chose the law – an upwardly mobile career for clever young men who lacked connections – serving an apprenticeship as an attorney's clerk and becoming a barrister in 1823. A dour, hard-working intellectual, he was heavily influenced by the social and political theories of the Utilitarian philosopher Jeremy Bentham. Many of Chadwick's acquaintances were 'Benthamites', including the young John Stuart Mill, and he would work as Bentham's secretary during the final year of the philosopher's life. Above all, Chadwick shared Bentham's enthusiasm for accumulating facts and statistics: the comprehensive collection of data both revealed hidden truths and served as a catalyst for change. This applied universally, even down to inculcating morality:

> Returns displaying, as they must do if collected properly, the consequences of vicious peculiarities and habits would effect more in the way of reformation with the old, and of prevention with the young, than the most inflammatory preaching . . .[1]

Chadwick would make good use of 'returns' throughout his career, particularly in sanitary matters. He first achieved national prominence, however, as de facto architect of the Factory Act of 1833 and the Poor Law Amendment

Act of 1834 (also known as 'The New Poor Law'). It would be the latter that led him – by a curious and circuitous route – to sanitation and sewers.

The Poor Laws were the nation's ancient parish-based welfare system. Different parishes provided different types of 'relief' for the old, sick, orphaned and unemployed. These included keeping the poor in workhouses, in return for the 'Benefit of their Work and Labour'; 'farming' them out to private work-house contractors; 'outdoor relief' of money, food and medicine; even subsidising agricultural workers' wages. By the early 1830s, government ministers were growing alarmed at the rising costs of relief to ratepayers, the negative effect of subsidies on wages, and welfare dependency.[2] They appointed a Royal Commission to suggest possible reforms. Chadwick, looking for useful employment after Bentham's death, took a post as a lowly 'assistant commissioner'. He then proceeded to dazzle his superiors by volunteering a comprehensive written report, a complete solution to the Poor Law question. Ultimately, he became principal author of the Commission's findings, which, in turn, formed the foundation of the 1834 legislation. The New Poor Law, therefore, was largely Chadwick's invention, a remarkable testimony to both his intellect and ambition – and possibly the most hated piece of legislation of the nineteenth century.

The Act itself contained three main elements. First, it established a central Poor Law Commission, run by three Commissioners, with authority over local parish administrations. Second, it grouped small parishes into amalgamated 'unions' for the purposes of poor relief, and laid the groundwork for the creation of large 'Union workhouses'. Finally, it abolished wage supplements and attempted to regulate and restrict outdoor relief, with a view to channelling all paupers into the new workhouses. These were to be vast, prison-like, administered on harsh, authoritarian lines, with strict segregation of the sexes and a subsistence diet. Chadwick's plan was that union workhouse life should be 'less eligible' than 'the situation of the independent labourer of the lowest class'.[3] The aim was to deter scroungers: only those who truly *needed* relief would choose to enter the grim, forbidding 'Union'; the rest would go and find work. Critics – of whom there were many – considered this, at best, uncharitable; at worst, a species of cruelty, eroding the traditional social compact between the wealthy and the poor, replacing local beneficence with a soulless, state-sponsored machine. Chadwick, on the other hand, judged it a perfect Benthamite mechanism: the would-be pauper would stand at the workhouse door, and reach the right conclusion about his need for state support, based on a fine calculation of pleasure and pain.

Indeed, Chadwick was rather proud of his new creation, and harboured great hopes of being placed at the helm of the Poor Law Commission. He was, therefore, both astonished and insulted to be informed that he would not be considered for a post as one of the three Poor Law Commissioners, due to his 'station in society' – such berths were reserved for the well-connected elite. There was, however, a consolation prize: the role of Secretary to the Poor Law Commissioners. Chadwick accepted, after receiving assurances that he would be 'the fourth commissioner' in all but name.

A meticulous administrator, well organised and energetic, Chadwick ought to have thrived in his new role. Instead, he found himself constantly thwarted by his more pragmatic, far less zealous superiors, for whom 'lesser eligibility' was not a strict article of faith. Another man might have found a common purpose with the Commissioners; but Chadwick was naturally abrasive and uncompromising. Gradually, he was virtually ostracised by his supposed colleagues, who grew irritated with his demands – the impudence of a mere *secretary*. He did his best to guide the workings of the Poor Law from behind his desk, but he lacked executive authority. This impotence was doubly galling, since the New Poor Law bore his stamp and he remained the butt of all its critics. *Blackwood's Magazine*, for example, fulminated against the mere '*Barrister*, late penny-a-liner' (Chadwick had worked as a jobbing press reporter) and contrasted his 'well paid secretaryship' with the fate of the poor. 'Is he of the class or of the antecedents, or of the repute from which a paternal government would have chosen a guardian for helpless infancy, or for poverty, honest and not less helpless?'[4]

Such barbs must have stung. Edwin Chadwick, brooding on his fate at the Poor Law Commission, stymied, sought out a new purpose, an outlet for his reforming zeal. He found public health.

The subject of public health did not naturally fall under the aegis of the Poor Law Commission; nor did it belong to any other government body, nor was it claimed by any medical body. The very concept barely existed. Nonetheless, it had been at the back of Chadwick's mind for some time. His very first published essay, printed in 1828, was a piece on mortality and life assurance, which noted that, if detailed recordings were made of sickness, 'the operation of causes which cannot now be clearly detected in single instances, would be pointed out for removal'.[5] Doctors, he believed, had their own pet theories about causation of disease, but ignored the bigger picture – tangible environmental factors, such as overflowing cesspools and open sewers. A rigorous assessment of sufficient data would reveal cause and effect; and provide boundless opportunities for preventing illness. Chadwick's views were not entirely born of theory. They were informed by the experience of a close acquaintance, Thomas Southwood Smith, physician of the London Fever Hospital – a charitable institution, which had sought to publicise the relation between slum conditions and contagious disease ever since its inception.[6]

It is perhaps too much to claim that Chadwick nurtured a strong interest in preventive medicine from 1828 onwards. Rather, this was one abstract Benthamite idea amongst many, carefully stored away for future use. Then, in 1838, it transpired that certain East End Poor Law Guardians were spending money on measures to improve drainage in order to prevent the local spread of fever (principally typhoid, typhus and influenza). Chadwick determined to support their efforts. He made no great claim to humanitarian motives – the real benefit lay in lessening the 'pecuniary burden' that medical treatment entailed upon Poor Law Unions.

He managed to persuade his superiors that the subject warranted detailed attention. He promptly commissioned three eminent medical men, drawn from his circle of Benthamite acquaintances, to write reports – Dr James Phillips Kay, Dr Neil Arnott and Dr Southwood Smith – and despatched questionnaires to Poor Law medical officers. He collated the material in the Commission's annual report, and laid it before parliament. This practice of authoring detailed, telling reports was his trademark – and proved a remarkably effective means of setting the wheels of state in motion.

Chadwick demonstrated that the fundamental problem in the East End was not poor health but money: epidemic disease rendered perfectly good working men a burden on the parish. The medical officers of Whitechapel, for example, had been obliged to attend over 2,000 cases of fever in a single year, all treated at Poor Law expense. Local administrators could not be blamed for addressing the issue (chiefly, by taking legal action against landlords for allowing filthy ditches and the like to persist on their property) and such preventive activity was 'good economy'. It was, after all, perfectly possible to remove the causes of disease. Chadwick laboured this point, glossing the words of a medical officer to make his own case: 'not only the existence of disease, but of particular diseases, may be inferred from obvious physical and removable causes'. Medical men might fuss and theorise but disease was no mystery: it sprang from 'obvious' environmental causes – filth, generating dangerous miasma – which could be *removed*. The poor themselves were not to blame, as they had 'little or no choice of their dwellings'. The answer, at least in the short term, was to allow Poor Law medical officers to act as health inspectors, and Poor Law Guardians to indict irresponsible landlords.

There was no immediate response from government. Cholera had already exposed the condition of London's slums; the reports revealed nothing that had not been uncovered and swiftly reburied in 1832. Chadwick, nonetheless, proceeded to lobby the Commissioners for further investigative work; and when that failed, he went above their heads, persuading the Bishop of London to move for a government inquiry as to the extent and impact of fever, not only in London but throughout the nation. The Bishop was known for his interest in social reform; he was a Privy Councillor during the cholera epidemic and had chaired the investigation into the Poor Law. The Home Office was suitably impressed by his support and asked for a full written report. Thanks to his dogged persistence, Edwin Chadwick now had a new role, albeit still within the Poor Law Commission: he would become the nation's sanitary investigator.

Chadwick was an ambitious individual and his motives have often been questioned. Undoubtedly, he saw removing the causes of fever not only as economically imperative but as a means of accruing political capital: a new sphere of influence for the much criticised Poor Law Commission; he also saw it as a novel means of making the mechanics of Poor Law administration (himself, the central authority and its local officials) invaluable to the nation. Indeed, the 1838 reports he collated were not straightforward investigations of slum life – they were commissioned for a purpose. The initial question-naires sent to Union medical officers presented the 'good economy' argument as a given, and demanded examples to illustrate it.[7] Similarly, it was inevitable that the final documents from Arnott, Kay and Southwood Smith would provide a useful medical endorsement of Chadwick's own views on preventing disease: he carefully chose medical men from his acquaintance who would not contradict his belief in 'physical and removable causes'. This very Benthamite insistence on manageable environmental factors also indirectly addressed damaging claims that the poor were starving rather than submit to the grim horrors of the workhouse. Accusations of starvation under the New Poor Law were threatening to completely undermine the model of 'lesser eligibility' – or, at least, make it morally unpalatable. Poor Law doctors were even prescribing food as emergency medical relief. It was important to Chadwick that disease was not perceived as a measure of the dire physical condition of the poor – i.e. a symptom of the New Poor Law's failure to care for the most needy. The focus on 'removable causes' provided a useful alternative interpretation, a scapegoat for the prevailing suffering in the slums.

The 1838 reports did not prescribe any single response to dire slum conditions. Arnott and Kay's report suggested improved sewers, street watering, public burial grounds and refuse collection; ventilation of streets and houses; the removal of nuisance occupations (such as slaughterhouses); and reducing overcrowding in lodging-houses.[8] Southwood Smith's report included a good deal on improving ventilation in buildings, fumigation and, his pet subject, the need for local fever hospitals.[9] Neglected sewers, cesspools and privies were conspicuous in the reports – but not to the exclusion of all else. If one compares the issues considered in the East End reports with the comprehensive 'primary elements of public health' enumerated by the 1831 Central Board of Health, then the only obvious omission is food and clothing. Food – diet – poverty – starvation – these were subjects to be avoided, i.e. the ones that the introduction of the New Poor Law was supposed to have resolved.

Chadwick was still setting out his stall. He had not yet settled on sewers and cesspools as *the* great sanitary concern – that would come next.

The 1840s would actually be punctuated by four separate government-sponsored inquiries into public health. The first – a select committee report on the 'Health of Towns' – was completed in 1840, and beat Chadwick to the punch. It was the brainchild of Robert Slaney MP, a benevolent Liberal land-owner from Shrewsbury, who was increasingly concerned about political unrest in the industrial North – not least the nascent Chartist movement. His original intention was to inquire into health, housing, education and unemployment – all areas in which he felt parliament had neglected the working man – but he found himself gently steered towards sanitation by a government that feared his report would only stimulate further agitation. Slaney's report would bring forward various cogent proposals for legislation; but none were given adequate parliamentary time to reach the statute book. Chadwick – who had offered 'many useful suggestions' to Slaney's committee – breathed a sigh of relief. He had already spent months working on his own project; he had his own agenda.

Chadwick's own compendious report, *An Inquiry into the Sanitary Condition of the Labouring Population of Great Britain*, finally appeared in 1842. It came out under Chadwick's own name, reflecting the tetchy disapproval of his superiors, a snub which only redounded to his credit. For the report's contents were rapturously received. *The Times* and *Morning Chronicle* serialised crucial sections. Others offered their own ringing endorsements: 'The Report itself should be in the hands of every legislator, or administrator, every philanthropist, and every employer of labour in the community.'[10]

The report recounted the sanitary sufferings of the poor at unprecedented length, and did not stint on detail:

> . . . in many of these places are to be seen privies in the most disgusting state of filth, open cesspools, obstructed drains, ditches full of stagnant water, dunghills, pigsties, &c. from which the most abominable odours are emitted. But dwellings perhaps are still more insalubrious in those cottages situated at the back of houses fronting the streets, the only entrance to which is through some nameless narrow passage, converted generally, as if by common consent, into a receptacle for ordure and the most offensive kinds of filth . . .[11]

Some of the detail was shocking: Glasgow slums where the only income was from the sale of dung heaps ('the dwellers in these courts had converted their shame into a kind of money'); houses where women lay 'imprisoned under a blanket', lacking money for clothes, obliged to share one dress between half a dozen individuals. But it was the depth and breadth of information which most impressed Victorian readers, Chadwick's trademark marshalling of facts and figures. It was now impossible to claim that insanitary dwellings were the lot of a few unfortunate souls in the East End of London, or the backstreets of Manchester or Glasgow. Poor drainage, lack of ventilation, filthy houses, open sewers – it was clear from the report that these were problems afflicting thousands upon thousands, blighting and destroying lives across the nation.

Chadwick presented both the problem and the solution. He reiterated the lessons of 1838: epidemic disease was caused by miasma, arising from 'decomposing animal and vegetable substances, by damp and filth, and close and overcrowded dwellings'. Poverty, he stressed, was not the *cause* – disease supposedly struck the employed with the same frequency as the unemployed; but poverty was, rather, the *result* of disease, and cost the nation dearly. The active worker was reduced to a burden on the state; his wife and children followed him into the workhouse. The solution was straightforward: the removal of miasmatic filth from streets and homes. The means: a triumvirate of improved sewerage (including the replacement of all cesspools with WCs connected to the main drainage); universal constant supply of water (both for domestic cleanliness and to flush out dirt from clogged sewers); and the recycling of waterborne sewage by piping it to the countryside, to be sold/ distributed as liquid manure (cutting costs and increasing efficiency, perhaps even making a profit).

None of this was entirely new. There had long been demands for improved water supplies (for example, John Wright's campaign); the superiority of the WC to the privy/cesspool was hardly contentious; and Chadwick himself acknowledged Martin's existing plan for sewage manure (whilst maintaining that his own system of piping liquid manure would be a more cost-effective method of distribution). Yet the report deftly combined all these desiderata into a single entity, which Chadwick would later dub 'the venous and arterial system'.[12] Constant running water, available in the home, and running through the sewers, was presented as a unifying force, the lifeblood of a healthy urban environment – or the oil in the urban machine. Despite talk of veins and arteries, Chadwick conceived the city more as a broken mechanism which required running water to operate efficiently and which, correctly calibrated, would churn out a valuable product: sewage manure. The parallels with the highly profitable dust trade – where the refuse of the town was sold at a profit in the countryside – were also obvious.

For those who had doubts, the report contained ready-made rebuttals. The universal introduction of WCs would be expensive; but it had to be offset against the annual cost of emptying cesspools, and the dilapidation caused by neglected drainage. The Thames would face increased pollution, as Chadwick considered removing cesspools the first priority – even before new sewers might be built – but this was 'an evil of almost inappreciable magnitude' compared with retaining miasma around people's very homes. Besides, eventually, sewage would not enter the river: it would be piped away and sold to farmers, at a cost 'not a tithe the expense of cartage'. There were also important collateral benefits: all street sweepings might be swept down into gullies, if there was sufficient, fast-moving water below to flush away the filth, saving yet more money.

There were sections of the report dealing with other sanitary matters. Chadwick made clear he considered proper ventilation of streets and houses to be important – as a miasmatist he could hardly argue otherwise – and he recognised the need for improved street scavenging and refuse removal. There were even some sections of the report that were allowed to contradict Chadwick's views. Medical officers in Lancashire, for example, listed every possible cause of disease in their respective districts, from miasma to the wholly un-Chadwickian: poor diet, lack of clothing, lack of hospitals. He did not attempt to incorporate and reconcile such differences in the report's conclusions – he just ignored them. There was no room for doubt. The 'venous and arterial system' was another finely tuned Benthamite mechanism – a neat way of increasing benefit and reducing costs – and its proud author would not rest until everyone understood its merits.

For the most part, the public, press and politicians were convinced. There were clearly question marks over the technicalities, and a need for proper costing, but few dismissed the report out of hand. The only serious dissenters came from the capital's Commissions of Sewers. Chadwick's plans trespassed on their domain, and he had gone out of his way to revive old accusations and lambast them as incompetent. The angry chairman of the Westminster Commission fought back, letting loose with both barrels in a lengthy public harangue. The report, he suggested, was a transparent attempt to ensure the continued survival of the faltering Poor Law Commission, 'whose meddling interference and heartlessness have drawn upon them the merited contempt and antipathy of every man in whose heart there remains one pulse of benevolent feeling'.[13] The Westminster Commission had built over 20,000 feet of improved sewers since 1800, plus 11,000 feet of new sewers in the last eight years. Accusations in the report that the Westminster Commission used outmoded flat-bottomed sewers were, he claimed, ridiculous – no such sewers had been constructed for fifty years. Other sewer authorities supported West-minster's stand.[14] Richard Kelsey, Surveyor of the City of London, wrote a long private letter to Chadwick declaring himself 'deeply injured' by the report's claims, and providing a point-for-point chronological rebuttal of his own commission's supposed technical failings ('In 1775 and 1778 the Sewer of Bishopsgate Street Without was built with a semicircular top and bottom . . .').[15] No other species of metropolitan local authority had been singled out for such hostile treatment. The Commissioners of Sewers feared – quite rightly, as it turned out – that Chadwick was bent on their destruction.

In theory, Chadwick's work was done; but his sanitary solutions begged further questions, particularly in the metropolis. It was all very well to talk of improved sewerage, but the chaotic conditions in the capital reflected diver-gent custom and practice between different districts; and disagreements amongst engineers and surveyors about design, hydraulics and the impact of sewerage on public health (e.g. whether gullies should be trapped to prevent odour). The supply of water lay in the hands of multiple commercial interests; the sewers belonged to multiple commissions; the streets were managed not only by separate parish vestries but by seemingly innumerable paving boards, trusts and commissions. These were miniature local authorities – often estab-lished by local landowners to take control of their own estates – sometimes governing as little as a single street or square. It was far from clear, therefore, who could orchestrate any overall improvement. No central authority existed; and the experience of introducing the New Poor Law showed that the present authorities would be very hostile to 'centralisation'. The existing vestries and paving boards valued local autonomy above all else, considering 'local self-government' a hallmark of the English constitution. This was a highly self-interested, self-important view of the value of vestrydom, but it was widely held.

The immediate outcome of the publication of Chadwick's magnum opus, therefore, was the establishment of a government commission – another sani-tary inquiry. The subject matter of the new commission was ostensibly the same as Chadwick's investigation, the remit subtly different. The commis-sioners were to be 'men of science, engineers, medical officers and persons skilled in the construction and arrangements necessary for carrying out a complete system of drainage'.[16] Their purpose was to review Chadwick's recommendations and assess their practicability. Hearings would be detailed and technical, covering everything from the chemical analysis of water to using the Ordnance Survey to determine levels for sewerage. Chadwick contributed information and assistance behind the scenes, and waited with bated breath.

The Commission's final thoughts appeared in 1845 as *The Second Report of the Commissioners for Inquiring into the State of Large Towns and Populous Districts* (there was a preliminary report in 1844). The Commissioners resolved that causes of disease were indeed 'capable of removal'. Their principal recommendation was to create powerful unitary authorities for sewerage in the nation's towns and cities, supervised by central government. These local bodies should be 'co-extensive with the natural areas for drainage' and manage not only sewerage but scavenging, including the removal of dust and night soil from private properties. Additional responsibilities should include the removal of nuisances; smoke prevention; making equitable arrangements with water companies for domestic water supply (with powers for securing their own supplies, where necessary); the appointment of local medical officers – and a good deal more besides. Chadwick would later reveal the full extent of his assistance to the Commission: he helped draft these conclusions himself.[17] They certainly provided ample scope for the introduction of the 'venous and arterial system' nationwide. They also confirmed the existing Sewer Commissions' worst fears about their imminent obsolescence.

All that was needed now was legislation. The government obliged with a 'Health of Towns Bill'. The bill, however, struggled to pass through parliament – other matters, not least famine in Ireland, were more pressing – and it would not appear on the statute book for three years, much diluted, as the Public Health Act of 1848.

Chadwick, meanwhile, was surprised to find his own position suddenly made unexpectedly precarious. In 1846, accusations of the maltreatment of paupers at the Andover workhouse led to an official inquiry into the supervisory failings of the Poor Law Commissioners. Chadwick himself willingly – and treacherously – gave evidence against his inimical superiors, which proved a mistake. For the government determined to make a clean sweep, dissolving the entire Poor Law Commission. Chadwick desperately scrambled to regain lost ground. He made it quite clear that he would not withdraw from his post gracefully; the threat of further revelations about the Commissioners' erstwhile maladministration hung in the air. Future employment under the forthcoming Health of Towns legislation was proffered, but Chadwick recalled the pie-crust promise of being 'fourth commissioner'. He required something more tangible and immediate.

Lord Russell, the Prime Minister, intervened. Typhus and influenza were again rife in the metropolis, yet vested interests had guaranteed that the forthcoming Public Health Act would not extend to the capital. The complaints of metropolitan vestries and the City of London against 'centralisation' had been too loud. Little parliamentary time had been available; the existing, overlapping divisions of London between the various sewer commissions, paving boards and parishes had seemed far too convoluted for a quick fix. Would Chadwick now consider leading a 'Metropolitan Sanitary Commission' to decide, once and for all, the capital's sanitary fate?

Yet another government inquiry. It did not matter. London was always the greatest sanitary challenge – reforming the metropolis a long-held ambition. This was a consolation prize not to be refused.

The intervention of the Prime Minister – to secure the support of a civil servant whose 'station in society' once marked him as unfit for office – needs explanation. Russell had no love for Chadwick personally, and considered his revelations at the Andover inquiry to be rank disloyalty. But Chadwick had become a totemic figure – the leading light in a national, loosely defined 'sanitary movement' that transcended politics. In part, this was simply a tribute to his work on *An Inquiry into the Sanitary Condition of the Labouring Population of Great Britain*, which had made a lasting impression. Support for Chadwick's grand designs had also been bolstered by determined lobbying – public meetings, pamphlets (often reprinting key sections of the various government reports), speeches and debates – all in favour of his sanitary reforms. Some of this was Chadwick's own doing; but much of this activity was organised by friends and sympathisers, particularly Thomas Southwood Smith.

Smith was physician not only at the London Fever Hospital but at the Eastern Dispensary and Jew's Hospital in Whitechapel. All three institutions brought him into frequent contact with slum-dwellers, and his *Treatise on Fever* (1830) was the leading textbook on the subject. A staunch miasmatist, he had obliged Chadwick with his East End report in 1838, and provided tours of

Whitechapel fever dens to any who doubted the urgency of the problem (his most famous convert being Lord Normanby, the Home Secretary, in 1839). He differed from Chadwick only in motivation. Chadwick's creed was, above all else, utilitarian: improved administration and reduced costs. Southwood Smith, on the other hand, was a Unitarian minister, driven by deep religious conviction. Regardless, his support for the sanitary cause was unwavering. His greatest contribution was the establishment of the Health of Towns Association in 1844. Its avowed mission was to disseminate information on the benefits of sanitation, 'assisting the Government to the utmost of their power in any contemplated legislation, by preparing the public mind for the change'.[18] The Association boasted leading members of parliament, clergymen and doctors amongst its founding fathers. By 1847, there were affiliated branch organisations in a dozen major towns and cities. Whilst Chadwick himself largely remained aloof from its business, there were remarkable congruities between the views expressed by the Association and those of the nation's most famous 'sanitarian'. In short, the Health of Towns Association was a formidable political pressure group, firmly behind Edwin Chadwick and all his works.

To dismiss Chadwick, then, was to dismiss a sanitary campaign – a sanitary ideal – to which many highly reputable individuals had now pledged allegiance. Russell decided it was more politic to move him into a new role – one for which, in any case, he seemed eminently qualified – as the arbiter of the capital's sanitary future.

The first report of the Metropolitan Sanitary Commission – the final general 'sanitary inquiry' of the decade – was published in November 1847. It was little more than an emphatic reiteration of what had gone before. The competency of London's existing Commissions of Sewers was again questioned; technical data were presented on sewer building, sewer flushing, drains and hydraulics. But one new topic was given pride of place at the beginning of the report: the treatment and prevention of cholera. A fresh cholera epidemic was travelling across Europe and it was plain that the capital would soon face a repeat of the turmoil of 1832. Chadwick must have cursed his luck. His newly acquired influence over metropolitan sanitation had become a poisoned chalice. He had spent nigh on a decade proclaiming that epidemic disease had 'removable causes'; he was now obliged immediately to make good on his promise.

The Commission's recommendations made clear what was needed: an end to the existing sewer authorities, whose works were uniformly 'uncertain, erroneous, and defective in their general principles of construction, injurious in their action, and unduly expensive'; their replacement with 'one competent executive body'; and the employment of the Ordnance Survey to provide a complete survey of metropolitan drainage, with a view to planning future works. Chadwick was not foolish enough to claim that he could save the capital from cholera; only that a single body would be more capable of effecting the requisite comprehensive cleansing of sewers and drains. The government, thoroughly prepared for this conclusion, yielded. The ancient Sewer Commissions had, after all, been under hostile scrutiny since the 1820s. In their stead a single Metropolitan Commission of Sewers (MCS) was established in November 1847, including not only Chadwick, but a number of like-minded 'sanitarians' amongst its ranks. It was to be chaired by Lord Morpeth, a founding member of the Health of Towns Association.

During the following months, Chadwick was at the height of his powers. He was presented with the honour of Companion of the Bath, at the urging of Prince Albert. He would also become one of three commissioners forming the new General Board of Health (the body supervising the workings of the long-awaited national Public Health Act). The other two were Lord Morpeth and Lord Ashley (shortly to become Lord Shaftesbury), both of whom held Chadwick in high esteem. The General Board would not only support and regulate sanitary improvements in provincial towns and cities but deal with the coming threat of cholera throughout the nation, including London. The time for writing reports and lobbying was finally over. Chadwick had unprecedented power to realise his sanitary vision in the capital.

Yet this ascendancy was itself a source of discontent. The London vestries were hostile to Chadwick's centralising agenda and feared for their own future. More particularly, rancorous internal disputes soon began to brew within the MCS. The great troublemaker was John Leslie, a tailor to the aristocrats of Mayfair, who objected to Chadwick's status as first amongst equals. Ironically, Leslie had received his post from Morpeth in the hope that his appointment would placate the local authorities in the capital. Leslie was a West End vestryman and had been a member of the Westminster Commission of Sewers, so seemed the ideal candidate to assuage vestries' concerns about their lack of representation on the new body. Moreover, he had won a certain fame for his vehement denunciation of the Westminster Commission's failings and might have reasonably been supposed to be sympathetic towards Chadwick's mission. In fact, he proved quite the opposite: determined to oppose anything he thought interfered with vestry interests and keen to take Chadwick down a peg or two. His boorish, obstructionist tactics damaged working relationships. In particular, he helped stoke a rivalry between the Commission's surveyors – Messrs Roe and Phillips – over the initial design for London's new sewers. When Chadwick brought in his own favourite civil engineer as a consultant to smooth over the dispute – Henry Austin, Secretary of the Health of Towns Association – Leslie promptly accused him of corruption (the very same 'jobbery' he purported to have uncovered in the Westminster Commission).

The engineering experts on the new Commission would remain at odds. By the summer of 1849 there were two complete, rival plans for sewering the capital, even though Roe had retired. Austin, now permanently employed, proposed creating capacious sumps dotted throughout the metropolis, connected to a network of pipes, pumping out sewage manure on all sides. Phillips, on the other hand, plumped for a large, deep intercepting tunnel sewer, 'under the whole of London from Chelsea to Greenwich, passing under the Thames twelve times and under the West India Docks once'.[19] Moreover, he publicly damned Austin's ideas as impracticable. There were other technical (not to mention often highly theoretical and unproven) arguments over the size of sewer pipes; the viability of sewage as manure; the cost of the rival projects. Most of all there was a clash of egos. Chadwick backed Austin's scheme, convinced of its relative cheapness and its proximity to the 'venous and arterial' ideal. Leslie, on the other hand, supported Phillips who, in fact, had been his crony when he sat on the Westminster Commission. None of this was conducive to genuine progress.

And then there was cholera.

The epidemic found a capital that had changed little since 1832 – except that the population had increased; and the slums had grown more dense and crowded. An investigation by the paving commissioners of Holborn found familiar evils: less than 10 per cent of slum properties possessed a water closet; the remaining privies and cesspools were rarely cleaned or emptied; makeshift drainage troughs and channels lay hidden in cellars; houses were filled with the stench from poorly constructed clogged sewers. Landlords in the worst street in St Giles had actually destroyed privies to avoid the expense of regularly clearing the cesspools below.[20] Elsewhere, residents, fearful of miasma, drew the moral that a complete lack of sanitation was the safest option: 'We were stunk out of the last house in which we lived by the drains, and we think ourselves very lucky in not having any drains here.'[21]

Amongst the wealthy, the fear of disease spreading from slum to garden square was rife:

Grosvenor-square must care for Bermondsey; Belgravia can no longer think slightingly of Bethnal-green . . . The filthy spots we have named, if they be allowed to generate and spread abroad their noisome miasmata, under favourable atmospheric influences, may gradually infect other quarters of the town.[22]

Chadwick's response to the epidemic would follow the pattern of 1832 – cleansing the slums – but with an important shift in focus. Drainage would be *the* great concern. He would tackle what he had long believed were the great causes of miasma: the cesspool and the sewer. Moreover, he would use the latest discoveries of sanitary science: cesspools would be disinfected and sewers flushed.

Introducing chemicals to cesspools was nothing new – it was an old nightman's trick to use quicklime or charcoal to reduce the overpowering noxious smell – but there were now patent brands of 'disinfecting fluid' on the market. These mixtures could be pumped into the pit, simultaneously agitating, diluting and deodorising the contents. The resultant odour-free mixture could then be unobjectionably and swiftly pumped out, down a street gully. Chadwick, with typical thoroughness, expended much effort on evaluating different brands and analysing the results. The MCS would ultimately employ six gangs of roving pump-men, available to householders for a modest fee (less than the cost of traditional hand-labour and cartage). They reportedly gave almost universal satisfaction, with customer comments meticulously recorded – 'cesspool cleansed; will recommend the pump to all his friends'.[23]

Sewer flushing, on the other hand, tackled foul-smelling blockages in the sewer network – both excrement, and rubbish indiscriminately dumped down gullies – and was deployed more extensively.[24] It had been shown to be cheap and effective by the Holborn Sewer Commission in the decade before its dissolution.

The process was simple: underground workers used wooden boards to create a dam in the sewer, building up a head of water. Releasing the boards produced a sudden forceful torrent that swept away any solid matter. The Holborn Commission had even begun to introduce fixed iron 'flushing gates' but there was no time to spread this innovation; wooden boards would suffice.

Chadwick embraced these twin solutions not simply because he wished the MCS to appear forward-thinking. Their success would hint at the full potential of his complete 'venous and arterial system' – where cesspools were abolished and water flowed abundantly beneath the streets. Fellow commissioners fell in behind their guiding spirit. Even John Leslie dubbed cesspools 'indeed, the greatest nuisances in the country (hear!); and that they ought to be done away with, and their contents taken away by small tubular drains into the sewers (hear, hear!)'.[25] By September 1848, the Commission had flushed 163 miles of the 'worst conditioned sewers'. By the end of 1849, they had spent over £18,000 on the work, with a particular focus on the south London slums.[26]

Chadwick also used new powers granted the General Board of Health under the hastily passed Nuisances Removal Act of 1848 to deputise Poor Law Unions and paving boards. They were instructed to employ medical men to engage in house-to-house visits and root out nuisances, much like the local boards of 1832. Some local authorities were industrious. The paving board of small, wealthy St James's personally inspected the coaching inns of Piccadilly, warning landlords about the state of their privies and dung pits.[27] The City of London co-opted its police force, who reported on sanitation in over 15,000 households.[28] But many of the Poor Law authorities were reluctant to spend their time and money. The Poor Law Guardians of St Pancras, hauled before a magistrate, brazenly conducted a lengthy defence of their neglect, claiming the General Board's 'interference' was illegal. This was ironic: Chadwick's sanitary directives scuppered by the penny-pinching functionaries of his own New Poor Law. Fortunately, all eyes were on the uncooperative Guardians; the General Board received praise for making the best of a bad job.

Indeed, the MCS and General Board made every effort – but the cholera raged on, seemingly unabated. The death toll would be significantly higher than in 1832.[29]

The record of the MCS now began to be called into question. During the summer of 1849, at the height of the epidemic, *The Times* was unashamedly hostile. Why had eighteen months passed with no agreement on an overall plan for sewerage? Lengthy experiments had been undertaken on disinfectants, the width of sewer pipes and the cheapest sort of WC; but nothing had been achieved. Sewer flushing had some merit – but it could only further pollute the Thames, making the river a giant open cesspool for the whole capital. Worse, the water companies still drew supplies from the river. Chadwick repeatedly and doggedly argued that the Thames pollution was a necessary evil – i.e. miasma from cesspools was more dangerous than diluted filth. The leader writers countered that the Commission had only spread and diffused the danger throughout the metropolis. The residents of Bermondsey – a riverside district prone to fever – were a case in point. They petitioned the Commission to cease their works (both emptying cesspools and flushing sewers) because the net effect seemed to be more miasma from the disturbed filth rising up from the gullies, 'disseminating death and disease . . . stenches which were scarcely endurable'. Camberwell swiftly followed suit.[30]

A more united Commission might have withstood such buffeting. John Leslie, however, continued to plough his singularly awkward furrow, determined to end Chadwick's dominance. The results were sometimes farcical. When Chadwick opined, perhaps somewhat optimistically, that flushing sewers cost 6d. per cubic yard, against 6s. 6d. spent by the Westminster Commission on manual removal and cartage, Leslie demanded an inquiry into the scandalous allegation. This was a peculiar sensitivity given his own repeated and determined efforts to publicise the old Commission's failings. Nonetheless, his relentless opposition proved effective. Complaints that Chadwick attempted to corral opponents into working on particular MCS sub-committees – leaving the key Works Committee packed with his supporters – revealed a rather clumsy attempt at legerdemain. Chadwick was painted as running the MCS as his own private fiefdom. The other Commissioners grew restless. Hoping to resolve the impasse over the rival surveyors' schemes – and prove there was no 'jobbery' – they announced that they would consider sewer plans from anyone who cared to submit them. This only made them appear weak and indecisive.

Lord Russell concluded that enough was enough. By the autumn of 1849, public confidence in the Commission seemed to have evaporated. *The Times* was positively relentless in its criticism ('they dribble away their own time and the public money in measuring house-pipes and reporting upon patent commodes').[31] Russell knew the London vestries were antagonistic – even without Leslie's self-appointed one-man crusade – and would prefer a body that represented their own interests. There were also vociferous complaints from civil engineers, who resented Chadwick's theoretical certainties about how to build proper drains and loathed the fact that the Commission's lucrative survey work was to be handed to the military Ordnance Survey. William Haywood, the City surveyor, remarked dolefully: 'It is rumoured they are to fill in the detail of Metropolis itself. If so, the occupation of the Land Surveyor is at an end.'[32] Russell, faced with all this vexation, would adopt the strategy applied at the Poor Law Commission: the MCS would be dissolved, then reconstituted without either John Leslie or Edwin Chadwick.

This came as a heavy blow. Chadwick, plagued by illness, aggravated by the stress of his work, nonetheless still determined to press on. He concentrated his flagging energy on the General Board of Health. He could still use the General Board to introduce his sanitary programme elsewhere. Numerous towns and cities had already sought the expert advice and government loans promised by the Public Health Act. As for London, he would focus on the other aspect of the venous and arterial system – the supply of water. The rest might still somehow follow.

There would be one last roll of the dice. Chadwick did what he did best: he produced another report, even though the metropolis was no longer within his remit. He employed a dubious legalistic argument to show that the brief of the moribund Metropolitan Sanitary Commission had passed to the General Board, and ploughed ahead.

The 1850 *Report of the General Board of Health on the Supply of Water to the Metropolis*, like John Wright's pamphlet, threw down the gauntlet to the water companies. *The Dolphin*, however, had been aimed squarely at the well-to-do of Mayfair, designed to raise anxieties about the quality of water pouring into middle- and upper-class homes. Chadwick, on the other hand, dived headlong into slums, and showed the problems of vitiated water – and lack of water – for the working class (which, in turn, would spread miasma amongst the general populace). The intermittent supply provided by water companies was a particular bugbear. It led to storage in large, communal cisterns, which were open to every abuse:

Besides the ordinary sources of pollution from the dust and smut in the atmosphere, and from slops thrown out of the top windows, this cistern is resorted to by boys in the street, the house door being always open during the day, to wash their hands, and play all sorts of pranks; such as dipping sprats, when they are in season; drowning mice, &c. &c.[33]

For some of the poorest Londoners, even polluted cisterns were an impossible luxury. They were obliged to queue at standpipes, quarrelling with their neighbours over their place, storing water in 'pails, old fish-kettles, and casks', lugging them up flights of stairs to badly ventilated, overcrowded rooms. The remedy was obvious: a constant supply of tap water in every home, the only way to inculcate cleanliness and decency in the labouring population.

Chadwick's proposed method for implementing reform was 'constant supply by consolidated management', i.e. compulsory purchase of the existing water companies, bringing London's water under a single state-run authority. He also recommended finding new supplies, away from the contaminated Thames, plus 'combination ... with the works for the removal of the soil water and the general drainage'.[34] In other words, he proposed dissolving the MCS and bringing both water and sewerage under a new unified authority. In short, the 'venous and arterial system' in all its glory. There was one notable departure: polluted water, particularly soakage from cesspools, poisoning wells, was acknowledged as a strong 'predisposing cause' of cholera. Chadwick still stressed that atmospheric impurity was a necessary condition, but he was keen to incorporate every possible objection to the existing metropolitan water supply, even if it undermined his long-cherished miasmatic theories.[35]

There followed months of lobbying from the water companies, inventors of new schemes for bringing water to the capital, and metropolitan vestries – all of whom proposed alternative plans for the future, whilst simultaneously sniping at their opponents, the government and the General Board of Health. The water companies, in particular, had huge financial clout, using the press to vilify Chadwick and decry his 'dictatorial' lust for power. They were not altogether wrong. The following year, Chadwick abandoned talk of constant supply and new sources of water and proposed, in vain, a single executive authority for 'Drainage, Water Supply, Paving and Cleansing in the Metropolis' – all under the control of the General Board of Health.[36]

The Metropolis Water Act which finally appeared in 1852 bore little relation to Chadwick's plans. There would be a restriction on drawing water from the Thames, below Teddington and an obligation to filter and cover reservoirs, which would come into force in 1855/56. There was a nod to constant supply, but the criteria under which it became obligatory were nigh impossible to meet. The water companies themselves would survive quite untouched – but they would not forgive or forget. The agitation over water reform stirred up a hornet's nest of opposition. Chadwick's influence on the sanitary future of London was at an end, and his reign as chief sanitarian at the General Board of Health precarious.

Hostility to both the General Board of Health and the post-Chadwick MCS began to intensify. The Metropolitan Commission of Sewers had looked set for great things after Chadwick's departure in 1849, with a new group of commissioners dominated by experienced civil engineers. There were, however, problems on numerous fronts: allegations of non-attendance at meetings (the engineers on the Commission all had their own lucrative commercial practices); a disastrous sewer-building project in Victoria, plagued by subsidence, which obliged the Commissioners to pay out thousands in compensation to landlords of damaged property; major problems with funding (it proved impossible to raise sufficient loans for a London-wide project against the promise of returns from a threepence sewer rate).

What *did* eventually emerge from the MCS was a workable, fully fledged scheme for building intercepting sewers, drawn up by Joseph Bazalgette (who was appointed Assistant Surveyor to the MCS in 1849, then Engineer in 1852) and William Haywood, based on earlier plans. But the Commission remained perpetually vilified by those who claimed the body had achieved little of any practical value: '[their] deepest anxiety, for a long time past, has been to escape out of office by a quiet back door, without even attempting to commence, or even lay down definitely, any really comprehensive system of drainage'.[37] Some local works had been completed; but no overarching solution to metropolitan ills. By the end of 1854, it was clear that the government had a mind to abolish the MCS – membership had already been repeatedly reconstituted – and, once again, start from scratch.

Chadwick, meanwhile, had his own battles to fight. The inspectors of the General Board of Health – who visited towns and assessed what work was required – were being accused of corruption. Like the civil engineers on the MCS, they had their own private practice, and were finding profitable employment as engineers on projects they themselves had approved. There were also complaints from voluble provincials who objected in principle to the Board's 'despotic interference' and called for 'self-government'. In part, this was due to the terms of the Public Health Act. The Act allowed the Board to set up a local public health authority wherever 10 per cent of ratepayers demanded it, even in the teeth of 90 per cent opposition. For some, this seemed genuinely undemocratic. For others, opposition was simply a question of self-interest. Slum landlords – the petty owners of rented tenements, concerned more about their rates than the welfare of tenants – resented paying for new WCs and drains. Complacent ratepayers resented the cost of *any* public health measure. Dickens's *Household Words* would satirise the rallying cry of the 'dirty party' in the provinces:

> Ratepayers, Cess-cum-Poolton! Rally round your vested interests. Health is enormously expensive. Introduce the Public Health Act and you will be pauperized! Be filthy and fat. Cess-pools and Constitutional Government! Gases and Glory! No insipid water!!![38]

The General Board of Health faced a large-scale typhoid outbreak in Croydon in November 1852, something of a public relations disaster. This had been one of the first districts to adopt the Board's preferred plans for modern sewerage (Croydon was not yet geographically part of the metropolis, and so did not fall under the MCS). The works included extensive use of ready-made earthenware pipes (a new technology, much smaller than traditional brick tunnels), which were found to have cracked, most likely because they were poorly laid. The press damned Chadwick for his well-documented obsession with cheap, narrow pipes. The real and imaginary failings of 'the tubular system' would dog the General Board for the remainder of its existence.

In 1854, the General Board of Health's initial five-year term of office was over. Proposals for its renewal faced a predictable barrage of opposition. Local authorities bemoaned 'centralisation'. The disgruntled engineering profession, resentful of Chadwick's powers of patronage, aghast at his haughty

FLVMINI · VINCVLA · POSVIT

Sr JOSEPH BAZALGETTE CB
ENGINEER OF THE LONDON MAIN DRAINAGE SYSTEM
AND OF THIS EMBANKMENT

1 Joseph Bazalgette (1819–91), who designed and built London's great network of intercepting sewers during the mid-nineteenth century, is memorialised on the Thames Embankment, with a bronze bust and the legend 'flumini vincula posuit' ('he placed chains on the river'). The inscription refers to the building of the embankment itself – containing both intercepting sewer and underground railway – which reclaimed more than 30 acres of land.

2 From an 1831 broadside entitled 'Salus Populi Suprema Lex' ('The welfare of the people is the supreme law'), this cartoon drawn by George Cruikshank shows the sewage of south London flowing into the Thames, whilst the chief of Southwark Water Co. (which drew drinking water from the foul river) poses mid-stream, like a filthy complacent Britannia.

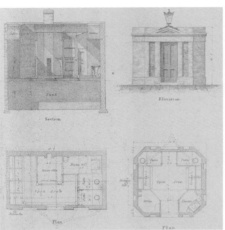

3 Bazalgette submitted a plan for building public toilets, as part of his application for the post of Assistant Surveyor at the Metropolitan Commission of Sewers in 1849. Bazalgette's appealing classical conveniences (for men only) would have contained water closets and urinals, monitored by an attendant. Tanks beneath would have collected the urine, which would have been periodically pumped out and utilised as fertiliser. The toilets were never actually built. Nonetheless, Bazalgette found employment with the MCS which ultimately led to him designing London's new sewers.

4 Charles Cochrane (1807–55), founder of the National Philanthropic Association, exhausted his personal wealth promoting, amongst other projects, the street orderly system of continual road cleansing. He also established two soup kitchens (which included the first public toilets for the poor), publicised workhouse abuses and the state of slum accommodation in his radical illustrated magazine *The Poor Man's Guardian*, and supported George Walker's campaign to abolish interments in overcrowded urban graveyards. Cochrane styled himself 'The Agitator of the Metropolis' and was criticised for his rabble-rousing, confrontational approach.

A LONDON NUISANCE. Pl. 1st

Passing a MUD CART.

5 The 'scavengers' who cleared mud off the streets were not terribly fastidious about their work, or its impact on the public. This 1820s print, entitled *A London Nuisance*, shows a well-dressed young man being spattered by mud, shovelled up by street-cleaners.

6 An 1860s photographic portrait of Edwin Chadwick (1800–90), the civil servant and public health reformer, 'father of the sanitary movement', author of *An Inquiry into the Sanitary Condition of the Labouring Population of Great Britain* (1842). Chadwick persuaded the nation that improving sanitation was imperative. He was, however, a divisive figure, disliked by both commercial interests and representatives of local government for his 'tyrannical' centralising agenda. Engineers and surveyors, likewise, resented his dogmatic certainties about sewers and sewerage. One of his many critics remarked: 'No one was to be clean except by Chadwick's patent soap.'

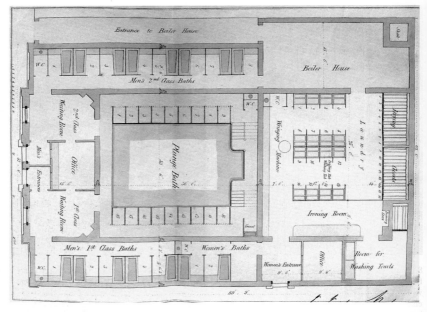

7 An 1850 model plan for public baths and washhouses, costing £2,000, by Price Pritchard Baly. The plan was published (with alternatives costing £4,000 and £8,500) by the Committee for Promoting the Establishment of Baths and Washhouses. Note the typical features: separate entrances for men and women, and different classes of bathers; and a modestly sized 'plunge bath' (as opposed to the grander swimming pool of the late-Victorian period).

8 Enon Chapel was opened as a burial speculation in the 1820s. The proprietor made money from funerals and interments in the vaults below the chapel building. Thousands were buried in a space which could barely hold a few hundred coffins. In fact, bodies were regularly cleared and dumped elsewhere. This lithograph was published in 1847, by which time the chapel had closed but was being used as a dancing saloon. The burial reformer George Walker proceeded to buy the lease and end the impious entertainments. He took the public on tours in the grim bone-ridden cellars, before paying for reburial of the remains at Norwood Cemetery.

9 London's commercial cemeteries of the 1830s and 1840s adopted various architectural styles and were not prescriptive about the design of individual monuments. Augustus Pugin (1812–52), the pioneer of Gothic Revival, mocks the result in this satirical sketch, which juxtaposes rather tasteless Egyptian-style gates (reminiscent of Abney Park Cemetery) and a classical chapel. There are also various other ill-matched details and nods to the vulgar nature of the enterprise. These include an unlikely advertising sign-board posted on the gates, which reads 'OBSERVE THE PRICES!!! . . . FOR READY MONEY ONLY'.

10 George Alfred Walker (1807–84), also known as 'Graveyard Walker', was convinced that miasma from full, badly-managed graveyards was a major factor in the ill-health of the poor. He launched a decade-long campaign to close metropolitan burial grounds, and supported Edwin Chadwick's scheme for government-run 'national cemeteries', beyond the boundaries of the capital. Chadwick's plans faltered, and parish vestries would retain control of burials. Walker, nonetheless, successfully made the case for burial reform. Following legislation in 1852, pestiferous ancient graveyards were closed by order of the Home Secretary, and spacious extramural parochial cemeteries became the norm.

11 The General Cemetery of All Souls, Kensal Green, opened for interments in 1833, the first commercial extramural cemetery in the metropolis, inspired by Père Lachaise in Paris. It was designed to provide a cleanly, orderly contrast to city churchyards, which were full to the brim with corpses, forcing gravediggers to regularly expose and clear recently-interred remains.

12 Local boards of health were appointed by the government to visit slums, promote cleansing of neglected courts and alleys, and seek out cholera cases. Before the outbreak of disease in 1831, however, there was scepticism that such measures were needed. This cartoon presents respectable middle-class gentlemen scouring the slums as a risible spectacle. One board member remarks: 'Positively we must find something; it won't do to lose our Twenty guineas a day' (there was a widely-held view that doctors and officials were profiteering from cholera panic). Another man exclaims: 'Oh! if I can but find a smell' (a reference to the insistence of miasmatists that vitiated air was the source of the disease).

TO THE INHABITANTS OF THE PARISH OF
CLERKENWELL.

His Majesty's Privy Council having approved of precautions proposed by the Board of Health in London, on the alarming approach
OF THE

INDIAN CHOLERA

It is deemed proper to call the attention of the Inhabitants to some of the Symptoms and Remedies mentioned by them as printed, and now in circulation.

Symptoms of the Disorder;

Giddiness, sickness, nervous agitation, slow pulse, cramp beginning at the fingers and toes and rapidly approaching the trunk, change of colour to a leaden blue, purple, black or brown; the skin dreadfully cold, and often damp, the tongue moist and loaded but flabby and chilly, the voice much affected, and respiration quick and irregular.

REMEDIES;

All means tending to restore circulation and to maintain the warmth of the body should be had recourse to without the least delay.

The patient should be immediately put to bed, wrapped up in hot blankets, and warmth should be sustained by other external applications, such as repeated frictions with flannels and camphorated spirits, poultices of mustard and linseed (equal parts) to the stomach, particularly where pain and vomiting exist, and similar poultices to the feet and legs to restore their warmth. The returning heat of the body may be promoted by bags containing hot salt or bran applied to different parts, and for the same purpose of restoring and sustaining the circulation while wine wey with spice, brandy and water, or salvolatile in a dose of a tea spoon full in hot water, frequently repeated; or from 5 to 20 drops of some of the essential oils, as peppermint, cloves or cajeput, in a wine glass of water may be administered with the same view. Where the stomach will bear it, warm broth with spice may be employed. In every severe case or where medical aid is difficult to be obtained, from 20 to 40 drops of laudanum may be given in any of the warm drinks previously recommended.

These simple means are proposed as resources in the incipient stages of the Disease, until Medical aid can be had.

THOS. KEY,
GEO. TINDALL, } Churchwardens.

Sir Gilbert Blane, Bart. in a pamphlet written by him on the subject of this Disease, recommends petatos to guard against the approach by moderate and temperate living, and to have in readiness the prescribed remedies; and in case of attack to resort thereto constantly but the great preventative in atoto, is found to consist in a due regard to Cleanliness and Ventilation.

N.B. It is particularly requested that this Paper may be preserved, and that the Inmates generally, in the House where it is left may be made acquainted with its contents.

NOV. 1st, 1831.

T. GOODE, PRINTER, CROSS STREET, WILDERNESS ROW.

13 This poster, dated 1 November 1831, from the parish of Clerkenwell, is typical of warnings that appeared throughout the metropolis, at the behest of the government's Central Board of Health, anticipating the coming epidemic. The gruesome description of the symptoms of cholera – hitherto unknown in England – served to inculcate an expectant atmosphere of 'extravagant terror' amongst the populace. The medical advice, focussed on maintaining warmth and circulation of the blood, was misguided. Doctors did not realise that cholera killed by rapid, extreme dehydration.

THE CROSSING-SWEEPER NUISANCE.

14 Young crossing-sweepers, ragged and bare-footed, flock together and overwhelm a pedestrian with their appeals for alms. One boy says, 'Now, Sir, Gi'us a Ha'penny & I'll stand on my Nose!!' An older, female sweeper stands to one side. This cartoon from *Punch* (26 January 1856) emphasises the beggarly nature of the sweeper; but they did perform a genuinely useful function, clearing mud from streets, paved crossings and pavements.

15 Paved crossings, generally six to nine feet in width, were laid down at road junctions by local authorities or, on occasion, private interests. They were constructed from durable stone and swept by mendicant crossing-sweepers, whose efforts allowed pedestrians to cross mud-drenched streets in relative comfort. The *Punch* cartoonist Linley Sambourne was an enthusiastic street photographer and captured this example at the turn of the century.

16 Dustmen at work in the back streets of late-Victorian Whitechapel (Old Montague Street). The dustmen have the tools of the trade: a shovel for scooping out ashes from fixed household bins, and a wicker basket for taking the dirt to the high-sided cart. Note also the protective wide-brimmed hats, and trousers tied at the knee – to prevent ashes entering clothing.

17 A carefully posed late-nineteenth-century photograph of a chimney sweep, together with his tools. The 'machine' of connecting wooden rods, topped by a brush (made from durable whalebone strips) was invented by a carpenter, George Smart, in 1803. He won the prize offered by the Royal Society of Arts for 'the most simple cheap and proper apparatus . . . for cleansing Chimneys from soot, and obviating the necessity of children being employed'. Unfortunately, it would take decades before abolition of child labour in the trade became a reality.

18 E.H. Dixon's watercolour *The Great Dust Heap* (1837) captures the grey, volcanic aspect of a large dust-yard on a plot of open ground, near King's Cross. Cinders and ashes, the largest component of household waste, were sold on to brickmakers in the countryside, and could realise large profits. King's Cross (or Battle Bridge) was, therefore, an ideal location to hoard 'dust' in the 1830s, close to the edge of the metropolis, and near to the Regent's Canal, for even wider sale and distribution of this valuable recyclable material.

DIRTY FATHER THAMES.

FILTHY river, filthy river,
Foul from London to the Nore,
What art thou but one vast gutter,
One tremendous common shore?

All beside thy sludgy waters,
All beside thy reeking ooze,
Christian folks inhale mephitis,
Which thy bubbly bosom brews.

All her foul abominations
Into thee the City throws;
These pollutions, ever churning,
To and fro thy current flows.

And from thee is brew'd our porter—
Thee, thou gully, puddle, sink!
Thou, vile cesspool, art the liquor
Whence is made the beer we drink!

Thou, too, hast a Conservator,
He who fills the civic chair;
Well does he conserve thee, truly,
Does he not, my good LORD MAYOR?

19 A *Punch* cartoon, *Dirty Father Thames*, from 7 October 1848, decrying the polluted, filthy condition of the Thames ('Thou, vile cesspool, art the liquour, When is made the beer we drink!') and criticising the City of London, as legal conservator of the river. Father Thames himself is portrayed as a ragged scavenger, amongst the dead fish, old boots and rusting iron at the bottom of the river. The accompanying poem, with its 'sludgy water', 'reeking ooze', 'mephitis' and 'foul abominations' makes clear the river also contains the capital's putrescent sewage.

FATHER THAMES "HIMSELF AGAIN."

"LOR BLESS YER R'Y'L 'IGHNESS! I AIN'T THE SAME RIVER SINCE I GAVE UP SCAVENGING, AND TURNED WATERMAN!"

20 *Punch* marked the occasion of the Prince of Wales opening Bazalgette's sewer system at Crossness with a whimsical picture of the Prince greeting Father Thames (15 April 1865). Instead of a dirty scavenger, picking through the muck, Father Thames is now in the traditional coat of a waterman (workers who were licensed to carry passengers on the river). The river has been transformed; freed from filth and miasma, safe for public use. For good measure, the water teems with regal swans and presents a pleasant contrast to the dirty factory chimneys in the background.

21 A comical suggestion from *Punch* (22 September 1849) on how to avoid the miasmatic stench of the metropolis – a rubber breathing tube. The tube should be worn in the neighbourhood of 'slaughter-houses, cattle-markets, graveyards, bone-boilers, soap-makers, and cat-gut manufacturers'.

INDECENCY.

22 In Isaac Cruikshank's caricature *Indecency* (1799) a woman relieves herself in the street, and asks the reader 'What are you stareing at?' The street is in St Giles, one of the worst slums in London, and the woman is a whore – an advertisement for Leake's Pills appears on the wall (a supposed cure for venereal disease). The picture contains coarse puns – the reader can see a 'pussy'; the word 'Leake'. The 'F.P.' notice indicating the proximity of a 'fire plug' (water company hydrant) adds another layer of humour. The 'indecency' lies not only in the act but the very public location – this a paved street, improved by local ratepayers, not a secluded yard or alley.

claims that sewers were 'beyond ... ordinary professional engineering and architectural practice', highlighted the purportedly grave dangers of earthenware pipes. Even parliamentary agents joined the fray. These were middlemen who made money from introducing and promoting local legislation in parliament, previously the only way of getting up local sanitary measures. The General Board was accused of being 'intolerant of all opposition, utterly careless of the feelings and wishes of the local bodies with whom they are brought in contact'.[39]

The post-Chadwick MCS faced similar hostility. One of the loudest voices for 'metropolitan self-government' belonged to Sir Benjamin Hall, MP for Marylebone. Indeed, he had agitated for the abolition of the MCS ever since its inception, leading three separate contingents of 'anti-centralisation' vestrymen to meetings with Lord Morpeth, the Home Secretary and the Prime Minister respectively.[40] Hall's hostile stance was rooted in the vestries' deep insecurity. This was a period when the reform of London's antiquated metropolitan local government, regardless of sanitary matters, looked increasingly likely. The Municipal Corporations Act of 1835 had created elected town councils in the provinces; and, by 1854, two Royal Commissions had contemplated wholesale change in the capital.[41] Vestrymen dreaded losing their influence under the ancient parish system to some newfangled central municipality. Chadwick was already a natural enemy because of the centralisation of Poor Law relief in 1834. Then, in 1847, he had actually managed metropolitan reform by the back door: the abolition of the Commissions of Sewers. The Marylebone vestry, which had even produced its own sanitary report, 'praying that the Sewer Commission be based upon the truly English principle of representative right' (i.e. members selected from the London vestries), was horrified at this development.[42] The constitution of the first MCS – all government appointees, largely loyal to Chadwick – had only confirmed their worst fears. Chadwick and all his works were an abomination.

Hall, therefore, was merely following the lead of his most eminent constituents. He was determined to guarantee the survival of the Marylebone vestry, and vestrydom generally. He campaigned in parliament for 'the representative principle' for the MCS and damned the current incumbents whenever possible. Likewise, in debates over the renewal of the General Board of Health – which had attempted to extend its power to the metropolis – he accused Chadwick of every possible failing, from incompetence to self-interest and corruption. In an intensely personal and vitriolic attack, Hall claimed that Chadwick 'had managed to render the Board of Health well nigh as unpopular as he had rendered the Poor Law Board, and consequently to render it ineffectual for the valuable purposes to which, under sound and honest management, it might be applied'. Chadwick, he declared, was an expert in finding himself paid government employment, but 'what the practical services were which he had rendered to the public remained to be discovered'.[43] Ultimately, Hall helped administer a parliamentary *coup de grâce*, together with 'directors and shareholders of the trading companies supplying gas and water to the metropolis . . . [and] wealthy engineers who raised a subscription with which the press was largely subsidized to get up an agitation'[44] – all the vested interests Chadwick had annoyed over the years – which saw the General Board of Health dissolved.

Supporters like Lord Shaftesbury and the Bishop of London vainly defended Chadwick's honour in the House of Lords. Chadwick's career as a public servant was over. He was pushed into retirement, albeit with a golden handshake: a comfortable pension of £1,000 p.a.

On his own terms, Chadwick had undoubtedly failed. There was still no London-wide system of sewerage in place; no single authority for water; no real commitment to a constant supply of water; no scheme for utilising sewage as manure. The sanitary movement itself was no longer lively and evangelical. The Health of Towns Association was no more, its object accomplished with the passing of the Public Health Act. The Metropolitan Sanitary Association – founded in 1850 – had flourished only briefly. In 1851, members of the latter association, including Lord Ashley (of the General Board), Viscount Ebrington (of the MCS), Charles Dickens, George Cruikshank, Robert Slaney, Charles Cochrane and 'about 170 other gentlemen' had gathered in the Kensington banqueting hall of celebrity chef Alexis Soyer and drunk toasts, late into the night, to 'The Metropolitan Sanitary Commissioners', 'The Sanitary Reformers in Parliament' and 'The Board of Health'.[45] By 1854, the Association held no public meetings and produced only the occasional petition and circular, no match for the vigorous lobbying of the vestries. The questionable management of the MCS; the endless rows over sewer tunnels vs pipes – the grim practicalities of sewerage – had dampened enthusiasm.

In truth, though, a good deal had been achieved. For a start, Chadwick had commissioned the first Ordnance Survey map of London 'on such a scale as to admit of the course of the capillaries, or house drains be seen for the purpose of inspection'.[46] Chadwick's campaign to empty cesspools was rightly criticised for polluting the river, but he had successfully persuaded many in the capital to modernise their conveniences. Landlords and householders, increasingly fearful of the cesspool's noxious vapours, took steps to improve their properties. For example, the owner of an estate of eighty-seven houses in Peckham – 'in a most filthy condition from the want of drains' – sought MCS guidance and introduced small drainpipes and water closets. The houses contained 181 cesspools, which were all emptied by pump, and filled in.[47] Such voluntary improvement works would continue and multiply. By the end of the 1850s, cesspools were all but extinct in central London.[48]

For the less conscientious jerry-builder and slum landlord, there was also new legislation. The 1844 Building Act – a product of the early sanitary agitation of the 1840s – placed restrictions on cesspools underneath new buildings, enforcing their drainage to nearby sewers, if these lay within 50 feet.[49] The Metropolitan Sewers Act of 1848 (which created the MCS) prohibited the creation of a cesspool if there was a sewer within 100 feet. The Nuisances Removal Acts of 1848 and 1849 – hastily drawn up to combat cholera, followed by a more substantial revision in 1855 – made it easier to prosecute owners of foul dwellings, and enforce local improvements in drainage. In 1855, the cesspool was outlawed entirely, in favour of a 'sufficient watercloset' and 'suitable water supply and water supply apparatus'.[50] Local authorities, empowered to intervene wherever they discovered poor drainage, began to make full use of their powers. A report from 1870 gives an overview of how much vigorous and proactive work was carried out.[51] In the fifteen years following 1855, Camberwell removed 4,352 cesspools and replaced them with 4,222 water closets 'through the direct action of the vestry', and boasted 'there is scarcely a cesspool or privy in the parish'; Mile End cleared 2,000 cesspools in the same period; the vestry of Chelsea reported that cesspools were now 'scarcely to be met with' – such prolonged, concerted activity would have been unthinkable in 1832.

This was Chadwick's great achievement: not engineering works, but promotion of the sanitary ideal; making improved sewerage seem *imperative*.

One might argue that this was done by questionable and imperfect means: the sufferings of the poor quantified as 'pecuniary burdens' upon the state; the dogmatic insistence on the miasmatic cause of disease; the stubborn refusal to consider any methods beyond the 'venous and arterial system' of 1842 (not least the time wasted on the investigation/promotion of sewage manure, which would never become a viable economic proposition). Chadwick's blinkered, authoritarian streak was also glaringly obvious. As one critic put it: 'No one was to be clean except by Chadwick's patent soap.'[52] The more astute of Chadwick's contemporaries were well aware that the serried 'facts' in his sanitary reports were carefully selected to frame ready-made arguments. William Haywood, violently opposed to centralisation, wrote to the architect William Tite:

> I know every trick of his most able most unscrupulous pen: his specious argument, his traps for the understanding by which the readers of his reports almost inevitably make false inferences, his selection of portions of evidence which suit the furtherance of his preconceived and predetermined opinions and the falsification of that evidence which does not suit him . . .[53]

Nonetheless, for all his flaws, Chadwick's unflinching certainty provided solutions to the problems that had dogged would-be reformers in the 1820s and 1830s. His anti-contagionist insistence on miasmatic theory gave a definitive explanation of the cause of disease, when one was most needed. Likewise, the destruction of cesspools and the promotion of waterborne sewerage provided a clear way forward, a very practical goal.

Ultimately, the great measure of Edwin Chadwick's success in London would not be the number of sewers flushed or cesspools filled. It was the fact that no one was prepared to abandon sanitary reform of the metropolis *after* Chadwick was dethroned – even, quite literally, his worst enemy.

Sir Benjamin Hall, Chadwick's nemesis in parliament, was appointed president of a reconstituted General Board of Health. Hall's unlikely repositioning as poacher-turned-gamekeeper was the surest way to ensure the quiescence of vestrydom. Chadwick instantly maligned him as 'a huge imposture [*sic*] of a man who will be engaged ten hours a day in parliament, who will have what he calls the duties of society to attend to, and his constituents'.[54] But Hall was no dilettante; nor was he a pompous blowhard like Leslie. If his opposition to Chadwick was intense, it reflected a genuine dislike of the man and his methods, not the sanitary ideal.

Hall took his new role very seriously. When cholera came again to London, only a couple of weeks after his appointment, he personally visited the site of the Soho outbreak, commending the Poor Law authorities for their efforts at cleansing – and met with 'much gratitude' from people in the street.[55] His tone with the Poor Law Guardians was emollient ('While the Board would deprecate any diminution of local responsibility or interference with local efforts, it is possible that their assistance and advice may be acceptable . . .').[56] He formed his own advisory medical council of senior physicians (as well as William Farr, the chief statistician of the Registrar General's Office), sending a 'Committee for Scientific Inquiries' to make chemical and microscopical examination of water supplies and the atmosphere. Yet, lacking Chadwick's know-all streak, he also readily adopted the instructions for the prevention of cholera issued by his predecessor. Inspectors were despatched across London to look into water supply and the state of the local sewers – to discover 'whether in those places that were the seats of disease in former years, the epidemic has appeared in a less virulent form where drainage and general improvements have been carried out'.[57]

Hall would continue to pay visits to the slums, becoming more and more convinced of the importance of sanitary reform. He wrote to the Home Secretary, Palmerston, in January 1855, at the conclusion of the cholera epidemic, offering a vision for the future. He dismissed Chadwick's efforts as having polluted the Thames; and made clear that the MCS could not continue in its present form. He concluded that the heart of the problem was 'the multiplicity of local authorities and the want of sufficient powers in such authorities to deal with these evils'.[58] The answer, however, was not more Chadwickian centralisation. Hall proposed sweeping away 'the existing chaos of local jurisdictions' – but simultaneously keeping the parish vestry in control of London's future. Vestrydom itself would finally cleanse the metropolis.

This was a way forward Chadwick had overlooked. He had always assumed that any local objection could be quelled by brute force: that a strong central authority could make its will felt through legislation, abolishing/replacing those who stood in the way – the steamroller approach. Hall, on the other hand, wanted genuine sanitary reform that would also guarantee the future of the vestries. Moreover, as the darling of the metropolitan vestries, he gambled that he could afford to suggest radical change without fearing accusations of 'despotism'. This assumption proved true. Hall's legislation, the Metropolis

Management Act of 1855, passed through parliament with barely a murmur of complaint. It encompassed the abolition of the plethora of small paving boards; the creation of large standardised vestries and 'district boards' (amal-gamations of smaller authorities), together with electoral reform; and, crucially, the creation of a central sanitary authority – the Metropolitan Board of Works (MBW).

The MBW, at first sight, looked like Chadwickian centralisation. In fact, it was more like a new tier of local government above vestrydom – a municipal authority with administrative power over the entire capital – yet *of* vestrydom. Members of the MBW would be elected by the vestries and district boards *from amongst their own membership*. Consequently, the London vestries could hardly object to its decisions – something of a masterstroke. There was only one check on the MBW's power: it had to pass any sewerage plans for approval by a government official, the First Commissioner of Works, a post recently obtained by none other than Benjamin Hall himself. This was plain chutzpah. If Chadwick had given himself the same final veto, he would have been accused of tyranny. But there was great enthusiasm for the new system. Joseph Bazalgette, who had accumulated extensive experience at the MCS, was chosen as the MBW's chief engineer; everything seemed to have fallen into place.

There were teething troubles. Loquacious vestrymen, accustomed to play to the gallery, relished their new platform. The MBW swiftly acquired the soubriquet 'The Metropolitan Board of Words'. Bazalgette's plan for inter-cepting sewers was, at least, swiftly approved. This was not Martin's two inter-cepting sewers parallel with the Thames, but multiple lines, converging on twin pumping stations, east of the capital. In the northern section, for example, the 'high-level' sewer would run from Hampstead, through Stoke Newington; the 'middle level' from Paddington, progressing along the line of Oxford Street and Holborn; the 'low level' from Pimlico, along the river. All three would then converge on the Abbey Mills pumping station at Stratford. The pumping station was there to raise the muck high enough to flow onwards towards an outfall, further down the Thames.

The location of the outfalls into the Thames, however, became something of a sticking point and created a rift between the MBW and Hall. No one was certain where to place the outfall pipes so that sewage would not flow back too far upstream with the receding tide. And every extra mile of pipe would add considerably to the huge costs of the project. Another difficulty arose: it transpired that City financiers would not risk lending the MBW money against the security of future sewer rates. Londoners despaired – these were the selfsame issues that had bedevilled Chadwick and his successors for nigh on a decade, seemingly incapable of resolution.

Then came a stroke of good luck. The problems of the MBW would be solved by a spell of hot weather.

For Chadwick, the Thames had been a perverse sort of sanitary barometer. The presence of more filth in the river, more complaints about stench from increasingly turbid waters, was proof that miasma was being carried away from the home. But the stink increased year on year, and, by the late 1850s, the logic of Chadwick's argument seemed topsy-turvy. Why, asked Londoners, was 'miasma' from the Thames any better than that of the household cesspool? The Thames diluted filth to some degree, but did not carry it swiftly downstream. On the contrary, the estuarine tide kept the contents of the capital's privies bobbing back and forth for days on end. London seemed to possess the world's biggest 'elongated cesspool' – hardly a proud boast. For the average inhabitant of the metropolis, this did not seem like progress.

High temperatures, naturally enough, made matters worse. June 1858 was particularly warm – an 'Indian heat' – and the river responded, generating an aroma that became known as 'The Great Stink'. The public baulked at using Thames steamboats, 'afraid not only of prospective disease, but of immediate nausea, headache and giddiness'.[59] Parliament, sitting on the banks of the river at Westminster, was possibly the worst-situated building in the capital. In 1857, members had complained of 'poisonous effluvia' causing headache, nausea and loss of appetite.[60] In the burning heat of 1858, the building was filled with the reeking stench of sewage – 'pregnant with disease and perhaps with death'. The government had still not approved a final scheme for London sewerage, fearful of costs, uncertain over the outfall problem. Some thought the miasma a kind of poetic justice: 'If Parliament can only be made to interfere by its own decimation, we must make up our minds to the dreadful sacrifice.'[61] The law courts, also situated at Westminster, echoed with complaint. A medical man, attending the Court of Queen's Bench as witness, declared that the atmosphere would produce typhus fever. The Lord Chief Baron noted in the Court of Exchequer, 'We are now sitting to try a most important cause in the midst of a stinking nuisance.' MPs sat, bilious, in the debating chamber and committee rooms, trying to concentrate on the passage of legislation. Those venturing into parts of the buildings overlooking the river were driven back, handkerchiefs clasped tight to their faces. Further down the river, a waterman was declared to have died from cholera, brought on by 'inhaling the noxious vapours of the Thames'.[62]

The Stink was urgently debated in the Commons. As a stopgap, orders were given for extensive 'deodorisation': the placing of deposits of 250 tons of lime daily near the mouths of all the sewers at a cost of £1,500 per week.[63] By the beginning of August, the government had made up its mind. The Metropolitan Board of Works was given full authority to proceed, allowed to choose its own sewer outfalls without government interference, with government bonds enabling it to raise up to £3 million. At last the great sewer work could begin. *The Times* gave full credit to the weather:

> That hot fortnight did for the sanitary administration of the metropolis what the Bengal mutinies did for the administration of India. It showed us more clearly and forcibly than before on what a volcano we were reposing.[64]

The attempts at deodorisation would continue for several years while the new sewer network was under construction. Success was mixed, with *The Lancet* describing the results as 'a peculiarly uninviting variety of sanitary lime-soup'.[65]

The construction of Bazalgette's intercepting sewers, and associated works, was not entirely without incident, plagued by problems with contractors, from bankruptcies to allegations of corruption. In 1863, Bazalgette himself became embroiled in a scandal, having taken a lucrative commission for recommending a contractor to the Ukrainian city of Odessa, then supposedly giving the same firm preferential treatment in London.[66] Some critics feared the new sewers would only spread miasma, and warned that the capital was creating 'A MONSTER CESSPOOL, from which every inhabitant . . . shall be obliged to construct a duct by which shall be conveyed a slow and sure poison to his family'.[67]

Nonetheless, nothing could derail the great undertaking, which would also come to include the construction of the Victoria Embankment. Bazalgette's steady progress soon won over many of his doubters. He was both a skilled engineer and a meticulous project manager, very particular about quality control, a practitioner of 'rigid economy and stern prudence'.[68] The MBW was so gratified with his success in 1865 that it seriously contemplated giving him a £6,000 bonus, before being taken to task over wasting public funds.

The official opening of the great sewer project – although the Embankment, with its built-in low-level sewer and underground railway was not yet complete – took place on 4 April 1865. There were formal sightseeing tours to both the Abbey Mills and Crossness pumping stations. The guest of honour was the Prince of Wales, accompanied by members of parliament, archbishops, aristocrats, members of the MBW; even Edwin Chadwick, a ghost at the feast. Guests marvelled at the last great crypt-like reservoir, as yet unfilled by sewage, illuminated by lamps, 'an underground Valhalla, where the streets of columns, lights and arches spread around in all directions'. The royal party were informed that only a single sluice gate separated them from 'five acres of the filthiest mess in Europe', and, perhaps a little nervously, praised the quality of the masonry and brickwork. Glasses were raised and a toast was given: 'Success to the Main Drainage!'[69]

London finally had its new sewers.

Proofs of the project's success were not lacking. For a start, the Thames swiftly returned to its glum, muddy, unodiferous self. There was also epidemiological evidence of the benefits of the new system. A cholera epidemic in 1866 spared much of the capital, but ravaged the portion of the East End which was still unconnected to Bazalgette's sewers. The primary source of the outbreak seemed to be the East London Water Company's reservoirs – which ought, in any case, to have been properly filtered – infected by the tidal flow of the River Lea, 'the common sewer of a large mass of the metropolitan and suburban population [of the East End]'.[70] There could be no better demonstration of the dangers of polluted water, and benefits of decent sewerage. In turn, these findings in east London contributed to a growing awareness of waterborne pollution. The conservative politician Frederick Spencer Hamilton, born in 1856, recalled his childhood in Mayfair in his autobiography.[71] The well on his father's property, renowned for the water's taste and purity, brought a 'long daily procession of men-servants in the curious yellow-jean jackets of the "sixties", each with two large cans in his hands, fetching the day's supply of our matchless water'. During 1867, Hamilton's father decided to have the water chemically analysed, regardless of its clarity, and found it contained 15 per cent 'pure sewage'. The well was sealed immediately.

The completion of Bazalgette's work was not, however, the panacea some-times suggested. Slums did not disappear overnight due to the appearance of a water closet and drain. Landlords were still perfectly capable of neglect. David F. Schloss ('Honorary Secretary of the Sanitary Committee of the Board of Guardians for the relief of the Jewish Poor') visited the poor in Whitechapel in the 1880s and found only one in ten houses with a 'flushing apparatus of any description'.[72] The broken or cistern-less 'water closet' would become as much a hallmark of slum housing as the old neglected privy and cesspool. The quality of closets was also often poor, with widespread use of old, cheap 'pan closets', which relied on a hinged copper pan that flipped down when the toilet handle was pulled. These were difficult to clean, and tended to accumu-late gas from badly trapped sewers beneath the pan-seal, resulting in 'a kind of explosion of water and foul gas' with every flush, 'bursting both water and effluvium to sometimes a considerable height above the seat'.[73]

London's sewers themselves likewise remained imperfect since they were a mixture of old and new. Local improvement works would continue for decades and expanding suburbs created new challenges. Wandsworth District Board, for example, had to build 105 miles of new sewers to connect with Bazalgette's new system, and a further 88 miles in the 1870s and 1880s, to keep up with its suburban sprawl.[74] Many tunnels, old and new, still needed regular 'flushing' to remove street-mud, rubbish and industrial pollutants. John Holl-ingshead conducted a lengthy exploration of 'underground London' in 1860, before the completion of Bazalgette's project. He made inquiries of the MBW, hoping to see sewer flushers at work, and was given his pick of locations:

They had blood-sewers (a delicate article) running underneath meat-markets, like Newport Market, where you could wade in the vital fluid of sheep and oxen; they had boiling sewers, which were largely used by sugar-bakeries, where the steam forced its way through the gratings in the roadway, like the vapour from the hot springs in Iceland, and where the sewer-cleansers get something very like a Turkish bath at the expense of the ratepayers . . . they had sewers of different degrees of repulsiveness, such as those where manufacturing chemists and soap and candle-makers most do congregate.[75]

The risks associated with 'flushing' and repair work under such conditions were considerable: drowning, explosions and suffocation or poisoning by gas. Smaller sewers – which could be only three or four feet high – might fill with water with astonishing rapidity during spells of bad weather. Flushers had to be aware of both the Thames's tidal flow and whether there had been any recent heavy rainfall. A certain Alfred Ash and one Joseph Rutherford, for example, were at work in a sewer in Kilburn in 1884. Ignoring one warning to leave, they were overwhelmed as storm waters flooded the tunnel. Their bodies were found the next day at the Chelsea outfall.

The principal cause of explosions was a build-up of 'carburetted hydrogen' – methane – which, of course, was highly inflammable. A typical case in Bermondsey in 1858 involved three men 'dreadfully burnt about the head, face and neck and arms, their eyebrows and hair being almost completely burnt off', as well as half a dozen others with minor burns. The gas was ignited by a sewer flusher's lamp.[76] Other gases from the decomposition of waste included toxic sulphuretted hydrogen (hydrogen sulphide) – the source of the familiar 'rotten eggs' smell of drains – and 'chokedamp' (carbon dioxide) which could have an astonishingly swift effect on the lungs. Labourers connecting an old sewer to a main sewer in the Whitechapel Road in 1857, opening up the tunnel, received 'a rush of foul air'. The man nearest to the bottom of excavation 'fell forwards'; another man went down to investigate and likewise fell immediately unconscious; three more followed, until five men lay in a heap – and had to be pulled up by grappling hooks. The first three men were found to have died.

Poisoning cases also arose from the outpourings of factories, chemical agents which reacted with the sewers' existing contents. In 1875 a gang of flushers, employed by the Wandsworth District Board, entered a local sewer near to the works of 'Messrs. Wallace, manufacturing chymists'. The works had already been the subject of an 'indignation committee' formed by local residents, prompted by the 'ventilators in the road . . . emitting dense hot vapour in the evening' which made passers-by feel ill. Inside the sewer, drains from the works emitted a 'blue substance which burnt their hands fearfully and turned them all sorts of colours'. Whilst attempting to clear some debris, the men were overcome by a burst of steam, 'a hissing noise like opening ginger beer', together with a sudden smell of sulphur, 'like brimstone going down their throats'. All four men were knocked unconscious, with one fatality.

Such were the manifold dangers of sewer gas that 'stench pipes' were constructed – tall, lamppost-like iron tubes that stood on the pavement above, either simply carrying the gas into the atmosphere, or burning it off whilst simultaneously serving as a street lamp. A lofty cast-iron ventilation pipe was even introduced into the clock tower of the Houses of Parliament, where it remains to this day.[77]

The accumulation of noxious gases, of course, only truly plagued sewer workers. The more fundamental flaw in Bazalgette's project was that it operated on the time-honoured sanitary principle of 'out of sight, out of mind'. The main object of the grand scheme was simply to move the capital's waste a little further to the east – so that it might flow out to sea, unnoticed. But the sites of the outfalls at Beckton and Crossness – the subject of much debate between Hall and the MBW – were not *that* distant from the heart of capital (about nine miles, as the crow flies). As London's suburbs expanded eastwards, the distance between the outfalls and the inhabited metropolis steadily diminished with every passing year; and the volume of sewage entering the Thames steadily increased.

The continuing presence and proximity of this river-borne filth were dramatically brought home by a tragedy on the Thames in the late 1870s – the collision between the paddle steamer *Princess Alice* (overloaded with several hundred passengers returning from a day out at Rosherville Gardens in Gravesend) and the coal ship *Bywell Castle* (returning to Newcastle). The crash occurred on the evening of 3 September 1878 at Gallion's Reach, a spot where the river was frequently thick with sewage pouring from the outfalls. The *Princess Alice* was split in two by the larger vessel, plunging several hundred men, women and children into the cold, murky water. There were one hundred and thirty survivors; some five or six hundred drowned in the filthy water. One would-be rescuer, rowing a boat to the site of disaster and nearly overwhelmed by the sheer numbers scrabbling to get on board, noted grimly that 'it was necessary to quench their hopes by knocking them off the sides with the oars'.[78] The state of the river water was much disputed. Some claimed that the wretched victims drowned in sewage; others that the water poisoned fourteen unlucky souls who died subsequent to their rescue.

The MBW carried out two exploratory cruises along the river, taking samples along the route to prove that press reports were exaggerated. They noted the 'interesting spectacle' of 'some men in a boat, "fishing" with nets to catch the fat carried out with the sewage from the outfall'. They also found a large number of lucifer matches and corks, bobbing around with the deposits of fat. But the river itself – at the very site of the disaster – was deemed relatively unpolluted.[79] The public remained unconvinced. In 1881, a deputation from riverside districts presented a petition signed by over 13,000 individuals to the Local Government Board (the body which now had responsibility for London's public health) asking for abatement of the foul condition of the Thames. The pleasure-cruise companies were said to be suffering; servants refused to work in riverside properties; the owners of docks and basins were frequently obliged to dredge out substantial deposits of sewage. The descriptions of the water which had circulated at the time of the *Princess Alice* disaster were corroborated: 'The gases seemed to explode in the bed of the river and come up like mud volcanoes . . .'[80]

A government commission was convened, reporting in 1884. Sewage was found as far upstream as Greenwich. The MBW held out against making any change until the end of 1885, but finally conceded that the outfalls could not continue in their present condition. It was decided to precipitate and chemically treat the solids, creating a sludge that could be dumped out at sea, and leave harmless liquid effluent entering the river. New tanks and pipes were built at Beckton and Crossness. Boats were ordered, 'capable of carrying 1,000 tons of sewage sludge and discharging the same out at sea in all weathers'.[81] The first boat would be named, amusingly enough, *Bazalgette*. There was some opposition to the idea, suggestions that the sludge could be turned to manure; or that pipes could be extended 40 miles through Essex to the sea. The latter, of course, was impossibly expensive; the former economically futile. Attempts to convert the sludge into 'cake' fertiliser for farmers proved that sewage manure was still not a money-making proposition. Farmers demanded to be paid for removing the tons of fertiliser and the overall cost per ton was five shillings, as opposed to 3½d. for despatching it into the North Sea.[82] There was no arguing with the numbers. Ultimately, by the mid-1890s, under the aegis of the London County Council, five boats – 'a fleet of fine sludge ships' – were working the estuary making over two thousand trips per year to Barrow Deep, just off the Essex coast. The LCC boasted that it no longer received complaints about the state of the Thames, and the river was suddenly teeming with life: 'fish are found enjoying themselves in the effluent at Barking.'[83]

At the very end of the century, London was finally purified; John Wright's vision of a clean Thames had been realised.

The Victorians' sewers have stood the test of time, although Bazalgette bequeathed the capital a problem. The great engineer sensibly let certain tunnels double as overflow drains, to cope with heavy rainfall and ever-increasing volumes of domestic water, with emergency outfalls running along the length of the river. He did not expect the system to reach capacity very often, and allowed for a population of four million in his calculations of that capacity. This was double the number of inhabitants of London when the sewers were built. Unfortunately, London's population has now almost doubled again, to eight million. Consequently, Bazalgette's tunnels grow too full and raw sewage spills over into the river throughout the year. Thames Water has proposed a new 22-mile-long 'super sewer' to resolve the problem – a project costing over £4 billion. Thus, over the next decade, sewerage will once again become the great metropolitan engineering project. The scheme has not been delayed by dilatory modern-day 'commissioners' – rather, it faces extensive planning objections from local and environmental pressure groups.

Marine dumping of sludge, meanwhile, was banned by the European Union in 1998. The noxious material now undergoes anaerobic digestion, creating biogas; some is burnt to generate electricity; and the great majority recycled as sewage manure – as John Martin and Edwin Chadwick once proposed – albeit sadly not at a profit.

5

VILE BODIES

THERE WAS ANOTHER 'waste removal' problem which plagued the capital as it agonised over sewerage: the disposal of the dead. There was little dispute about the means. Burial was the norm; cremation a peculiar foreign custom. The difficulty lay in finding room for an ever-increasing number of corpses. The capital's burgeoning population, upon their decease, were filling up its small churchyards, burial grounds and vaults. The consequences, wherever demand exceeded supply, were decidedly unpleasant. Coffins were stacked one atop the other in 20-foot-deep shafts, the topmost mere inches from the surface. Putrefying bodies were frequently disturbed, dismembered or destroyed to make room for newcomers. Disinterred bones, dropped by neglectful gravediggers, lay scattered amidst the tombstones; smashed coffins were sold to the poor for firewood. Clergymen and sextons turned a blind eye to the worst practices because burial fees formed a large proportion of their income. Macabre scenes awaited those who pried too closely into the gravedigger's work:

> I saw them chopping the head of his coffin away; I should not have known it if I had not seen the head with the teeth; I knew him by his teeth; one tooth was knocked out and the other was splintered; I knew it was my father's head, and I told them to stop, and they laughed . . .[1]

Clearance of long-buried bones had always taken place; but the growing demand for burials in crowded grounds meant that the work became ever more grisly.

Churchyards were not the only sites open for burial. There were other general locations for interment, not restricted to the members of particular parishes, churches or chapels. Bunhill Fields, on the edge of the City of London, had long served as a general unconsecrated burial ground for Dissenters and Nonconformists.[2] Other modestly sized grounds, established by enterprising undertakers and clergymen as commercial speculations, were dotted throughout the suburbs. Islington and Southwark, for example, each boasted their own so-called 'New Bunhill Fields', opened in 1818 and 1820 respectively.[3] A few parishes had what we might now call 'overspill' grounds. St Giles – a slum-ridden district near Covent Garden – created a new burial ground in St Pancras in 1803. This was something of a radical departure, since it was more than a mile from the parish it served.[4] Famously, the 1830s would also see the creation of large commercial cemeteries in semi-rural districts bordering the metropolis – beginning with the Cemetery of All Souls, Kensal Green in 1832.

Nonetheless, despite these welcome additions, the burial problem persisted. Moreover, by the 1840s London's overcrowded churchyards (and the older, small commercial grounds) were not only seen as posing a logistical challenge, but damned as a source of 'miasma'. Sanitarians, quite mistakenly, believed that the stench from poorly interred decaying bodies was poisoning the metropolis.[5] The practice of urban burial was touted as a profound menace to public health, just as pernicious as the household cesspool.

The story of how this came about – how dead bodies became a category of metropolitan filth, and how London responded to the challenge – begins in the 1820s with George Frederick Carden, like Edwin Chadwick an ambitious young barrister, the self-styled 'Founder of the system of ex-urban sepulture'.

Concern about insanitary churchyards was nothing new. John Evelyn, writing in the mid-seventeenth century, believed the Great Fire had been a lost opportunity for London to build a 'universal cemetery to all parishes' beyond the walls of the city. Evelyn lumped the existing small churchyards together with 'kennels, sinks, gutters, lay-stalls and other nuisances' – in other words, they stank.[6] In 1817, the Methodist biblical scholar Adam Clarke, commenting on Luke 7:12, condemned the practice of burying in churchyards and vaults. Speaking seemingly from personal experience, Clarke declared churchyards 'perfectly unwholesome', denouncing 'gas which is disengaged from putrid flesh' as both foul-smelling and potentially fatal.[7] George Carden, however, was the first to widely publicise the supposed danger of graveyard gases for a purpose – to promote his own commercial schemes for metropolitan burial.

Carden became interested in such matters during a trip to Paris in 1818.[8] Like many foreign tourists, he visited the 'garden cemetery' of Père Lachaise. By the time of Carden's visit, this non-denominational cemetery, which had opened in 1804, was already widely acclaimed as the exemplar of how to deal with metropolitan interment. It was not only situated beyond the city precincts and rather spacious – extending over 110 acres – but cleverly landscaped, neatly planted with shrubs and flowers, with artistically designed tombs and classical monuments, 'all neat, decent and appropriate to the solemnity of the scene'. Père Lachaise was ornamental, a carefully planned Romantic spectacle – a stark contrast to the 'narrow, close, filthy and almost indecent' churchyards of London.[9] Carden returned home, suitably impressed, and wondered if something similar could be achieved in the English metropolis. Still a young man, he spent the next few years dabbling in both law and medicine, studying the latter in Edinburgh, between 1822 and 1824.[10] When he returned to London in 1824, his thoughts turned again to the problem of burials. He found the capital gripped by frenzied stock market speculation. This was a period of frenetic activity, producing many dubious 'bubbles', 'when a joint-stock company for establishing steam carriages to the moon would have succeeded'.[11] Carden spied a business opportunity. Now was the time to reform the existing system of metropolitan interment – and make a profit in the process.

Carden launched the Economic Funeral Society in 1824/25 ('Capital 150,000*l.* in 6000 shares of 25*l.* each'). This joint-stock company would provide funerals and burial plots across the metropolis at moderate, fixed prices. Undertakers were notorious for persuading grieving widows and widowers of the 'propriety' of all sorts of extraneous trappings – 'best black feathers', '2 porters at the door in gowns, staves, silk covers, halberds and gloves', 'use of seven superfine cloaks', etc.[12] Carden believed that the public would willingly switch allegiance from well-established firms 'to secure themselves, their friends and dependents from unreasonable and extravagant charges'.[13] The company prospectus would ingenuously solicit undertakers, owners of hearses and horses, wholesale merchants of black feathers etc, to offer their services ('it being the intention of the Directors to distribute the business as much as possible throughout each district'). Carden seems to have naively believed that undertakers would willingly undercut/undermine their existing highly profitable trade in return for his company's custom. Potential investors, however, were not convinced, and so Carden revised his plans. The company name was changed to the General Burial Grounds Association; the capital required was doubled to £300,000. Rather than manage funerals, the new company would build a London version of Père Lachaise. The new cemetery would be an elegant resting place for the dead beyond the built-up city, with neat lawns, beautiful monuments – and high walls to deter the body-snatchers who made their living from stealing corpses for the anatomical schools.

Security of the grave was an important prerequisite. The measures taken to thwart 'resurrectionists' in existing grounds were manifold: watch-houses; night-watchmen; high walls topped with broken glass or iron spikes; families taking turns to maintain a nocturnal vigil (until the body decayed); 'Brigman's Patent Wrought Iron Coffin' (capable of deflecting the resurrectionist's crowbar); the occasional use of 'spring guns' – booby traps, laid amongst the tombstones. Some grieving families were even willing to add quicklime to the interior of coffins to render the body unfit for dissection. Carden, however, would claim that the public health benefits of his new scheme were 'the most important consideration of all'.[14] He chose *salus populi suprema lex* as the company's motto, and used the prospectus to wax lyrical on the dangers of the stench from exposed or poorly buried corpses. In particular, drawing on his own experience, Carden outlined an incident in a City churchyard (which, in later years, he would identify as St Sepulchre) when putrefying remains were exposed to the atmosphere by workmen. The noxious gases issuing from the corpses left several labourers confined to their homes for days afterwards, and the author himself 'violently affected by fever'.[15] Surely, he argued, this was ample proof of the danger of graveyard miasma. The general public, Carden noted, 'cannot be aware of the extent of the evil'.

Once again, however, the venture did not prosper: the General Burial Grounds Association did not survive the great stock market crash of December 1825. Indeed, according to one latter-day critic, the scheme 'did not catch a single stray deposit of 2*l*. 10*s*'.[16]

The pricking of the stock market bubble undoubtedly played a major part in discouraging Carden's potential investors. There were, however, other factors. Firstly, the size and, hence, vulgarity of the speculation was a stumbling block. No one doubted that individual undertakers made a healthy, even excessive profit from funerals – but at least they provided a personal service. The idea of a joint-stock company organising burials on an almost industrial scale was an uncomfortable proposition. There was also the question of propriety. True, the London churchyard was frequently a rather grim place, but this was 'no unbefitting preparation for the solemnity of the church'.[17] Père Lachaise had swiftly become a fashionable promenade. Nearby taverns and drinking houses catered for the more secular needs of those who had finished contemplating the eternal verities in its neatly manicured grounds. Some wondered if such things were decent.

Above all, there was an underlying suspicion that the proposed cemetery was a Continental innovation, innately foreign and unwelcome. There were two similar projects already under way in Liverpool but no English precedent on a comparable scale.[18] This was a period when anything French smacked of unbecoming ostentation. The Romantic idyll presented by Père Lachaise was quite alien: 'An honest John Bull would only laugh at the knavish fool whom he saw blubbering and groaning over a grave stuck with daffadowndillies.'[19]

There were at least two separate printed spoofs of Carden's prospectus, playing on these anxieties, mocking the 'Parisian' scheme to 'rob death of its terrors and make it delightful', deriding it as a mere vehicle for speculators.[20] One offered a rather unlikely vision of the facilities that a 'General Burying Company' might make available to mourners:

> . . . a convenient hotel and tavern on the spot . . . a table d'hote will be constantly prepared at five shillings a-head, for cold meat and Vin de Grave will be furnished: and on Tuesdays, Thursdays and Saturdays, during the summer, after burying hours, COLINET's band will be regularly engaged for quadrilles, and the grounds illuminated with variegated lamps.[21]

To a modern reader, this seems a peculiar conceit. It is, in fact, a description of an archetypal London 'pleasure garden'. These landscaped grounds, which, in the evening, became a peculiar mixture of theme park, hotel and dance hall – essentially al fresco nightclubs – ringed the metropolis in the 1820s, the most famous being Vauxhall Gardens. Some pleasure gardens were more respectable than others, but most were morally dubious, known as nocturnal haunts of prostitutes. Of course, no one truly expected licentious carousing and 'Vin de Grave' amidst Carden's tombs – but the joke reveals how strange the garden cemetery was to the English imagination. The pleasure garden was, after a fashion, the nearest point of comparison; and a far more lively and appealing proposition.

Carden's public health claims – the perils of graveyard miasma – were also met with scepticism. Some critics reluctantly accepted that such smells *might* be dangerous to health, whilst others would remain determinedly disbelieving – 'Where is the proof that disease EVER HAS been communicated to the living by the buried dead?'[22] John Wright would experience the same problem in 1827/28 when arguing that polluted water caused disease – there was no unimpeachable way to link cause and effect, only anecdotes and appeals to 'common sense'. Wright would ultimately be proved correct by medical science; Carden and fellow miasmatists wrong – but scientific clarity would not emerge for decades. In the meantime, when it came to such matters, Londoners relied as much on gut instinct as medical science. In 1825, few believed that graveyards were *that* dangerous. The fetid aroma of death had always lingered in certain poorly managed churchyards as just another irritating metropolitan stink.

The public perception of risk, however, would soon change.

Carden's dismal failure in 1825 did not put an end to his ambition nor prevent others from coming forward with their own ideas. One Thomas Willson, an architect, proposed a rather striking solution to the burial problem. This was not a conventional cemetery, but a giant pyramid mausoleum, to be situated on Primrose Hill (the site which Carden had proposed for his grand design). Willson first exhibited plans for the building at the National Repository – a showcase gallery for manufacturers and inventors – in 1827.[23] He would spend the next few years touting his prospectus. The enormous structure would cover 18 acres, with 'four cyclopean flights of stairs ascending from the pavement to the pinnacle . . . surmounted by a plain characteristic obelisk, having a circular stone staircase, and terminating in an astronomical observatory'.[24] There would be additional land around the pyramid in which small monuments might also be situated. Inside, there would be catacombs in each level of the building – with room for 147,360 coffins in the base, and just 480 at the very peak. The building would tower above the city at well over double the height of St Paul's Cathedral. It hardly needs saying that this was a fanciful and fruitless scheme – somewhat bizarre, even allowing for the contemporary enthusiasm for Egyptiana – but it may well have spurred Carden to renew his own endeavours. He had spent the late 1820s finishing his legal apprenticeship (he was called to the Bar in 1829) but never entirely abandoned the idea of an English Père Lachaise. Discussions with Willson about somehow uniting the two plans came to nothing.[25] Instead, returning to the fray, Carden obtained backers for a new joint-stock company to accomplish his old purpose: it would be dubbed the 'General Cemetery Company' (GCC).

Launched in 1830, the GCC was the 'English Père Lachaise' scheme revisited. Influential supporters included Andrew Spottiswoode, the king's printer and a member of parliament; Viscount Milton, also a well-respected member of parliament; and the wealthy banker Sir John Dean Paul, who would come to dominate the company's board.[26] Carden despatched a petition to parliament, noting that London burial grounds were 'offensive to public decency and dangerous to the health of the people', highlighting the state of the worst churchyards in the metropolis.[27] This was swiftly followed by a public meeting at the Freemason's Tavern, which confirmed that an ornamental, spacious, public cemetery was the solution. The Bishop of London broadly declared his support, as long as the clergy did not lose their accustomed burial fees. The company was advertised in the national press, and a prospectus was issued. The public health case seemed a little stronger than in 1825. *The Lancet* noted the lectures of Dr Armstrong of the London Fever Hospital, who had linked typhus to burial grounds, and concluded that the cemetery was an important 'sanatory [*sic*]' measure, which 'may save the lives of thousands'.[28] Other useful support came from J.C. Loudon, the noted landscape gardener and architect, who hoped the new cemetery might also contain 'as many hardy trees and shrubs and herbaceous plants, as room could be found',[29] providing an inspirational botanic garden for the masses. King William himself vaguely indicated his approval.

Carden's insistence on the public health benefits of the garden cemetery would, second time around, prove particularly fortuitous. For, during the summer of 1831, the notion of well-ventilated suburban grounds suddenly became infinitely more appealing to the general public. The cause was fear of cholera. The newspapers were filled with feverish anxiety about its approach. Scepticism about the dangers of miasma was replaced with generalised terror about atmospheric corruption. Even contagionists – who believed the disease spread through touch – must have been a little wary of attending small churchyards and burial grounds, where corpses were frequently disinterred and grisly relics lay scattered on the ground. The much touted extra-urban cemetery, on the other hand, seemed to offer a safe haven to mourn the dead. More cynical would-be investors must also have noted the epidemic's potential to generate large numbers of additional customers. The GCC was certainly alive to the fact that cholera might boost support for their scheme. Viscount Milton, whilst purporting not to spread alarm, gave a speech in support of the new cemetery, noting 'it was as incumbent on the people of London to guard against internal sources of infection, as Government had found it necessary to prevent the introduction into the country of contagion from abroad'.[30] The modern cemetery, in other words, was a safeguard against the enemy within – the corruption of the city churchyard. This sufficed to overcome much of the reluctance felt in the 1820s. As Henry Morley, Dickens's favourite sanitary correspondent for *Household Words*, would later note: 'if it had not been for cholera, it is doubtful whether the cemeteries would have proved to be a profitable speculation'.[31] It was during these months that the fledgling GCC became confident enough to purchase a plot of land, selecting a site at Kensal Green, on the Harrow Road, rather than Primrose Hill.

Fears that cholera was bred in urban graveyards persisted into 1832, when the epidemic finally reached the metropolis. The residents of Russell Court, off Drury Lane, took a petition to local magistrates – and, later, their local board of health – complaining about an adjoining burial ground, anxious that it might produce the disease. The foul-smelling, crowded site had been repeatedly excavated for graves and topped up with earth to such an extent that it was 'elevated above the back parlour windows facing the same'.[32] Unfortunately, after much musing, nothing was done. The Central Board of Health, meanwhile, reported to the Privy Council that close-packed grounds, insufficiently covered with earth, were 'an evil of serious consideration'.[33] The Central Board vainly urged all London authorities to adopt the precaution of creating separate burial grounds for cholera victims. For most small parishes, however, the cost of land was too high. Larger parishes did not relish the prospect of such a burden on the rates. In any case, many landowners were unwilling to allow their property to be used for such a pestiferous purpose. Cholera victims were buried hurriedly, in existing locations.

The necessary legislation to incorporate the GCC – An Act for Establishing a General Cemetery for the Interment of the Dead in the Neighbourhood of the Metropolis – was finally passed in July 1832. The cemetery grounds at Kensal Green were consecrated at the start of the following year, with the first burial at the end of January 1833 – 'Margaret, wife of Bernard Gregory, esq. of Great Russell-street' – for whom the directors of the GCC promised to erect a memorial tablet at their own expense, to commemorate their first customer. Carden's vision of an English Père Lachaise was realised. By this time, however, the threat of cholera had receded. There was a collective sigh of relief across the metropolis. Sanitary anxieties were put to one side with the passing of the epidemic.[34] A government offer to purchase five acres of the Kensal Green site, solely for victims of the disease, was hastily withdrawn. Likewise, a City of London plan to open a new 22-acre cemetery in Holloway was abandoned.[35] Indeed, since Carden had touted the new cemetery as the solution to mismanagement and overcrowding, some assumed the burial problem was now solved.

Fetid graveyards did not attract much attention during the years that followed. One reason was that Carden himself, despite his focus on miasma, was no ardent campaigner for public health. He was undoubtedly a genuine miasmatist – his experience in St Sepulchre's churchyard seems to have convinced him that graveyard gases produced disease – but his ultimate goal was to sell the garden cemetery to the public. By the end of 1832, this work was done. At the same time, he was growing increasingly disillusioned with the GCC, which he had expected to provide him with more in the way of respect and remuneration. There would be a very public split between the self-styled 'founder' of Kensal Green and the GCC Board of Directors. It manifested itself in various ways, including arguments over suitable architects and styles for the cemetery buildings. By 1838, the dispute had blown up into legal proceedings in which Carden attempted to sue the company for his 'services and expenses'.[36] GCC lawyers would settle the case for £1,000 the following year.

Carden would later attempt to paint himself as a conviction sanitarian *avant la lettre* (' "Salus populi suprema lex" was my motto of 1824'),[37] a claim which is hard to take seriously. Certainly, the contemporary response to his early ventures suggests he was perceived as a speculator. Carden preferred to present his initial failures in a more heroic light – 'Mr. Carden, it seems, never contemplated personal gain . . . he *singly* and at his *own* cost set about the task, with the exertion, risk and chance of ridicule all his own, when the authorities would not, and others did not, set about the task.'[38] Yet, significantly, recounting his early efforts, he always removed the Economic Funeral Society from the story. The budget funerals scheme did not fit quite so well into the 'reformer' narrative.

There is further evidence against Carden's self-declared sanitary enthusiasm. He owned a number of houses in Lambeth (amongst other places) and, during the 1850s, was repeatedly indicted by the local authorities for the emptying of night soil into the street and poor maintenance of privies. He blamed the parish, the sewer authority and tenants for the trouble – and took great pleasure in personally defending himself in court, laying into his accusers with a rather crude, bludgeoning wit: 'I wonder what sort of a privy this Dr Bushell has, and whether it smells different or more sweet than other persons'.'[39] Yet the Metropolitan Commission of Sewers had already put 320 feet of pipe sewers in the very street in which Carden's houses were situated. We can only assume that Carden did not care to pay the cost of making a connection to the new mains. Such persistent neglect hardly suggests a man tirelessly devoted to the cause of public health. Indeed, Carden was so careless of the Lambeth properties that the freeholder – the Duchy of Cornwall – eventually took the unusual step of bringing a court action to recover the buildings, lest they collapse.[40] In short, this public-spirited projector of luxurious resting places for the dead was also a slum landlord.

This actually makes a certain sort of sense. Kensal Green and subsequent imitators were squarely aimed at the middle classes, charging up to double the fees of the parish grounds.[41] It is significant that Kensal Green truly began to prosper when the Duke of Sussex was buried there in 1843. Cemetery burial offered not only salubrity but a certain social exclusivity, away from the riff-raff. One's choice of burial site reflected social class and religious scruples: 'People like to be buried in company, and in good company.'[42] Joint-stock company cemeteries removed the corpse of the respectable tradesman and prosperous City clerk from the squalor of the crowded churchyard; they did not provide for the humble factory worker or manual labourer. If Carden was a 'proto-sanitarian', providing wholesome graves for his fellow Londoners, then he had a rather circumscribed constituency: the comfortable and the wealthy.

In truth, Carden was, first and foremost, a man of business. It is notable that amongst the very first potential rivals to Kensal Green was the Great Western Cemetery Company, projected in 1834 – by Carden himself. This was another episode on which the 'founder of ex-urban sepulture' would rarely dilate in later years. Carden, alienated from the GCC, was the scheme's 'projector, treasurer and registrar'.[43] The proposal was to purchase a substantial site in Notting Hill on the Norland Estate, to build yet another garden cemetery in the manner of Père Lachaise. The location – only a mile and a half from Kensal Green – lay somewhat closer to affluent west London, carefully chosen to trump the existing company. The Norland grounds were opened for public inspection in 1834, much to the annoyance of the sitting tenant, who used the land for an archery school. This, in turn, led to a dispute over bringing a model of the cemetery on to the site, during which the somewhat irascible Carden drove his horse into two men, and was hauled before a magistrate. Nothing ever came of the speculation beyond this court appearance; the land would be gradually covered by housing from the late 1840s onwards.[44]

Others would successfully imitate Kensal Green: the South Metropolitan Cemetery Company opened Norwood Cemetery in 1837; the London Cemetery Company opened Highgate Cemetery in 1839 and Nunhead in 1840; Abney Park, Brompton and Tower Hamlets cemeteries swiftly followed. But the creation of this 'magnificent seven' (to borrow a phrase from twentieth-century cemetery enthusiasts) did nothing to put an end to crowded parish burial, nor to remove small privately owned burial grounds where frequent disinterment was the norm. Consequently, the poor would still struggle to find decent sites for their dead.

It was concern about the interment of the poor that would return urban graves to public scrutiny at the end of the 1830s. Reformers would reaffirm Carden's link between the churchyard, miasma and disease – not for commercial gain, but hoping to effect wholesale improvement in public health.

The principal agitator was George Alfred Walker – who would acquire the nickname 'Graveyard Walker' – a surgeon who took up practice in Drury Lane in the mid-1830s.[45] The district was a poor one. Half a dozen badly managed burial places lay within a short distance from the doctor's premises – including the site adjoining Russell Court. Walker came to the conclusion that these foul-smelling grounds produced much ill health in the neighbouring population. He did not deny the influence of sewers, poorly ventilated housing, etc., but he was certain that graveyard miasma was an important, much neglected predisposing cause of disease. In 1839 he began a long campaign to end 'intramural interment',[46] commencing with a pamphlet entitled *Gatherings from Graveyards*.

Walker's public health claims in *Gatherings* – and, indeed, all his later work – were not dissimilar to Carden's. He provided, however, more extensive examples, authorities and evidence. The key to the problem was gas emanating from rotting corpses. The existence of such gases was undisputed. Sextons and undertakers were often called up to 'tap' coffins in church vaults, drilling a hole to prevent them breaking open with explosive force. Walker dutifully recorded the effects of leaking miasma on the constitution of gravediggers, ranging from general ill health ('pain in the head, heaviness, extreme debility, lachrymation, violent palpitation of the heart, universal trembling, with vomiting') to sudden death. Gas could, indeed, prove fatal: graveyard workers who broke into bloated coffins were occasionally suffocated by the release of 'cadaverous vapours'. Walker republished the 1771 experimental findings of Dr Haguenot of Paris, which proved the dangers of graveyard miasma in the most dramatic fashion ('Third experiment. – Cats and dogs thrown into this grave, were strongly convulsed, and expired in two or three minutes, – birds, in some seconds').[47] He also quoted Robert Bullen, a parish medical officer in the City, who thought graveyards 'the great cause of contagion', belching out the 'mephitical effluvia of death', and had submitted his impressions to Chadwick's East End inquiry of 1838. Walker's overall argument in *Gatherings* was that concentrated graveyard gases caused instant death in man and beast; foul-smelling grounds, constantly releasing more diffused miasma, did not produce sudden death – but they debilitated those living nearby, according to their level of exposure and individual resistance.

This would prove a persuasive proposition. It helped that Carden had already made the connection between graveyard miasma and cholera – something Walker never acknowledged, since he feared being linked to the commercial interests of the cemetery companies.[48] Walker would attempt to ally himself with Chadwick's nascent sanitary campaign, even aping his language – 'that many of these sources of disease are removable I am certain . . .'[49] He was also a skilful propagandist in his own right, adept as utilising grisly detail to grab the attention of the reader. His favourite example of malpractice was Enon Chapel, situated in slums north of the Strand. This dubious place of worship, established in the 1820s largely as a burial speculation, contained a modest cellar in which the deceased were laid to rest in their thousands (i.e. corpses were regularly surreptitiously cleared away). Mangled coffins in the chapel vaults produced unclassifiable 'body bugs', which sprang from the corpses and lurked in hair and clothing. Worshippers reported foul aromas and 'a peculiar taste' during services, praising the Lord with a handkerchief pressed to their nostrils. Some redundant remains were dumped in a sewer that ran directly under the building.[50] The latter was a detail worthy of a penny dreadful, except that it was not fiction.

Walker appeared before Robert Slaney's 'Health of Towns' committee in 1840. He then met the Bishop of London ('no satisfactory conclusions could be arrived at').[51] Others drew inspiration from his much publicised campaigning. The City of London's Lands Committee produced a report in 1841 that recommended prohibiting urban burial, and petitioned parliament the following February. Walker, not to be outdone, wrote to the Home Secretary and worked up his own petition, denouncing graveyards as 'laboratories of malaria[52] . . . so many centres of infection, constantly giving off noxious effluvia'. It was, he claimed, only the differences in locality, atmosphere and individual constitution that rendered such gases a 'slow or energetic poison'.[53] The MP William Mackinnon, who had listened to Walker's evidence at the Slaney inquiry, presented the petition and successfully moved for a select committee on the subject. Thanks to Walker's agitation the burial problem would receive detailed parliamentary scrutiny.

The Mackinnon inquiry of 1842 covered similar ground to Walker's reports. Amongst other things, the select committee confirmed the reality of Walker's accounts of gross and gruesome scenes in churchyards and vaults:

> I have seen them play at what is called skittles; put up bones and take skulls and knocked them down; stick up bones in the ground and throw a skull at them as you would a skittle-ball.[54]

The medical evidence, however, was not emphatic. James Copeland, Censor of the Royal College of Physicians, stated that burial grounds were probably the most important factor in generating ill health amongst the poor, but focused on the effect of liquefying, decomposing bodies on local wells and water supply. George Collier, another doctor, affirmed that graveyard miasma would 'depress, impair and enervate the human frame', and was a predisposing cause of fever of the 'low typhoid kind'. The committee chairman agreed – that there was a link between miasma and fever – but would only go so far as to say: 'I should presume that over-crowded burying-grounds would supply such effluvia most abundantly.' The connection, in other words, seemed likely but not definite. Others noted alternative explanations for the prevalence of fever in the slums – the stench from sewers and the general dirt. A doctor at King's College Hospital, located next to a notoriously ill-managed burial ground, said that his patients suffered 'no inconvenience'.

Despite these equivocal findings, the select committee ultimately endorsed Walker's miasmatic claims. Distrust of stench won the day – for there was no doubting the awful aroma that arose from certain grounds. As one gravedigger eloquently declaimed: 'I [have] emptied a cesspool, and the smell of it was rose-water compared with the smell of these graves.'[55] Mackinnon recommended immediate action: the prohibition of urban burial, with legislation requiring parishes (or unions of parishes, as under the Poor Law) to build their own large cemeteries at a safe distance from the centre of the metropolis. If necessary, he would bring forward his own bill in parliament, recommending a penny rate to pay for new cemeteries, and a central board of health to oversee parish arrangements.

Mackinnon's bill was necessary – i.e. the government did not volunteer – but it did little to move matters forward. In fact, the bill became a magnet for vehement opposition. Vestries criticised the bill for proposing new burial boards – composed of rectors, churchwardens and two parishioners, with the power to settle burial fees and levy rates – because 'it took all power out of the hands of the vestry'.[56] Clergymen complained that they would not have exclusive control over deciding their fees and perquisites. The most angry critics were the Dissenters, who did not bury their dead in parish grounds. They largely relied on sites contiguous to their own churches and chapels, Bunhill Fields, and numerous small commercial grounds. The prohibition of urban burial would close all such venues and, according to Mackinnon's plan, replace them with a handful of large cemeteries superintended by Church of England clergy. Most existing parish grounds either refused Dissenters burial outright or penalised them with excessive charges. There were fears that this religious prejudice would be extended on a grand scale. There might be some unconsecrated ground set aside for those beyond the embrace of the established Church, but this approach – which had been adopted at Kensal Green – was characterised as ghettoisation. As one opponent of Mackinnon's scheme put it:

> Are we next to have Church and Dissenting carriages on our railways? Are we, then, to have Church and Dissenting compartments on the decks and in the cabins of our steamboats? . . . Why, then, attempt to classify the bodies of mankind upon principles which the Judge of all flesh will not apply to their immortal spirits?[57]

Mackinnon still plugged away in parliament. James Graham, Home Secretary, made vague noises that the government might bring forward its own legislation, but then issued an unexpected demand: first there must be a further report, from Edwin Chadwick. The subject had been omitted by Chadwick from his 1842 sanitary report, in deference to the Mackinnon committee. A charitable interpretation is that Graham had decided that burial might form part of 'Health of Towns' legislation and hence required Chadwick's detailed attention. More likely, however, he intended to kick the contentious topic into the long grass. Mackinnon dutifully yielded to the claim that the subject was now actively under government consideration, and withdrew his bill. After all, Edwin Chadwick's public health plans revolved around removing sources of 'miasma' – he would surely back the campaign.

In fact, Chadwick's report, which appeared in 1843, went too far. Indeed, it positively reinforced Graham's reluctance to address the burial problem: 'nothing convinced him more of the extreme difficulty of dealing with the subject'.[58] Chadwick's proposal was typical of his centralising approach: he declared the parishes were incapable of executing such large-scale work; moreover, that they had shown themselves incapable of managing burials in a hygienic fashion, and that any *parish* cemeteries would inevitably become a public nuisance. The only rational alternative was a national scheme managed by central government with state-run cemeteries and fixed fees established by legislation – and the abolition of all existing commercial concerns. This was not simply regulation but wholesale nationalisation of burial, replacing commercial interests with officials who would certify deaths and ensure that corpses were buried promptly. Graham, unsurprisingly, could not contemplate such a radical, intrusive scheme, which comprehensively divested the clergy of their supremacy in all things funereal, and excluded the parish authorities from the equation. Instead, he came out in favour of the status quo, declaring that 'he was not prepared to admit that the public health was endangered' and that the subject was 'so distinct and disconnected from all other causes productive of temporary disease' that it should *not* be included within any wider 'Health of Towns' measures.

Mackinnon would doggedly raise the need for legislation over the next few parliamentary sessions, only to be repeatedly rebuffed. Walker, meanwhile, although he had hoped for more from the government, refused to be downcast. He was a remarkably determined individual and continued his campaign in letters, pamphlets, petitions and lectures. His technique was repetition, constantly assailing the public with ever more gruesome facts, recycling tales of graveyard degradations, seeking out new examples. He formed a Society for the Abolition of Burial in Towns, modelled on the Health of Towns Association, which attracted a small but dedicated membership. Then a particular instance of egregious practices came to his attention, which he felt sure would spur the government to action – the Spa Fields scandal.

Spa Fields, immediately south of Exmouth Market in Clerkenwell, was a typical small burial ground. Covering not much more than an acre or two, it first opened in 1778. By the 1840s, it was maintained by private speculators as a business concern, wholly divorced from the abutting Dissenting chapel. Customers came largely from the local poor, since the owners charged competitive prices – 'so extremely low, that the poorer class of people from all the surrounding parishes buried their dead at this place for cheapness'.[59] Unfortunately, low prices meant low standards. Walker, surveying the site in the late 1830s, had already noted that it was 'absolutely saturated with dead'.

In December 1843, two local women – 'highly respectable inhabitants of Clerkenwell' – brought Spa Fields to the attention of their local magistrate. They alleged that recently buried bodies were being disinterred and destroyed to make room for fresh interments. In particular, the body of an infant had been chopped up, the body and coffin burnt in the ground's 'bone house'. Bone houses, or charnel houses, were resting places for disinterred remains – storage for the ancient skeletons, which might be occasionally disinterred when breaking ground for new graves. The accusation was that the Spa Fields bone house was more akin to a butcher's shop and crematorium.[60]

Walker spotted the case in *The Times* and immediately rushed to offer himself as an expert witness; but the magistrate was uninterested. Walker persisted and talked to the local residents who believed that recently interred bodies were being consigned to the bone-house furnace. The manager of the ground, Mr Bird, threatened a libel case if Walker publicised the claims; but this only goaded the good doctor into action. Walker encouraged the local residents to raise further complaints and petitions – this 'community activism' was part of his regular modus operandi. At the start of 1845, Mr Watts, a pawnbroker, brought the problem, once again, before the local magistrate. Numerous residents testified to the foul-smelling smoke constantly billowing from the chimney of the bone house, and stated that they had been obliged to quit their homes on account of the stench. The magistrate, on this occasion, despatched a constable to investigate, who confirmed that coffin wood was certainly being burnt but found no evidence of dead bodies. Mr Bird claimed the smell came from the pitch used to seal coffins. A fireman – who had, on occasion, been called to put out the bone-house furnace, when it raged too strongly – stated that he believed the smell 'seemed as if from burnt bones or flesh'.[61] One woman swore that she had seen 'gravediggers throw up parts of a human body and then chop it up with their shovels'.

The dubious goings-on at Spa Fields swiftly became something of a cause célèbre in the national press. The visceral aspects were not *that* novel; but the suggestion that large numbers of bodies were being *burnt* was unusual. There was a generally heightened interest in sanitary matters in the mid-1840s, and Walker was doing all he could to publicise the case, issuing condemnatory handbills throughout the Clerkenwell district. He would later publish an entire pamphlet. Another reason for the unusual amount of publicity was that the ground's manager, Bird, was determined to loudly rebuff all claims of impropriety. He bluntly stated that the site buried eight bodies in each grave ('We put in two coffins of adults lengthwise, and then put three children's coffins at each end'); that bodies were disinterred as soon as the gravedigger could spear a metal rod through the earth below (which produced gasps from spectators at a crowded magistrates' court, although the use of such rods was common practice throughout London); and denied the key accusation of dismembering and burning corpses. The only problem for Bird was damning evidence from the marvellously named Reuben Room, a former gravedigger, which cast serious doubt on his claims:

> I have severed head, arms, legs, or whatever came in my way, with a crowbar, pickaxe, chopper and saw. Of the bodies, some were quite fresh and some decomposed. I have had as much as 1.5cwt. of human flesh on what we term the 'beef board' at the foot of the grave at one time. I have often put a rope round the neck of the corpse to drag it out of the coffin . . .[62]

Room was the star witness and whistle-blower. He only conceded that he had burnt coffin wood with flesh 'adhering' to it – but the surrounding detail was so gruesome that it hardly mattered. Similar revolting practices undoubtedly happened elsewhere, but Spa Fields was now infamous.

The case received so much publicity that the Home Secretary intervened, despatching an assistant police commissioner to investigate. The inhabitants of nearby tenements testified to gruesome sights ('I saw what appeared a mash, which seemed to me to be the bowels of a corpse, which the gravedigger attempted to gather up in a shovel . . .'). Bird made a foolhardy attempt at regaining public confidence, which proved utterly counter-productive. He offered to open any graves to prove that bodies had not been disinterred – perhaps thinking that few would actually want to witness the decomposing remains of their nearest and dearest. When one grieving widow had the temerity to ask to see her dead husband, calling his bluff, he refused to pay his labourers to undertake the work, reportedly telling her 'she had got enough teeth to dig a grave herself'.[63] With the stratagem failing, graves were then promiscuously opened – to prove the site had nothing to hide – drawing a crowd of distraught relatives and angry neighbours, together with the idle and curious. The unseemly melee that followed did nothing for Mr Bird's reputation; and the ground lost much of its custom. Finally, at the end of March 1845, after much magisterial and police investigation, the owners, managers and employees were prosecuted.

The conclusion to the scandal, however, was rather unsatisfactory. Mackinnon once again raised the burial question in the House of Commons, but the Home Secretary declared that the prosecution of Bird was evidence that existing legislation was quite sufficient, that there was no need for further regulation. The prosecution itself, after various indictments were raised and then dropped, turned into a legally complex arbitration procedure under the aegis of the Queen's Bench, which would not be resolved until September 1846. In the meantime, burials continued, albeit in nothing like previous numbers. The Clerkenwell parish clerk, who had decided the ground ought to be closed, presented evidence before the arbitrator that the soil was frequently waterlogged, and that neighbouring streets contained typhus, diarrhoea and fever 'in a more aggravated form in this than in any other part of the parish'.[64] The arbitrator concluded that the worst part of the ground should be closed to interment; with a minimum standard of five feet of earth on top of coffins – but that a small section could still remain open to burials. The whole ground would be temporarily closed by the General Board of Health during the cholera epidemic of 1849, when a servant living in neighbouring tenements succumbed to the disease. Once the cholera epidemic passed, Spa Fields actually survived as a burial ground until the autumn of 1853.

All in all, therefore, the Spa Fields case was something of a hollow victory for Walker and Mackinnon. The publicity for the cause was valuable. The ground became a byword for graveyard horrors ('In the immediate vicinity . . . the exhalations will produce sudden death; a little further off, typhus fever . . . and more remotely still, eruptions for instance, generated in Spa Fields, will perhaps disfigure faces in May Fair').[65] Yet it did not provoke the government into drafting new legislation; the much delayed and rather tepid justice meted out to Bird and his confederates was not sufficient to deter others; and, above all, the ground remained open for burials.

Why were the poor willing to have their loved ones buried in such sites, with all their well-known failings? The truth was that they had little alternative. They could not afford the fees, mourning displays and travel expenses associated with the likes of Kensal Green; nor even to spend time 'shopping around' the various parish and commercial grounds which were open to them – the cheapest, nearest site usually won out. The alternative – the indignity of a pauper's funeral, paid for by the parish – was considered far more humiliating. The parish typically buried paupers en masse, with the briefest collective funeral service ('Paupers were buried by contract, and the hearse came for coffins every Tuesday and Friday').[66] Mass graves would gradually be filled over a period of weeks, the coffins concealed after each burial by wooden boards covered with a smattering of earth. Miasma loomed large and mourners were generally few in number.

Spa Fields and its ilk prospered, therefore, because the poor would do anything to avoid this final indignity. Chadwick and others bemoaned this – as they saw it – false pride; for it encouraged the poorest families to retain dead bodies at home (which often amounted to one or two crowded rooms in a tenement) while they scraped together sufficient funds for a 'proper' burial.[67] The clergy condemned the moral consequences: 'The body, stretched out upon two chairs, is pulled about by the children, made to serve as a resting place for any article that is in the way . . . the hiding-place for the beer bottle or gin if any visitor arrives inopportunely.'[68] Chadwick was more concerned about the public health issue: the corpse produced dangerous domestic miasma. The poor, regardless, preferred to pay for burial, wherever possible, whether they kept the body for a week or even longer. Yet, whilst they put up with revolting burial grounds, it is worth noting they were not necessarily content. Mourners at a commercial ground in the East End began a near riot in September 1850, when told that the coffin of a deceased child would have to share a grave with another. The family attempted to fill the grave themselves, and the funeral ended up in a violent affray between 'mourners, spectators and grave-diggers . . . all struggling and fighting together'.[69]

Walker could at least take heart that he was swimming with the tide. The sanitary cause was prospering, and burial reform became part of more general agitation. Mackinnon would speak on several occasions at Health of Towns Association meetings, talking both about graveyards and other sanitary questions. Charles Cochrane's National Philanthropic Association also took up the cudgels, publishing an exposé of the fate of the Enon Chapel, Walker's favourite bad example. The chapel, having finally closed its miraculously capacious vaults, now housed a Temperance Society. The Society held regular dance nights: 'quadrilles, waltzes, country-dances, gallopades, reels, &c. are danced over the masses of mortality in the cellar beneath'. The impiety and miasmatic danger of 'dancing upon the dead' – complete with an illustration of the scene – made good copy for Cochrane's campaigning newspaper, the *Poor Man's Guardian*.[70]

Cochrane was, in fact, an active member of the Society for the Abolition of Burial in Towns; and he timed the publication of the article to coincide with Walker's own endeavours. For the doctor had decided to end the horrors of the ill-famed chapel with a blaze of publicity. A couple of months previously, in October 1847, Walker had negotiated with the building's trustees to take on the lease, promising to remove the accumulation of corpses and coffins. This might have been a quiet, decorous affair, a generous charitable intervention. Instead, Walker stage-managed a remarkable stunt. The public were invited to come and view the infamous 'Golgotha' beneath the dance hall, an object lesson in the perils of urban burial.

There was, despite Walker's protestations to the contrary, something of the fairground sideshow about this supposedly educational experience. A man was placed at the chapel gate, 'who walked about with skulls in his hand, apparently with the view of increasing the excitement of the persons assembled outside'.[71] Once inside, the public were treated to various revelations, including visiting the neighbouring out-house, where bodies had once been quietly removed from the vaults for the purpose of sale and dissection. Most bizarrely of all, the former proprietor, who had offered so many dubious cheap burials, was the highlight of the tour: ten years deceased, 'a stark and stiff and shrivelled corpse' resembling an Egyptian mummy, propped up for public inspection, recognisable by his 'screw foot'.[72] The press lapped up the Gothic spectacle, lovingly describing not only the exposed bones, skulls and coffins in various stages of decomposition, but the slumland location: 'windings of narrow and dirty lanes . . . an obscure and choked-up market . . . a gloomy and frowsy court was pointed out to us by squalid children playing round a stagnant puddle'.[73] The parish churchwardens, on the other hand, whilst conceding Dr Walker's eminent respectability, complained about the propriety of the undertaking, and the size of the mobs that gathered for a viewing. Walker countered that the only money taken – at the end of the visit – was at the discretion of the individual. Any cash would, he claimed, contribute towards a fund for removal of the bodies to a decent cemetery. In fact, after the exhibition had run for several months, Walker would pay £100 of his own money – there is no record of whether or not it came from the show's takings – to transfer the remains for burial in Norwood Cemetery.

This was an unusual venture for Walker – perhaps he took the idea from the showman-like Cochrane – and it is doubtful that it had any lasting impact on the case for burial reform. Nonetheless, a decade of campaigning would soon bear fruit.

By the late 1840s, it was generally accepted that urban graveyards were a danger to human health. There was a growing orthodoxy about miasma (as Chadwick famously put it, 'All smell is, if it be intense, immediate acute disease'); and Walker himself had done much to convince the public. *Punch* magazine would personify graveyard miasma, in doggerel, as 'The Vampyre (NO SUPERSTI-TION)', ('To work vengeance and woe is his mission of dread. Upon those mid the living who bury their dead').[74] Dr Walker must have expected the government to take some action on burial. Sanitary reform was the great popular cause: the Public Health Act had been passed; the General Board of Health created. Then cholera returned to London – an additional stimulus.

Most cheering for Walker was the fact that noxious burial sites were included in nuisance removal legislation cobbled together to meet the cholera emergency. The General Board of Health was given powers to inquire into the state of grounds; apply 'disinfecting substances' where necessary; and recommend burial elsewhere (whether in cemeteries like Kensal Green or other parishes' grounds) with the cost coming out of the poor rate. The General Board, upon an inspection, could also prohibit interment in parish grounds and recommend schemes for new cemeteries (although they were not given power to enforce these recommendations).

These new powers would be tested immediately. The results were somewhat mixed. Whilst many parishes complied readily with the Board's instructions, many did not. St Saviour's Southwark, for example, told to close the Cross Bones burial ground, simply refused. The vestry claimed its condition had been much exaggerated, and any closure would entail greater expense on the poor. The chairman of the vestry noted complacently, 'there was room in the Cross-bones ground which would last a hundred years'.[75] Critics suggested the truth was that the parish incumbent would mourn the loss of his burial fees.

Parish authorities were not the only problem. The Whitefield Chapel on Tottenham Court Road was equally defiant regarding its Dissenters' burial ground. Indeed, their legal representatives proved that the somewhat hastily drafted nuisance legislation did not contain sufficient powers to close a Dissenting ground (as opposed to a parish churchyard). The magistrate remarked dryly that it was 'one of the most lamentable instances of legislative bungling that they had ever met with'.[76]

When the General Board began the extensive use of disinfectants – which they hoped might prove a simple alternative to closure notices – they were met with further complaints. St Paul's, Covent Garden noted that no one living near the churchyard had caught cholera or diarrhoea in the last twelve months. Residents objected to the inspector's recommendation that their entire ground be strewed with three inches of quicklime – it would steam in wet weather, and fill the streets with dust in the dry. Chadwick's officious micro-management also militated against his actual purpose. The demand that parishes only bury reinforced lead coffins, 'at least six pounds to every superficial square foot', prompted local authorities to wonder if churchwardens were expected to possess a pair of giant scales.

The overall effect was chaotic and, after the epidemic had passed, there was a clear need to create a more coherent system. The General Board of Health was instructed to draft further legislation. The parishes had shown themselves to be obstructionist, hostile to improving their burial grounds. The General Board, on the other hand, appeared more sinned against than sinning. Thus, once again, the interment question passed into the hands of Edwin Chadwick. Parochial authorities in Lambeth, fearing imminent government intervention, slashed their burial fees – the '1st class ground' reduced from 27s. to 16s., the '2nd class' from 16s. to 6s. – a rather grim clearance sale.[77]

The resultant 1850 Metropolitan Interments Act was Chadwick's attempt to bring in his earlier plan for 'national cemeteries'. It was still a remarkably radical scheme, but the public's enthusiasm for the sanitary cause, and the threat of cholera, persuaded the Whig government of the day to hastily accept what the previous administration had so emphatically rejected. The stated intent of the legislation was to close church vaults, churchyards and burial grounds within the metropolis. One or more large public cemeteries would be established in their place, situated beyond the built-up city and managed by a central commission. The ground would be divided into consecrated and non-consecrated, with one chapel for the established Church, another for Dissenters – just like at Kensal Green. The price of funerals would be regulated on a sliding scale, suitable for the different social classes and the clergy compensated for the loss of burial fees, based on their income over the previous three years. Likewise, owners of closed burial grounds and cemeteries would be awarded appropriate compensation. This included the 'magnificent seven' of Kensal Green etc. – none of them anywhere near full – which Chadwick might easily have proposed to nationalise. Instead, he preferred to buy them out, close them and start from scratch.

Chadwick's most novel proposal – attempting to address the complaint that the poor would struggle to afford travel to distant cemeteries – was to suggest that the 'chief metropolitan cemetery should be in some eligible situation accessible by water-carriage'.[78] The suggestion that new cemeteries might be located alongside railway lines – conveying coffins and mourners by rail – had long been mooted as a solution to the expense of travel, although some considered the idea lacked dignity.[79] Chadwick, whilst not ruling out contracting with railway companies, believed that steam-boat funeral barges would resolve the issue in a stately fashion. He was perhaps inspired by Kensal Green's never-realised plans for a water-gate by the Regent's Canal.

Walker rejoiced – this was the scheme he had long supported as the solution to the burial problem.

It would prove completely unworkable.

Hostile voices were inevitable. There was, naturally, opposition from the parishes. Likewise, the undertaking profession railed against artificial restrictions on their fees. The fundamental problem, however, was not shrill critics, but the scheme's financing. Chadwick had sold his plan to the government on the basis that it would ultimately pay for itself, via fees received from burial, topped up, if necessary, from the rates. The requisite initial loan would come from the City – whose financiers would surely recognise the vast profits available to anyone who could claim a monopoly of metropolitan burials.

The City, however, was not convinced. Chadwick's all-or-nothing approach created a raft of problems. For a start, the government had not anticipated that Chadwick proposed to buy up all the joint-stock companies simultaneously. This would ensure the 'national cemeteries' instant monopoly, but also generate a vast burden of debt before any income had been received.[80] Moreover, according to Chadwick's plan, this mass purchase had to happen before *any* parish burial grounds were closed. Securing the monopoly would guarantee investors; investors would provide money to build a cemetery; then the parish grounds could be abolished. Ministers, reviewing the situation, began to worry that the scheme was both incredibly expensive and unlikely to effect any sanitary change in the near future. Financiers questioned whether the Board had sufficient government backing.

The putative national cemeteries also faced an unexpected new commercial rival. The London Necropolis Company proposed to open a cemetery on Woking Common, beyond the metropolitan monopoly granted in the 1850 Act, and would convey funeral parties by rail from Waterloo. The possibility of the Necropolis Railway, and other companies, opening up new sites beyond the newly defined metropolitan burial district – yet taking customers from within its bounds – completely undermined the monopolist *raison d'être* of Chadwick's scheme.

No amount of persuasion, or tinkering with the Board's legal powers, would persuade the City to loan money. In 1851, the Treasury, equally unwilling to foot the bill, ordered Chadwick to immediately cease his work on the scheme. This was not before the General Board had made a rash legal commitment to purchase Brompton Cemetery from the West London and Westminster Cemetery Company. The company was struggling financially and its backers were jubilant at the government buyout. Indeed, they took legal action that actually forced the Board to complete the purchase.[81]

All in all, after two years of Chadwick's work, the government had spent £70,000 on a west London cemetery that nobody wanted; and not a single urban graveyard had been closed. The management of metropolitan burial, much to Chadwick's chagrin, was removed from the General Board of Health. The government, at least, felt morally obliged to do something in order to make matters right. An Act to Amend the Laws concerning the Burial of the Dead in the Metropolis was passed in July 1852. The legislation of 1850 was repealed, and replaced with a far simpler arrangement. Parishes were empowered to take out twenty-year loans, backed by the Treasury, to build extramural cemeteries – or rent space in the joint-stock company grounds. Meanwhile, existing *individual* burial places – whether parish or private – could be closed by order of the Secretary of State.

George Walker did not approve. Like Chadwick, he firmly believed the parishes were not competent to manage burial, and maintained the need for national cemeteries. The Metropolitan Sanitary Association expressed deep disquiet that the Act contained 'no distinct assertion of principle' and left everything to the discretion of the government minister involved, on a site by site basis; nor did it seek to regulate cemetery fees.

In fact, Lord Palmerston, the Home Secretary, would prove extremely willing to close offending grounds. The government was keen to show that the new legislation was practical and effective. Within the first year of the Act's operation, Palmerston had issued notices to nearly two hundred sites. This produced harsh words from the Bishop of London, who noted that 36 out of 43 available grounds had been closed in the East End, creating intense pressure on the remaining sites, whilst parochial cemeteries were still under construction:

> . . . the corpses of children were frequently carried to the places of sepulture in cabs, and that it was no uncommon sight to see a string of such vehicles, filled with dead bodies, waiting at the gate of an unconsecrated burial-ground, until they could be admitted. He need not say that on such occasions the solemn services of the Church were performed in a slovenly, irregular and indecent manner . . .[82]

The owners of private grounds closed by the government were not inclined to go quietly; they were, after all, losing the entirety of their business. A certain Mr Jones, proprietor of the New Bunhill Fields in Upper Street, Islington, proclaimed (quite falsely) that Lord Palmerston's notice had instructed him not only to close but to clear the ground. He began to disinter bodies, perhaps hoping to build on the site. The children in a nearby school were treated to the sight of broken coffins, bones and 'slimy matter, alive with maggots'.[83] In 1856, Jones was found to be taking down tombstones and monuments, 'selling them for what they would fetch'.[84] The instructions from the Home Office were that the site should be covered with two feet of earth, sown with grass and intercut with asphalt paths, to create pleasant walks for the public. Instead, by 1858, the walls had been demolished, brickwork removed, and the ground given over to a local scavenger, to use as a rubbish dump. The local Sanitary Inspector noted, 'It was about sixty yards square, and there were from 6,000 to 10,000 loads of rubbish on it.'[85] Abandoned burial grounds, like any empty plot in the metropolis, were liable to become dumps – whether for household rubbish or, in the worst districts, 'ankle deep . . . with excrement, thrown out from the houses'[86] – and other sites would meet the same fate.

Fortunately, whilst the owners of speculations lived down to their rather grubby reputation, London's vestries defied Walker's low expectations.

St Pancras, a large and prosperous parish, bought Horse Shoe Farm in Finchley in 1853 – two miles from its northern boundary – and opened it as the first large-scale parish cemetery in June 1854. The cemetery itself was very much in the 'garden' style, 'visited by large numbers of persons, as it is laid out like a splendid park, and its walks afford the advantages of a perfect promenade'.[87] Fees in new parish cemeteries varied from district to district, but a common grave at the City of London Cemetery at Little Ilford, for example, cost only 8s. 6d. when the cemetery opened (albeit with '1st class' graves going for 17s. 6d.). This was no trifling expense – and there were travel costs – but the price was comparable with what might have been paid at small commercial grounds in the East End.[88] Those vestries unwilling to or incapable of making their own separate arrangements to build a new cemetery could either amalgamate into unions, buy space in the joint-stock-company cemeteries or cut deals with their neighbours. St Mary Islington, for example, home to Jones's rubbish dump, bought some of the St Pancras cemetery for its own use.

Within the space of a few years, large parochial cemeteries, nestling on the edge of the city, were an accepted part of the London landscape. They were spacious, well ventilated, and proper regulations ensured that graves were deep and well maintained: any threat from miasma was neutralised. George Alfred Walker surveyed the scene, then quietly withdrew from the public eye. He would eventually retire to North Wales, where he died in 1884. An anonymous 1890s' memoirist, recalling Walker and his 'doctor's shop' on the corner of Drury Lane and Blackmore Street, would describe him as 'a great favourite in the neighbourhood . . . on account of his kindness to the poor'.[89]

The 1852 legislation, limited in scope, did not solve every problem. It dealt with the supposed public health impact of crowded grounds, and created much needed space – nothing more. Funerals, even reasonably priced, remained a grievous expense for the likes of the casual dock labourer or the needlewoman making her living by piecework. Bodies, therefore, were still retained in crowded tenements while the family struggled to obtain funds to bury them. Likewise, pauper funerals – the grim alternative to finding that money – continued to incentivise retention of the body.

Parishes buried their paupers by contract with undertakers, who would typically make two collections per week of bodies. Corpses continued to be taken en masse to the cemetery, with the minimum of ostentation. Some parishes hired 'funeral omnibuses' – 'half hearse, half omnibus' – containing both mourner and mourned.[90] This was a practical solution to the transport difficulty associated with distant cemeteries, courtesy of the Shillibeer bus company; but hardly elegant or seemly. Graves were still large pits, kept open until they contained sufficient numbers, with coffins roughly arranged by a gravedigger, 'as though he were adjusting a stowage of packing cases in a cellar'.[91] Paupers' graves were, naturally, at the far end of the garden cemetery, by the wall – i.e. the most neglected part of the ground. Some parishes, attempting to address the sanitary issue of retaining decomposing bodies in the home, began to introduce mortuaries. This was also partly for the benefit of coroners and doctors performing post-mortem examination. The poor, however, were nervous about releasing relatives to the safe keeping of the local authority, largely because the 1832 Anatomy Act allowed unclaimed paupers to be sent to the anatomy schools. The parish of St Anne, Soho, first to open a dedicated mortuary in 1856, circulated reassuring handbills stating that 'coffined dead will be strictly guarded and watched day and night by a resident attendant'.[92]

A peculiar social problem also arose as a result of the 1852 Act: it became difficult for the poor to bury stillborn infants. The ancient custom was to tip the local gravedigger a shilling or two. The dead child would then be secreted in an open grave or coffin, while the gravedigger went about his work. This saved burial fees, and appears to have been a very common practice. Once burial began to take place at some distance, this informal arrangement became impossible. In 1855, one south London coroner noted that he was dealing with increasing numbers of dead babies exposed in the street. The following year, jurors at another coroner's inquest on a dead child recommended sympathetically that 'the old system of interring still-born children in the burial grounds of parish of Lambeth ought to be continued'.[93] In due course, undertakers would quietly adopt the role for themselves – a fact which occasionally came to light, when there were suspicions of foul play or when particular individuals abused parents' trust. There were instances of stillborn children being placed in coffins, both with and without permission from the family of the deceased. ('The friends of Mrs. Aycock did not know that I had put a second body into her coffin.')[94] Some undertakers took gruesome liberties. In 1883, one Mr Camden, an undertaker of Bermondsey, was found to have a cache of dead babies in his shop, all of whom he had previously promised to secretly bury in various parochial cemeteries for the sum of five shillings. An angry mob gathered, and the premises required police protection. There was, however, no crime committed under English law and Camden himself escaped punishment, receiving only the thunderous disapprobation of the magistrate.

The poor, in other words, continued to struggle.

There can be no argument, however, that George Carden's vision triumphed. By the 1860s, garden cemeteries surrounded the metropolis on all sides, both commercial and parochial. Many of the old, disused private burial grounds would also eventually become garden cemeteries, of a sort. During the 1880s and 1890s, local authorities, the LCC and the Metropolitan Public Gardens, Boulevard and Playground Association[95] began to clean up and reopen old burial sites. Their tombstones cleared to one side, they were remade as public parks, small breathing-spaces for Londoners. Spa Fields, for example, was landscaped and reopened as a park and playground for the children of the poor in 1885 (although the 'gymnastic appliances' fell victim to an arson attack by local youths in 1888).[96] The public park survives to this day, directly opposite the London Metropolitan Archives.

In some cases, decay would follow. The pioneering 'magnificent seven' cemeteries filled up, failed to pay dividends to shareholders, and fell into disrepair during the twentieth century, suffering from theft, vandalism and general indifference. Some of their grand chapels were demolished; others now stand forlorn and ruined amidst the tombs, ghostly hollow shells. The grounds themselves are much changed. The managed decay of the likes of Highgate Cemetery bears little relation to the pristine plans of its progenitors. The forest that has swallowed Abney Park mocks the original design for an arboretum, where every plant was carefully labelled, to elevate the public taste. Indeed, the notion of the cemetery as 'a great theatre for public taste' – a phrase used by John Bowring, MP, in the Mackinnon inquiry – has fallen completely out of fashion. Victorian statuary crumbles away. Plain tombstones and grass lawns are now the unchallenged norm; minimalism is the key. The greatest change in the post-Victoria era, of course, has been not aesthetic, but the gradual acceptance of cremation (first proposed by a few radical thinkers in the late nineteenth century).

Yet, despite the ravages of time, changing customs, vicissitudes of fashion, the Victorian garden cemetery still survives in its various forms, one of the great legacies of the nineteenth century.

6

THE GREAT UNWASHED

NOWHERE WAS DIRT more visible in the nineteenth-century metropolis than on the hands, face and clothing of the poor. Soot in the air; mud strewn on the road; grease, dust and grime in the factory, workshop and warehouse – all of this clung stubbornly to the person. With good reason, 'the great unwashed' would become a droll description of the lower orders from the 1830s onwards.[1]

Not every working-class family lived in abject poverty; but most struggled to wash themselves and their clothes. First and foremost, finding water was a challenge. Many tenements lacked even a single tap. Supplies, therefore, were limited to parish pumps; purchased by the bucket from shop owners or publicans; or communal stand-pipes, which were turned on for only a few hours each week. Penny-pinching landlords paid a small sum to the water companies for the latter basic level of provision. Women were obliged to queue to fill buckets with rather murky liquid – 'quarrelling for their turn, the strongest pushing forward'[2] – which they would carry back home to serve as their pathetic ration for washing, cooking and laundry combined. Sometimes 'articles too disgusting to be named' had to be used on clothing in lieu of expensive soap – this meant stale, concentrated urine, valued for its ammonia.[3] John Liddle, medical officer of the Whitechapel Union, would report the olfactory consequences of attempting to do laundry in slum conditions:

When they are washing, the smell of the dirt mixed with the soap is the
most offensive of all the smells I have to encounter. They merely pass dirty
linen through very dirty water. The smell of the linen itself, when so washed,
is very offensive, and must have an injurious effect on the health of the
occupants. The filth of their dwellings is excessive, so is their personal filth.
When they attend my surgery, I am always obliged to have the door open.[4]

There were grades of deprivation. The inhabitants of Red Lion Street,
Wapping, thought themselves lucky to be able to wash their clothes in the
kennel (central gutter of the street) because the hot water waste from a nearby
factory's steam engine flowed freely along the road.[5] Some tenement-dwellers
had access to a separate 'washhouse or sort of kitchen appropriated to the
house for the use of washing at times' – for a small additional payment to the
landlord.[6] Some working-class women washed at home, but could afford to
'put out to mangle' (i.e. drying) for a few pence. Many, however, were obliged
to wash and dry clothing in the same space in which they ate and slept. For
the worst-off, this was a small, single room. Henry Mayhew, writing in 1849,
describes meeting a family of eight, living in a space seven feet square with the
wife busy at the washtub. The items at her disposal: 'a saucepan . . . two flat
irons . . . a broken ginger-beer bottle filled with soda', and string draped across
the ceiling to serve as a washing line.[7] Whilst women did hang lines outside,
across alleys, or on the roof, such locations exposed washing to 'chimney
blacks' (soot) as well as 'pigeons, sparrows, playful cats – all war with clean
drying on the roof, even if she has command of it'.[8] In the poorest districts, it
was not uncommon for husbands to stay in bed on a Saturday afternoon while
wives washed their one suit of clothes.[9]

Wealthier folk, naturally, did not suffer the same sorts of privations and
indignities. They possessed servants who did the household laundry, supplied
with running water on tap, sufficient fuel to heat it up and plentiful
soap, starch and 'blue' (brightener). Many householders also hired a
washerwoman, who would come and provide additional skilled labour on
washdays. Some purchased labour-saving appliances – e.g. large 'coppers' for
boiling or hand-turned washing machines – devices which became more
common as the century progressed. These were advertised with ringing
endorsements from satisfied customers: 'My servants wash more clothes and

much better in one day with your Machine than they used to do in three days without it.'[10]

Alternatively, there was the luxurious possibility of 'sending out' to a washerwoman or, later in the century, larger more mechanised laundries. This was more expensive and, according to health experts, dangerously unhygienic. Individual washerwomen not only did laundry in their own home but dried it in backyards, 'frequented by the lowest class of persons', close to their dustbin and water closet.[11] Still, sporadic reports of such conditions communicating diseases like smallpox did little to stifle the trade. There was no escaping the fact that, for the middle-class housewife, it was 'very much pleasanter to send it out'.[12] There were many advantages: servants did not have to spend an entire day or more in the scullery, subjecting laundry to a vigorous series of washes, boilings and rinses; the master of the house did not have to forgo his usual comforts ('dinner late, and ill-dressed, owing, you are told, to the washing');[13] in winter months, the house was not turned into a 'vapour bath' filled with drying clothes.

Respectable households, unlike the poor, also possessed washstands for personal ablution. These were, typically, wooden stands, kept in the bedroom, which contained basin, water jug, soap and 'slop basin' for dirty water. Daily washing routines did not necessarily involve anything more than applying soap and water to one's hands and face – but servants made sure fresh water was always available, and dirty water regularly cleared. For those desirous of more thorough cleansing, sponges could be applied to the body. *Cassell's Household Guide* of the 1870s – a bible for the aspiring middle-class housewife – advised sponging oneself daily, 'soap to the arm-pits, the groin and parts about, and the feet', but only 'if persons can afford the time and have the inclination'. An alternative/additional skin-cleansing process involved rubbing one's skin with a rough cloth, or 'flesh brush' or 'flesh glove' (a mitten, covered with coarse hair, 'used from time immemorial in Hindostan, Persia and throughout the East').[14] For those actually inclined to bathe the full body – very much a minority pursuit in the nineteenth century, even amongst the wealthiest in society – once a week was considered more than ample. This would typically take place in a portable metal bath, placed before the fire in the bedroom or dressing room. Only gradually were dedicated bathrooms incorporated into houses during the second half of the century.[15]

Indeed, bathing the entire body was considered more of a stimulant than a hygienic necessity. Medical men agreed that judicious bathing could help rebalance an ailing constitution – although they argued about whether hot, tepid or cold baths were suited to particular cases – with seawater believed to have particularly sterling qualities. Bathing was, in short, a tonic: 'Wash the body at least once a week,' a women's magazine advised its readers in 1842, 'the vigor and hilarity of feeling you will experience will amply repay you for the labour'.[16] The cold shower, likewise, had some famous adherents, largely on account of its 'bracing' quality. Thomas Carlyle, the great man of letters, installed 'the noblest shower bath' in his back kitchen ('only a bucket and cylinder on pullies against the ceiling; no case around it, but as good as the King's') and directed his wife Jane to take a daily 'submission under the shower-cataract'.[17] Dickens, a firm believer in shocks to the system, had his brother-in-law, the sanitary engineer Henry Austin, design a shower-bath for his new home in Tavistock Place in 1851 ('But what I want is a Cold Shower of the best quality, always charged to an unlimited extent, so that I have but to pull the string . . .').[18] But Dickens and Carlyle were not typical. As *Cassells* would note regretfully, 'the majority of people are quite unacquainted with such a thing, from childhood to old age as the morning dip or the cold douche'.

The wealthy at least had a choice. The poor could hardly do more than wash their hands and face; and many did less ('There are those who pass through life and never wash any part of the body but their hands and face, and these but seldom').[19] Some, certainly, found daily washing an unaccustomed nuisance, when it was imposed upon them. An out-of-work spinner on a 'temperance tour' in Lancashire remarked, 'what punished me most was, I was obliged to wash every morning.'[20] Bathing was even more alien. An 1848 report on the readiness of metropolitan workhouses to treat cholera cases found many examples of unwillingness to bathe. Several workhouses reported that regulations that required would-be inmates to take a bath (even with ample supplies of warm water) were 'one of the most effectual modes of diminishing the number of applicants'.[21] Bodily dirt could even be a point of pride. In the 1860s, Thomas Wright, self-styled spokesman for the working man, would claim that the working classes had come to embrace the term 'the great unwashed'. Dirty hands differentiated them from 'counter skippers' (shop workers) and the like, whose work did not involve honest physical labour.[22]

Yet, whilst some might take pride in dirt – serving as proof of their hard graft – this is not to say that they abhorred cleanliness. The 1837 case of Benjamin Broadway, an apprentice to a spectacle-maker in Clerkenwell, provides an interesting example of contemporary attitudes. Seventeen years old, Broadway came from the workhouse, and starved to death in squalid living conditions after ten years in his master's employ. The spectacle-maker, pleading at the Old Bailey, contended that Broadway was 'naturally dirty'; that pauperdom had habituated him to filth. As proof, he brought forward a witness – a spring-maker in a clockmaker's business, who had worked with the boy for a time. The spring-maker confirmed that he had remonstrated with the boy and told him to wash, 'but he used to laugh at me – I told him of it twice – our business is not very clean'. He continued: 'when I speak of his being dirty, I mean his face and hands . . . I have known him go three days without washing his hands and face.'[23] There was, in other words, an expectation in the workshop in question, even though the work was 'dirty', that one should start the day with a clean face and hands. The witness thought a jury would consider this reasonable. Thus, *pace* Thomas Wright, even 'the great unwashed' – or, at the very least, the skilled artisan or 'mechanic' class – had some standards.

Indeed, cleanliness was an established element of the respectability to which the artisan worker aspired. Middle-class moralists and medical experts had long expounded the moral and physical benefits of personal hygiene. Dr William Buchan's *Domestic Medicine*, for example, a best-selling mid-eighteenth-century health manual, asserted that dirt on clothes or the skin hampered perspiration and thus produced illness, sending toxic matter inwards ('when that matter which ought to be carried off by perspiration is either retained in the body or reabsorbed from dirty clothes, it must occasion diseases').[24] In the church and chapel, preachers repeated the old saw, popularised by Wesley, that 'Cleanliness is next to Godliness'. This was not only spiritual metaphor – the echo of spiritual purity in physical cleanliness – but practical moral instruction. Mankind was made in the image of God; to be dirty was to befoul that image and diminish one's faith in the eyes of others – believers had to keep clean and not 'stink above the ground' (the smell of decay belonged to the dead). For women, the hard work of removing dirt was also a moral duty to one's family. The failure to keep a clean home drove a husband to the comforts of the public house, which led to intemperance and vice. The failure to clean clothes meant that families, lacking their 'Sunday best' could not attend church or chapel. To quote one horribly pious moralist, 'a dirty wife or a dirty mother is one of the most disgusting of objects'.[25]

True, such moralising would increase in the wake of the sanitary movement and the rise of evangelical Christianity, but it was not uniquely Victorian. In other words, the Victorians did not abruptly awaken the masses to their own filth. Even at the beginning of the nineteenth century, the more aspirational members of the working class – those who listened to the preaching of their betters – were far from ignorant of the manifold merits of personal cleanliness. The problem was that they could do little about it – apart from occasionally splash their hands and face under the parish pump.

There were various commercial baths in London, but they were not intended for the lower orders. At the top end of the scale were the likes of the Royal York Baths, near Regent's Park, which, unusually for the metropolis, offered baths for both sexes. Refurbished in 1829, this urban spa presented the nobility and gentry of the West End with a range of luxurious, health-giving treatments. Baths included not only hot water but 'real sea water' (7s. 6d.); 'medicated sulphurous' (7s.); 'private cold bath' or 'a cold shower bath' (1s. 6d.); and the chance to imbibe Genuine Harrogate Water (i.e. mineral water) at 1s. 6d. per bottle. Cheaper venues existed outside the West End, but they still priced themselves beyond the pocket of the average working man. Peerless Pool, an open-air swimming pool near Old Street, particularly spacious (50 yards by 30), was known as a 'democratic' bathing venue. First-class bathing still cost a shilling; second-class, sixpence. The prosperous City clerk would be expected to buy a first-class ticket; the artisan, second-class. There was no third-class option – the labourer and factory worker were effectively excluded. The poor, therefore, tended to improvise. In the summer months, working-class men and boys plunged into the capital's canals and lakes, whether to keep clean, cool or simply enjoy themselves. These were not necessarily terribly wholesome stretches of water. Some were desperate enough to resort to brickmakers' flooded clay pits.[26]

One oft-repeated objection to these makeshift proletarian public baths was their indecency, since male bathing was traditionally done in the nude. This was the case even at the seaside resorts frequented by the middle classes[27] – and, in any case, the working man could hardly afford a bathing costume; and had no wish to go to work or return home with his clothes all sopping wet.

The likes of Hyde Park, therefore, had to be avoided by respectable women at dawn and dusk, when the Serpentine became 'obscene with bathers'.[28] Yet, although some complained about this 'obscenity', the authorities tolerated the use of the parks for this purpose, merely limiting bathing to set hours (canal bathing was more likely to result in prosecution).[29] The view was taken that the poor needed *somewhere* to bathe – or, at least, working men did (no one believed it would be decent for women to disport themselves in such a brazen fashion). To this end, when Victoria Park opened in the East End in 1845, designed for the working man, provision was made for bathing. The lakes – often now described as 'ornamental water' – were actually given over to bathers from 4 a.m. to 8 a.m. daily and provided with a conveniently sloping beach-like shore. The park even had its own 'swimming master', whose day-job was selling ginger beer and sugarplums to the owners of miniature yachts, who occupied the lakes during daylight hours.[30]

It was not only the park authorities that were willing to overlook 'indecency' in favour of cleanliness. Whenever complaints about public bathing reached the press, they were generally drowned out by vociferous champions of the poor. Some supporters were gentlemen-bathers who wanted to promote the cause of swimming as health-giving, hygienic exercise, and resented the intrusion of prudes and authority ('Persons of cleanly habits and of real delicacy of feeling seldom complain that others try to be clean and comfortable').[31] Many, however, simply wished to express sympathy with the great unwashed, asking of those who inveighed against nudity, 'What are the poor people to do?'[32]

In the 1840s, sanitary reformers began to contemplate this question and ask whether anything could be done for those mired in filth.

At the start of the decade, it looked as if a model scheme might be found in an existing commercial venture in Lambeth. The 'National Baths' in Westminster Bridge Road, Lambeth, were laid out with the working man in mind. Opened in 1836, the Lambeth site contained three swimming pools – but the bulk of business was done in the 'Operatives bath'. This was a lavish 500,000-gallon affair, with a threepence admission – pricing aimed squarely at local factory workers. The price was immediately recognised as a dramatic shift in making bathing more accessible to the humbler classes, whether for pleasure, stimulating the body or washing off dirt (most contemporaries believed that all forms of bathing, including swimming, encompassed all three of these ends). As one admiring letter-writer, dubbing himself *Natator*, put it: 'I will not allow any working man to say he cannot afford threepence. Let him take a glass of gin a-day less, and he may bathe once a week.'[33] The same anonymous writer urged the government to take heed, and build public baths across the nation, noting, 'P.S. Similar baths might be constructed for females as well as males.'

The proprietor of the National Baths, a certain Mr Sowten, was interviewed by Robert Slaney's Health of Towns Commission in 1840, precisely because of his pricing policy. Sowten confirmed that there were three classes of bathing in Lambeth – costing 1s. 6d. for the 'subscription bath' kept at 84°F; 1s. for the 'middling classes' at 80°F; and 3d. for 'the humbler classes' at 70°F. Sowten claimed that '180,000 mechanics' visited the 3d. baths each season (the baths were closed during the winter months, when there was considerably less demand), many of whom learned to swim in the capacious pool. This was a roaring trade but Sowten declared himself frustrated that 'instead of being used as matters of health, they have merely been used as matters of pleasure in a very great degree'. He also described his customer as 'not at all the description of persons that I reckoned upon when I fitted up the place' and wondered whether raising his prices might reduce 'vagabondism and noise'.[34] The moral benefits of bathing for the poor were, therefore, somewhat disappointingly unproven – but, at least, it appeared that workmen's baths could make a profit. This profitability alone suggested the Lambeth scheme as a paradigm for future projects. Robert Slaney's report, however, would not prove influential; and would ultimately be overshadowed by Edwin Chadwick's, with its focus on sewerage.

Instead, the stimulus for providing bathing and laundry facilities for the London poor would come from the north-west of England.

The Corporation of Liverpool opened combined public baths and washhouses in Upper Frederick Street in May 1842, with twenty-six washtubs, which could be hired for a penny, and ten individual bathtubs – cold baths for a penny, and warm baths for tuppence. The inspiration was purportedly Kitty Wilkinson, a poor local woman who had turned her basement into a communal laundry during the cholera year of 1832, letting her neighbours have boiling water from her copper for a penny. She was hailed as a folk heroine by reformers on the council, a status which may not have been entirely deserved.[35] Regardless, although small in scale, within a couple of years a second Liverpool baths and washhouse was under construction. The Bishop of London happened to see Upper Frederick Street during a visit to the city in 1844 and was suitably impressed. He returned home, determined to agitate for something similar in the metropolis.

The Bishop's decision would mark the birth of the public baths and washhouses movement in the capital.

Bishop Blomfield was an influential figure – he had persuaded the government to commission Chadwick's sanitary report – but the omens were not particularly good. There had already been one failed philanthropic attempt to set up a 'public laundry' in the vicinity of the Clare Market slums in 1840 – 'with washing-troughs, steaming-box, drying-closet and other conveniences'.[36] Similarly, an 1833 Select Committee on Public Walks, chaired by Robert Slaney, had recommended, amongst other things, establishing 'Public bathing places' along existing rivers and canals, to legitimise pre-existing working-class bathing – to no avail. An 1835 private member's bill, inspired by Slaney's committee, had also proposed creating public baths, discreetly out of view, 'adapted to teach the art of Swimming, as well as to afford the means of ablution' – but did not pass its second reading.[37]

Regardless, the Bishop gathered together like-minded individuals, called a public meeting at the Mansion House, and stated his case. Citing the revelations of 'poverty, squalid wretchedness, filthiness, and moral as well as physical degradation' in Chadwick's 1842 report, he praised the Liverpool model as capable of elevating the worst-off in society. Others offered similar contributions, testifying to the grim sufferings patiently endured by the poor and denying that they were indifferent to cleanliness. It was noted that the ancient Romans did not neglect to provide baths for their citizens; could Britannia do any less?

This was stirring stuff and the meeting proved a rip-roaring success. An action committee was formed. Cheques for ten and twenty guineas were hastily written by the enthused; plans for three baths/washhouses in north London, and one in the south, were discussed (only one would eventually be built). *The Times*, the following day, added the full weight of an editorial stating that the poor could not be blamed for their dirt, that they were victims of their circumstances, offering a cheeky counter-factual proposition to illustrate the point:

Take, for instance, the House of Lords, probably the cleanest assemblage of men which could be found; condemn them to cold water and no soap, and to wash all their own clothes with their own hands in their own drawing-rooms for a single twelvemonth, and how would they look at its termination? Isabella-colour would, we suspect, become fashionable for shirt-fronts, and white would yield to drab of divers shades.[38]

There followed a flood of support, including a £200 cheque from Queen Victoria.

There were a few dissenting voices. A certain Alderman Lawrence gave a speech before the City of London's Common Council objecting to a donation of money towards the project. Respectable working-class women would be obliged, at *public* washhouses, to associate with 'the most abandoned of the sex', who would introduce them to the gin shop and general debauchery. The City still voted £200 in aid. The Secretary of the Bishop's newly formed committee, John Bullar, nonetheless wrote to *The Times* to assure potential subscribers that there would be a 'barrier between each pair of tubs, to insure to every washer the greatest practical amount of privacy'[39] – this had to be a respectable enterprise. Another letter-writer, signing herself 'A WOMAN', suggested that the poorest possessed only a single ragged garment, and that they baulk at having to wash their laundry half-naked. The *John Bull* newspaper – very much of the Lawrence persuasion – believed the 'great unwashed' would ignore the new institutions entirely, preferring to spend money on beer. Likewise, would women leave their children and home merely to wash clothes? A 'Journeyman Engineer' wrote to *The Times* to state that – himself excluded – the average working man had no great wish to keep clean.

Yet, for every hostile comment, there were two in favour of public baths. The 'Journeyman Engineer' received several rebuttals in the letters pages: pointing out that the average working man did not possess the thirty-shilling weekly salary of an artisan and questioning the veracity of his claims. Another correspondent, with only one room for himself, wife and five children, stated that doing laundry at home cost him nearly a shilling – a public washtub at a penny an hour, supplied with piped hot water, would be a great saving.[40] The general tenor of press reporting was highly supportive. The only question was what the new 'Committee for Promoting the Establishment of Baths and Washhouses' would do with its funds.

The first small-scale experiment would take place in Glasshouse Yard, Whitechapel. 'The Association for Promoting Cleanliness Among the Poor', an 'offset' of the original Mansion House Committee, resolved to set up a rough-and-ready establishment for immediate use in the East End.[41] The Association chose a location convenient not only for the poor of Whitechapel but for the casual labourers at the nearby docks.

The site, whose facilities were free, opened in the summer of 1845. The venue was a building owned by a night refuge, the Asylum for the Houseless Poor, whose 'cribs' remained, separated from the washhouse by makeshift wooden walls. Women were given free access to a wash-trough, hot water, an ounce of soap and a piece of soda for doing their laundry, as well as ironing boards, and a 'drying room' warmed by hot air. Next door, visitors could enjoy the 'Eastern luxury of a warm bath' – i.e. the individual 'slipper bath' (so called because of its shoe-like shape, with a raised back for sitting up, and the front section covered, preventing the spillage of water). Initially there were just two baths, and 'six persons were obliged to use the same water successively',[42] until funds permitted half a dozen baths to be installed and the water replenished with each visitor.

The Association made every effort to ensure the poor attended. They made available striped gowns for women to wear, so that they might wash and dry the clothing in which they arrived – although this outfit must have smacked rather of the House of Correction. The attendance figures were promising: within the first six months, 13,538 had bathed; and 15,543 had come to wash their clothing. The demographic was very much the poorest in society – it was found that just over half the visitors were Irish immigrants – and some travelled several miles just to use the facility. An experimental section was also introduced where customers had to pay a small sum for the same facilities. It was thought this might attract a more select clientele, since the slightly better off working man and his wife would resent receiving outright charity. This proved not to be the case: few paid money for what otherwise might be obtained for free. A certain 'E.M.' a letter-writer in *The Times* – presenting a lengthy piece of investigative reporting – declared that Alderman Lawrence's qualms were groundless. The 'strictest order and decorum prevailed' and the customers had embraced washing and bathing with enthusiasm: 'love of filth does not exist, as many suppose, in the minds of the poor, but they are dirty from the lack of means of fuel, of tubs, of soap, water and conveniences'.[43]

As Glasshouse Yard opened for business, two further experiments were on the drawing board, designed to establish larger, purpose-built baths and washhouses. These would both charge a small fee, as in Liverpool; but still be cheaper than the existing commercial baths. The first, in George Street, near Euston Square, was the work of a charitable committee established by house-holders in St Pancras with the support of local landowners, such as the Duke of Bedford. It included not only slipper baths and a washhouse, but communal plunge baths (60 by 20 feet) and sauna-like 'vapour baths'. It threw open its doors in August 1846.

The second experimental building, located in Goulston Square, Whitechapel, belonged to the original Mansion House Committee but was much delayed by uncertainties about cost and design. Finally opening in July 1847, it was intended as a 'model' institution, which might be copied by others – i.e. parish vestries. The Committee had no desire to go into business running baths and laundries; rather, it wanted to persuade local authorities to follow the example of Liverpool. Indeed, while the building was still under construction, the Bishop and his supporters – most active was Sir Henry Duckinfield, vicar of St Martin-in-the-Fields – proposed legislation which would allow individual vestries to establish their own baths and washhouses without having to obtain costly individual local acts. In June 1846 they presented a series of petitions before the House of Lords, including one signed by City merchants and bankers, another by the managers of the London Dock Company and another by the massed parochial clergy of the metropolis – all in favour of legislation to promote public baths. The following month, with remarkable alacrity, a Baths and Washhouses Act was passed.

The Act allowed parishes to take out government-backed long-term loans for building new premises. Facilities for men and women, separated into first and second class, were obligatory, charging 1d. for a cold bath and 2d. for warm, whilst 1d. an hour bought time in the washhouse. The Rev. Duckinfield's parish was the first to adopt the Act, borrowing £11,000 for the purpose, and the legis-lation itself became known as 'Duckinfield's Act'. The Act would be amended in 1847, so that parishes could charge slightly larger sums for first-class bathing (up to 6d. for warm; 3d. for cold), which might attract 'many little tradesmen to whom cleanliness was a great object, but who did not like to go into the same bath that had been used by coalheavers or porters, or their own menial servants'.[44] It was also hoped this might provide useful additional income.

The Baths and Washhouses Act was an impressively easy win for the reformers. Just two years had passed between proposing the baths and washhouses idea and enshrining it in legislation. In retrospect, compared with the long-running campaigns to improve sewerage and burial grounds, this seems rather remarkable and in need of an explanation.

One factor was that the legislation was merely permissive – and it required two thirds of a vestry to agree on the measure in any given parish. Equally, the cause itself – personal cleanliness – was incredibly straightforward and popular, certainly when compared to the technicalities and complexities of Chadwick's sewer schemes. There were also no anxieties about vested interests. Laundresses and proprietors of existing public baths had – it hardly needs stating – no great influence in parliament. Naturally, this did not prevent objections from interested parties. Mr Sowten of the Lambeth baths, and the proprietors of Peerless Pool, presented their own petitions against the legislation but they were not heeded.[45] More seriously, Lord Brougham raised doubts over loans being secured against the poor rate – i.e. if baths and washhouses were not profitable, the balance would come from the rates. He was assured by the Bishop of London that baths would most likely run at a healthy profit of 7–10 per cent.[46] This confidence, probably based upon early reports from Liverpool, would prove to be wildly optimistic.

In fact, despite many claims to the contrary, it was soon doubtful whether baths and washhouses could ever be made entirely self-supporting. The Glasshouse Yard site was free and patently unsustainable without large ongoing donations; it closed in 1848 or 1849. The model institution built in Goulston Square was overly ambitious and expensive, and suffered due to its rather obscure location. A fund-raising dinner, held at the height of sanitary fervour in 1848, co-opted Edwin Chadwick to offer his seal of approval to the Committee and their model baths. He gave the requisite toast – 'Health and prosperity to the bankers and traders of the city of London' – before quickly and clumsily returning to his preferred topic of sewerage. The event still raised the astonishing sum of £7,500. Even with such backing, it proved nigh impossible to service the debts attached to the Goulston Square building (amounting to £27,800). The Committee would end up attempting to sell the baths to the City of London as a going concern in the mid-1850s – only to be rebuffed. The Goulston Square baths would struggle on, relying heavily on donations, closing in 1871. The Whitechapel Vestry would revive it in 1878 – but with no great hope for profit.

The George Street baths near Euston Square were little better, as a perusal of the early accounts from 1846/47 reveals. The receipts from baths, wash-houses and the plunge baths amounted to almost £3,000, but salaries, wages, fuel and other incidental expenses cost £1,700; advertising alone cost almost £800. Water was initially provided free by the local water company, then heavily subsidised. This was the gift of the New River Company, which had likewise provided the site at a nominal rent – but such largesse hardly provided a model for other sites. Repairs and maintenance costs were also very high. The hope that cash from artisan bathers (paying a shilling for a warm bath) would amply subsidise the working-class baths proved a chimera.

Several parishes built their own baths before these financial realities hit home. St Martin-in-the-Fields baths opened first, in 1849, behind the National Gallery, followed by Marylebone in the same year; sites in Westminster, Poplar and Greenwich in 1851, until ten parish baths and washhouses were in opera-tion by the end of 1855. Then the ball stopped rolling – no more public baths were constructed until King Street, St Pancras, in 1868, and only three further examples in the 1870s.

This is not to say that enthusiasm for baths and bathing waned – merely that vestries grew wary of committing themselves. Sanitary claims as to the merits of the new baths continued to be repeated in numerous publications and pamphlets. Even if the ratepayer had to subsidise baths, it could be justi-fied along Chadwickian lines: 'Clothes impregnated with the debris of the human body must attract disease, and when once this comes, the rates are burdened beyond conception.'[47] The Mansion House Committee continued to publicise the cause, although its model baths had singularly failed to live up to expectations, romantically extolling the benefits to the poor from 'luxuries that have hitherto been enjoyed only by the rich – and which are associated in the popular mind with affluence and expense'.[48]

The experience of using public baths was not actually incredibly luxurious, especially in the early years. The mere presence of hot and cold running water was the real luxury. In the slipper baths, a lot depended on the assidu-ousness of individual bath attendants. *Pick Me Up* magazine – a lower-class version of *Punch* – would chronicle the perils of a '1st class' public bath in 1890: 'the soapsuds of the previous gentleman are waltzing on the top of the water . . . I wonder how many have been in that bath before me, and how many have used the brush with the long handle . . . the last chap's left his soap!'

The differences between first- and second-class facilities were also highly cosmetic. Individual first- *and* second-class slipper baths were made of the same material (typically zinc or copper, though occasionally cement or tiled; later in the century, porcelain); likewise the walls or divisions between them (usually faced with slate or tiled). It was only the accoutrements that varied. The first-class bath cubicle might include carpet or a mirror or extra towel; the second might not. Smaller establishments enforced a class distinction by making Monday, Wednesday and Friday for first-class bathing only, and second-class on the remaining days – which shows how little 'class' related to the actual experience of bathing. It was simply that, according to the mores of the period, the social classes were to be kept separate in all things, even if this only amounted to segregating the 'tradesman' from the 'coalheaver'.

The same superficial distinctions applied to first- and second-class plunge baths and swimming baths for those parishes which decided to build more extensive facilities. Whilst the 'bathing box' in which one both changed and left one's clothes (what we would now called a cubicle) varied a little on class lines, the pools themselves were usually identical in size and layout (sometimes a single pool with a partition; occasionally a single shared pool). Typical signifiers of class distinction in the bathing boxes included whether they were painted or had a mirror and comb. Similarly, whether they had a door/curtain or were left open to the baths.[49] This latter difference may have been as much about defining an enclosed personal space for clothing and valuables as reflecting different expectations of modesty. The second-class customer was less likely to possess items worth stealing – hence there was no need to cordon off their personal possessions. Some baths did allow one to leave valuable possessions with the ticket office clerk; but this was not universal.

In the 1840s, 'changing' for men, of course, simply meant disrobing. There seems to have been little in the way of fretting about nudity and public morals in the pool. Regulations demanding 'bathing drawers' (loose-fitting trunks) were gradually introduced; but this reflected a general trend across society rather than any specific concern about swimming pools and morality (the seaside resort of Margate, for example, would prohibit nude bathing in 1862).[50] Trunks, like towels, could usually be hired from bath attendants. When swimming baths were added to Goulston Square in 1886, posters were printed that stated the rules in the first-class bath: 'All bathers to use bathing drawers either their own or those provided for their use, for which 1d charged.' There seems to have been no such restriction in the second-class bath. Either the managers considered the humble labourer was too accustomed to nude bathing in parks and rivers; or they simply thought he could not afford the additional penny.

One local magistrate, Sir Peter Laurie, inspecting the George Street baths upon their opening, did complain that the plunge baths allowed 'indecent exposure' and said 'he had seen two or three dozen bathers . . . whose gambols were indecent and disgusting', an indirect allusion to homosexual activity. He was, however, flatly contradicted by the superintendent who had taken him round the building; and the popular press mocked him for preferring 'Prudery' to cleanliness: 'there is no more likelihood of finding any disgusting indecency than amongst a parcel of Eton boys amusing themselves in the Thames'.[51]

This is not to say, however, that there were no concerns about behaviour. Washhouses, in particular, were carefully superintended by matrons to ensure there was no stealing, arguments or general rowdiness; and there were wooden divisions between washtubs which rather resembled the 'separate system' of the model Victorian prison, preventing gossip and distraction. Likewise, individual separate 'drying closets' were abandoned with reluctance when it became clear how inefficient they were in comparison with large heated 'drying rooms'. Outside the building, there were usually entirely separate entrances to the men's and women's baths to prevent casual mixing of the sexes; inside, bath attendants were expected to keep good order. Maintaining discipline was one reason why the water supply to slipper baths was generally controlled by the attendants, using turncocks on the outside of cubicles. As one attendant, asked about dealing with troublesome bathers in Goulston Square, explained: 'When they refused to be quiet at my request, I turned off the water from their baths and they found themselves dry at the bottom.'[52] Bathers in the cubicles were generally enjoined not to talk to each other.

Decoration in public baths and pools was typically plain tiling or glazed brick, with some modest motif. The walls of the City of London swimming baths in Golden Lane, however, were 'painted over with pious texts' which, noted an 1870s' visitor, were not in keeping with the rather more earthy language of the local bathers.[53] Public health propaganda also appeared in poster form and on flyers within and without the baths: 'Sickness is Often Brought on by Having a Dirty Skin'; 'Dirty Clothes are Like a Second Dirty

Skin, and Help to Make the Body Sickly'.[54] An early poster publicising the George Street baths in Euston Square gives an indication of the high-minded sentiments foisted upon the mid-Victorian working class during their ablutions. Talking up the danger of a new cholera epidemic, the 1848 notice reads:

> To raise yourselves to the proper position in the social scale, you must practice sobriety, morality and cleanliness . . . Remember, a filthy person indicates filthy habits; dirty in his apartments, he will be dirty in his mind; profligate in his amusements, unfit for a higher sphere. If you have any feelings for your present and eternal interests, or for those connected with you, think on these things.

The expectation was that the poor would not simply wash, but develop 'a regard for decency and personal cleanliness'.[55] A superintendent of the wash-tubs at St Martin-in-the-Fields washhouse noted with satisfaction in the early 1850s, 'there is a most decided improvement in the character of the women who wash'.[56]

The manners of the working class may well have improved. There is, however, little evidence that the bathing public were deeply concerned with the much trumpeted medical, moral and spiritual benefits of ablution. They simply wanted the comfort of a wash, clean clothes, and relished treating the baths as a leisure activity – whether enjoying the luxury of warm water or the amusement of swimming. Indeed, even Mr Sowten's 1830s' customers used his facilities as a 'matter of pleasure' – much to his surprise – and this trend would continue throughout the century. We still tend to think of the Victorians as terribly stern and self-denying: the facts rarely bear this out. At the grand first-class swimming pool in Lambeth, during the 1860s, the warm-water-spewing fountain at the centre was the prime spot for 'a group of devotees [who] may generally be seen luxuriating'.[57] The use of the word *luxuriating* suggests that – at least, for some – swimming baths were as much about pleasure as purification. Likewise, the statistics collected by parishes for the use of slipper baths show that the cold dip, recommended by many a medical authority, was never terribly popular. In the parish of St George, Hanover Square, between 1874 and 1887, less than 5 per cent of second-class bathers chose the cheaper cold bath option (and when they did, it may often have been out of financial necessity); and less than 3 per cent of the first-class bathers.[58]

In fact, the growing popularity of swimming as a sport and recreation during the second half of the century began to redefine the perceived purpose of bathing. Leisure certainly became as important as cleanliness. The Lambeth Baths – a privately owned successor to Mr Sowten's baths, built when the local vestry refused to adopt the 1846 Act – would be at the forefront, promoting swimming both as sport and entertainment. Lambeth hosted innumerable club competitions and 'fetes', and possessed a particularly famous 'Professor' in the form of Frederick Beckwith. Beckwith not only taught students swimming, but raced competitively and led his family, both wife and children, in spectacular underwater aquatic displays. The family were dubbed 'The Beckwith Frogs' and performed in a specially constructed glass tank at various places of public entertainment, including Cremorne Pleasure Gardens (although reporters were quick to assure the reading public that these bathers were 'clad in fleshings and drawers, after the fashion of acrobats').

Some sought to cash in on growing public enthusiasm for 'natation'. In 1875, the Floating Swimming-Baths Company Ltd. built and installed a wooden-bottomed floating bath, covered in iron and glass, like a miniature Crystal-Palace-on-Thames, on the site of a former steamboat pier by Charing Cross Station. The pool relied upon pumped-in river water, filtered and heated – 'which completely removes all mud and other matter that may be in suspension in the water, but still allows water to retain its natural salts and soft refreshing qualities'.[59] This extravagant construction was, naturally, not aimed at the working man – admission was one shilling – but it prospered for a decade or so, whilst serving as a floating ice-rink in the winter months.[60]

London's vestries, in turn, began to lose enthusiasm for the slipper bath as swimming grew more fashionable. Swimming, according to its advocates, not only produced cleanliness but was good exercise; and, of course, given a certain square footage, one could fit more people in a swimming pool than in a set of partitioned slipper baths (there was no question of malingering in the pool, as the bather was usually restricted to a half-hour session). Whilst no local authority actually abandoned slipper baths, grand swimming pools increasingly became the focal point in new buildings. This was acknowledged in an 1878 amendment to the Baths and Washhouses Act ('to extend the Act for the establishment of Public Baths and Washhouses to covered swimming baths, gymnasia, and other means of healthful recreation').

Thus, by the 1880s public pools tended to be larger than their modest 'plunge pool' predecessors of the mid-century. Exercise, sport and leisure were now the keynote. The *Daily Mail* proudly announced in 1898, 'amongst the Lambeth youths, water-polo is almost as much of a hobby in summer as is football in winter'.[61] Springboards became commonplace for practising diving. Spectator galleries for watching races and other 'aquatic spectacles' were a given. The 1890s even saw a vogue for 'chutes' (water slides), 'both for amusement and learning diving', with instructions carefully provided:

1. Get yourself into position by the use of the ropes.
2. Do not hold the sides of the chute while sliding.
3. Keep the head well down and the body stiff.
4. Do not run down the chute.
5. Not more than two persons must use the chute at one time.
6. Do not crawl up the chute.[62]

These slides were named after an American log-flume amusement ride, 'The Chute', which had opened at Earls Court pleasure ground in 1893. This was a long way from the stern injunctions to cleanliness of the 1850s.

There was also increasing provision for women swimmers (as opposed to merely providing slipper baths), with Paddington the first vestry to introduce a ladies' swimming pool in 1874, following a petition by female ratepayers. Women's use of baths – both individual slipper baths and swimming pools – still remained substantially less than men's. Indeed, Hackney would turn over its women's swimming bath to men and boys on a Sunday, such was the lack of demand (sometimes only a single customer for the whole day). It was also considered that the solitary female attendant would have little work, except on 'school days and club nights', and so could devote much time to mending bathing drawers and dresses.[63] Nonetheless, separate women's swimming baths began to be seen as a socially necessary accompaniment to any new development – although mixed bathing remained inconceivable.

Finally, after a lull of two decades, the 1880s and 1890s saw a boom in new public baths and washhouses – often built by vestries that had formerly rejected the Dukinfield Act in the 1850s – as well as the reconstruction of old baths on a grander scale to accommodate the growing enthusiasm for swimming pools.

This was not because public baths suddenly became profitable. The Bishop of London's hope that baths would return 7–10 per cent on the investment – sufficient to swiftly pay off a government loan and make a small profit – had proved illusory. By the 1880s, it was quite clear that initial loans of £20,000–£50,000, repaid over thirty years, could rarely be recouped from admission fees, without some burden on the rates. Nor was there new sanitary enthusiasm. Rather, under the flowering of late-Victorian 'municipal socialism', public baths were redefined by progressive authorities as a civic good, along with dust destructors, public libraries, and other facilities for the masses – and the cost and size of parish facilities increased to match the ambition of local councillors. Swimming baths became a particular source of municipal pride, opened with great fanfare. For example, new baths in the parish of St John, Hackney, would be visited by the Prince and Princess of Wales during their construction, and opened in 1897 by the Lord Chief Justice, with a reading from the local vicar, 'aquatic displays' and a stirring rendition of the Hallelujah Chorus.

Not everyone approved. Some commentators believed that the grander buildings were deterring the very poor ('poor persons shrink from contrasting their wretchedness with this display of wealth and the wealthy bathers they would naturally imagine that they would meet in such palatial entrance-halls').[64] The architect Alfred Hessell Tiltman, who gave several lectures on the subject of baths and washhouses during 1899, agreed. He proposed constructing multiple smaller 'People's Baths', containing only washhouses and 'rain douche baths' (i.e. showers) dotted throughout the backstreets of the metropolis. Large swimming baths were all well and good, but the poor were not sufficiently educated 'as to the necessity and benefits of the bathing habit'. They needed small-scale baths situated in the very streets in which they lived, not as part of some overbearing municipal complex. Tiltman, in short, wanted a return to the sanitary focus of the 1840s – something more like the original Liverpool model. Yet, despite these reservations, he still put the existing annual attendance at metropolitan baths and washhouses at 1.5million.[65]

Did the public baths and washhouses movement make a significant difference to public health? The question is very hard to answer. Improved personal cleanliness surely must have helped reduce the incidence of communicable diseases like typhus, spread by lice which flourished in filthy clothing. Yet, on the other hand, epidemic typhus had vanished in London by the 1870s, far too soon for the very limited number of washhouses to have made a profound impact. In the late-Victorian period, there were also unnoticed problems with what we would now consider basic hygiene. Swimming baths contained no disinfectants and, in many cases, were emptied only when they looked dirty, a case of fine judgement ('It is stated by the Superintendent that 250 bathers require a change of water').[66] This could lead to contamination and infection. In the early 1900s, the London County Council would trace large outbreaks of conjunctivitis in schoolchildren ('pink eye') to infection in public baths.

At the very least, a good deal of dirt was removed from clothes and bodies making life more comfortable for countless Londoners; and, perhaps, as they slid down chutes, jumped off springboards or played water polo, life also became a little more amusing. This was not exactly what Bishop Blomfield had intended when he first proposed cleansing the London poor, but it was still progress.

7

The Public Convenience

THE VICTORIANS INVENTED another type of sanitary amenity for the benefit of the masses: the public toilet. From the mid-1880s, unobtrusive underground conveniences were constructed under street corners and mid-road pedestrian refuges. These new facilities were a focus of municipal pride, just like public baths. Past iron railings, down a flight of steps, there was often surprising luxury. Sinks adorned with marble; stalls made from solid mahogany or teak; brass fittings on the doors. The visitor to London could now seek relief in a pleasant environment, staffed by a uniformed attendant. The capital's backstreets and alleys would no longer be polluted by those unable to find a water closet.

However, even at the end of the Victorian age, many Londoners still objected to having public toilets near *their* home or business; and provision for women remained a rather suspect innovation. Public conveniences for men and women were actively promoted by various interested parties from the 1840s onwards, but arguments about demand, dirt and decency meant that they only appeared in the final years of Victoria's reign.

In the early 1800s, there were few public places where a stranger could legitimately answer the call of nature. There was an obscure, historic 'house of easement' in the City of London: the medieval 'Whittington's Longhouse' (originally containing a capacious, communal toilet funded by the estate of Richard Whittington). It still functioned as a public privy as late as 1851, albeit much reduced in size.[1] In poorer districts, one might stumble across common privies in courtyards or alleys, erected by slum landlords and serving whole tenements – but these closets were not strictly public, and often foul. Coaching inns and public houses might oblige the casual visitor but such generosity was not guaranteed. The man in the street, therefore, often had recourse to the nearest alley, at least when it came to urination. Some, of course, were bolder than others. There was an angry letter about Trafalgar Square being 'polluted by some brutes in human shape' within days of its opening.[2]

Parish vestries received frequent complaints on the subject. Residents of Staple Inn, Holborn, were particularly vexed by well-attended political reform meetings at the Mechanics' Institute on nearby Chancery Lane. Staple Inn was an old 'Inn of Chancery', containing offices and living quarters for lawyers and men-about-town, nestling around a charming rose garden. When working men came out of the Mechanics' Institute, satiated in their thirst for knowledge, they had a habit of retiring from the main thoroughfare 'to satisfy any call of nature against the low wall as immediately below the rails of the Inn'.[3] This was despite prominent notices demanding they 'Commit No Nuisance'. The parish's paving committee could only suggest that the Inn erect an additional set of railings.

Similarly, in 1832, a shopkeeper in Kingsgate Street, Bloomsbury, demanded that something be done about a doorway adjoining the County Court:

> the constant resort of men for the purpose of making Water . . . my Wife and Family whose occupation is from necessity a great part of their time in the shop are consequently subject to great annoyance by this indecency, because of the unwholesome accumulation of filth which it occasions in so confined a situation.[4]

Such complaints – often citing offence to females – reflected a growing demand for 'respectable conduct'. Indeed, the Georgian squares of Bloomsbury, neatly laid out and carefully managed by their aristocratic landlords, were meant to be better regulated. Some streets even boasted a dedicated 'street-keeper' whose job was to keep out the riff-raff. Their middle-class residents expected a certain degree of cleanliness and decorum. They raised petitions not only about offensive micturition but the work of night-soil men; the proximity of noxious-smelling manufactories; the keeping of livestock and blood-soaked slaughterhouses. The genteel inhabitants of the newly built Brewer's Estate even demanded action from their local authority on the amorous proclivities of the bullock grazing opposite their new-built houses – 'bulling other cows on this ground, in the face of the respective inhabitants of Perry Street and Brewers Street, and their children'.[5] They had, after all, paid good money to enjoy refined suburban living.

Unfortunately, when it came to public urination, vestries and paving boards could do little more than post warning notices. The police did interfere ('our police constables are required to wage incessant war against nature, modesty and health, without advantage to any, and to the mutual discomfiture of all'),[6] but the problem was endemic. Property owners, therefore, tended to adopt their own measures. Walls that were habitual haunts were affixed with 'barricadoes and shelves, grooves, and one fixed above another, to conduct the stream into the shoes'.[7] These were reportedly a feature of 'every alley and court, and every piece of blind wall'[8] – which suggests how prevalent was the nuisance. Only one set of these shelves survives – along Clifford's Inn Passage, EC4, the same retired spot in which Rokesmith draws Mr Boffin aside from the bustle of Fleet Street in *Our Mutual Friend* – unnoticed by even the most assiduous modern chroniclers of London's street furniture. The would-be malefactor could, of course, simply move to somewhere less obstructed; but the 'urine deflector' (I can offer no better description) provided some small localised deterrent.

Women, of course, had the same needs as men. The statement by one late nineteenth-century source that lack of facilities for women meant working-class women ' "didn't go out, or didn't "go" '[9] – i.e. resigned themselves to suffer painfully in silence – should be treated with caution. For a start, the attitudes of the Board School-educated working class of the 1890s were not necessarily the attitudes of their grandparents. The late-Victorian memoirs of the anonymous 'Walter', entitled *My Secret Life* – elaborately pornographic, but convincing and detailed in their description of daily life – provide something of an earthy corrective. They contain a lengthy section, drawn from the author's boyhood, in which he describes secreting himself in a coal vault in a cul-de-sac in the East End. He observes from below 'the pissing place of the gay women' (prostitutes) – a convenient recessed grating, above the vaults. Possibly such obscure backstreets were exclusively the haunt of prostitutes, scorned by other working-class women; but this seems unlikely. In a metropolis pock-marked with insanitary slums – their clogged privies filled to the brim with excrement – the poorest in society must have resorted to similar spots, when the need arose.

The middle-class attitude to such behaviour, naturally, was disapproving. Any woman seen urinating in public degraded herself; much more so than a man – the softer sex were meant to possess more innate modesty. An Isaac Cruikshank caricature from 1799, showing a brutish-looking prostitute brazenly relieving herself in the street, is indicative. It is simply entitled *Indecency*. But Cruikshank's illustration also has a wider moral purpose, asking the onlooker to extend his instinctive revulsion at the sight of public urination to prostitution – both, he implies, should provoke horror. The actual indecency portrayed is also as much about the location and brazen attitude as the gross act itself. The woman crouches, in broad daylight, on a *paved* public street – i.e. one that has been 'improved' at cost to the ratepayers. She looks out at the reader, saying 'what are you stareing at? [*sic*]' Would Cruikshank have considered a humble laundress or seamstress, finding a quieter spot to discreetly answer the call of nature, similarly 'indecent'? Whilst discussing female bodily functions was considered highly indelicate, the more thoughtful and charitable members of respectable society must have realised that the poor had to 'go' somewhere.

There were, fortunately, alternatives for those women whose higher social standing would simply not permit al fresco relief. The coach-owning classes were not above keeping a 'bordalou' (a gravy-boat-shaped chamber pot) and drawing the vehicle's blinds to use it in private. Equally, female shoppers might pay a call at a confectioner's or milliner's, buy some trifle and politely request use of the owner's privy.[10] An expensive business – but it provided a solution.

Building public conveniences was an obvious way to tackle these annoyances, simultaneously addressing complaints about indecent behaviour; providing comfort to travellers and preventing pollution of the streets. The idea was mooted quite early in the century by various individuals. In 1809, a writer in the *Farmer's Magazine* suggested that large cities should invest in 'temples of

Cloacina erected in convenient situations, and each under the superintendence of its owner or his lessee', from which a small profit might be made by selling collected manure to farmers.[11] There was briefly some kind of commercial public water closet in the City of London, circa 1830.[12] In 1832, J.C. Loudon, arbiter of horticultural taste, would present two elegant classical designs for public toilets for 'Scotch towns' in his *Gardener's Magazine* (again, presuming that accumulated waste might be sold to farmers). The notion of the public toilet, therefore, was already in the public domain before the sanitary agitation of the 1840s; and examples of such facilities on the Continent were praised. Yet, remarkably, it would be decades before such conveniences became commonplace in the metropolis.

In fact, the first widely available 'public toilets' in London were not privies or water-closets, but simple urinals for men. Publicans led the way, constructing urinal accommodation because they were annoyed by the perpetual pools of urine and foul-smelling brick and woodwork outside their premises. Parishes followed suit, trying to address a public nuisance which caused so many complaints. Bizarrely enough, this often involved sanitary committees of prosperous vestrymen paying visits to particular walls to establish whether they stank sufficiently to merit intervention.

Urinal building seems to have begun around the start of the nineteenth century, although precise dates are very hard to establish (prior to this period, 'urinal' meant a glass vessel used by doctors for collecting and inspecting patients' urine). A parishioner's letter to the Holborn vestry in 1814 mentions 'the Urinal set up by the Committee at his request at the side of his House'. By the 1830s, Holborn not only possessed several parish urinals, but employed a labourer to clean them, at three shillings a week (paupers, previously employed at two shillings a week, had failed to perform the task with sufficient enthusiasm).

These early urinals were not complex affairs. They were typically nothing more elaborate than slates or a stone fixed to a wall, situated outdoors, sometimes with an upright stone slab to conceal the lower half of the man's body.[13] Many of the public house models lacked any system of drainage – i.e. they were essentially just to preserve the condition of the building to which they were attached. The City of London, perhaps the most enthusiastic sanitary authority in the metropolis, ensured that all its public-funded urinals drained to the sewers; but even by 1850, only a handful of these had running water.[14]

We know a good deal about the City's sanitary provision thanks to a survey by William Haywood. In 1850, there were seventy-four urinals in the 'Square Mile'. Forty belonged to public houses, with the remainder erected by the Corporation and its various adjuncts – as well as one established by the Dean and Chapter of St Paul's and another by the Bank of England. Haywood, employed as the City's Surveyor, earnestly requested the Corporation to invest in more of these conveniences, noting 'Public opinion has changed and is still changing upon this subject'.

This was, in fact, a rather over-optimistic assertion. Most Londoners did not share Haywood's enthusiasm. An 1850s' petition, from over 150 inhabitants of aristocratic Mayfair, gives a flavour of typical complaints. The well-to-do residents in question opposed a urinal being placed 'opposite Her Majesty's private entrance to Buckingham Palace':

> *Firstly*, The position is unsuitable and ill chosen.
>
> *Secondly*, It is not required by the cabmen there being a closet at each Public House at either end of the cab rank . . .
>
> *Thirdly*, There are several milliner's establishments overlooking the spot . . .
>
> *Fourthly*, Being in the direct road of Her Majesty and the Inhabitants of Belgravia it would certainly cause a diversion of the traffic . . .
>
> *Fifthly*, The Class for whose accommodation it is designed not having very refined notions of public decency, continual annoyance to residents would be an inevitable result.[15]

Nimby-ish petitions and legal challenges, drawn up along these lines, would dog the efforts of sanitary-minded local authorities throughout the century. For every householder who wanted to remove the unseemly spectacle of public urination, or simply the pools of urine accumulating by his wall, another would raise objection. Obstruction to foot or road traffic; drawing more men to the spot; offence to public decency and the delicate sensibilities of innocent females; attracting dubious characters – all of these would be cited again and again as reasons *not* to provide public facilities.[16] Well-meaning vestrymen must have torn out their hair in frustration. The public wanted a solution to public urination; but they did not want it near their own property. How could these opposing demands be reconciled?

Whilst urinals were, at least, being constructed throughout the capital during the first half of the century – despite innumerable local objections – public water closets remained few and far between.

The sanitary 1840s did produce one champion of the public convenience: Charles Cochrane, the originator of the 'street orderly' road-sweeping system. He would proclaim the need for 'public cabinets d'aisance and urinals' in poorer neighbourhoods, at National Philanthropic Association rallies.[17] Suggesting that the poor, rather than the middle classes, might benefit most from such facilities was a typically radical gesture from the would-be political firebrand.

In 1848, Cochrane decided to prove his point. He had constructed two public water closets in Ham Yard, Great Windmill Street, in the same premises where he had established a soup kitchen and night refuge for the homeless. They were opened to the public on 22 May 1848. By the following summer Cochrane had tallied 135,916 visits from men, 27,508 from women and 2,796 from children. Most were very poor folk, since large numbers came from the casual (overnight) ward of the nearby workhouse. They were reportedly very keen to avail themselves not only of the WCs, but of the six washing basins, soap and towels, as well as razors, hairbrushes, combs, clothes and shoe brushes.[18] Cochrane made sure to advertise in the press, extravagantly (to say the least) declaring the closets 'Under the Patronage of HRH Prince Albert the Board of Ordnance, the Board of Admiralty, Bank of England, &c'.[19] There had been, Cochrane proudly proclaimed, no thefts – the lavatories were staffed by attendants – and, once again, the theory that the poor 'loved dirt' was shown to be false.

Cochrane also orchestrated a stunt to publicise the project: a petition from 'respectable females' objecting to a nearby urinal. Having received no satisfaction from the paving board that authorised the urinal, Cochrane encouraged the women to address their complaints to the Metropolitan Commission of Sewers. The respectable ladies described the urinal as rendering the spot in question 'one of the most disgusting and offensive that can possibly be conceived . . . no Lady or woman servant can possibly pass the spot without the fear of witnessing indelicacies impossible to describe'. The pavement was reportedly covered 'with all that is offensive' – a suitably vague and ominous phrase – whilst Mr Cochrane's fastidiously clean toilets were only a few yards distant. What did the Commissioners intend to do about it?

The Commission responded by engraving the following words upon the urinal:

YOU ARE ENTREATED TO PUT YOUR CLOTHES IN ORDER BEFORE LEAVING THIS PLACE

In other words, men should be sure to conceal their members before turning to face the houses opposite. Cochrane considered this response most inadequate. There was a further letter from the outraged ladies to *The Times*, which went unpublished – perhaps because the topic, particularly when openly discussed by females, was considered too indecent.[20]

Another soup kitchen, inspired by the Ham Yard building, opened in the City of London in 1852 – replete with public closets – but it did not survive Cochrane's near-bankruptcy and inglorious flight from the country in 1853. Ham Yard itself survived as a charitable concern until the 1880s; but its groundbreaking provision of toilets for the masses would be forgotten. Cochrane, writing in 1850, consoled himself that his campaign was instrumental in persuading the Commissioners of Sewers to introduce two sets of public closets, in Soho and the notorious Church Lane slum in St Giles – although nothing much came of the experiment.

There was another attempt to persuade the Metropolitan Commissioners of the merits of public toilets. Joseph Bazalgette, soon to be famed as the engineer who built London's new sewers, applied for the post of Assistant Surveyor at the Commission in 1849. He supplemented his testimonials with details of a scheme for 'establishing public water-closets and urinals throughout the metropolis'.[21] These were to be distinctive purpose-built structures – neatly designed miniature classical temples, topped with a gaslight – placed at the junctions of major thoroughfares. Each temple would contain urinals, water closets and 'private' closets with superior fixtures and fittings, including a sink. The sink was a luxury item, since, prior to the acceptance of germ theory, hand washing was not considered a hygienic necessity. An attendant would manage the building, his income coming from a twopenny charge made for use of the private closets, and the sale of toilet paper for a halfpenny. Bazalgette also proposed, like others before him, to make the toilets financially self-supporting by collecting and recycling the waste – in this case, urine. This would be stored in tanks below, then pumped out into water carts, and conveyed to 'four large reservoirs situated in the north, east, south, and west suburbs of the metropolis, carefully constructed so as to avoid any possible annoyance', where it might ferment and then be sold on to farmers and market gardeners as liquid manure.

Applicants for the post of Assistant Surveyor had been asked to submit a paper of some sort, describing how they would remedy urban drainage.[22] Hence, the features of Bazalgette's scheme were calculated, somewhat clumsily, to satisfy Edwin Chadwick – i.e. covering the whole of London; only recycling urine (excrement would not accumulate quickly enough; and prolonged storage would be too reminiscent of the dreaded cesspool). There were, however, some peculiar aspects to Bazalgette's design – not least that most of the structure, apart from the 'private' closet, should not be roofed but open to the elements for ventilation – very airy, but hardly pleasant for customers in the public closets. The idea that suburban Londoners would accept vast reservoirs of fermenting urine in their midst – no matter how carefully constructed – must also have raised a few eyebrows. Most importantly, the plan did not actively engage with Chadwick's enthusiasm for narrow-piped sewers. To the modern reader, it also seems peculiar that Bazalgette entirely ignored women – each temple was to contain urinals, and so women were, de facto, excluded. Doubtless anything touching upon the subject of the female anatomy was too delicate to discuss in communication with a potential employer. Perhaps Bazalgette would have addressed the question, if the scheme had ever been taken forward but – as we shall see – addressing women's needs was always a fraught business.

Chadwick was, in fact, impressed enough to have the paper published; and Bazalgette got the job, although his plan was shelved. The need for some sort of metropolitan scheme for public toilets, however, would soon become more obvious and more pressing – for in 1851 London would host the Great Exhibition.

From its inception, it was clear that the grand showcase for national manufacturing and design, housed in a 'crystal palace' in Hyde Park, would bring thousands of tourists to London (in the event, an astonishing six million tickets would be sold during the six months the Exhibition was open). This would create various logistical problems, not least the provision of toilet facilities. The

Exhibition's 'Commissioners' (the management team) responded to the challenge, unimaginatively, by searching for more places throughout central London to erect urinals – and found few residents or shopkeepers willing to oblige them with sites.

There followed various expressions of anxiety. In February 1851, three months before the Crystal Palace opened, a petition was raised. It was signed by eminent members of the Royal Society of Arts (RSA), the body which had first proposed an industrial exhibition. The petitioners urged upon the Commissioners the erection of 'waiting rooms or halting places' inside existing shops and commercial premises. These would be comparable to similar facilities at railway stations (a cloakroom, toilet and washing facilities). The Commissioners might pay for 'a dozen establishments throughout the metropolis . . . as an example'; others might follow, as private speculations.[23] Meanwhile, readers fretted in the letters columns of the newspapers. A scare-mongering writer to *The Times* declared all foreigners 'not particular when certain calls of nature press, where they stop to relieve themselves' and suggested constructing suitable buildings beneath the trees in the park. The alternative was that 'doors, porticoes, and railings of our squares and public buildings will become receptacles of impurity'.[24]

Ultimately, the Commissioners decided to take a limited view of their remit, and not concern themselves with the defilement of the metropolis, or even the park. They would build water closets for both men and women, but only within the Crystal Palace itself, attached to the various refreshment rooms. The most central facilities would cost a penny; those in the building's wings a halfpenny (to discourage congestion in the central 'transept'). It is unlikely, therefore, that the phrase 'spend a penny' can be attributed to these arrangements, as often claimed, since most of the 'waiting rooms' fell into the halfpenny category. The Exhibition may, however, have inaugurated the custom of labelling toilets 'Ladies' and 'Gents.' or 'Gentlemen' – which is how they appear on the official floorplan. The manufacturer of the toilets was to be George Jennings, a Blackfriars-based sanitary engineer, who was also exhibiting within the building (his other products included 'a patent shop shutter shoe for securing shop shutters without a bar, improved mops and brushes for cleaning railway and other carriages, patent joints for plumbers').[25]

Some have mistakenly suggested, based on his work in 1851, that Jennings 'invented' the public toilet – a distinction which might better be lavished on either Loudon or Cochrane. The notion that Jennings (or the public) dubbed the toilets 'monkey closets' – a rather brutish and comical term – is also fallacious. This was a latter-day trade name for the type of 'wash-out' toilet basin which Jennings tested at the Exhibition. There is no indication that it was used by the general public of the sedate and dignified 'retiring rooms'. What Jennings's toilets did reveal, however, was that the public were more than willing to use the facilities – a total of 704,528 visits were paid to the ladies' waiting rooms, and 827,820 to the men's (countless more in practice, since the urinals were free of charge, and therefore there was no tally of their usage). Reporting on the Exhibition in 1852, the Commissioners stated that the figures revealed the want of such accommodation in the metropolis, and 'the sufferings which must be endured by all, but more especially females' for the lack of somewhere to relieve themselves. If anyone were willing to build public toilets, such establishments could be made 'perfectly remunerative'.

In fact, within days of the Exhibition opening, various parties had already embarked upon their own private speculations. A certain Mr Davis established a 'large portable urinal . . . which looked like a monster of the omnibus kind . . . gaudily painted', and parked it on the busy shopping street of Cheapside. City of London officials claimed they had been duped into giving it their blessing. A model, presented to the Sewers Commission, was 'excessively modest and unobtrusive', whereas the actual covered vehicle was sufficiently large and startling to attract large crowds of onlookers, gawping at gentlemen disappearing inside to relieve themselves.[26] The charge was one penny (ladies were not catered for). Mr Davis was ordered to remove the vehicle with all possible haste.

A 'Metropolitan Sanitary Convenience and Advertising Company' was also registered. The company prospectus cited the medical harm done by excessive restraint of bodily functions and the success of such undertakings on the Continent. The prospectus promised its toilets would 'add a leading feature to the metropolitan improvements, and the health, morality and comfort of the public'.[27] The project would include free urinals ('of a superior standard') and paid water closets for both men and women, with lucrative advertising space on the outside of the structure. Potential investors, however, stayed away.

Strangely enough, the body most keen to prove that public toilets could be made profitable was the Royal Society of Arts. Founded in 1754, the Society's mission was to encourage excellence in 'Arts, Manufactures and Commerce', offering prizes for innovative ideas. Several of its members, including the leading railway engineer Samuel Peto, still remained convinced that 'public waiting rooms' in existing shops and businesses would most readily meet the needs of the metropolis. The receipts from the public toilets at the Great Exhibition seemed to prove their hypothesis. A 'Waiting Room Committee' was formed to take things forward. There would be an experiment with waiting rooms for ladies and gentlemen, located in appropriate shops, suitably segregated on opposite sides of the street. Charges would be gradated from a penny for the urinals, to threepence for full use of a water closet and lavatory (sink). Proprietors of premises in central London were asked to volunteer: 'The shops which appear to be most suitable for waiting-rooms for ladies are staymakers', bonnet-makers', milliners', &c.'[28] For gentlemen, there was a different masculine list: 'hairdressers', tailors', hatters', taverns', &c.'[29] In short, this was to be a middle-class counterpart to Cochrane's Ham Yard experiment.

The project would take some time to get off the ground, not least because the RSA Council grew wary of the expense involved. Peto would eventually volunteer to underwrite the scheme against any pecuniary loss, although it was hoped that profits would render such insurance unnecessary. A gentleman's waiting room was fitted out with water closets and cloakroom and opened on 2 February 1852, within the Old Bell Tavern at 95 Fleet Street. An attendant was hired at 20 shillings a week to keep the place in order; and it was verbally agreed that the landlord would take over the convenience, once it was proven to be self-supporting. The ladies' waiting room opened a week later at 57 Bedford Street, off the Strand, in a failing 'milk and butter shop', to be managed by a Mrs Grant, the sitting tenant. Every effort was made to publicise these twin ventures, with an advertisement intended for *The Times* (although it never seems to have appeared, for reasons unknown) and 50,000 handbills distributed amongst the public. 'Tickets of Admission' were issued gratuitously to RSA members over a period of weeks, circulated with the Society's published papers. The details were even inserted into 'a guide to the conveniences of London called "Where is it" ' – the fact that this remarkable publication has not survived is a minor tragedy for sanitary historians.[30]

The trial, in any case, turned out to be a complete disaster.

During the first month, only 58 men and 28 women made use of the facilities. The entrance fee for using the WC was lowered from tuppence to a penny; but it made little difference, and after six months, the total receipts came to £15 – an abysmal sum, compared with nearly £500 spent on setting up the premises and advertising. Mrs Grant, having failed both at the butter *and* toilet trade, begged to be allowed to use the shop as a milliner's. The ladies' waiting room would be closed in June 1852, after only five months. The men's establishment lasted only a couple of months more. The RSA committee, shocked, commissioned a report from Henry C. Owen, who had been General Superintendent at the Crystal Palace. He was the very same enthusiastic official who had written the Commissioners' report that stated 'such establishments may be made perfectly remunerative'. Peto and his colleagues were mystified. What had the RSA done wrong?

Owen blamed neither management nor the publicity material. His verdict would become the fixed view of officialdom on public toilets for the next three decades:

> An Englishman rarely requires anything more than an ordinary urinal in the streets. From the class of customers thus limited, are then deducted those who can step into a public-house, a hairdresser's shop, and many other places, where, for a few pence to the servant or a small purchase in the shop, all that is necessary may be obtained.[31]

In other words, if respectable folk could easily give 'a few pence to the servant', what was the point of trying to improve upon the existing arrangements? Owen also noted there were free urinals not far distant. Yet, although the presence of urinals nearby might explain men's lack of interest, he offered no explanation as to why middle-class women had shown such reluctance to use the facilities. They had used the toilets at the Exhibition enthusiastically.

Perhaps provision for women in shops *was* relatively adequate, as long as one knew which businesses would discreetly reward one's patronage. Perhaps, alternatively, the advertising campaign was actually a failure. The progenitors of the project must have believed that Bedford Street was sufficiently respectable, with enough 'passing trade' to bring in more than one or two women per day. But there seems to have been no signposting of the facilities; no advertisement on the front of the premises – probably on the grounds that it might offend female modesty. Did the Society's handbills reach the right audience? One possibility is that respectable women were simply too embarrassed to specifically seek out and use the establishment. What seemed acceptable amidst the bustling throngs of the Exhibition – unfamiliar territory, where countless others were doing likewise – may have seemed more socially awkward, alone on the Strand.

The sanitary legacy of the Great Exhibition was, therefore, more negative than positive. Whilst the sheer numbers using Jennings's closets *initially* suggested that more public accommodation might appeal to the masses, the RSA's high-profile experiment demolished the idea. The great and the good of the metropolis became convinced that public toilets would simply not be used. Shop owners and others would occasionally attempt something similar – e.g. a 'boot-cleaning saloon', opened in Covent Garden in 1855, with public lavatories and dressing rooms attached[32] – but generally there was scepticism. A 'Metropolitan Lavatory Company' published its prospectus in 1863, promising accommodation of men and women, 'with every regard to taste and comfort, in which newspapers and writing materials will be constantly supplied', spread over sixty sites near theatres, law courts, public buildings etc. Shareholders would receive a free ticket of admission.[33] The company sank without a trace.

Letter-writers to the medical press would occasionally advert to the need for better facilities and the particular discomfort to women – 'There are three grounds upon which a large extension of public urinals and latrines is imperatively required. These are – convenience, public decency, and public health'[34] – but no local authority seemed willing to repeat the RSA's brave effort.

Urinals, at least, continued to be installed throughout the metropolis. To answer local objections, vestries looked to improved designs, built to conceal all activity within. Self-contained structures, which did not rely on being next to an existing wall, began to appear in all shapes and sizes – including circular, cuboid and octagonal. Cast-iron urinals would dominate by the end of the century, the metal perforated with geometric patterns for both decoration and ventilation. Inside, glazed stoneware urinal basins and marble divisions began to replace the humbler iron and slate of previous decades.[35] As the capital expanded, these cast-iron conveniences would become a distinctive feature of suburban street life, usually painted dark green (in his play *Candida*, George Bernard Shaw glumly describes 1890s' Hackney as 'well-served with ugly iron urinals').[36] A good example still survives in the grounds of York

House, Twickenham, with an intimate instruction firmly stamped into the metalwork: 'Please Adjust Your Dress Before Leaving'.

Like the RSA's shop-based facilities, signposting the existence of urinals was problematic. There was a certain squeamishness; 'modesty' had to be observed. No one wished to remind respectable folk of bodily functions any more than was necessary. Gaslights, at least, were usually placed at the entrance (although an 1860s' court case makes passing mention of a boy going round a urinal, putting lighted candles in each compartment, hoping for a small gratuity). The City of London helpfully added the word 'Halt' to its urinal lamps, which William Haywood considered 'sufficiently, without being offensively, suggestive'.[37] The 1850s' Board of Works for St Giles contemplated providing 'finger indicators' (painted 'pointing hand' signs) to guide the public to their new facilities ('an indirect allusion only being made to them on the indicators'), but it is not clear if such signs were ever introduced.[38] Haywood would repeatedly plead with the City to make sure new urinals appeared on major thoroughfares, where they would be noticed by the public. But many vestries seem to have felt that the less visible the better – the more discreet the location, the less chance of giving offence.

In fairness, the unwelcome association between urinals and various types of 'nuisance' was not entirely illusory. William Haywood, writing to an acquaintance in 1851, noted that there was a trade-off between privacy and morality.[39] In other words, the more one hid the act of urination in 'suspicious iron cages',[40] the more one created a space which might conceal other misdemeanours, including robbery, illicit advertising and homosexuality.

This was not a uniquely Victorian concern. Dubious bills had long been posted in water closets and houses of easement; and this continued throughout the nineteenth century – mostly advertisements for prostitution and its unwanted consequences. As one *Times* reporter genteelly described it, when a bill-sticker and his employer were prosecuted for defacing a Shoreditch urinal, the advertisements in question 'related to the defendant's ability to cure certain diseases'.[41] Quack doctors relied on urinals, amongst other locations, as places to post their contact details, hinting at cures for venereal and other embarrassing complaints.

Likewise, there was a long-standing association between 'houses of easement' and cottaging. Such activity continued in the nineteenth-century urinal – as did countless instances of attempted blackmail, whether based on real or imagined illicit homosexual liaisons. Easy money could be gained by accusing a nervous gentleman of an unwelcome sexual advance and demanding payment for silence. If the gentleman refused – and found a policeman to take the accuser into custody – then courts were obliged to hear very graphic details ('the prisoner was in the next place, and put his hand round and took hold of my penis in a very indecent manner, and turned round and exposed himself to me . . . he did not lay hold of me till I had pumped ship').[42]

Vandalism was also an ongoing problem. William Haywood, having persuaded the City authorities to invest in more urinals, was disheartened to find them the target of wanton destruction – 'damage which could only have been effected by a wicked intent, a strong arm and a heavy instrument'.[43] The urinals of St James's vestry, in the West End, were likewise regularly trashed by the public ('The pleasure to the perpetrators is beyond the comprehension of any man claiming common sense').[44]

As for general 'indecency', even at the end of the century some 'traditional' urinals remained outside public houses, overlooked by neighbouring properties, exposing men to passers-by. A survey of St Pancras in 1884 found 40 out of 113 public houses had outdoor urinals, ten without any door or screen whatsoever.[45]

In a sense, therefore, ongoing public hostility towards urinals, wherever they were placed, was inevitable. One interesting solution was proposed as early as 1858 – by none other than George Jennings – but it would be decades before it was adopted.

Jennings deserved a hearing, since he had valuable experience. He had provided water closets for not only the Great Exhibition but for the Dublin Exhibition of 1852; and he had persuaded those in charge to include his toilets at the resurrected Crystal Palace in south London (after initially being told 'persons would not come to Sydenham to wash their hands'). In 1856, he turned his attention to the idea of establishing public conveniences on the streets of the capital, offering his own design for a building next to the Royal Exchange. This was rejected, but two years later he had a flash of inspiration. He repeated his proposal to the City Commissioners of Sewers, offering to erect a convenience at his own cost (including gas, water, and the attendants' wages) 'and carry out every detail, under your Engineer's direction, provided the attendants I furnish are allowed to receive a small gratuity for use of

Towels &c. as at the Crystal Palace'.[46] He felt confident he had resolved all possible moral and practical objections. Firstly, just as at the Exhibition, attendants would keep order, and ensure both cleanliness and decency ('who on pain of dismissal should be obliged to give each seat a rub over with a damp leather after use').[47] Secondly, the new structure would not interfere with foot or road traffic, nor force passing citizens to contemplate the delicate subject of their bowels – for it would be *underground*. Jennings proposed to construct a convenience that both met the bodily needs of citizens and quite literally buried a distasteful and annoying subject.

Yet, once again, the City declined to take the matter any further. Jennings would later claim that this was down to nothing more than 'false delicacy' – City officials displaying an exaggerated concern for 'public morals', parading their own refined sensibilities. These were 'individuals, who if measured by their obstructive policy, one would suppose that they themselves never required any convenience of any kind'.[48] Certainly, there was a good deal of such sentiment in circulation, particularly with regard to the fear of offending 'modest' females. According to some, public toilets – and what people did inside them – were a shameful, indelicate subject: 'English ladies should not be shocked by seeing in the open streets such objectionable contrivances.'[49] Unfortunately, the Sewer Commissioners' actual response does not seem to have survived in the City archives, but this was not many years after the RSA's failed effort. The City Commissioners may also have believed there was no great demand for water closets; that their existing provision of urinals was sufficient. Men, after all, already had somewhere to urinate. As for the rest, both men and women could contain themselves – as they had always done. In truth, the needs of women, relatively thin on the ground in the mercantile/ corporate hub of the metropolis in the 1850s, were not a great concern.

Jennings lamented this short-sightedness, but he was not alone in receiving a rejection. The City's Sewer Commissioners received numerous letters from would-be commercial partners as soon as William Haywood publicised his ideas about expanding the number of urinals in the City. Many believed they could make a profit from toilets – whether from charging for their use or pursuing Bazalgette's idea for recycling urine. A certain Mr D'Angely of Paris, patentee of a secret deodorising process (which supposedly both removed all smell and created an instant fertilising agent), promised to build and maintain an experimental urinal for fifteen years, as long as 'the urine deposited should during that period become his property'.[50] A Mr Classon proposed to collect both urine and faeces from a public closet on Cheapside, promising that it would be painted an 'unobtrusive colour' and be financially self-supporting.[51] Several others followed suit and all seem to have been refused. Indeed, for almost three decades, the City was content to rest upon its laurels; and other metropolitan authorities did likewise. There was a standard response whenever better accommodation was demanded, as a critical 1880s' report noted: 'Two or three public urinals are put up, in such positions as to disfigure their surroundings, and then the business is regarded as satisfactorily completed.'[52]

Agitation for change would come from the very women whom the paterfamilial City worthies hoped to protect, courtesy of the Ladies' Sanitary Association (LSA).

The LSA was founded in 1857 to tackle matters of domestic public health. True, civil engineers might build improved sewers; parliament might legislate about overburdened cemeteries; but there remained 'the personal habits of the people'. The LSA, managed by an all-female committee – a largely aristocratic committee, naturally – would consider how to improve the home life of the poor. This was an inquiry deemed uniquely suited to well-bred women, i.e. conveying valuable sanitary messages to the slums, encouraging hard-pressed wives and mothers to adopt habits of personal cleanliness.

There was some focus on practical help at the birth of the organisation. 'Bible women' visited slums to read religiously uplifting material to the poor, but also armed themselves with soap, pails and scrubbing brushes, which could be hired for a farthing.[53] Other 'sanitary' activities came and went, including taking Ragged School children to London Zoo for 'healthful recreation'; and promoting the use of parks. Public lectures 'affording instruction to ladies in the laws of life and health' were also part of the LSA mission. The main focus, however, soon became printing and distributing tens of thousands of tracts with titles like 'How to Manage a Baby', 'The Black Hole in Our Bedrooms', 'Never Despair' and 'The Power of Soap and Water' (a bestseller). An excerpt from an LSA pamphlet, entitled 'Hints on Your Health' – an abecedarian poem, priced at one penny – gives a flavour of the advice on offer:

Let dust on the furniture never be seen;
Much illness is caused by the want of pure air,
Now to open your windows be ever your care.

Old rags and old rubbish should never be kept,
People should see that their floors are well swept;
Quick movements in children are healthy and right,
Remember the young cannot thrive without light.
See that the cistern is clean to the brim,
Take care that your dress is all tidy and trim . . .

Yet, in 1878, the LSA ventured beyond the domestic, albeit still contemplating intimate female matters. Supported by the campaigning journal the *Woman's Gazette*, which championed the rights of women workers, the LSA contacted every London vestry and district board with a proposal: that they build public water closets exclusively for the use of women.

The LSA's secretary, Rose Adams, writing later in the year to Bethnal Green vestry, acknowledged the universal truth that there was often hostility to new conveniences of any kind, and listed all the possible 'public' sites over which the authority had complete control and which might accommodate women's toilets ('park lodges, cemeteries, recreation grounds, model lodgings, hospitals, laundries, baths, dispensaries, workhouses, School Board schools, tram and omnibus stations, churches and chapels'). Alternatively, there were 'small shops where articles are or could be sold in which women are interested' (the lessons of the RSA's scheme were now apparently forgotten). The 'best plan', however, would be custom-built structures 'in a well-frequented part of the parish, not in a mews or middle of the roadway, or close to a public house' (i.e. somewhere fairly respectable, not too exposed to the gaze of others). The aim of the proposal was to assist not only middle-class but working women – so that whilst there should be an attendant, charging for full use of the 'lavatory' (sink) and watercloset, '*a free W.C. should always exist* at a paying station'. This, claimed Miss Adams, was an urgent matter: 'The increasing number of women (working) of all classes who travel about London daily renders such provision of serious moment.'[54]

Bethnal Green bounced the idea around various committees. The vestry's Medical Officer of Health noted that such provision was envisaged in the 1855 Metropolis Management Act, but had never been taken up in the capital.[55] Women could only call on 'confectioners' shops and the waiting rooms of railway stations' (as opposed to the wide availability of urinals). He dubbed this difference a 'selfish inequality'.

James Stevenson, the Medical Officer for Paddington, went one stage further, producing a widely circulated and extensive written report. Stevenson testified to the increasing numbers of women in the workforce, as well as more women independently shopping and visiting London as tourists. The modern metropolis, he claimed, created new social arrangements, which demanded new provisions:

> No one would think of proposing latrine accommodation for women in a town where most of the inhabitants are known to one another, and are within an easy distance of their own homes. London is a populous wilderness, and nowhere is the sense of solitude at times more keenly felt.

Stevenson denied that women were physically better able to exercise self-control – a popular myth. Rather, he claimed, they were simply more uncomplaining of discomfort. Daringly, he even alluded to pregnancy and menstruation, albeit ever so opaquely: 'there are periods and conditions peculiar to sex, when latrine accommodation would be specially convenient; and as at such times the requirements of nature are apt to be more urgent and more frequent'. The physical consequences of excessive self-restraint were severe: 'cerebral and cardiac disturbance'.[56]

This was powerful stuff, a rare acknowledgement of the physical needs of the female sex. London's vestries ultimately chose to ignore the LSA's plea but the topic of public toilets, particularly those for women, became a talking point. In the same year, the City's Medical Officer of Health also asserted the need for more 'urinals, necessaries and other conveniences'.[57] The Bishopsgate Ward Club – a group of local businessmen and merchants – wrote to the City's Commissioners of Sewers, suggesting that public toilets be constructed for both sexes.[58] And, at the start of 1881, the City of London finally yielded to the latest commercial speculator who insisted that he could make public toilets pay.

The time had at last come for the public convenience proper, not in shops or exhibition halls, but upon the streets of London.

Mr Alfred Watkyns had been touting his 'Chalets de Nécessité' – modelled on similar conveniences in Paris – around virtually every large municipality in Great Britain and had met with the same mixture of unease and anxiety that ruled the metropolis. How much would these things cost? Surely decent women would be offended at the very sight of them? To acquire a contract with the City of London, therefore, was something of a coup. After some discussion, it was agreed there should be two trial buildings at Ludgate Circus – one for men only on the north side (with urinals and a single WC); and another with entirely separate sections for both men and women, on the south side.

The buildings were designed in the style of rustic Swiss chalets, with extensive decorative woodwork, and measured around 20 feet by 12. It was envisaged that the outside of the chalets would incorporate a seat for passers-by, a kiosk selling small items, and advertising boards (original advertisements for the first City chalet included a safe company, painkillers, toothpaste, and Pear's 'Dirty Boy' soap). The kiosk and seat were soon dropped from the plans – presumably because it was felt they would attract loiterers and deter customers. The euphemistic 'Halt' sign, adopted by William Haywood for his urinals, would be replaced with 'Ladies' Lavatory' and 'Gentlemen's Lavatory' painted on the roof. This, too, was something of a euphemism in its infancy. Previously, 'lavatory' merely meant a place for washing one's hands and face, not a toilet (hence, when detailed descriptions of Victorian public toilets refer to a 'lavatory', they generally mean a sink area).

The usual hostile petitions came flooding in, though with a slightly different flavour than in some areas of the capital, as this was an exclusively commercial district. Businesses complained that their premises were obscured; that the advertisements were inappropriate (they would be removed in June 1884). The *Pall Mall Gazette* suggested that shop owners were piqued that passers-by no longer had to 'enter shops and buy things they do not want' in order to use their toilets.[59] A further chalet experiment, erected in Bishopsgate, attracted a solicitor's letter about men who 'commence to disarrange their attire before entering and come out of the Urinal with their clothes disarranged and complete their attire in front of our client's property'.[60] A hairdresser took up residence in the Ludgate men's chalet, much to the chagrin of local barbers. Nonetheless, the City stuck to its intention of giving Watkyns a fair trial, and declined to interfere.

For the first time, men and women had equal access to public toilets on the streets of the metropolis – even if only in a single location. Unfortunately for Watkyns, few other districts were willing to make the same trial. Worse, the City Sewers Commission was now in an experimental mood. In 1884,

they also authorised the creation of the first underground public convenience, at the Royal Exchange – the selfsame idea that George Jennings had
proposed some twenty-six years previously. It proved inoffensive to passing
pedestrians – the very advantage Jennings had foreseen. Originally, the water
closets were free of charge but there was heavy use by 'men who undoubtedly
could go elsewhere, but preferred the most perfect accommodation provided
gratis by the Commission'.[61] The charge of one penny was then introduced.

Other local authorities, suitably impressed, began to draw up similar plans.
Commercial rivals to Watkyns came forward. There was soon a convenience
in Oxford Street, opened by a newly formed 'Ladies Lavatory Company',
'tastefully arranged with a good entrance, convenient dressing room and every
other requisite'.[62] The Chalet Company had barely begun its trial run, when
suddenly it had public and private competitors.

It is interesting that the City adopted Jennings's scheme in 1884, rather than
in 1858. There does seem to have been a new mood of experimentation – a
urine-collection scheme was finally trialled in the same period. The growth of
the underground railway had, perhaps, accustomed Londoners to stepping
beneath the streets. There may also have been a personal incentive for the City
worthies on its streets and sewers committees. The Lady Mayoress at the
Mansion House was repeatedly taken ill in 1883, complaining at the stench of
a urinal situated beneath her bedroom window. The Lord Mayor, in turn,
complained bitterly to the Commissioners of Sewers – which may well have
incentivised them to seek alternatives.[63] The urinal in question would be
removed in 1884; the new facility at the nearby Royal Exchange opened
shortly afterwards on 23 January 1885.

For members of the Ladies' Sanitary Association, however, the Royal
Exchange toilets looked less like progress. The new underground convenience
made no provision for women; and, worse, two years later, William Haywood
actually produced a report which claimed to show that toilet accommodation
at workplaces, railway stations and confectioners' shops, etc., was quite
adequate for females within the City. This was a preamble to cancelling
contracts with the Chalet Company – which went bankrupt at the end of the
decade. Haywood replaced the mixed Ludgate toilets with another underground structure – entirely for the male sex. There was also disheartening
news elsewhere. Paddington vestry had a vestryman keen to introduce both

male and female underground conveniences; but his plan was rejected by his fellows.[64] The Parish of St Margaret and St John, Westminster, proposed a joint 'urinal and retiring rooms for women' with St George, Hanover Square, but the latter demurred.[65]

For a brief moment in 1888/89, it seemed that another commercial venture might provide for women. This was not the Ladies' Lavatory Company (which seems to have flourished for the briefest time) but 'The International Hygienic Society'. Based in Berlin, the company promised to construct elegant Italianate 'kiosks'. In the West End, these would contain lavatories, dressing-rooms, space for the storage of shopping, facilities for letter-writing and reading the daily paper – a sort of ladies' club in miniature. Two such buildings were actually constructed on the Duke of Westminster's estate in Mayfair, and another, probably rather less grand, opposite the Clerkenwell Sessions House.

The latter survived until 1899, but all three were effectively made redundant in the early 1890s. For London's local authorities finally began to take notice of women's needs. The vestries of the West End, in particular, realised women shoppers were increasingly important to local businesses – and whilst new department stores provided some toilet facilities, the charge of 'selfish inequality' in existing provision was hard to deny. The West End vestries also had no wish to be bettered by the City of London. Thus, they decided to copy the much praised model of the Royal Exchange – the underground convenience – while also providing for both sexes.

St James's Westminster took the lead, opening an underground convenience at Piccadilly Circus in 1889 – a project planned during the building of the new Shaftesbury Avenue in 1885 but delayed by various difficulties (not least the indifference of the Metropolitan Board of Works).[66] The women's section would include 'two mirrors, brushes, combs &c., the idea being to provide all necessary accommodation for ladies shopping or doing business in the West End'.[67]

Marylebone followed, determined to supply a treat for shoppers at Oxford Circus, both male and female:

The entrance steps at each end are surrounded by an ornamental cast-iron railing. The walls of the interior are faced with white glazed bricks, the floor being of colour incaustic tiles. In the men's department, a double range of urinals occupy the centre, formed of polished rouge royale marble, with dove marble backs and white stoneware basins, and on either side are placed the W.C.'s – twelve in number, the doors and partitions of which are of pitch pine. Lavatory accommodation is also provided. In the women's department, the construction is much the same. The convenience is well lighted by day, by means of pavement lights, and at night made brilliant by the electric light . . .[68]

During the same period, the egalitarian London County Council, created in 1889, began building free public lavatories for both sexes, principally in its public parks. The LCC's election literature for 1892 would boast, with marvellous exaggeration, 'Thanks to the Council, 5,000,000 Londoners can now do their daily business without running an almost ludicrous but still very real physical danger.'[69]

The bodily requirements of women were now in the spotlight. In 1892, *The Times* would run a long correspondence concerning public toilets. For many letter-writers, the recent introduction by railway companies of automated penny-slots in lavatories was an indignity too far. It was bad enough that ladies were always expected to pay for WCs – whilst men used urinals gratis – but broken locks, dirty waiting rooms and general misery seemed to accompany this supposed mechanical improvement. One woman complained that, stymied by a locked waiting room at Euston, she was obliged to undertake a seven-hour journey to Bangor without any relief (only first-class carriages had lavatory accommodation in this period).[70] A particularly frank, if pseudonymous, female testified that she could not use the few existing public conveniences situated in the middle of streets, near cab ranks – the shame of passing the cabmen and loitering males was too great. Was it, she asked, surprising that some women preferred to use 'retired streets', even if they were obliged to dodge the patrolling policeman?[71] Finally, after several weeks of discussion in the Letters page, a *Times* leader demanded the end of payment for female toilet facilities. Failing that, the railway authorities should at least remove the 'mean and pettifogging slot'.[72]

By the end of the century, the subject was so much 'out in the open' that lavatory accommodation for women was a rallying cry for progressives in local elections.[73] There were, admittedly, still reactionary elements who insisted that women were too pure, angelic and modest to require public toilets. George Bernard Shaw, who served as a St Pancras vestryman, would detail his fellow vestrymen's astonishing reluctance to allow a female convenience on Camden High Street in 1900. One objected that poor local flower-girls would only use the toilets to wash violets. Another claimed that any women who wanted such accommodation had 'forgot their sex'. A wooden mock-up of the lavatory, erected to show its effect on traffic, became – according to Shaw – the object of deliberate vandalism by every passing omnibus and cart, a joke 'kept up for fun by all and sundry'.[74] The matter would not be resolved until a woman's underground lavatory was finally erected in 1905. Shaw's account is interesting, because it paints a picture of ageing vestrymen engaging in repulsive schoolboy sniggering over the female body – and also a certain class bias. It was one thing to provide toilets for respectable middle-class women in the West End; another for the flower-girls and factory workers of Camden, who would hardly know what to do with such luxury. Shaw's description tallies with the 'false delicacy' of the City of London, which so irritated Jennings in the 1850s. The City, in fairness, would revert to building women's toilets – underground – from 1893 onwards.

It does seem to have been true that many women struggled to enter highly visible public conveniences, on grounds of modesty – inadvertently propagating the myth that such structures were simply not desired by respectable women. Messrs Davis and Dye, advising fellow plumbers on lavatory construction in 1898, warned that women's lavatories were often sparsely attended:

> This strange form of modesty still prevails however with the weaker sex as public conveniences for women are, as yet, more often failures, financially and practically, than a success; and in building such places with sections for either sex, it is commonly provided that the whole can be easily converted to the use of men only.[75]

Busy venues – like the Great Exhibition and its successors – may have given anxious women more 'cover'. Similarly, the underground conveniences built by St James's, Westminster, at Piccadilly Circus received 87,643 female customers in the first eight months of operation – not far short of the male total, discounting use of free urinals. Ironically, slightly more retired situations may actually have made women feel more isolated and vulnerable to scrutiny.

Regardless of modesty, by the end of the Victorian era the basic demands of the LSA had been met – although the provision of fewer toilets for women than men was the norm (and continues to this day). Women, too, were still generally required to literally *spend a penny* whilst men could make use of traditionally free urinals. There was an attempt to address this issue with a device which might be used gratis, like the male urinal, by poorer females. Plumbers came up with the 'urinette' – a miniature toilet bowl, situated behind a curtain, into which women could discreetly reverse (slightly easier than it might sound, since Victorian female underwear was crotchless, with drawers on each leg only joined at the waist). In fact, when installed in Shoreditch in 1896, a charge of a halfpenny was made, although the attendant was allowed 'to use her discretion as to their free use by poor persons'.[76] But urinettes never really became popular, not least since many potential customers reportedly recoiled in horror at the immodest contrivance.[77]

What has become of the Victorians' urinals and underground conveniences? The former have all but vanished from London (though some survive in the provinces, particularly in Bristol); and a handful of underground lavatories remain. A few of the latter have period fixtures and fittings (see South End Green, Hampstead, for a rare example). Many, however, have been entirely remodelled; many more have closed or been demolished. Some examples have been converted to other uses. These range from an 'award winning urban day spa' to a recently opened café in Fitzrovia, where modern-day bohemians can sip their coffee while leaning against a row of specially modified urinals.

More generally, the very idea of the public toilet is under threat. A report from UNISON has recently condemned local government cost-cutting for its impact on public toilet provision, with hard-pressed councils closing numerous sites – causing unnecessary distress to mobile workers (postmen, paramedics, bin men et al.) as well as the general public. The legacy of forwarding-thinking Victorian vestries, stung into action by feminist campaigners, is falling prey to twenty-first-century 'austerity'.

8

WRETCHED HOUSES

THROUGHOUT THE VICTORIAN era, intrepid social reformers ventured into London's slums and came back with horrifying first-hand accounts of urban poverty, written to prick the conscience of respectable society. Following the various government sanitary reports of the early 1840s, Charles Cochrane was one of the first to engage in this new investigative journalism. He made a series of forays into workhouses and lodging-houses for the *Poor Man's Guardian*, including lodgings in Field Lane, Holborn, the haunt of Irish immigrant labourers, where he uncovered 'dirt and effluvia both sickening and disgusting. . . . the smell so truly overpowering that I thought I should have been compelled for my own preservation to have immediately retired'.[1] Cochrane's published article included a striking accompanying illustration: a 'cutaway' drawing of a typical Field Lane lodging-house, the exterior stripped back to show the corruption beneath. Attic rooms packed full with single beds; a ground floor bereft of furniture, with bare boards and crumbling masonry; twenty or so wretches huddled around an open fire; a basement lined with excrement and filth, with an open privy. Sewers and sanitation might improve such places; public baths might cleanse the bodies of the poor; but there was a larger truth to lay before the public. The very fabric of slum housing was decrepit and filthy – ancient buildings on the verge of collapse, let and sublet to the verge of extinction – soot, grease and grime omnipresent – the legacy of decades of neglect by heedless landlords and impoverished, transient tenants.

Numerous 'social investigators' would follow Cochrane's example. Dramatic exposés of slum conditions would become a standard campaigning tool for social reformers, appearing in ever greater numbers from the late 1840s onwards. Authors would assure the reader that they were entering terra incognita, a netherworld, previously hidden from view:

> The condition of large sections of its inhabitants is wholly unknown to the majority of those above them in the social pyramid, the wide base of which is made up of poverty, ignorance, degradation, crime, and misery.[2]

Historians of the period have tended to take this assertion of unfamiliarity at face value, as if our ancestors were wholly incurious about the homes of the poor before Chadwick's inquiries of the 1840s.

In fact, Edwin Chadwick was not the first to posit a link between poor housing, dirt and disease; nor the first to propose a practical remedy.

The Society for Bettering the Condition and Increasing the Comforts of the Poor was an evangelical charity, founded in 1796. Its guiding lights included the Bishop of Durham, Sir Thomas Bernard, treasurer of the Foundling Hospital, and William Wilberforce, nemesis of the slave trade. Established in a period of poor harvests and unemployment, the charity disseminated pamphlets on practical improvements to help the lower classes through difficult times – 'cottage gardens for supplying the family with milk'; 'less exceptionable modes of assisting beggars'; 'public rooms for the industrious in cold weather' – documenting particular schemes which had been tried in different parts of the country. The Society's main tenet was that increasing domestic and workplace comforts would foster industrious habits and independence in the working man. This, in turn, would help to tackle a worrying dependency culture amongst the poor, who were increasingly reliant on parish relief. Chadwick would address the same issue by introducing the dehumanising utilitarian calculus of the 1834 New Poor Law. The Society had a more positive view of human nature. The aim was to stimulate 'that master spring of action on which equally depends the prosperity of individual and empires – THE DESIRE IMPLANTED IN THE HUMAN BREAST OF BETTERING ITS CONDITION'.[3] The Society was originally solely an information exchange for like-minded philanthropists and local officials. In 1801, however, its members resolved to embark upon their own practical scheme to aid the poor of the metropolis: establishing a fever hospital.

The fever in question was typhus, otherwise known as 'gaol fever' or 'hospital fever', a potentially fatal contagion, with a mortality rate of between 20 and 45 per cent.[4] Typhus was a disease that flourished periodically in dirty and overcrowded locations – ships, military encampments, hospitals, prisons, workhouses – and especially in slums. Symptoms included sore limbs, a weak and irregular pulse, profound headache, mental confusion and a high temperature. Whilst these symptoms were familiar, much else remained a mystery. Doctors believed that a range of 'predisposing causes' decided whether particular individuals might catch fever (which could include anything from negative emotional states to diet), but the precise mechanics of causation and transmission were impossible to fathom.[5] Breathing vitiated air seemed the most likely immediate 'exciting cause', particularly the exhalations of fever patients. Some argued that typhus was not contagious; others confused it with typhoid. Its true nature – *Rickettsia prowazekii* bacteria, carried by lice, infecting the patient through scratching or inhalation of lice faeces – would not be known until 1909.

The Society decided to set up a fever hospital for two reasons. First, London was in the throes of a typhus epidemic.[6] Second, despite uncertainty about typhus's aetiology and transmission, there was growing consensus about its treatment. Dr John Haygarth's rules on treatment of fever patients were becoming widely accepted: the necessity of ventilation; the need to cleanse clothes and the sickroom, avoid intimate contact and isolate the infected. The project was an opportunity to put the latest theory into practice; and it had every chance of success. In his practice at the Chester Infirmary in the 1780s Haygarth had proven the effectiveness of isolating fever patients and enforcing meticulous cleanliness. Isolation wards had begun to appear in other hospitals in the North of England. Manchester had gone one stage further and opened a separate 'House of Recovery' for its fever patients in 1796, which had proved highly successful.[7] The capital, on the other hand, although it had a dedicated smallpox hospital from 1746 onwards, possessed no special facilities for 'contagious malignant fever'. London hospitals only isolated their venereal patients – a moral stand rather than a medical one; and, in fact, many refused fever patients admission.

The Society assembled over a dozen doctors from metropolitan hospitals and dispensaries who all testified to the need for a specialist fever hospital in London. There were also encouraging signs from another quarter. The Smallpox Hospital, which already practised inoculation, had just begun to conduct trials of vaccination using cowpox. The practice was controversial but promised to be successful. With vaccination for smallpox, and isolation wards for typhus, it seemed possible that two long-standing scourges of the urban poor might be dramatically reduced or even eradicated. As one eager supporter put it: 'What a diminution of misery and mortality does such a prospect hold out to mankind!'[8]

The site chosen for the London 'House of Recovery' was Constitution Row, a terrace of houses along the northern-eastern portion of Gray's Inn Road. Neighbours were dismayed at the prospect, fearing it would only serve to spread disease. Legal advice was required, before the hospital had even opened, when local residents threatened to sue the charity for creating a public nuisance. The location, however, was a good one. Firstly, it was only a brief walk from the Smallpox Hospital at Battle Bridge, allowing the doctors to share expertise. Secondly, although the plot opposite the hospital was still open fields, the site was only half a mile from one of the greatest breeding grounds of fever in the capital: the slums of Holborn. This district, which Cochrane would investigate half a century later, was known locally as 'Little Ireland'. The proximity was important, for the doctors planned not only to treat patients in hospital but to arrange 'cleansing and purifying of the apartments[,] furniture and clothes of those in whose habitation a contagious disease has subsisted or is likely to appear'.[9] The infamous backstreets of Holborn would provide a conveniently situated test-bed for a novel public health programme; a groundbreaking exercise in preventive medicine which might eventually be extended to the whole metropolis. Thus, the very first practical measure undertaken by the new hospital – before the building itself was prepared – was the despatching of a 'sub-Committee' of three doctors to seek out fever cases, 'with authority to direct the white-washing with hot lime' – to disinfect London's slums.

The sub-Committee was in action for several months before the House of Recovery opened. We know this from minutes and a series of published case studies, disseminated by the Society, dated between July and October 1801.[10]

In these studies, the circumstances of individual fever patients are described in detail:

> Nicholas Terry, his wife, and two small children, reside in a narrow room, on the ground floor, in Lumley's Rents, near Chancery-lane. They had very lately arrived from Ireland, when the wife was attacked by fever, from which she partially recovered in a few days; but, at the end of about a fortnight, relapsed; and, at the same, the man became affected in a violent degree. From the closeness of the room (occasioned chiefly by impossibility of opening the windows) and the evident infectious nature of the disease, none of their neighbours would venture to their assistance . . .[11]

Nicholas Terry's case was typical of conditions the sub-Committee encountered: a poor Irish family – a slum in Holborn – the house in bad condition – 'vitiated atmosphere'. Terry was first encouraged by a relative to apply to a hospital 'said to admit fever patients at all times, *as accidents*' (many hospitals refused contagious cases point blank; some took them in as emergencies). He travelled there in a hackney coach – an expensive business, risking transmitting disease to future occupants – only to discover he had been misinformed and was obliged to return home.[12] A bed was then found in another institution; and, after recovery, he returned home again. But re-infection followed; and, on the second occasion, the entire family was afflicted. The sub-Committee, upon inspection, found the family's accommodation 'extremely close and offensive, and the walls very dirty'. They persuaded the landlord to fix the windows, limewashed the walls – using a solution of lime in water, applied with a brush – and all was well (i.e. no further re-infection occurred).

The Terry case and others like it seemed to demonstrate the efficacy of cleansing slum apartments. The sub-Committee roamed through the capital during the summer and autumn, actively seeking out patients in their own homes – finding fever victims and cleansing rooms in Holborn, Clerkenwell, Finsbury, Covent Garden, Westminster, Whitechapel and St Pancras. In truth, they treated no more than a few dozen cases in total – but they seem to have met with little objection from the poor or their landlords.

Then the hospital itself opened its doors. Members of the sub-Committee were required to attend the wards and, frustratingly, there was no one to take their place. The hospital lacked manpower and funds to continue its more proactive efforts and investigate places where disease was 'likely to appear'. Whilst it retained an inspector to organise the limewashing and fumigating of homes of patients, i.e. those admitted to the hospital, wider ambitions had to be scaled back. Plans for multiple Houses of Recovery, dotted throughout the capital, were shelved.

The doctors, however, did not abandon hope. They looked to London's parish vestries and Poor Law authorities. Victims of fever were, after all, a drain on the public purse, filling workhouse infirmaries, spreading disease. The new hospital created new opportunities: the chance to identify the alleys and courts which were the recurrent sources of fever, by tallying up admission records. Once such hotspots were identified, the parish could wash and fumigate rooms, just as they cleansed roads outside. The hospital's founders would stress in their published literature that the poor might pass on typhus to their acquaintances – particularly those in service – who might, in turn, endanger the middle-class family. With parochial co-operation, the rot could be expunged at its very roots.

The first appeal to parish assistance was sent to St Andrew and St George, Holborn. A certain backstreet – Spread Eagle Court – had come to the Fever Institution's notice. It had furnished the House of Recovery with twenty-five patients within twelve months. The road lay just north of Holborn, on the eastern side of Gray's Inn Lane (a couple of hundred yards north of the modern-day Chancery Lane tube station). It was a long, dead-end courtyard, surrounded by old four-storey houses and accessed via a narrow entry between two shops. There were twenty properties in total, lining the sides of the court, inhabited largely by the Irish poor.[13] They lacked gardens or yards, and the population's accumulated filth went into the streets or cellars. In 1803, the Fever Institution's inspector reported wearily, 'patients are still frequently sent from the same place in every Stage of Fever, notwithstanding the repeated use of Nitrous Fumigation and Whitewashing'.[14] The court was too filthy for a merely reactive approach in individual apartments. Thorough cleansing was required throughout.

The hospital's committee contacted the workhouse authorities for Holborn, and asked them to oblige. They received a half-hearted response. The officials in question were 'sensible of the advantages likely to result to the

THE CELLAR.

THE MODEL LODGING-HOUSE.

23 and 24 *Punch's Almanack for 1850* contrasts the accommodation offered by slum landlords, with that provided by model housing charities. In the slum, a dirty windowless cellar houses an entire family, as well as a coster's donkey. Rats swarm around the floor, the children are gaunt and sickly. One child carries a broken pitcher, containing the family's meagre ration of water. The model lodging-house, on the other hand, contains a stove for heat and cooking, the walls are papered, the floor has a rug, there is a dinner table with cloth and cutlery, and the family are full-faced and jovial. Signs of cosy domesticity abound – one child even spies a present, a doll, in her father's coat pocket. Books on shelves signify education and improvement, and the rooms have running water.

25 Annoyed by public urination against their buildings, the owners of private property in Georgian and Victorian London constructed 'ridiculous barricadoes and shelves, grooves, and one fixed above another, to conduct the stream into the shoes of the luckless wight who shall dare to profane the intrenchments.' These were reportedly in every alley and court, whereas now only a solitary row of these shelves survives in Cliffords Inn Passage, off Fleet Street (the building to which they are attached dates from the 1830s).

26 One of numerous estates of 'model dwellings' built by the Peabody Donation Fund, provided by the American entrepreneur and philanthropist George Peabody (1795–1869). These carefully managed estates provided flats for the working class at 'moderate rentals'. Peabody buildings were criticised by some as resembling workhouses or barracks, rather than homes, and here we see the railings, warning notices and monolithic apartment blocks which drew such criticism. The only disorderly element in the picture is anti-Semitic graffiti, partially hidden by the parked cart: 'No Jews Allowed'.

27 The Victorian slum encompassed everything from jerry-built workers' cottages to decaying, neglected middle-class homes, fallen into multiple occupancy. Here we see the latter category. Clare Market, north of the Strand, was a notorious slum of crumbling tenements, known for its cheap butchers' ('It is meat, and you take it on faith that it is meat of the ox or sheep; but beyond that you can say nothing.') The area would be levelled for creation of the broad avenue of Kingsway and the graceful curve of the Aldwych in the early 1900s, combining road-building with slum clearance. Clare Market, in turn, would become home to the London School of Economics.

28 A slum scene at the end of the nineteenth century. The wallpaper and framed pictures suggest this is not absolute poverty, but the floor is dirty, the children have ragged clothes, and a bed is squeezed into the corner of the room. The mother and daughters are engaged in piece-work, putting together brushes, working fibres into ready-made holes, and securing them with wire. Such work, returned to a wholesaler when completed, would typically earn a meagre halfpenny per brush.

29 Link-boys appeared whenever there was a thick fog. These were youths with flaming torches, offering to guide Londoners through the impenetrable darkness, for a small fee. Pea-soup fogs were also a boon to criminals, not least the so-called 'garotters' who performed street robberies (the stranglehold was supposedly the mid-Victorian mugger's favourite technique). Hence the gentleman in this *Punch* cartoon from 1865 is armed with a pistol – although the cheeky torch-bearing youths are not impressed.

THE FOG, JANUARY 21ST., 1865.

Link-boys (Masters of the Situation). " IF YER DON'T GIVE US A SHILLIN' WE'LL SINGE YER WHISKERS ! "

IMPORTANT MEETING OF SMOKE MAKERS.

30 *Punch* (20 August 1853) depicts a gathering of 'smoke makers' of the metropolis, debating the Smoke Nuisance Abatement Bill of 1853, which demanded breweries, factories and steamboats introduce smoke consuming furnaces. The picture not only includes comic caricatures of the commercial interests who were actually opposing the bill, but a young swell smoking a cigar, and a chimney sweep.

Loox on London with its Smells—
Sickening Smells!
What long nasal misery their zealous foe—
tells!
How they trickle, trickle, trickle,

On the air by day and night!
While our thoraxes they tickle,
Like the fumes from brass in trickle,
Or from naphtha all alight!
Making stench, stench, stench,
In a worse than witch-broth drench,

Of the musk-maladoration that so nauseously
wells
From the Smells, Smells, Smells, Smells,
Smells, Smells, Smells—
From the fuming and the spuming of the
Smells.

31 A *Punch* cartoon from 1 November 1890, bemoaning the 'Smells, Smells, Smells' of the metropolis. The aroma of rotting rubbish, sewers and chimneys combine to create a fearful mephitic spectre. The accompanying rhyme, however, focuses more on the nuisance of the stench ('nasal misery . . . our thoraxes they tickle') rather than any medical danger. By the 1890s, the mid-century terror of 'miasma' as the source of disease had somewhat receded.

"IT'S AN ILL WIND THAT BLOWS NOBODY GOOD."
Scene—*A Suburban Road after the last Snow.*
Chorus of Small Boys. "Yer *must* 'av it dun now, Mum. Th' P'liceman's a-comin'!"

32 The Metropolitan Paving Act of 1817 made it obligatory for all householders to clear snow from the pavement in front of their home. Householders, however, were loathe to carry out the task, and servants thought it beneath their dignity. Hence the work was performed – if at all – by enterprising gangs of men and boys, 'usually far from prepossessing in appearance, or in language', as in this cartoon from *Punch* (8 March 1879).

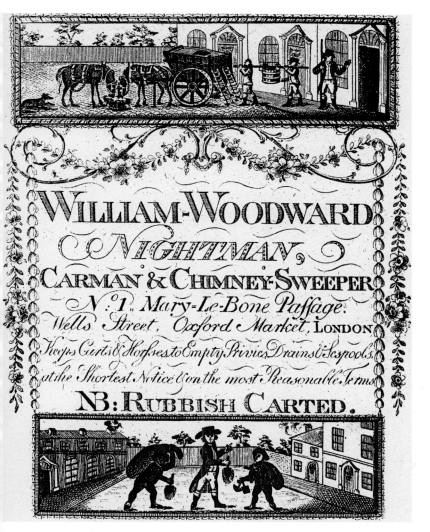

WILLIAM·WOODWARD

NIGHTMAN,

CARMAN & CHIMNEY·SWEEPER

Nº 1, Mary-Le-Bone Passage,
Wells Street, Oxford Market, LONDON
Keeps Carts & Horses to Empty Privies Drains & Cesspools,
at the Shortest Notice & on the most Reasonable Terms

NB: RUBBISH CARTED.

33 A trade card for a London nightman, William Woodward, advertising his availability to empty drains and cesspools. Cesspools were only emptied once a year or so, and hence being a nightman was rarely a full-time job. Instead, the work was normally undertaken by those whose day job had some connection to household dirt (chimney sweeps, scavengers, and even the bricklayers, who built cesspools). The work involved shovelling and scooping the accumulated filth into buckets, transferring it to carts, ultimately to be sold as fertiliser. It was restricted to the hours of darkness, as the smell was a public nuisance, thus *night*-soil, *night*man.

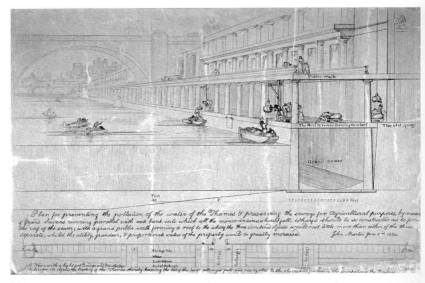

Plan for preventing the pollution of the water of the Thames & preserving the sewage for Agricultural purposes, by means of grand sewers running parallel with each bank, into which all the minor drains should fall. Wharfs should be so constructed as to form the roof of the sewer; with a grand public walk forming a roof to the whary the three combined objects would cost little more than either of the three separate; whilst the utility, grandeur, & proportional value of the property would be greatly increased.   John Martin June 2ª 1834

34 The painter John Martin (1789–1854) presented his plans for a Thames embankment, composed of tiered colonnades, to the 1834 Select Committee on Metropolis Sewers. The classical splendour would conceal a 'grand sewer' running alongside the river, anticipating Joseph Bazalgette's intercepting sewer built into the 1860s Thames Embankment. Martin's obsession with drawing up plans for London's water supply and sewerage contributed to his near bankruptcy in the 1830s.

35 Joseph Whitworth (1803–87), the famous mechanical engineer and inventor, patented a besom cart in 1842. The horse-drawn machine, which had rotating brushes sweeping up street mud into its central container, was adopted by some metropolitan authorities. The machine was, however, expensive to operate and cumbersome, unable to reach nooks and crannies. It was cost-effective on wide, flat stretches of road, but its bulk meant that it was liable to damage the easily-pitted macadam that covered most of London's streets.

36 A group of City of London officials and a *Strand Magazine* reporter exploring the Fleet sewer in 1898, one of London's oldest sewers. All are wearing the sewer worker's safety clothing: 'thick woollen stockings . . . huge waterproof boots reaching to the thighs . . . a rough blue smock, very similar to those worn by coastguardmen . . . oil-skin "sou'-westers" on our heads . . . and rough gloves, as we had to seize hold of things not very pleasant to touch.'

37 A model 'washing and drying compartment' for a public washhouse, by Price Pritchard Baly (published 1850). The idea was to provide neatly segregated units in which every woman could wash and dry clothes, without any contact with her neighbour. This would avoid any association with undesirable elements, and reduce the risk of theft. However, the use of individual heated drying closets proved uneconomical. Individual washing troughs were retained, but public baths and washhouses were increasingly constructed with communal drying-rooms.

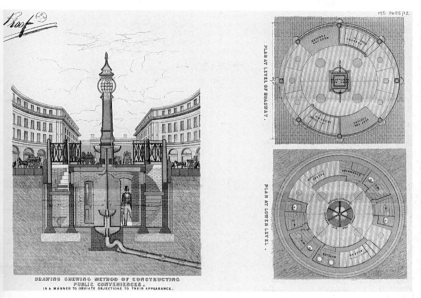

MS 1685/12.

PLAN AT LEVEL OF ROADWAY.

PLAN AT LOWER LEVEL.

DRAWING SHEWING METHOD OF CONSTRUCTING
PUBLIC CONVENIENCES.
IN A MANNER TO OBVIATE OBJECTIONS TO THEIR APPEARANCE.

38 A plan for building underground public toilets, by sanitary engineer George Jennings (1810–82). This copy was despatched to Capt. Francis Fowke, Director of Works at South Kensington Museum, with a view to it appearing in the 1862 International Exhibition. Jennings' scheme was originally brought before City of London officials in 1858, but rejected. Jennings blamed their squeamishness about discussing bodily functions. The City would eventually reverse its decision, three decades later. The first metropolitan underground convenience opened outside the Royal Exchange in 1885.

39 and 40 Photographs of the first- and second-class men's pools at Lambeth Baths, opened in 1897. By the 1890s, local authorities competed to build large and ornate swimming baths, symbols of municipal ambition. The typical first-class pool of the 1890s was much more splendid than its mid-century predecessor and hence more differentiated from second-class. Here we see ornate ironwork and lamps, a comfortable viewing gallery for watching sporting events and competitions. Note also the archetypal Victorian signifier of first- and second-class bathing: private changing-cubicles were the preserve of the middle-class.

poor by promoting more general admission of Patients into the house of recovery' (i.e. infectious patients not entering the workhouse) and committed to pay two guineas towards the treatment of any pauper afflicted by fever. This was welcome, although not what had been intended. The parish's paving committee, furthermore, promised to ensure that the yard would be thoroughly cleansed by their contractor. There was, however, no commitment beyond carrying out the exterior 'scavenging' – the removal of filth from the road, according to the already existing arrangement. The interior of the fever-ridden apartments remained a matter for the landlord or the hospital.

Admittedly, the response could have been worse. The parish officers of St Giles had been asked, earlier in the year, to arrange for the burial of a pauper who had died in the House of Recovery. They had responded dourly 'where the tree had fallen, it might lie'.[15] The doctors persisted, undaunted. When hotspots of fever were located, their inspector would contact the relevant local authority.[16] Typhus flared up again in Spread Eagle Court in 1805 and, following advice from the hospital, St Andrew's ordered their officials to keep a stringent check on street cleaning and rubbish collection, demanding 'an extraordinary degree of cleanliness'.[17] Again, this was not going as far as the doctors hoped; but it was something. Other parishes were more grudging. The parish clerk of St Sepulchre's, for example, notified about the dirty condition of Wright's Buildings, Chick Lane, took six months to reply. He claimed the street was 'frequently attended unto by the Scavengers and not in such a filthy state'; he blamed any dirt on 'the lowest sort of Irish People . . . very far from being cleanly in themselves or dwellings'.[18]

By the end of the decade it had become obvious that the relationship between parishes and the Fever Institution would never develop into any kind of serious partnership – most parishes adopted the attitude of St Giles and St Sepulchre. There were exceptions. The managers of workhouses were generally keen to despatch infected paupers to the House of Recovery, even if they were obliged to pay a couple of guineas. The riverside parish of Shadwell, facing an outbreak of typhus in its workhouse during April 1812, would eagerly submit the entire building to cleansing and fumigation, under the watchful eye of Dr Bateman, the Fever Institution's chief physician. The workhouse, however, was parish property, its expensive management a subject of intense interest to the ratepayers. The slums themselves were another matter – private property, not public business. It was difficult enough to arrange for normal scavenging, let alone cleansing of whole buildings. Parish contractors were consistently loath to engage with the poorest areas.

The early ambition of thoroughly cleansing the capital's slums of fever would, therefore, remain unfulfilled – a victim of lack of resources and parochial inertia. The homes of Fever Institution patients would receive a visit from the hospital's inspector; as well as an offer to wash all the household's clothes. Neighbours, no matter how pestiferous their conditions, would not be disturbed.

For a while, this actually seemed enough. From 1805 to 1816, the House of Recovery treated fewer than a hundred patients per annum, although there were concerns that its existence had not been sufficiently publicised. The Society looked fondly on its offspring and blithely declared that it had annihilated typhus in the capital, suggesting that 'without gross neglect and inattention, it is likely never again to be a prevalent or fatal disease in the Metropolis'.[19] Such hubris could not go unpunished.

The winter of 1816/17 was a time of scarcity and general distress which saw an unexpected rise in fever cases. This prompted relocation of the hospital to larger premises, containing 69 beds instead of 16. The following year, the new House of Recovery would treat a record 800 patients. Anxious parishes, faced with a new epidemic, became slightly more co-operative. They assisted in removing clothes and bedding from the worst-afflicted locations, destroying the infected articles and supplying fresh ones. The Fever Institution's annual reports, meanwhile, would continue to stress the need for comprehensive intervention in the slums, 'an undertaking of no small difficulty, requiring the co-operation of zeal, intelligence, and labour; of professional, parochial and perhaps legislative support'.

Parishes, however, always lost interest. Localised outbreaks of fever subsided; and no one wished to engage in expensive ongoing cleansing. Vestries did occasionally interfere and take steps to cleanse individual apartments, but only rarely – for example when rotting bodies had been kept too long amidst the living ('coffins have been sent and the bodies removed and placed in a vault under the church until interment, and the rooms limewashed at the expense of the parish').[20]

The most depressing aspect of the resurgence of typhus – at least, for the medical men of the Fever Institution – was that it haunted the same locations where it had prospered in 1801. In other words, after nearly two decades of treatment, limewashing and fumigation, there was no sign of progress; dirt and slumdom seemed to have triumphed.

This was more or less the view that prevailed at the time; and partly explains the relegation of the Fever Institution's early work in the slums to the footnotes of history. Yet the doctors' ongoing efforts would have an important sanitary legacy. Thomas Southwood Smith would be appointed as the Fever Institution's chief physician in 1824. His experience of fever patients – and the hospital's intervention in their homes – would inform his writing on fever and public health, heavily influencing Edwin Chadwick's views on 'removable causes'.

Chadwick, of course, became consumed with reforming sewerage; but he did not dismiss household cleansing. Indeed, he took an early and active interest in its sanitary possibilities. In 1839, under the authority of the Poor Law Commission, he recommended that Poor Law Unions should employ the Metropolitan Police Courts Act to enforce interior cleansing of filthy properties. The legislation, a single sanitary clause tacked on to a bill regulating magistrates' courts, was rather imperfect, not least in that it put the onus on occupiers rather than landlords.[21] Nonetheless, it allowed Chadwick to demonstrate a possible way forward in the wake of his 1838 East End reports. Parish officials often visited the homes of the poor to assess or provide 'relief' and could serve as a makeshift medical police; and the threat of prosecution could prompt improvements. In Bethnal Green, one landlord readily submitted: 'the furniture of the houses was taken out and washed; the houses were lime-washed'. The Strand Union found likewise, that the necessary cleansing was performed by the owners at the mere threat of legal action.[22] Others were more truculent – but, for Chadwick, this only showed the need for better legislation and more rigid, centralised medical policing.

Ten years later, Chadwick still believed in the merits of cleansing individual apartments. The General Board of Health, which included Southwood Smith as its medical expert, faced with a new cholera epidemic, would stress the benefits of house-to-house visits and limewashing filthy rooms. Just as in 1801, the poor were generally grateful, appreciating 'the fresh smell of the lime, and its light and agreeable effect on the black and dirty walls'.

Support from parish vestries and Poor Law authorities, however, varied from district to district. The 1850 report of the General Board on the epidemic stressed that cleaning rooms was 'more effectual than had heretofore been understood'.[23] The question was how to make vestries' and paving boards' sanitary efforts consistent and universal, rather than reliant on the whim of individual districts and prompted solely by outbreaks of disease. In 1850 this was not easily resolved, given the hostility of the London parishes to Chadwickian centralisation. Indeed, for all the sanitary reports of the 1840s, and the establishment of the General Board of Health, this was the problem that had thwarted the Fever Institution in the early 1800s, whether in Spread Eagle Court or elsewhere – parishes' lack of enthusiasm for spending money on sanitary improvement. Lord Ashley, serving on the General Board, recognised the difficulty all too well. The 'obstinate and parsimonious wretches' who composed parish vestries, the Poor Law authorities and paving boards, had no long-term interest in sanitary matters. Shaftesbury reflected dolefully, 'The cholera, thank God, has passed – is not the wholesome fear passing also?'[24]

There were other approaches to removing filthy slums: one radical possibility was demolition.

Government finances were tight in the 1830s, but there remained parliamentary enthusiasm for the expensive business of 'metropolitan improvement', repeating the grand success of Nash's Regent Street and driving broad, straight new roads through the old, congested quarters of the capital. It would be wrong to claim that street improvements projected in the 1830s, and carried out in the 1840s, were designed principally to clear the capital's 'rookeries' – the great goal was to open up new traffic routes – but the side-benefits of wholesale destruction were well recognised. These included clearing out the undesirable elements who tended to congregate in the oldest, most neglected parts of the city; and destroying the 'plague spots' in question. Moreover, the poor lived where rents were cheapest; and the government preferred to buy up land where landlords needed the least compensation. Thus, slums were always in the path of development.

The most famous example of slum clearance in this period took place in St Giles (the district immediately south of the British Museum). This decaying warren of narrow streets, alleys and courts – known for hooliganism and vice – was the principal obstacle to easy communication between Oxford Street and the City of London and an obvious location for a new thoroughfare. Thomas Donaldson, chairman of the Westminster Commission of Sewers, testified before a select committee as early as 1835 that a new street cutting through St Giles 'would relieve this neighbourhood from a very vile class of occupants'.[25] It did not matter, he argued, that this had long been a 'low' district. The new street, with fine new buildings, would bring 'a more respectable class of occupants' and a domino effect would induce landlords in the surrounding roads to improve their property and acquire more lucrative tenants. A local resident confirmed the prevalence of filth, poverty, crime and disease, declaring St Giles a source of dangerous miasma, and noted that, 'owing to its ruinous and dilapidated condition, the district is incapable of improvement except by pulling the whole down'. He added, rather optimistically, that it would be for the residents' own good – they would retire to healthier parts of the metropolis and its suburbs. Others noted that a new road might clear 'all the low brothels in Buckeridge Street, Bainbridge Street, Church Street and the adjoining rookery'.[26]

A scheme for a new road through the slum – 'New Oxford Street' – was approved and negotiations with existing landlords began in 1841. The level of compensation awarded by juries to freeholders and lessees, particularly shop-keepers, was higher than the government had hoped, and the Commissioners of Woods and Forests (the managers of Crown estates allotted the work) were obliged to borrow heavily.[27] Slum-dwellers were not keen to relocate: 'in some of the houses, though the roofs have been taken off, they still remain'.[28] Nevertheless, the street was finally opened in June 1845, with plate-glass-windowed shops on the ground floor of the new buildings on either side of the thorough-fare. By the following year, these were 'furnished with inviting wares and peopled with trim assistants'; and by 1847 an entire new road through to Holborn was completed. Some quibbled at the 'meanness' of the architecture, compared with Regent Street, but the *Illustrated London News* remarked that the new street had 'swept away the filth of St. Giles's' and possessed a 'splendid appearance'.[29] The *Lady's Newspaper*, keen to plug a new shopping street, waxed lyrical: 'the most loathsome of the haunts of vice and infamy . . . St. Giles converted into streets of palaces, is a transformation that outvies any in the marvel-abounding Arabian Nights'.[30]

It soon became clear, however, that the 'filth of St. Giles' had been, as it were, only swept under the carpet. Half the original slum had been spared the sledgehammer, to keep costs down. The result was that Church Street, to the south, just yards from the Arabian delights of New Oxford Street, offered a marked contrast to its commercial neighbour: 'a roadway strewn with every species of filth, the playground of children, covered with rags, and the loitering place of their idle and squalid parents'.[31] The road had never been pleasant but many of the residents evicted during the clearance had simply moved next door into its already foul and crowded houses. Twelve properties, which contained 277 inhabitants in the 1841 census, were found to contain 463 in 1848. Rooms were overcrowded and dirty ('the loaded atmosphere having reduced everything to a dull earthy tint'); drainage non-existent; cesspools overflowing. Rents, perversely, grew higher due to the competition for space, even as conditions grew worse ('he had had the greatest difficulty in finding a place to shelter his head at 2s. 6d. a week or 3s. 6d. a week').[32] Residents wrote a pathetic, semi-literate letter to *The Times*, which the newspaper dutifully printed with misspellings intact ('Preaye Sir, com and see us, for we are livin like piggs, and it aint faire we shoulde be so ill treted').[33] The paper then published details of the absentee landlords who owned the property in Church Street (an aristocratic member of parliament and a colonel) and attempted to shame them into action with a public lesson in slum economics:

> . . . no less than 2850 persons crammed into 95 wretched houses, on 1 1/10th acre of ground. Sir John Hanmer is, we believe, the proprietor of these houses, and underlets them in batches, at the rate of about 20*l*. per house per annum, to lessees who sublet them singly at 35*l*. each to a third class of speculators, who again let out the single rooms at a further advance, to a fourth order of tenants, whose lucrative trade consists in a fifth subletting of the space, as nightly shelter, at 3*d* per head, to those wretched outcasts whom crime or misfortune has reduced to the very lowest grade of the social scale . . .[34]

The street remained, however, notoriously bad; landlords and their middlemen indifferent. With cholera rearing its head again in 1849, the residents of New Oxford Street even raised 'hoardings 20 feet high' to keep 'the loathsome exhalations of this urban jungle' from their windows.[35]

Demolition, in short, was no answer to slumdom without provision for the displaced; it only concentrated the poison.

There was a third way of tackling the slum problem which seemed to offer more hope: building new, improved housing. Whilst some argued that the 'pig made the stye' (that it was the low morals and slovenly habits of the poor that always ruined their accommodation), others took the contrary view. They conceded that the poor might need education in habits of cleanliness, but no amount of scrubbing would repair rotten floorboards, fix broken windows or replace crumbling plaster. The basics of housing had to be rendered decent and wholesome; and it was simplest to start from scratch.

Chief amongst those interested in housing was Lord Ashley, a reforming politician, who had already campaigned on factory working hours and child labour. Ashley, like Southwood Smith and many others, was driven by his evangelical beliefs. He saw housing as an arena in which Christian charity might effect not only physical but moral improvement – and, indeed, save souls. Living amidst filth and decay was morally degrading. It distracted one from higher things, particularly the message of the Gospel. It led to intemperance, because the public house offered superior comforts. There were also fears, in the age of Chartism, that it bred revolutionary discontent. The comforts of a clean home, on the other hand, created a placid proletariat: 'the man who loved his home was generally a man who loved his country'.[36] The powerful, beneficent moral influence of 'home' extended to personal morality. Those who possessed decent homes, perhaps with a neat window box to add a little gaiety, were softened by their environment. As a latter-day sanitarian remarked: 'I do not believe that a man who is fond of his flowers could ever thrash his wife.'[37] For Ashley, the idea of placing the poor in decent housing had an enduring appeal that went far beyond public health – a fresh start for both body and soul.

The only question was: who might provide this new accommodation. The idea of central or local government providing housing for the poor was anathema in the laissez-faire 1840s. The state had no business interfering in the Englishman's castle. Such a move would undermine the workings of the New Poor Law and the position of existing landlords, the 'little shop-keeping class of persons' who also tended to dominate parish vestries.

Could charities play a part? Or private enterprise? The answer was both – simultaneously. Lord Ashley's solution was to combine philanthropy and speculation into a hybrid – and produce 'model housing'.

The model housing movement began at a public meeting on 15 September 1841 with a scheme to beat the slum landlords of London at their own game.

The Metropolitan Association for Improving the Dwellings of the Industrious Classes would build modern, clean and decent accommodation for the poor as a social enterprise. Rents would not exceed existing levels, and the return to investors would be restricted to 5 per cent of net profits (with limited liability for investors in the event of financial disaster). The proposal was for a commercial speculation of sorts, but 'of a very safe and honourable kind' – what we might now dub an ethical investment. The Metropolitan Association would aim to provide housing both for its own sake and as a 'model' for other right-minded speculators; and shame existing landlords into making improvements. Leading lights of the new association included Lord Ashley, the Earl of Devon; Lord Ebrington, Lord Morpeth and Lord Russell. Many of these notables had previously been taken on tours of the slums by Southwood Smith, following his report on the East End in 1838.[38] The doctor had shown them the despicable conditions in which families were paying three shillings a week for a single room, and they had been suitably astonished.[39] They were persuaded it was possible to construct 'buildings, airy, comfortable, well-drained and well supplied with water' for the rent that currently purchased dirt and degradation.

The accumulation of sufficient capital for a large-scale experiment, however, proved a long and drawn-out business. Lord Ashley, impatient for progress, embarked on a smaller scheme, which would focus more on 'models' (rather than creating large numbers of properties). He staged a takeover of an existing, moribund national charity – the Labourer's Friend Society, previously concerned with agricultural poverty. He reinvigorated it as the Society for Improving the Condition of the Labouring Classes (hereafter SICLC), whose first object would be 'the improvement of the Dwelling-houses of the poor in town and country'. Ashley would reference both the tracts of the Society for Bettering the Condition and Increasing the Comforts of the Poor and Chadwick in his inaugural speech – and impress upon his audience the need for taking practical steps, rather than mere pamphleteering.[40]

In truth, there was little difference between the Metropolitan Association and the SICLC. Both had plans for developing model housing and establishing savings banks; they shared many of their patrons and supporters. The SICLC touted a scheme for allotments for the poor, which soon proved impracticable in the metropolis (the savings banks idea, likewise, came to nothing). There was little else to tell them apart. It would be the SICLC, however, that became the first body to complete purpose-built housing for the poor in London. It acquired a strip of land from Lord Calthorpe, one of its supporters, and built a small 'model street' of two-storey terraced houses, just off the Gray's Inn Road (the site is now occupied by the King's Cross Holiday Inn). The street's architect, Henry Roberts, noted that local residents complained about the project, although the district, behind the Middlesex House of Correction, was only borderline genteel. They feared 'a non-descript pile of pauper buildings'.[41] Instead, in the spring of 1846, they got a very plain street of 'two-up, two-down' workers' cottages, somewhat cramped, some split into two-room flats, others serving as two-bedroom houses, as well as a lodging-house for poor widows. There was nothing particularly innovative in the design beyond ensuring the provision of water, water closets and wash-houses for laundry – but it was a start.

The Metropolitan Association, having finally acquired a royal charter and sufficient funds, would open its first buildings on Old St Pancras Road in 1848. This was a larger endeavour: a five-storey block of two- and three-room flats – 110 units in total – in a grand but somewhat barrack-like building. Each set of rooms contained a water closet, boiler, oven and dust-shoots to a communal bin. The grounds were railinged off so that children could play outside (and so that strangers did not intrude); and a washhouse and drying ground were provided at the rear. References were required from those seeking accommodation, and strict rules of conduct laid down – but this proved no deterrent to would-be tenants. There was soon a long waiting list for tenancies. The Metropolitan Association continued its work with a second development, in Spitalfields, principally containing rooms for single men, with an extensive coffee-room (alcohol being strictly forbidden) and reading room, 'warmed by open fires, and furnished with some of the daily papers and popular periodicals'. Communal kitchen and cooking facilities included 234 individual meat safes, one for each resident; as well as the option to purchase hot meals from an in-house canteen. Inhabitants were required to be 'domestic, methodical, and clean; to live by rule; and, above all, to pay one's rent punctually at the stipulated time'.[42] This was quite typical of the model housing movement: the 'model' provided was more than model housing; it was also a model of respectable conduct.

Other buildings would follow. Ashley succeeded in interesting Prince Albert in the work of the SICLC. Ashley felt sure that royal patronage would not only be good publicity but would accomplish a moral purpose – to bring the common people and aristocracy back into sympathy and 'stifle Chartism'. The Prince famously would sponsor a pair of semi-detached model houses for families, designed by Roberts, to be displayed in the grounds of the Cavalry Barracks in Hyde Park during the Great Exhibition (then reconstructed in Kennington Park, where they remain to this day). Model dwellings now had the royal seal of approval.

The accommodation provided in model housing was undoubtedly superior to what was on offer in their immediate surroundings. They were also seemingly successful as sanitary projects. Southwood Smith later noted, triumphantly, of the 1848/49 cholera epidemic, that 'no case of cholera occurred in any one of these [model] dwellings, though the pestilence raged in all the districts in which they are situated'.[43] The figures for infant mortality and typhus also seemed to bear out the claim that model dwellings were innately healthy. Some had feared that packing the working classes close together would engender fever. In fact, the strict cleanliness, ready water supply and good sewerage proved the sanitarian belief in 'removable causes'.

Still, a handful of much trumpeted developments made little difference to the many thousands still living in poor housing. And whilst there was much praise for the philanthropy of Ashley et al., there was a problem. Capitalists did not pile into building model dwellings – there were larger profits to be had elsewhere, not least in the slums. Ashley was acutely conscious of this failing and the high cost of building from scratch. Therefore, in the early 1850s, he contemplated a new cheaper 'model' scheme: to reclaim and renovate existing slums. It would begin with Wild Court, off Drury Lane, and another ancient haunt of poverty – Tyndall's Buildings, formerly known as Spread Eagle Court.

The decaying courtyard in Holborn had not improved since it was first investigated by the Fever Institution. In the cholera epidemic of 1831/32, it was described as 'chiefly occupied by the lowest description of Irish people . . . a complete nuisance, and dangerous to the health of society'.[44] In 1834, a charitable school was established to provide a basic education for the 'children of the lower class in the neighbourhood' – who were promptly seen using their new-found book-learning to purchase 'books and pictures of an obscene description' (i.e. pornography) from a local shop.[45] Occasionally the violent antics of its denizens made the national press:

Two sisters, Honora and Eliza Foley, loose girls, who carry about fruit for sale, reside together in a disreputable way in Spread Eagle-court, with a fellow named O'Connell. On Wednesday they contrived to extract a sovereign from a man's pocket, when a dispute occurred as to the sharing of it between the three; a quarrel ensued, in consequence of Eliza Foley refusing to divide it, and a battle took place, in which knives, pokers, sticks and other weapons were used.[46]

The medical officer of the Holborn Union would single out 'Tyndal's Buildings [sic]' to Robert Slaney's 1840 inquiry as the most unhealthy part of the district, plagued by serious overcrowding and lack of drainage, as well as 'the filthy habits of the inhabitants'. Pigs were kept in the houses – a commonplace practice amongst the Irish poor, an investment which could be fattened, then sold or slaughtered.[47] Thomas Wakley, holding a coroner's inquiry into the death of a four-year-old child in a blaze in the court, was informed 'it was without exception the most filthy and abominable of all the dirty places in London'.[48]

The reason for the change of name to Tyndall's Buildings, c.1840, has been lost to posterity. Most likely it was the whim of a canny landlord, an attempt at 'rebranding' the street. Certainly, freeholders came and went with alarming rapidity. The properties, all in all, brought in around £200 p.a. in rent – a pleasant enough little income – and frequently changed hands.

Names of landlords come and go in the parish rate books; most too generic to trace – a 'Mr. Wright', a 'Mr. George'. There is passing mention of both a colonel and a clergyman – i.e. the unexceptional members of the middle class who inherited or invested in slum property. Samuel Addinsell, perhaps a little lower down the social scale, a Nottinghamshire-born tailor, held nos 1–16 during the mid-1840s. He had lived in the court in the late 1830s, but by 1843 removed to the rather more genteel Lamb's Conduit Street – perhaps on the strength of his profits as a landlord – only a five-minute walk to the north.

The most interesting identifiable landlord is one 'Mr. Gant', who held nos 17–20 from the late 1840s. This was Samuel Castle Gant, a Welsh civil engineer, elected to the Institution of Civil Engineers in 1839, erstwhile director of the Metropolitan Sewage Manure Company, son of the chairman of the Holborn and Finsbury Commissioners of Sewers. Gant was something of a sanitarian, publishing a rather inchoate commentary on the Public Health Act in 1855, in which he stated in his preface:

how little has been done to ameliorate the sanitary condition of any of our populous towns! . . . Another season of 'death, lamentation and woe' may probably soon appear when hundreds and thousands of victims may again be sacrificed to the absence of systematic sanitary measures, and the continued prevalence of laissez-faire.[49]

There is no mention in the many reports on Tyndall's Buildings that Mr Gant's properties were in a superior condition to their neighbours; or that Gant had made them the object of improvement. The posthumous charge of hypocrisy and cant is, therefore, hard to avoid. Indeed, many a respectable, middle-class Victorian had a similar dirty secret – as we have already seen with George Carden. It was easy enough to proclaim allegiance to the sanitary cause, harder to divest oneself of a profitable investment in some backstreet, alley or court.

Tyndall's Buildings first came to the attention of Lord Ashley and the SICLC through reports gathered for the General Board of Health during the cholera of 1848/49. In 1851, the Fever Institution was consulted. It was found that during a period of three months, the court had supplied 84 fever patients to the hospital.[50] The street's problems were long-standing – filth and overcrowding – but they had gone from bad to worse in the previous decade. In 1841, the court lodged roughly 120 men of working age. By 1851, there were more like 200 men, largely Irish labourers, many of whom had doubtless fled the Great Famine – not to mention, of course, women and children. In other words, the houses were full to bursting. George Godwin, campaigning editor of the *Builder*, was emboldened to pay a visit and found a single barrel of stagnant water serving all the domestic needs of two houses containing one hundred people.[51] Basements contained fetid refuse of every variety – 'ashes, rubbish, human faeces and offal of various kinds in great quantities'. The architect Henry Roberts, asked by the SICLC to look at how the court might be improved and remodelled, found himself almost incapable of stomaching the smell: 'returning home, I was, to use an expressive vulgarism, "as sick as a dog"'.[52] Ashley – now Lord Shaftesbury – testified that there were parts of the houses he could not visit, so 'utterly impossible was it for him to endure the virus and intensity of the horrible stench'.[53]

If the SICLC could reform such a place, then it could reform anywhere. Shaftesbury had an idea for Roberts to follow, apart from internal remodelling and renovation: knocking down the end houses to create a through road to the plot of land immediately to the east. This happened to be where a new church was mooted, to bring Christianity to the heathen slum-dwellers of Holborn (St Alban the Martyr, still standing). Clearing the two houses would serve a double purpose: street 'ventilation' – relief from miasma – and simultaneously, literally, leading the poor closer to God.

It would take some time to acquire the leases – Samuel Gant eventually settled on a rental of £60 p.a. from his new tenants, £10 or so above what he might have received from his slum-dwellers. The legal wrangling seems to have been settled by the end of 1855. There was some difficulty in emptying the filth-encrusted basements – three workmen were taken ill, afflicted by the 'foul effluvia' – but universal cleansing, plastering and whitewashing were soon under way: 'a set of dens and styes will be transformed into cleanly, orderly, and wholesome dwellings'.[54] In 1856, the *Builder* recorded the last days of the old buildings in a fine full-page sketch; and the following year included a picture of the improved street, with the two tumbledown houses at the end of the row replaced by a narrow, three-storey-high archway, providing the much desired ventilation.

The physical side of the remodelling was a success. Water closets, dustbins, properly ventilated rooms – all the features that created 'sanitary' accommodation were present and correct. The social aspect, however, was another matter. The sitting tenants were 'a dangerous company' whom George Godwin was happy to characterise as criminals ('who get a living, as a police officer said "goodness knows how, though you and I can guess, sir" '). The old inhabitants of Tyndall's Buildings 'did not care about changing, neither did they like to have much inquiry made'.[55] They had not been consulted about improving their dilapidated dwellings; and they did not wish to pay the SICLC's price for improvement in order to move back in. Partly this was a question of money. Whilst single rooms in the new buildings could be had for a range of prices comparable to the old, this equivalence was somewhat misleading. In the previous arrangement, no one cared how many friends and family shared a room – or even pigs. The cost of accommodation for any given individual was substantially increased by the scheme. There was also another unwelcome price to pay – conformity. The rules in SICLC accommodation were designed to enforce almost military order:

... no one will be allowed to remain on the lobbies or landing, or on the staircases at night. They must keep their rooms clean, and well-scrubbed once a week at least. They must keep their windows clean ... The stairs and landings must be scrubbed and washed down at least once a week; and the water-closets and galleries must be kept quite clean by the tenants in turn ... no persons will make their beds on the floor; nor will drunken and disorderly conduct be allowed, nor card playing nor gambling of any kind. The penalty for infringement of these rules is *instant dismissal.*[56]

Unsurprisingly, the ramshackle band of casual labourers and criminals who occupied the site were not inclined to remain. In a sense, this was all well and good – the Society had no objection to housing more select members of the working class, and by the 1861 census, only 15 per cent of male residents identified themselves as casual labourers (as opposed to about 70 per cent in 1851). But if the original tenants moved on, there was little difference between renovation and outright slum clearance – only that the cost of building was a little cheaper. The former tenants, moreover, would still spill over into the surrounding streets, increasing overcrowding – just as had happened in St Giles.

Tyndall's Buildings was, in fact, not terribly successful for the SICLC. Whilst the redevelopment of Wild Court on Drury Lane was making a healthy annual profit by the early 1860s, Tyndall's Buildings made an equivalent loss, and suffered from under-occupancy – most likely because of the sheer volume of cheaper slum accommodation in the vicinity.[57] For all the much publicised benefits of model housing projects – and many more schemes would follow, under the auspices of the Metropolitan Association, the SICLC and a slew of new organisations – their success and profitability were not guaranteed. Indeed, the Metropolitan Association would only manage to finally hit its target of a 5 per cent return to investors in 1873.[58]

Critics began to suggest that the economics of model housing did not quite add up. The requirement to turn a small profit and repay investors had one tendency: it induced associations to set rents which excluded the poorest of the poor – the very people who most needed assistance. In other words, it was nigh impossible to match or undercut slum rent *and* find profit for investors. Whilst philanthropy of any sort was praiseworthy, there was a danger that model dwellings provided help to those who could already help themselves – the artisan elite of the working class. Whether through clearance or 'improvement' – not to mention the large-scale demolition caused by the railways – the original slum-dwellers were being driven into worse and filthier dens.

The 1850s would, at least, see an attempt at regulating the worst buildings. In 1851, Shaftesbury introduced the Common Lodging Houses Act, which made police registration and inspection obligatory for the lowest class of nightly accommodation in the capital, containing about 80,000 'dossers'.[59] The keepers of lodging-houses had to regularly cleanse all surfaces, privies, drains and cess-pools, notify the local sanitary authorities and Poor Law authorities of any contagion, and apply limewash twice a year – or face hefty fines.

Benjamin Hall's 1855 reorganisation of London's local government, although designed to placate the anti-Chadwick lobby, also included a thoroughly Chadwickian sanitary measure: making the appointment of Medical Officers of Health obligatory for all the new vestries and district boards. Unlike pre-1855 parish medical officers, these would not be jobbing doctors, responding to the needs of the sick, but actual employees concerned with public health. They would report back to local government on the sanitary state of the district and enforce improvements.

The great inspiration – the proof that such medical policing might work – was Dr John Simon, Medical Officer of Health for the City of London since 1848. The legislation that established Simon's post – the City of London Sewers Act – had been drawn up to prevent the City falling under the central administration of the General Board of Health. Simon, however, was determined his role should not be a sinecure. He provided detailed and damning evidence of the need for reform, chiding the City Commission of Sewers, forcing them to fully employ the powers they had demanded for themselves, including 'the removal of offensive matter, the purification and whitewashing of premises, and the abatement of any nuisance arising in conditions of filth'.[60] The City soon gained a deserved reputation as the most sanitary-minded district in the metropolis, especially after a second act in 1851, which extended Simon's powers to include inspection of all houses and even allowed for demolition on the grounds of public health.

The role of the new Medical Officers was wide-ranging: gathering statistics on epidemic disease, monitoring the quality of food and drink, meat markets, slaughterhouses, and industrial pollution – but dealing with living conditions and dirt was fundamental to their work. They usually had assistance, supervising one or two Sanitary Inspectors, who visited premises, and served notices for improvement on negligent landlords ('It is requisite that the heaps of filth should be removed, the damp rotten woodwork of the ceiling cut away, and the remainder repaired, the lath and plaster made good, the walls painted or lime washed . . .').[61] The reason for inspection could include information provided by police or lodgers, but some districts also introduced regular systematic visits to the houses of the poor (the middle classes and above, of course, were exempt from such interference). Previous outbreaks of disease were a guide. The Medical Officer of St Giles, Thomas Hunt, a respected surgeon and skin specialist, began his term as Medical Officer with an inquiry into all the houses which were reported to have furnished victims in previous cholera epidemics.[62] Warning notices to landlords, drawn up by Sanitary Inspectors, would be approved by the Medical Officer, and possibly the district's Surveyor, depending on the nature of the complaint; then followed up by official letters. Finally, if no action was taken, there would be a prosecution before the local magistrate under the 1855 Nuisances Act or the London Metropolis Management Act. This was the system that would be used to ferret out the last remaining metropolitan cesspools, with each district keeping a proud tally of the number removed.

The Medical Officer also provided public health advice to the masses, principally via public notices pasted to the walls of the district. These 'Hints for the Preservation of Health' were widely distributed during outbreaks of contagious disease. A typical notice from St Mary Newington, drawn up in the cholera year of 1866, contains a virtual sanitarian creed for the working class:

> CLEANLINESS, domestic and personal is important. Limewash ceilings, passages, out-houses and privies. Sweep and scrub floors. Never let slops remain long about a room. Use soap and water freely to the body . . .
>
> FRESH AIR is necessary. Do not crowd together . . .
>
> WATER from a PUMP or WELL must not be drank [sic] . . .
>
> BAD SMELLS always have a cause, search for it at once . . .

This was the system so singularly lacking in the first half of the century. The Medical Officer of Health provided a standard means of monitoring and intervening in public health at the parish level, from prosecuting recalcitrant landlords to informing the general public of their rights and responsibilities.

By the 1860s, therefore, there was some cause for optimism. It seemed that everything was in place to improve the homes of the poor: local inspection would ensure that no one lived in insanitary conditions; model housing associations would provide improved accommodation. True, the problem of model housing being too expensive for the poorest had not been solved – but there were new bodies at work, pouring money into new projects. The Peabody Trust, established in 1862 by the American banker and philanthropist George Peabody, had a starting capital of £150,000, which its founder eventually raised to £500,000 – an enormous sum.[63] The Trust was persuaded by Shaftesbury to invest in model housing, and did so in style – constructing large, distinctive housing estates in yellow stock bricks, which are still used as social housing to this day. These were much criticised for their rather plain and brutal aspect ('costly edifices, in a style of building composed of the union workhouse and barrack orders of architecture').[64] The Peabody approach was also rather more spartan than the 'models' introduced in the 1840s, with shared lavatories and sculleries on common landings (supposed more 'sanitary' in that they allowed for easier inspection, and were marginally more distant from living quarters). Nonetheless, George Peabody's generosity promised to improve the living conditions of hundreds of Londoners, and model housing, two decades after its inception, once again became the focus of social reformers.

One such reformer, operating on a smaller scale, was Octavia Hill – the granddaughter of Dr Southwood Smith, who shared his evangelical bent. Miss Hill, with financial and moral support from family friend John Ruskin, invested in slum property – not as a speculation, but to show how it should be managed. She was convinced that existing model housing schemes were too expensive, both in construction and the rents they charged. She also considered the 'barracks' of Peabody et al. as impersonal and unhomely. The poor could not learn cleanliness and domesticity in such places. Her plan, therefore, was to purchase existing buildings in poor condition, but capable of restoration, occupied by the lower classes of workers. Unlike the SICLC, with its extensive remodelling, Miss Hill's idea was to use a gradualist approach, retaining as many current tenants as possible:

The repairs required were mainly of a superficial and slight character: slight in regard to expense—vital as to health and comfort. The place swarmed with vermin the papers, black with dirt, hung in long strips from the walls; the drains were stopped, the water supply out of order. All these things were put in order, but no new appliances of any kind were added . . .[65]

This would keep costs down and show other landlords that much could be achieved with minimal investment, whilst still making a profit. The tenants would be offered relatively low rents – at a price. They would be carefully managed, quizzed and inspected by female rent collectors, whom they would meet at least once a week. This somewhat inquisitorial regime (in which Miss Hill played an enthusiastic and active role) was intended to raise the moral and sanitary standards of residents. Miss Hill believed that 'the heavy incubus of accumulated dirt' was the result of neglect by landlord *and* tenant. She offered the poor a contract: she would act as the perfect landlady; they, in turn, had to be perfect tenants. They had to clean, maintain and brighten their homes according to her ideas of respectable domesticity. Those who preferred 'liberty, and dirt, and mess' to detailed scrutiny were swiftly evicted.

The great merit of Octavia Hill's work was that she catered for those a rung down on the social ladder from the artisan workers who tended to predominate in other schemes. Her tenants were not, as she sometimes claimed, the very poor – such folk remained in the lowest common lodging-houses, for a couple of pennies each night – but they were regular members of the working class. This was possible because rents were kept to a minimum; even to the extent of allowing whole families to live in single rooms, which others considered beyond the pale. Miss Hill, on the other hand, believed that any environment could be made good with due attention to cleanliness and a bit of gumption: 'I speak from experience when I say that I know numbers of the prettiest, happiest little homes, which consist of a single room.'

Miss Hill was an indomitable, forthright character – despite her fearsome matronly reputation, she began her life's work while still in her twenties – and became famous for her tireless efforts, adding more and more new properties with every passing year. Her methods appeared to offer a cheap 'self-help' solution to the problem of the slums without the need for massive investment. Rather, if landlords invested modest sums, and coaxed tenants into taking better care of their property, then both would profit.

The difficulty was that few slum landlords cared sufficiently about their tenants to invest even small sums in improving their tenements; and certainly not enough to employ rent collectors who took an active pastoral interest in their well-being. Even in a period not short on evangelical zeal, such efforts seemed too demanding: 'It requires very great personal attention. It is not everyone who is Miss Octavia Hill.'[66] For all Miss Hill's success, the funda-mental problem remained – larger profits could be made from exploiting insanitary slums to the hilt.

The model housing associations received a boost from the 1866 Labouring Classes Dwelling Houses Act, which allowed them to borrow government money cheaply for future projects. This was, in effect, a government subsidy for house building, although few dared put it so bluntly: no one was truly comfortable with the state interfering in such matters. One reason for this measure was that it was increasingly plain that the 'model' aspect of model housing was illusory – '5% philanthropy' had not exerted any moral sway over the property-owning class. Yet, even with this additional support, it was highly unlikely the associations could expand to replace the existing rented sector.

There was, of course, a radical alternative: the state itself might provide housing for the poor.

The idea had actually first been mooted in 1851, but with minimal response. Shaftesbury had pushed through 'An Act to Encourage the Estab-lishment of Lodging Houses for the Labouring Classes', which allowed vestries to build lodging-houses for the poor. Not a single London vestry had taken advantage of the legislation. The Act itself was too complex; the expense of legal proceedings too large. Vestrymen – many of whom, of course, were the owners of rented-out property – were not inclined to burden the rates. By the mid-1860s, however, the situation had changed. Vestries, thanks to the exer-tions of their Medical Officers of Health, were finally taking some interest in improving the slums. True, enthusiasm for sanitary matters varied from one district to another. Some Medical Officers complained that their employers provided little support for their efforts. But the principle that the slums *were* the concern of the local authority had been established. The MP William McCullagh Torrens then proposed moving things one stage further: a bill that allowed vestries to clear slum properties and build improved accommodation. If vestries were happy to build amenities like public baths, why not houses?

Torrens persevered with his bill in the face of relentless opposition – not least from several London vestries, which did not share his civic vision. After a tumultuous two years, during which time three versions of the bill were considered in parliament, the Artizans' and Labourers' Dwellings Act was passed in 1868. Unfortunately, the scope was much reduced from Torrens's original conception. Most importantly, the legislation only allowed local authorities to demolish, or compulsorily purchase, individual properties as 'unfit for human habitation' – *not* build new houses. There were issues of cost and complexity in utilising the legislation. Medical Officers of Health, whose professional association had supported Torrens, were also loath to demolish properties without having powers to rehouse. Demolition would only displace residents to nearby overcrowded dwellings – the old familiar problem. Medical Officers, charities and journalists criticised the inadequacies of the new law; more comprehensive legislation was required. The slums could not be tackled piecemeal: 'Whole blocks must be demolished, large spaces cleared . . . This is a great task, but it will have to be done, and the time perhaps is not distant.'[67]

Grudgingly, parliament paid heed. Yet more legislation was passed in the 1870s: the Artizans' and Labourers' Dwellings Improvement Act 1875 (also known as Cross's Act, after the Home Secretary who introduced it). The Metropolitan Board of Works, the great London-wide authority established in 1855, would be given the authority to carry out wholesale slum clearance (upon the receipt of a request from a local authority, and after obtaining permission from the Home Secretary). Two crucial provisions attempted to address the obvious objections: firstly, any scheme had to make provision for rehousing the displaced slum-dwellers after demolition; secondly, the building of new properties was to be the work of existing model housing associations. This was not unreasonable – housing associations were the experts in high-density housing for the poor. But it also indicated the reluctance of the government to get its hands dirty and actually build housing for the working class – that would be an unprecedented experiment in socialism. One member of parliament rhetorically declaimed: 'The next demand made of them might be to provide clothing, if not carriages and horses, for the poor.'[68] For many, whether Whig or Tory, house building was simply not the business of the state.

The 1875 Act would usher in a decade of slum clearance in the heart of the metropolis, albeit after a hesitant start on very familiar ground: the slums of Holborn.

Tyndall's Buildings had enjoyed two decades of the SICLC's benign administration, but it remained an oasis of cleanliness and working-class respectability, surrounded by some of the worst streets in London. Indeed, the condition of Holborn had worsened during the 1860s thanks to an influx of refugees from improvements made in the City of London. The creation of Farringdon Road, the Metropolitan Railway, the new Smithfield Market and the Holborn Viaduct and valley schemes had all pushed large numbers of the evicted poor into the nearest cheap accommodation – and many had sought refuge in the streets around Leather Lane and Gray's Inn Road. The Holborn District Board of Works made three separate entreaties to the City authorities in the early 1870s, reminding them that their improvement schemes had contained a commitment to rehouse the evicted.[69] In reality, the damage was already done.

Holborn, therefore, had been one of the few authorities desperate enough to make some use of Torrens's 1868 Act, ordering the demolition of a number of properties whose walls 'cracked and bulged so as to be in danger of falling'. In 1875, Holborn District Board likewise seized upon the new arrangements of the Artizans' and Labourers' Dwellings Improvement Act, and had their surveyor, Lewis Isaacs, draw up a proposal for a 10-acre slum clearance scheme (covering much of the ground between Gray's Inn Lane and Leather Lane – even the model lodgings of Tyndall's Buildings). This was to be wholesale improvement. Details were promptly forwarded to the Metropolitan Board of Works for approval and execution. The MBW conducted a thorough peram-bulation of the district. There was no disagreement that the area would profit from large-scale clearance – but then the difficulties began.

First of all, the MBW had doubts about the scope and legality of the project, since it included the widening of Gray's Inn Lane, which was not technically a housing improvement. This resulted in the original plan being reduced to a 4-acre scheme in committee – which the Home Secretary promptly rejected as a timid half-measure. Stung by this refusal, the MBW somewhat petulantly included Gray's Inn Lane as part of its programme of road improvements, under separate legislation.[70] They proposed widening the road from 30 to 60 feet, and stripping away the slum properties immediately adjacent (again, including Tyndall's Buildings). This did not require further rubber-stamping by the Home Secretary and compulsory purchase began in 1877. Unfortunately, compensation awards to landlords were substantial; and legal problems caused lengthy delays. The MBW's street improvement legislation limited clearance to fifteen houses at a time – and the rehousing of evicted tenants – before builders could move on to demolish more property. This was, theoretically, a safeguard against producing overcrowding in the vicinity. The practical impact was to made the clearance cumbersome, piecemeal and time-consuming.

The economics of the site also proved a stumbling block. Arbitrators began offering landlords full market value for their properties, regardless of their condition – with particularly large sums for those on the main thoroughfare of Gray's Inn Lane. The model housing associations, however, which the MBW hoped would then buy or lease the cleared space, could not afford to pay anything like commercial rates. This created an enormous deficit. The MBW estimated that utilising the land as model dwellings – i.e. selling the land at a price which would make the work viable for 5 per cent philanthropists – would involve a loss of £300,000 due to the high costs of compensation. This sum would ultimately have to be borne by the metropolitan ratepayer. The builders were told to stop work. Some houses, already compulsorily purchased, were left to fall into ruin, or demolished; others remained standing. Gray's Inn Lane, pockmarked by vacant lots and abandoned premises, became semi-derelict, 'a disgrace to London'.[71]

The chaos in Gray's Inn Lane led to relaxation of the legislative restrictions on how many properties could be simultaneously demolished by the MBW. Limits were placed on the level of compensation and the quota for rehousing was reduced to half the original residents (under the 1882 Artizans' Dwellings Act). Meanwhile, once the MBW finally accepted that making some loss on the deal was inevitable, the Peabody Trust stepped in. The Trust was a canny operator, and would acquire numerous sites throughout London at a knockdown price under the new regulations – much to the chagrin of its more financially straitened contemporaries.

All in all, this was an awkward period, with both the MBW and government fumbling to find a way forward. Finally, work went ahead. Tyndall's Buildings, the reformed slum, was itself quietly reformed out of existence, to allow for widening of the old thoroughfare. Gray's Inn Road (suddenly no longer 'Gray's Inn Lane' in its lower reaches) opened to the public in 1884, with the chairman of the MBW giving a rather partisan speech blaming central government for nigh on a decade of delay, beneath coloured flags and a banner bearing the word 'Progress'.

The Gray's Inn Lane debacle was something of a learning experience. The MBW would actually manage to clear 59 acres of central London during the 1880s and see 263 blocks of improved dwellings raised by the 5 per cent philanthropists.[72] The numbers entering this improved accommodation, however, were only a small percentage of London's workers. Moreover, the population of the metropolis was still growing; and other factors were putting pressure on housing and rents in the centre of the capital, not least a growing tendency to convert residential into commercial premises. One of the great debates in Gray's Inn Lane was whether the poor could be housed above commercial premises on the main thoroughfare. It was considered doubtful, even if entrances were placed at the rear. The lower classes 'might put objec-tionable things in their windows and deal with the property in all manner of ways', which would put off potential commercial tenants.[73]

There was, at least, one positive result of the MBW's struggles: the slum problem became the subject of renewed public interest. Campaigning jour-nalism also came back into vogue, with *The Bitter Cry of Outcast London: An Inquiry into the Condition of the Abject Poor* published anonymously by a Congregationalist minister, Andrew Mearns, in 1883. The sternly worded tract, written to promote Congregationalist missions in the slums, was much publicised by the sensationalist *Pall Mall Gazette*, and became a national talking point. Mearns denied that existing measures were improving the lives of the poor: 'THIS TERRIBLE FLOOD OF SIN AND MISERY IS GAINING ON US.' The poor did not attend church ('one street of Leicester Square contains 246 families, and only 12 of these are represented at the house of God'); their homes remained 'courts reeking with poisonous and malo-dorous gases arising from accumulations of sewage and refuse . . . dark and filthy passages swarming with vermin . . . black with the accretions of filth which have gathered upon them through long years of neglect'.[74] Many couples were unmarried; incest and sexual immorality were rife: 'no form of vice and sensuality causes surprise or attracts attention'; criminality was commonplace.

This was deliberately sensational stuff – although Mearns's pamphlet contained nothing particularly novel. The risk of incest when families shared a single bed had been aired in the 1840s. Regardless, Mearns did much to raise awareness, once again, of the living conditions of the urban poor. *The Bitter Cry* also marked something of a turning point in how the slum problem was conceptualised. In part, this was because the Chadwickian sanitarian agenda of the mid-century had reached its apogee with the completion of Bazalgette's sewers in the 1870s. Sanitary work now consisted of localised hard graft: small, gradual improvements in plumbing and sanitation; consolidation of legislation; Medical Officers of Health chipping away at recalcitrant landlords; the Board Schools and the likes of the Ladies' Sanitary Association educating the poor. It was well and good to be 'sanitary' – but not a cure-all.

In short, a more sophisticated argument began to take shape about the condition of the poor – their wages, rents, education, housing – and the role of the state. Was the free market capable of meeting the most basic needs of the 'abject poor' in the heart of the capital: the lowliest workers, who could not afford model housing? By the 1880s, the answer was plainly 'no'. Landlords, by and large, had refused to raise their standards. Equally, when standards were raised – by model housing – the poorest could not afford to participate. The rents and rules of the housing associations were not for the lowest of the low – and the poorest slum-dwellers fought shy of them. One maker of walking sticks, wife to a chimney sweep, told those who directed her to model housing that such organisations had no interest in her kind. Where would the sweep keep his dirty brushes? Or the costermonger 'dress' his fruit and vegetables, or tether the donkey that pulled his barrow? She was certain – with some justification – that such folk did not fit into the 'model' – they could not afford it; they were not wanted.[75]

Mearns believed that the state now had to intervene. The *Pall Mall Gazette*, in a leader entitled 'Is it not Time?', set the tone for future debate:

> What the evil is every one knows. It is the excessive overcrowding of enormous multitudes of the very poor in pestilential rookeries where it is a matter of physical impossibility to live a human life.[76]

As the 1880s progressed, 'overcrowding' gradually became the watchword, when once it had been 'miasma'. The sanitary requirement of cleanliness was now taken for granted; and it was not enough. In fairness, this process of redefinition – and more awareness of (un)affordability of housing – was partly thanks to the model housing movement. Four decades of housing association work had provided a modest 'model' of sorts – a definition of the basic level of provision required for the working man and his family (even if it was generally taken up by the artisan class). The question was whether everyone could obtain this minimum.

The 1890s would see the MBW's replacement, the London County Council, being given powers to build new homes – a chance to show that the state could do better than the 5 per cent philanthropists. There was also hope that the working man's trains, their cheap fares enforced by government diktat, would encourage the poor to move out to new working-class suburbs. Districts like Walthamstow, Leyton and West Ham would flourish precisely because of the Cheap Trains Act of 1883.

But the poorest Londoners did not benefit. They could not afford to commute; and, in any case, many had to live near the source of their irregular, casual labour. Moreover, the LCC followed exactly the same principles as the philanthropists, setting rents higher than slum-dwellers could afford. This may seem peculiar, but it was difficult to engage with the 'very low type' of occupant who haunted the slums; and the LCC could not force them to apply for tenancies. Nor, perhaps, was it overly keen for them to do so. The LCC wanted reliable residents, who paid their rent on time, just like any other landlord. Remarkably, on the famous Boundary Estate, the first great 'council estate' in London, opened in 1900 by the Prince and Princess of Wales, only eleven dispossessed residents of the demolished Old Nichol slum moved into the LCC's new Shoreditch apartment blocks.[77] Whether this was success or failure depended on how much one cared about the fate of the dispossessed.

After a hundred years of slum reform, the poorest in society remained firmly in the grip of the slum landlord, surrounded by dirt and decay.

9

The Veil of Soot

Smoke was produced in immense quantities in the nineteenth century capital, spewing from domestic and factory chimneys, 'that solemn gray canopy of vapour which sits like an incubus on the whole town'.[1] In theory, Nature provided the mechanism for its dispersal, scattering dirt on the breeze; and chimney sweeps attended to the residuum of soot. Yet, as the century progressed, it seemed that neither of these operations was entirely satisfactory. Soot-drenched fogs brought the metropolis to a complete standstill; Londoners literally struggled to draw breath. The sweep, meanwhile, was increasingly condemned for his brutal exploitation of children.

Two long-running campaigns would be fought against the backdrop of London's 'veil of soot': one to abate the 'smoke nuisance'; the other, to end the sweep's reliance on child labour. They were very different struggles and only one ended in victory.

The household fire was, in fact, a rather filthy and troublesome beast all round. There was the awkward business of removing ashes and cinders; general cleaning and maintenance; and, finally, ensuring the chimney remained unobstructed. Among the servant-owning classes, maids had responsibility for the hearth. This was not only a question of removing cinders and polishing the grate. Housemaids were also judged on their ability to light a fire without it 'smoking'. First, windows had to be opened – not too little, nor too much – to create a draught that would carry smoke up the chimney; then the right amount of wood, paper and coal had to be placed in the correct position on the grate. The consequences of failure were visible to a canny mistress:

> A difference may be seen at the end of the week in the furniture of a room where the fire is badly lighted. The soot hangs on the curtains, the books, and the little cracks of the ceiling; and the ladies wonder how it is that they cannot keep their finger ends clean.[2]

There was, however, only so much that could be done. Fires that did not 'draw' tended to trap smoke in the room; fires with too strong a draught pulled in currents of air from outdoors, laden with the soot of the metropolis, which collected around door frames and windows ('a fine fringe of soot pointing towards the fireplace').[3] Opening a window was always asking for trouble ('in come the blacks and cover our window-sills, our papers, our tables and our books').[4] Yet, on the other hand, inadequate ventilation, according to most medical men, was dangerous to health.

Technological solutions were offered to this conundrum. Ventilation tubes equipped with filters and valves offered some measure of control over the atmosphere inside the home. 'Tobin's tubes' were built into walls; some devices were camouflaged as decorative classical columns ('The "Imperial" Ventilating Tubes . . . ornamental in appearance, easily fixed and inexpensive').[5] Plants and more delicate ornaments were placed under protective glass 'bells'. A certain Mrs Priestley developed a hybrid ventilation system cum jardinière: a glass case, with stained-glass doors and a trough at the bottom for planting, which could be fastened tight to the frame of sash windows, 'the air being filtered through the growing plants'.[6] Completely keeping out airborne filth, however, was nigh impossible. Thomas Cubitt noted succinctly: 'everything gets so black in London'.[7] Only the endless cleaning routines of Victorian maid-servants could remove the atmospheric impurities which constantly settled on furniture, drapery and ornaments.

Servants were also expected to regularly remove congealed soot from the chimney with a brush or a broom. But there were limits to what could be achieved by domestic staff. To accommodate multiple fireplaces in a single dwelling, flues from individual fireplaces normally went upwards, then sloped at an angle towards a central chimney. It was in these angles, well beyond reach, that sooty deposits were most likely to form. Blockages of soot could send smoke billowing back into a room. Worse, they could be ignited by a stray spark, starting a chimney fire, destabilising the brickwork, setting light to an adjoining rafter or beam. The London Fire Engine Establishment – an early incarnation of the fire brigade – collated annual tallies on the causes of fires. During the 1850s, between 7 and 10 per cent of fires each year were caused by poorly maintained chimneys.

It was for this reason that regular visits by a chimney sweep were essential. The houses of the poor, naturally, were less acquainted with the sweep – the blackened walls of many a slum room were the necessary consequence. More prosperous households, on the other hand, would employ a sweep once, twice or even three times a year.

The sweeps' work was a messy affair, and so they would typically arrive at 3 or 4 a.m., waking up a servant to gain access to the main rooms of the house – the dining room, drawing room, kitchen – before the household proper awoke. Servants had to be a little wary. Nocturnal access to the better class of house was a tempting prospect, and it was not unknown for men masquerading as sweeps to perform extensive burglaries. Rather more commonplace was the danger of sweeps trailing soot round the floor, or accidentally marking the walls with the sacks of filth slung over their shoulders. Housemaids followed them nervously from room to room ('to have a handsome brussels carpet stained with soot is no light misfortune to a feeling heart, to trace the creature at every step is no pleasant journey').[8]

Brushing the chimney was done with a hand-brush as far as the sweep could reach, and then in one of two ways – by a young boy (very rarely a girl) or by 'machine' (a series of poles mounted with a brush). At the start of the nineteenth century, almost invariably it was a child 'apprentice' who scrambled up into the flue, with a hand-brush and metal scraper in hand.

The practice of using child labour to remove soot went back as far as the seventeenth century, although we now think of it as quintessentially 'Victorian'. This is largely because it was nineteenth-century reformers who repeatedly publicised the abuses to which the children were subject. The horrors inflicted on the child sweep remain shocking. The flues in London houses were generally no wider than 9 by 14 inches; and could be as small as 9 inches square (known in the trade as a 'notchy hole' or 'bare nines'). Children would not so much climb through these dirty spaces as wedge themselves into the gap, pressing their knees and elbows against the rough bricks and mortar to lever themselves up or down. The space was so tight that they would even remove their clothing, known as 'buffing it', to gain a little extra room to manoeuvre. Extreme physical hardship was the norm. George Elson, a child sweep in the 1830s and 1840s, suffered festering sores on his knees and elbows which took weeks to heal ('their scars, about the size of a shilling-piece, I bear to this day').[9] Child sweeps were frequently obliged to go barefoot, even in the dead of winter, because of their sores: soot worked its way into shoes and aggravated the wounds. Growing bones were also affected by hours in the cramped confinement of chimneys and it was generally accepted that sweeps were mostly 'deformed, as well as stunted and emaciated'. The legs of a typical sweep were 'an "S" more than an "L" in shape', with young sweeps 'limping and hobbling, for not one . . . could walk with that freedom and elasticity with which other children move'.[10] These injuries and deformities occurred in optimal conditions, but there were other potential dangers, which included burns (when the chimney was on fire or had not been allowed to cool after regular use); suffocation from falling soot (Elson used his climbing-cap, made of unbleached calico, as a face mask, breathing through the cloth); and, finally, the nightmarish and very real possibility of becoming trapped in the flue. In this eventuality, additional boys might be sent up to try and pull down the apprentice, or a bricklayer would be summoned to open up the chimney and pull the child out before he suffocated. Some unlucky souls expired before help arrived. Mature sweeps notoriously suffered from 'sooty wart' (a cancer of the groin and scrotum, caused by prolonged abrasive contact with soot).[11]

If such dire working conditions were not terrible enough, they were made worse by the practitioners who employed the boys. The brutality of some of the master sweeps was infamous. Most had been boy sweeps themselves and were convinced, no doubt quite rightly, that only beatings and threats of violence could drive a boy to perform such work. If boys panicked or demurred once inside the chimney, common stratagems included lighting some straw beneath their feet or pricking their soles with pins. One master sweep, George Ruff, testifying to the Children's Employment Commission of 1862, gave the following grisly description of making an injured boy ready for returning to work:

> Part of his knee-caps had got torn off, the gristle all showed white, and the guiders (tendons) all round were like white string, or an imitation of white

cotton; his back was covered with sores all the way up. To harden his knees, a lotion made of old 'netting' (i.e. urine kept long for the purpose) simmered with hot cinders, was put on them; and to make him hold his knees straight the while, he had a brush-tail tied up and down his back, and something else like it in front and he was made to walk in this way 20, 40, or 50 times up and down the room. It was like killing him, and I had to stand by and see it all. However, he was the clumsiest boy I ever saw and had no activity.[12]

The final comment shows how pragmatically many sweeps viewed their young charges.

It now seems almost incomprehensible that such cruelty was tolerated by respectable society. One reason that master sweeps could get away with this behaviour was that most of their apprentices were unwanted and abandoned. Many came from workhouses, and others were – for want of a better term – trafficked by their parents. Indeed, sweeps provided a very dubious sort of apprenticeship. Masters offered board and lodging, as was customary when taking on an apprentice; but this was the only type of apprenticeship in which masters were willing to pay parents for the privilege of obtaining their children, as opposed to the parents paying for the child's indenture. This rather venal arrangement reflected both the acknowledged dangers and risks for children involved, and how remunerative a young sweep could be for his employer. As one master sweep bluntly put it: 'You can buy boys by the dozen. Parents themselves go hawking their children about . . . Sometimes as much as 5*l.* has been paid for a boy, but very seldom. In Liverpool, where there are lots of bad women, you can get any quantity you want.'[13]

The middle and upper classes, meanwhile, ignored the abuse, sacrificing the health (and occasionally lives) of poor children to their own convenience. They were perfectly aware of the work being done by apprentice sweeps. An 1820s' pamphlet graphically describes a sweep's visit from the perspective of a curious middle-class child lying in his bed: 'I used to listen for the sound of his body rubbing against the sides of the chimney, and catch with eagerness every sound of his half-stifled voice as it answered the gruff call of the master from below . . .'[14] It was customary for the young apprentice to ascend to the very top of the flue and poke out his brush, 'waving it victoriously and shouting', to assure the master sweep (and any servants watching) that the work was done. Climbing boys were not kept hidden from respectable society. Indeed, child sweeps had their own festival on the first of May – as if to atone for their suffering throughout the rest of the year. The boys paraded the streets with a Jack-in-the-Green – a 'green man', symbolising spring and fertility. This was constructed by placing over an old sweep's body a conical wicker-work frame wreathed in laurels and evergreens (through which only the man's face and arms could be seen, so that he resembled a moving tree). There would also be a 'Lord' and 'Lady' (usually a boy in female attire) whilst the appren-tices, decorated in ribbons and makeshift finery, made noise with their brushes, dustpans and scrapers and sang songs, collecting money from passers-by. Some respectable folk denounced this traditional performance as a form of begging – and it seems that masters, not missing a trick, took a percentage of the donations – but the public readily contributed their coppers. Child sweeps, in short, were part of the fabric of daily life. For respectable folk, the use of child labour was deemed a regrettable necessity – but a neces-sity, nonetheless.

That said, there was a peculiar stigma attached to the sweep's filthy work, which undoubtedly helped to foster a lack of empathy for the children involved. It was almost as if outer dirt signified inner wrong – the negative of 'Cleanliness is next to Godliness'. Some aversion to the sweep's presence was, of course, eminently practical. Sweeps *were* famously dirty, constantly covered in soot – the boys from climbing chimneys; the masters from carrying bags of soot (which could be sold profitably to farmers and market gardeners as ferti-liser). Before the advent of public baths, many involved in the trade 'slept black' (i.e. never washed). Marylebone Public Baths reserved '5 baths for sweeps and others engaged in occupations of a similar character' – no one else would want to use a bath immediately after a chimney sweep.[15] *Punch* joked in 1858: 'HOW TO CARVE YOUR WAY THROUGH A CROWD – Get a chimney-sweep to walk before you'.[16] But popular hostility to sweeps extended beyond anxiety about being smutted by dirty clothing. George Elson, having run away from home and ended up a climbing-boy, recalled in his memoirs the shame he felt on returning to see his family, his mother in particular: 'Truly we were tradesmen, but in such a trade!' His parents were itinerant hawkers – but a sweep was still considered lower down the social scale. Travel-ling round the Midlands in his quest for work, Elson was also frequently pursued by boys, throwing stones, calling names and trying to upset his belongings. This was because sweeps, as well as being generally reviled for their dirt, were used as a bugbear to frighten children – 'If you are not good I shall give you to the sweep and then you will have to climb up the chimney.'[17] For poor children, this was a threat with considerable force, given the very real existence of trafficking in the trade, and the rumours that some sweeps practised child abduction.

To the Victorian popular imagination there was also something vaguely devilish about the black complexion of the sweep; his close association with fire; and the 'coal-black imps' who followed him. Black skin had other connotations. Reformers were wont to draw parallels between 'the chimney-sweeping soot-boy and the miserable negroe-slave' – the climbing boy was trafficked like a slave, kept in a form of a bondage by a cruel master, and the soot-blackened skin even created a passing physical resemblance to the 'miserable negroe'. It was a useful parallel, because, amongst the liberal-minded, the abolitionist cause was a popular one; but also telling – the sweeps were something of a race apart, separated by the colour of their skin. This all contributed to making the sweep an 'unclean' figure both literally and metaphorically – outside regular society – and made the very real evils of the trade somewhat easier to ignore.

There were some who refused to turn a blind eye. Admittedly, not everyone who called for change had entirely disinterested motives. The parish of St Andrew Holborn came out against the exploitation of sweeps' apprentices, whilst noting 'the burthen of maintaining as paupers those whose apprenticeships have expired or outgrown the size of climbing, and so far wounded in their limbs, or impaired in health from accidents and diseases, as to be incapable'.[18] The key reformers, however, were genuine philanthropists, who wished to protect boys from cruelty: the Society for Superseding the Necessity of Climbing Boys (SSNCB). Founded in 1803, under the patronage of the Duchess of Gloucester, the Society could claim the likes of the Bishop of Durham, the Duke of Bedford and William Wilberforce as leading members.

Mindful of the fact that many saw climbing boys as a necessary evil, the SSNCB immediately joined the Royal Society for the Encouragement of Arts, Manufactures and Commerce (RSA) in promoting a competition for 'the most simple cheap and proper apparatus . . . for cleansing Chimneys from soot, and obviating the necessity of children being employed'. Within a couple of years, a reasonably effective system of hollow sticks, surmounted by a brush, was put forward by one George Smart; and a superior version was developed by Joseph Glass in 1828. The 'machines' of Smart and Glass were not complex and solved the basic problem. They offered a new, humane means of cleaning chimneys. By the mid-century, the rods of a typical machine were 2 feet 6 inches long, made of lightweight cane or ash, connected by brass screws or 'ferrules'; and the top was a circular brush-head, made out of flexible whalebone strips, wide enough to entirely fill the flue. Different-sized brushes could be attached and a small wheel was fitted to the top of the stock to prevent the tip jamming in a corner. Mr Glass generously left his design unpatented. His model became the standard device, costing between two and five shillings (cane was more expensive than ash; and they were sold in either 60- or 80-foot sets).

Unfortunately for the SSNCB, the mere existence of 'machines' was not sufficient to persuade dyed-in-the-wool sweeps (and many householders) that new technology could replace a hard-working child. It was certainly not so economical for the master sweep – adult journeymen required wages to operate a machine; boys received nothing. Half a century of agitation and legislation followed, as master sweeps attempted to withstand the march of progress. The reformers produced a massive body of campaigning literature; held public meetings; spawned sister associations in every part of the country; and, by the mid-century, had broad support in parliament. The sweeps, doggedly, clung to their old ways.

The history of nineteenth-century legislative attempts to quash the employment of 'climbing boys' would be almost comical were the subject matter not so tragic. Again and again, legislation was passed, only to fail in its practical application. Early efforts to pass a bill in 1818 and 1819 were stifled in the House of Lords. An Act was passed in 1834 which set a minimum age of ten for apprentices; but it was widely ignored.[19] Lord Shaftesbury – long concerned with the welfare of child workers – pushed through more extensive legislation in 1840, laying down restrictions on the size and construction of new chimneys and, crucially, limiting apprenticeships to those over sixteen years of age.[20] This, too, was ignored by many in the trade – and their clients. In January 1843, *The Times* complained of the 'dishonesty of the common chimney sweepers who still retain their boys, and quietly put them up chimneys at the west end of the town and in other places'. The price for using a boy rose to offset the risk of prosecution. In one particularly embarrassing incident, the Children's Employment Commission of 1862 found that 900 badly constructed flues in the Houses of Parliament had only recently been cored (cleared of excess mortar) by five boys, in direct contravention of the law. The aristocrats of Mayfair were reputedly the most egregious offenders in London, with a particular objection to introducing soot-doors (hatches in chimney breasts to allow rods access): 'They don't go so far as to positively say they will have a boy, but they say "I won't have my house pulled about" .' Beyond the capital, the North Staffordshire Association for Suppressing the Use of Climbing Boys was obliged to concede in 1863: 'there is no very general strong feeling against the use of climbing-boys. Lords, squires, magistrates, and mayors have their chimneys so swept without shame.' It was discovered that sweeps had begun describing boys as 'assistants' rather than 'apprentices' to avoid prosecution.

Yet more legislation was passed in 1864, at the urging of Lord Shaftesbury: the Chimney Sweepers Regulation Act. The new Act stated that no child under ten could work in *any* context for a sweep, and, again, that no one under sixteen could work as an apprentice – and added imprisonment with hard labour as an alternative to the usual fine. Even after this, pockets of resistance lingered. It was revealed in 1875 that Liverpool Town Hall was still using boys to clean its difficult flues and paying the boys' master a premium – demanded on account of the acknowledged risk of breaking the law. In the same year, a fourteen-year-old boy climbed chimneys at a Norfolk lunatic asylum, and subsequently died from having inhaled and ingested soot.[21] His master received six months' hard labour. Shaftesbury pushed through a final piece of legislation, which introduced compulsory licensing for all sweeps.[22] Anyone employing an apprentice chimney sweep had to obtain an annual licence, cost 2s. 6d., from the police. London sweeps objected that they were being penalised for wrongs perpetrated outside the capital by a small minority of the profession. Their complaints were, fortunately, not heeded. Whether it was the introduction of licensing – or simply the tide of public opinion finally flowing in the reformers' direction – there were no further significant abuses recorded.

The soot, of course, remained, waiting to be cleared – but now it would only succumb to the struts of Glass's whalebone brush. By the 1880s, the thoroughly respectable *Sunday School Hive* considered the chimney sweep a changed man:

The sweep is quite a respectable-looking person compared with what he used to be. He no longer looks the ragged, shuffling sweep calling out in long, lazy, and doleful tones 'swi-eep'; and instead of walking rides in a neat little cart drawn by a sleek well fed and brightly harnessed little pony, of which he is the happy possessor. On the side of the cart he displays his sign-board, with his name in gaily-painted letters, stating that he sweeps chimneys, beats carpets, and that orders are punctually attended to.[23]

This was a rosy, exaggerated picture in a magazine for children, but reflected a real change, over the decades, from the more ragged, disreputable master with his troop of 'imps'. There would be further legislation in 1894 to prohibit sweeps touting for business door-to-door: the Chimney Sweepers Act. There was still filth – someone had to get their hands dirty – but the trade had been reformed.

The battle to remove soot from the atmosphere of the metropolis would prove equally arduous; but not so successful.

It began in June 1819, when the ambitiously christened Michael Angelo Taylor, MP for Durham, stood up in the House of Commons and declared that the nation was slowly being suffocated by the furnace and steam engine. Factories were the problem, powered by coal, belching out soot-laden black smoke 'prejudicial to public health and public comfort'.[24] The public mood was that 'the evil is incurable'.[25] Taylor, on the other hand, argued that all that was needed was a little effort and ingenuity. Parliament must force manufacturers to introduce the latest 'smoke consuming' machinery. Taylor had already successfully promoted legislation which had laid down a standardised system for prosecuting London 'nuisances' (a legal term for offences involving harm or annoyance to the individual or the public). The Metropolitan Paving Act of 1817 (known as 'Michael Angelo Taylor's Act') facilitated prosecution of hawkers blocking the pavement, flying dustmen, coach drivers committing traffic offences, and much else besides. Now, the Honourable Member for Durham intended to tackle the greatest curse of urban life – the very air itself.

Taylor's concern extended far beyond the metropolis. Indeed, by the early 1800s, industrial centres like Manchester and Birmingham had outstripped London in their production of noxious fumes. Nonetheless, the capital had its own problem with smoke. Small 'manufactories' were dotted throughout the city. Larger polluters congregated near the river in Lambeth and Southwark: glass-makers, breweries, potteries, tanneries and others. Tens of thousands of domestic coal fires, likewise, contributed to a decidedly carboniferous atmosphere. MPs might be unfamiliar with the grime of Manchester but they had all experienced the airborne filth that swirled around the Houses of Parliament: the 'blacks' – specks of soot – that sullied their clothes; the dark winter fog peculiar to the city, 'so different in its sensible properties from any in the country'.[26] Taylor had a point; a select committee was formed.

There were two questions before the committee: was smoke dangerous to health, and could anything be done about it?

Doctors were called who supported Taylor's contention that smoke was a public health issue. One stated that inhaling smoke did not cause particular disorders but interfered with the 'vital principle' of air and ultimately shortened lives. Another stressed the severe impact on those already afflicted by lung disease. Meanwhile, manufacturers and engineers were lined up to confirm that smoke consumption was both possible and desirable. It was, they claimed, perfectly feasible for smoke to be consumed within a furnace – i.e. burnt up as part of the process. Whilst owners might have to make adaptations or purchase new machines, investing in new technology had long-term advantages. The combustion of soot generated heat – the soot serving, in effect, as additional fuel – making for greater efficiency. Smoke consumption would actually save manufacturers money.

When the committee hearings were finished, Taylor gave an ardent speech to the Commons, warning that smoke 'propagated fever and disease' (although he had gathered no evidence to support such a bold claim about contagion). The wealthy, he noted, were increasingly inclined to flee to the suburbs, to avoid the dirt and the gloom; the general populace were left to suffer. The following session, he brought forward a bill to support legal prosecution of factory owners.[27]

The bill faced predictable opposition from the manufacturing interest in parliament, laissez-faire capitalists, who saw only interference and expense: 'If the plan of consuming the smoke of Steam Engines was a good one, it would find its way without any legislative enactment; if a bad one it ought not to be forced upon the country.'[28] Taylor's proposal was not, however, without precedent. Concerned residents had already drawn up local 'improvement acts' in the industrial Midlands, the North and Scotland, which included clauses designed to regulate factory smoke. Acts had been passed for Bradford in 1803; Paisley in 1806; Birmingham in 1812.[29] The Birmingham Act mandated all factories in the district consume smoke; and laid down a hefty £50 fine for owners whose chimneys occasioned 'any nuisance whatsoever'. Taylor's bill, in contrast, was far less exacting. If anyone successfully brought a prosecution for common law nuisance caused by smoke, the court could award costs to the prosecutor. Secondly, the court had the power to order factory owners to alter their machines to remedy the cause. This was the sum total of the proposed legislation: no definition of what constituted a smoke nuisance; no standard penalties. Every detail was left to the discretion of the magistrate. Taylor merely offered financial encouragement for individual nuisance prosecutions by anyone who felt aggrieved – which would take place in the traditional manner, under the common law.

The bill, hardly revolutionary, was passed. There followed an initial flurry of court cases in the industrial North, where the smoke problem was most acute.[30] Unfortunately, a ruling in *Rex* v. *Gott* (1824) thoroughly undermined the working of Taylor's already rather modest legislation. Benjamin Gott, owner of one of the first great woollen mills in England, based in Leeds, was 'one of the most opulent and respectable merchants in that town'.[31] His chimneys came to the attention of a group of concerned citizens, who wanted to use Taylor's Act to make exemplary prosecutions of the worst polluters in Leeds. Gott grudgingly carried out alterations and improvements – but not before legal proceedings had already been set in motion. This led to a much publicised trial, the courtroom 'crowded by fashionably dressed persons of both sexes', where the would-be reformers tried to recover the money they had already spent on lawyers' fees. The question of whether smoke was merely a filthy annoyance or a more serious public health issue was aired. The prosecuting barrister mocked the opinion of certain medical men who had testified that 'soot and smoke were wholesome', to appreciative laughter from the packed courtroom.

The judge, however, effectively ruled there was no case to answer – everyone agreed the chimneys had now improved – and Gott was declared 'not guilty'. Justice Bayley was clearly somewhat sympathetic to the harassed industrialist:

manufactories are of the greatest importance, and if they cannot be carried on with less smoke than they are in the habit of making, it will not in that case be a nuisance . . . In such a place as Leeds, which flourishes in consequence of these nuisances, some inconveniences are to be expected.[32]

Complex legal wrangling, relying on other legislation, eventually extracted £269 from Mr Gott – but only after a very costly dispute (the initial costs demanded had been in the region of £30).[33] More importantly, Michael Angelo Taylor's new Act was dealt a fatal blow. *Rex* v. *Gott* established a perverse precedent: if factory owners remedied the nuisance *after* they were served with legal proceedings, but *before* they appeared in court, they would not have to pay out to their prosecutors. The additional incentive to bring such cases vanished; and factory owners, with nothing to lose, had little reason to make changes until someone actually commenced proceedings. The new Act became something of a dead letter.

Smoke, therefore, continued to pour unabated from factory chimneys, 'abominable encroachments on the enjoyments of the people, their health and comforts'.[34] Indeed, the volume of smoke in the metropolis grew exponentially over the following decades. London's population surged from around 1 million in 1800 to over 2.6 million in 1851. In the same period, its coal imports rose from 1 million to over 3.5 millions.[35] Impenetrable fog – the infamous London 'peasouper' – became a more frequent occurrence (albeit still limited to an average of half a dozen days a year).[36] The 'soup' varied in colour, according to its particular chemical composition – 'grey-yellow, of a deep orange, and even black at the same time'[37] – smelt of sulphur and left a fine coating of soot upon every available surface. It was said of the sheep in Regent's Park that one could tell how long they had been left to graze by the blackness of their wool.

It was not until the sanitary 1840s that metropolitan 'smoke abatement' found new champions. The City of London took the lead, forwarding a report to parliament in December 1841. The report contained various methodologies for reducing smoke, put forward by forty-one separate correspondents ('by the Introduction of Fresh Air in Furnaces . . . by the method of coking or charring the coal . . . by introduction of a jet of steam in conjunction with a jet of air . . .').[38] The City was increasingly plagued not only by the outpourings from the factories which lined the Thames shore, but by those of the steamboats which plied the river – from smaller commuter boats to large ocean-going vessels entering London's docks. Nostalgic Londoners reminisced about the days when rowing boats manned by 'jolly young watermen' were the principal means of river travel – but those days were long gone. Instead, the 'silent highway' was filled with the raucous shouts of the steamboat crews, the roar of engines, and blackened funnels spouting dense clouds of dirt.

The City's report, and the accompanying petition asking for legislation, went unheeded – but it was widely circulated and others began to take an interest. After the report of Chadwick's sanitary inquiry was published in 1842, the newly formed Metropolitan Improvement Society – numbering amongst its members Southwood Smith, George Godwin, John Martin and George Walker – took up the cudgels. The Society bypassed the government and wrote directly to London manufacturers, engineering works, breweries and others, threatening that they would bring prosecutions against anyone with a smoking chimney. Letters were also despatched to the proprietors of steamboats. The move was inspired by similar efforts, and prosecutions, in northern cities – but these had proceeded under newly passed local Acts. In truth, the London letters were little more than a gesture. The Society lacked the resources to take countless factory owners to court, and could only rely on the common law or Taylor's legislation. The issue of atmospheric pollution was, however, grafted on to the emerging sanitary agenda.

William Mackinnon, MP, who had recently completed his report on urban graveyards, thought something more could be done in parliament. Despite the lacklustre government response to his recent proposals on burial, he demanded a new select committee – on smoke prevention. It was not many months since Chadwick's much lauded sanitary report had criticised 'the chimneys of the furnaces which darken the atmospheres and pour out volumes of smoke and soot upon the inhabitants of populous towns'. Smoke created 'deteriorated' air and affected the personal and household cleanliness of the lower classes.[39] Chadwick had concluded, in typical fashion, that local government and the magistracy were too incompetent and nepotistic to enforce anti-smoke measures – central government ought to intervene. Mackinnon's demand for an inquiry was, therefore, hard to refuse.

Mackinnon's committee began its hearings in 1843. More than twenty years had passed, but the medical evidence was remarkably consistent with that gathered by Michael Angelo Taylor. Dr D.B. Reid, engaged in improving the ventilation of parliament, stated that soot affected the lungs of those with 'a delicate constitution'; and recounted how he had hung a giant canvas veil to filter air coming into the House of Parliament, trapping '200,000 visible portions of soot . . . at a single sitting'. He also asserted that soot clogged the pores and, therefore, damaged the respiration of the skin. William West, a lecturer on chemistry, said that smoke particles adhered to the lining of the lungs and prevented breathing. West believed this 'mechanical' effect was more important than any possible chemical reaction. Another chemist complained bitterly of the 'black mucus expectorated from the lungs during a November fog'. J.E.N. Molesworth, an outspoken Rochdale clergyman and anti-smoke campaigner in Manchester, stated that all dirt tended to generate disease.[40]

There were dissenting voices. A few manufacturers asserted that smoke only caused mild inconvenience. There was also passing mention of the belief that smoke 'disinfected' the air, removing the smell of sewer gas and drains. The idea that smoke acted as a fumigant – that it was even bracing for the lungs – had some notable enthusiasts. Robert Angus Smith, for example, who discovered acid rain in 1859, was convinced that sulphurous acid in town smoke, whilst destroying buildings, kept down miasma. The assertion in a recent history of pollution, however, that 'most people – until the late nineteenth century – viewed coal smoke as benign' is questionable.[41] James Anderson's *A Practical Treatise on Chimneys*, for example, declared the smoke from Newcastle coals 'not only disagreeable but absolutely noxious, as many well-known facts too fatally declare' in 1776. Taylor expressed a similar opinion in 1819. The audience at Mr Gott's trial broke into laughter at mention of witnesses who described 'wholesome' clouds of soot. The majority of those who testified before Mackinnon's committee were of the same mind. Coal smoke was not 'miasma' – its sulphurous aroma did not arise from the decay of organic matter – but that did not make it harmless. Most of Mackinnon's witnesses believed smoke was inimical to health, and sometimes fatal, even if the mechanism was through aggravating pre-existing medical conditions.

The proposed solution, once again, was the installation of smoke-consuming machinery. There was also much praise for Welsh coal – anthracite

– which gave off little smoke, as opposed to the bituminous 'sea-coal' shipped from Newcastle. Meux's brewery in Tottenham Court Road reported that it had successfully adopted the more expensive Welsh fuel, after repeated prosecutions by the residents of Bloomsbury ('the gentlefolks in the squares') – a rare instance of a successful legal challenge.[42]

Mackinnon's inquiry, however, had one crucial limitation. Just as in 1819, there was no serious discussion of how to limit smoke produced by domestic fires. As one witness noted, any such measure would be 'very tyrannical' – i.e. far beyond the bounds of what constituted legitimate state interference. The Englishman's home was his castle; the blazing open hearth was the symbol of cosy domesticity, the great emblem of 'home'. Curtailing the fire – worse, confining it within some ugly Continental or American stove – was utterly out of the question.

In fact, the government of the day was reluctant to introduce any concrete measures. The Prime Minister, Robert Peel, suggested that 'a report should be made upon the 40 or 50 inventions for preventing the smoke nuisance which were most deserving of adoption' before any legal intervention (factory owners had complained that the bewildering array of patents made their lives impossible). The Home Secretary, James Graham, repeated the arguments he had deployed against burial reform – yet more information was needed; the government would certainly contemplate a measure – at some point. *The Times* damned Mackinnon as twice having been bamboozled by the wily Graham: 'Mr. Mackinnon's Smoke Prohibition Bill has ended in smoke, just as his Interment Prohibition Bill ended in its own burial.'[43] A second committee sat in 1845, hearing more technical discussion. Another report was commissioned in 1846 – written by the eminent chemist Lyon Playfair and the geologist Henry De la Beche – which added little to the government's knowledge. Graham, however, picked up on caveats that manufacturers needed protection from ill-informed or spurious prosecutions, and pronounced that the Playfair report, 'far from removing his doubts, had confirmed them'.[44] He would not support any bill.

Mackinnon doggedly persisted. Speaking at a National Philanthropic Association meeting, he declared smoke was one of the great sanitary concerns: 'The greatest obstacles to an improved state of health were the smoke nuisance, the wretched state of the dwellings of the poor, intramural burial, and defective sewerage.'[45] *The Times* was supportive, regularly publishing readers' letters on the topic and adding the occasional leading article. Graham would leave office in 1846. The new Whig government was better disposed to all things sanitarian. Nonetheless, smoke prevention was not ultimately included in the Public Health Act of 1848. Facing opposition from industrialists, the smoke question was dropped.

Mackinnon lacked sufficient political clout to force the issue, notching up a total of six failed attempts to bring forward legislation in half a dozen years. It would take new champions to keep up the pressure – beginning with John Simon, the City of London's Medical Officer of Health.

Simon included the problem of smoke in his sanitary reports of 1849 and 1850. He noted that Londoners could not ventilate their rooms due to the smoke-ridden atmosphere outside. As one letter-writer to *The Times* put it: 'it is impossible to open a window without everything in the house being covered with soot.'[46] In consequence, they breathed vitiated air and damaged their health. Simon was not quite willing to state that smoke produced ill health in itself – he felt there were insufficient data – but noted 'there are valid reasons for supposing that we do not with impunity inhale so much air which leaves a palpable sediment'.[47] Smoke also defaced public buildings, sculpture, and did immense damage to clothing – 'a very heavy annual tax on persons using clean linen'. Smoke was 'wasted fuel', which it was actually economical to consume. The City fathers were persuaded. The City Sewers Act of 1851 stipulated that every furnace within the Square Mile consume its own smoke. This was exactly the sort of legislation that Mackinnon had hoped to introduce nationwide. The act did not rely on the legal concept of nuisance – i.e. there was no need to prove harm to any given individual or the public – smoking factory chimneys were simply outlawed. The City demanded that all factory owners improve their machinery immediately. In the event of any prosecution, the onus was on the owner not only to abate the smoke, but to show that they had made permanent changes to their works.

Lord Shaftesbury then demanded in parliament that equivalent legislation be drafted for the whole metropolis. What was good enough for the City was good enough for Westminster and beyond. Smoke was 'the everlasting source of the thickness, darkness and filth of the London atmosphere', which exhausted the poor, ruined their dwellings and clothes, and drove them to the gin shop.[48] Shaftesbury, unlike Mackinnon, had considerable influence. Lord Palmerston would take up the cause as Home Secretary, proposing new legislation, whilst aiming a broadside at the manufacturers: 'Here were a few, perhaps 100 gentlemen, connected with these different furnaces in London, who wished to make two million of their fellow inhabitants swallow the smoke which they could not themselves consume.'[49]

Palmerston introduced the Smoke Nuisance Abatement (Metropolis) Act of 1853. Mills, factories, printing-houses, dyers, iron foundries, distilleries, brewers, sugar refiners, gasworks and waterworks – the majority of the capital's industries – now had to consume their own smoke, as did steam vessels operating west of London Bridge.[50] The police were given an active duty to monitor chimneys, under the ultimate control of the Home Secretary. Again, there was no need to prove 'nuisance' – if opaque smoke was emitted, there was strict liability.

Palmerston would show the same zeal in prosecuting recalcitrant factory owners that he applied to closing metropolitan burial grounds. Over eight thousand printed notices were distributed to the owners of furnaces. *The Times* gleefully described police watching the chimney-tops of Lambeth and Southwark, 'as a terrier would a rathole'. The policemen employed on smoke duty received printed test cards, depicting darkening shades of grey, to determine whether prosecution was required. Within a matter of months, the atmosphere of the capital had changed. In 1857, Mr Broome, the keeper of Inner Temple Gardens, boasted that he had cultivated 2,000 roses, instead of 200, thanks to reduction in factory smoke from the Surrey side of the river. The children of the poor – admitted to the lawyers' verdant lawns after 6 p.m. on weekdays, and on Sunday afternoons – could now frolic on the grass without 'rolling in clouds of smoke'.[51]

Palmerston's Act promised a new dawn. The reality, however, was that it delivered only a few glimmers of light. Mr Broome, carefully watching the chimneys of Southwark in 1857, was already noticing backsliding amongst factory owners – their chimneys still 'very bad at times' – even as he praised Palmerston's wisdom. New equipment failed; stokers fell back into less attentive habits; the cost of anthracite was found to be prohibitive – there were numerous reasons why a factory might lapse. Many factory owners just kept their heads down and hoped they would not be prosecuted.

In fact, there would be numerous court cases brought under the new act – several dozen a year, from 1854 onwards – but they were not necessarily terribly chastening. The courts had discretion to remit penalties, if smoke consumption had been effected 'as far as possible' in any given furnace. This was capable of wide interpretation, and it was easy for factory owners to claim technical difficulties. The new Act had created a legion of would-be innovators, keen to sell their latest inventions. Seventy-seven smoke-reducing systems were patented in 1855 alone and many of these designs proved inadequate.[52] Manufacturers complained that the government outlawed smoke without commending any particular remedy. In practice, magistrates often sympathised with the industrialists, and imposed small fines, even below the 40 shillings minimum prescribed in the legislation.

There was another important reason why the new Act was doomed to have a limited effect: the domestic grate still went unchallenged. It was perfectly obvious that smoke could never be properly tackled unless some restrictions were placed on household fires. No one really disputed the point. Few politicians, however, were willing to countenance such intimate interference in the domestic lives of the public. Not to mention the fact that adapting/replacing domestic grates, or enforcing the use of anthracite, would put every middle-class householder in London to trouble and expense – hardly a vote-winner.

The consequence of this unwillingness was that, despite the new regime of enforced 'smoke prevention', London remained a city of smoke and fog.

There was no great improvement in the 1860s and 1870s. The domestic hearth was still sacrosanct; factory chimneys belched out their contents, with only modest interference by police and magistrates. *The Times* noted that East End chimneys were seemingly permitted 'to belch forth thick smoke from morning till night'.[53]

Fog also seemed to be growing more troublesome. This was not merely a question of the dirt and foul smell ('that nauseous compound flavour of all the sulphates and phosphates').[54] Fog billowed into courtrooms, theatres, museums and galleries, interfering with public life ('it has only been at fitful intervals that visitors could obtain anything like a favourable inspection of the pictures exhibited').[55] In rare cases, these incursions could prove fatal. In December 1873, a dense haze settled on London for five days, 'simply abominable . . . with smoke and dirt'.[56] The cattle show at the Agricultural Hall, Islington, was halted by noxious fog gradually seeping into the building.

After prolonged suffering, several prize cattle died in the hall's choking air, not helped by the heat from the gaslights and crowds of visitors. Ninety-one animals had to be removed from the hall, many to be slaughtered. The show's champion beast, 'Lady Flora', was killed the following day (her head was stuffed and mounted for posterity by the leading taxidermist Royland Ward). A couple of days later, it was the turn of the 'toughest rhinoceros in the Zoological Gardens', whose demise was also attributed to the foul atmosphere. The *Globe* reported, with droll humour, that at least the pigs at the Agricultural Hall 'stood the fog, so to speak, like Londoners . . . and the sheep observed a comparatively calm demeanour'. Londoners, however, were not so hale and hearty as the paper suggested. The Medical Officer of Health for Hackney reported a 50 per cent increase in mortality. Many found it harder to breathe during the visitation.[57] *The Lancet*, tallying the returns of the Registrar General, pointed out that deaths across the metropolis from respiratory problems more than doubled during the relevant week, rising from 520 to 1,112 cases. Londoners were forced to 'consume their own smoke' quite literally – a care-worn but apposite pun. The city, remarked the paper, 'stews in its own gravy'.

The fog of 1873, typically, also caused numerous accidents and some fatalities due to the impenetrable darkness. Pedestrians feeling their way blindly along pavements, 'by a careful regard to the kerbstone', crossed the road at their peril. In central London, at least, one might meet an enterprising youth with a flaming torch, willing to offer safe conduct in return for a few pence ('boys with little red torches were prepared to pioneer the path to Euston station for twopence').[58] The most dangerous places were the docks and canals. On 20 December 1873, the Poplar coroner found himself conducting a hearing on the deaths of no fewer than seven men who had fallen into the West India Docks.[59] The jury returned a verdict of accidental death, whilst noting that guard ropes or chains, capable of being set up at short notice, were a necessity, 'to avoid a recurrence of such a melancholy catastrophe' – advice which, going by the number of similar accidents in subsequent years, was utterly disregarded.

Following another fog-blighted winter in 1879/80, a new generation of reformers would try to address the 'smoke nuisance'. Indeed, by the end of 1880, a lecturer at the RSA was moved to remark that a sea change had taken place, and the omnipresence of smoke and fog was finally 'recognised as dangerous to the whole community'.[60] In part, this was down to the increasing duration of severe fogs; but it was also partly because the mortality figures spoke for themselves. William Farr, the Registrar General of the 1840s, had felt that it was 'extremely probable' that smoke caused increased deaths from pulmonary conditions, but struggled to prove it.[61] By the late 1870s, prolonged fogs and improved statistics from Medical Officers of Health meant that the correlation became more obvious. Dr Arthur Mitchell, for example, published a paper in the *Scottish Meteorological Journal* focusing on the statistics from the London fog of the past winter, noting the impact on mortality from bronchitis, pneumonia, whooping cough and asthma; just as in 1873, mortality rates for chest complaints doubled.[62] Whether this was the result of the 'mechanical' action of soot in the throat and lungs or some 'chemical' factor, such as the proportion of particular gases in the atmosphere, was not clear – but death was the result.

One of the notable reformers from this period was Francis Albert Rollo Russell, born in 1849 (son of the Prime Minister, Lord Russell), who published his pamphlet *London Fogs* in 1880. Russell was a shy, reserved man, who would eventually quit his civil service career to write on public health, meteorology and the environment. In his pamphlet, he catalogued the effects of fog on health, focusing on lung diseases; and listed the damage to public buildings and monuments ('the sitting figures, for instance, on the north side of Burlington House might ... be taken for Zulus'). An earlier writer had once pondered, 'If the pecuniary injury done to the inhabitants of great towns by smoke could only be put in the form of a smoke rate, what unwearied agitation there would be against it!'[63] Russell did the next-best thing and estimated the loss to the capital in unnecessary cleansing and waste of fuel – more than £1.7 million per annum.

Russell also lavished much attention on the 'moral evils' of smoke:

> Wives of labouring men coming from the country find the task of keeping their houses clean too hard for them, and give it up in despair. A forced neglect thus eats into the domestic happiness, and disheartens the spirit of the best of them. Then there is the worry and trouble of smoky chimneys, chimney-sweeping, window-cleaning, renewing and cleaning dirty furniture, dress, &c. . . .

Smoke also deprived the poor of 'that glorious and almost universal privilege of looking upon the clear azure above them' – a nod to the Romantic notion that the urban masses were artificially divorced from Nature, and, by implication, God. Russell's solution to the problem, however, was not religion. He suggested taxing antiquated household grates and subsidising alternative smokeless fuels (including coke and Welsh anthracite); and to have the Metropolitan Board of Works nationalise gasworks, to supply smoke-free gas and coke to the metropolis at cost price. Regulation, he believed, could work, since the emissions from steamboats had been much reduced – but the government had to supply the right economic carrots and sticks. Dr Alfred Carpenter, a Croydon GP and much quoted lecturer on public health, would write to *The Times*, dispensing a very similar prescription – taxation of old grates, and state provision of gas for cooking and heating.[64]

The most active anti-smoke reformer of the 1880s was undoubtedly Ernest Hart, editor of the *British Medical Journal* and president of the National Health Society (yet another body distributing pamphlets and giving public lectures on household management and public health). Hart saw the problem largely as a failure by homeowners to adopt modern grates and stoves. In the summer of 1880, he joined forces with the Kyrle Society – originally the Society for the Diffusion of Beauty – founded by Octavia Hill and her sister Miranda 'to bring the refining and cheering influences of natural and artistic beauty home to the people'. Hart and Hill put together a Smoke Abatement Committee which obtained the patronage of Princess Louise. They would show the public how easily domestic smoke could be countered. The result was a 'Smoke Abatement Exhibition' in November 1881, in Kensington's exhibition galleries, adjoining the Albert Hall. Dozens of 'improved fire-grates' and other apparatus were placed on display. There was a competition of smoke-consuming grates, kept burning throughout, whose output of heat and gaseous products would be measured, and prizes awarded accordingly. Lectures were also given on related topics, including a talk by a Dr Neale on providing a 'chemical lung' for underground trains, with steam-driven fans circulating purified air through smoke-filled carriages.

The exhibition was considered a great success, albeit not quite breaking even financially, and received something in the region of 100,000 visitors during the three months it was open. Doubtless some visitors were encouraged to introduce smoke-free gas, anthracite or coke into their homes. Ernest

Hart would continue campaigning for the next two decades, until his death in 1898. Sadly, however, very little came of his efforts. The problem was not that technology was lacking; rather, that the public was apathetic. As long as severe fog appeared for only a few days per year – and the number of days varied considerably, beyond the predictive powers of any meteorologist – Londoners were loath to change the habits of a lifetime.

In 1887, Lord Stratheden and Campbell proposed a permissive bill to allow vestries to prosecute for domestic smoke nuisance. Parliament, as ever, would not countenance government inspection of private homes – nor were vestries trusted with such an intrusive role, which might impact more upon the middle classes than the poor. Like Mackinnon, Lord Stratheden and Campbell would bring his bill repeatedly before the House; and find himself continually rebuffed, at various stages of its progress. 'Moral suasion' was to remain the order of the day – which largely amounted to doing nothing.

There was discussion in the press as to whether innovative technology might provide an answer. The proposed solutions were rather impracticable, from 'smoke drainage' (connecting chimneys with the sewers, and using steam engines to suck smoke underground) to the discharge of electricity from specially erected lampposts, balloons or kites. More realistically, it was plain that gas and electricity in the home could reduce reliance on coal. Gas and electric, however, would not dominate domestic fuel until well into the twentieth century. Expense and inertia meant that most late-Victorian households retained the devil they knew. 'King Coal, The Fog Fiend, Baron Bronchitis & Co.' had triumphed over the reformers.[65]

By the end of the century, the pall of smoke and fog over the metropolis seemed inescapable, and Londoners were resigned to its presence. Parliament would not act; householders were apathetic. Some suggested the constant gloom contained the seeds of the capital's decline. Late-Victorian 'degenerationists' argued that vitiated air and lack of sunlight were creating an underclass of slum-dwellers, atrophying in the darkness. The most wretched poor were passing on an ever-accumulating collection of physical and mental defects to their rickety children, resulting in 'racial degeneration'. This dark parody of Darwinian evolution gained greater credence when thousands of young men were turned away for service in the Boer War on grounds of their poor physical condition. Smoke and fog were high amongst the possible culprits for what seemed a disturbing decline in physical strength. Commentators noted that the Boers had the benefit of a rural existence – 'big strong frames and the hard muscles developed by constant out-door exercise' – whereas the British lived in towns, which sapped their powers. The ideal would be to return men to the land; failing that, 'all accumulations of filth which corrupt the atmosphere of towns should be removed with the utmost celerity'.[66]

The *fin de siècle* pessimism of degeneration theory was matched by dark, lurid imaginings about fog itself. William Delisle Hay's novella *The Doom of the Great City* (1880) was the first and best of such tales, a story of urban apocalypse.[67] It describes in loving detail the entirety of central London being choked to death by toxic fog. Hay works into his narrative a general condemnation of the complacency of Londoners:

> Londoners were well accustomed to the inconvenience of these fogs, and looked upon them in the light of a regular institution, not caring to investigate their cause with a view to some means of mitigating them . . . no one seemed to think the 'institution' other than a huge joke, and not a serious evil to be earnestly combated by science.

The hero of Hay's story returns to the desolate metropolis, trying to find his mother and sister, but meets with corpses everywhere, 'a chaos of heads and limbs and bodies, writhed and knotted together into one great mass of dead men, dead women, and dead children, too'. Finally, reaching his destination, he discovers his family sitting in their comfortable parlour, tightly embracing each other – in death. *The Doom of the Great City* presages Wells's *The War of the Worlds* – not least in the figure of a solitary hero surveying the ruins of modern civilisation. The narrative also contains some tedious moralising, with the vices of modern London, prostitution in particular, seemingly demanding wholesale extinction. Yet, at heart, the novella is a striking cautionary tale, symptomatic of the fog-bound anxieties of the early 1880s – even if that caution was completely ignored.

Hay's imputation that Londoners lacked enthusiasm for tackling fog was not inaccurate. There was, outside the circle of reformers, a persistent tendency to regard fog as nothing more than a joke played by the weather. Doubtless, some of this was studied insouciance, the stiff upper lip. For example, the diary of arch-hypochondriac George Gissing, for January 1888, captures perfectly a certain wintry misery that must have been familiar to thousands:

> *Mond. Jan. 9.* Hideous fog; bad cold. . . .
>
> *Tuesd. Jan. 10.* Fog still; cold worse. . . .
>
> *Wed. Jan. 11.* Fog denser than ever. Cold so much worse, had to lie up in house. . . .
>
> *Thursd. Jan. 12.* A terrible day; the fourth that we have not seen the sky.
>
> *Frid. Jan. 13.* Fog hanging about still, until 3 in afternoon. then clearing. Got up at 10 . . .
>
> *Sat. Jan. 14.* Black fog at noon, then cleared, and at night thanked heaven for showing its stars once more. . . .
>
> *Thursd. Jan. 19.* Cold and cloudy. Must be several weeks since there was a single gleam of sunlight.[68]

But even Gissing, perpetually anxious about his health, did not fear that fog meant anything *more* than a bad cold and feelings of depression. Public opinion held that fog and smoke did not *cause* disease, only that they exacerbated existing complaints.

The consequence of this belief was that smoke abatement could never achieve the momentum of the sanitary movement of the 1840s. Smoke did not occasion the 'wholesome fear' generated by the workings of cholera – even after the public was exposed to Hay's purple prose. Fatalities from the fog, when they occurred, tended to be relatively predictable, amongst the already weak and infirm who had existing pulmonary problems. Smoke, moreover, had long been considered part of urban living. Londoners had grown accustomed to the nuisance, and saw it as the inevitable by-product of a modern society: 'the black canopy which it is the fashion in England to consider the proper attribute of a large town'.[69] London itself famously had become known as 'the smoke' or 'the big smoke' – the city synonymous with its own pollution.

There was, also, for better or worse, a genuine love for the 'cheerful' open fire that militated against change. It was, theoretically, possible to conceive of replacing it with a stove and slow-burning anthracite, but, as one mid-century writer put it, 'such a revolution in established national habits and associations is scarcely to be expected'.[70] Lord Salisbury, the Prime Minister of the day, would repeat this point half a century later, doubting that Londoners would 'condemn themselves and their children to sit by a flameless fire'.[71]

Some visitors to the capital even found the less severe doses of 'London particular' (that rather affectionate term for fog) quite charming. The Canadian journalist Sara Jeannette Duncan considered it pleasing to the nose: 'it gave a kind of solidity and nutriment to the air, and made you feel as if your lungs digested it. There was comfort and support and satisfaction in that smell.'[72] Claude Monet, an obsessive painter of the fog-heavy Thames, its bridges and the Houses of Parliament, rhapsodised, 'without the fog, London wouldn't be a beautiful city ... It's the fog that gives it its magnificent breadth.'[73] Fog, of course, posed real dangers, from walking heedlessly into traffic, plunging into the river or falling victim to criminals – pickpocketing and smash-and-grab robberies increased on foggy days. But, for more adventurous souls, it was fearfully exciting to navigate the pitch darkness. Breathless accounts of near misses and accidents populated the press. Stories with titles like 'Love in a Fog' and 'Flirtation in a Fog' regularly appeared in women's magazines, with social distinctions romantically blurring in the darkness ('Why! that was her serene highness Alexandrine, Princess of Saxe-Weisenach and Countess of Hennebourgh!').[74] Walter, the anonymous author of the pornographic *My Secret Life*, naturally put matters more bluntly:

> Foggy weather is propitious to amatory caprices. Harlots tell me that they usually do good business during that state of atmosphere, especially those who are regular nymphs of the *pavé*, and who don't mind exercises in the open air. Timid men get bold and speak to women when they otherwise would not. That is my own experience also, and recollect going along a main street on one such night, accosting nearly everyone in petticoats . . .[75]

At the end of Victoria's reign, amidst the choking gloom and the 'smuts' that floated in the air, the veil of soot concealed a multitude of sins – some of them rather exciting.

EPILOGUE

The colour of life is grey and drab. Everything is helpless, hopeless, unrelieved, and dirty. Bath tubs are a thing totally unknown, as mythical as the
ambrosia of the gods. The people themselves are dirty, while any attempt
at cleanliness becomes howling farce, when it is not pitiful and tragic.
Strange, vagrant odours come drifting along the greasy wind, and the rain,
when it falls, is more like grease than water from heaven.

Jack London, *The People of the Abyss*, 1903

This was the East End at the beginning of the Edwardian era, mired in poverty
and filth. The American writer Jack London, having investigated daily life in
Whitechapel and surrounding districts, considered 'the managing class' to be
incompetent and culpable, not merely for the dirt but for the degraded state
of the metropolitan poor. Certainly, there were parts of the capital where half
a century of sanitary reform seemed to count for nothing; and whilst the mid-
century sanitarians never promised they would eradicate urban poverty, they
had surely hoped for something better than a populace left 'helpless, hopeless,
unrelieved, and dirty'. The only saving grace was that the authorities had
tackled the one category of filth most intimately connected to epidemic
disease, the 'removable causes' identified by Chadwick and Southwood Smith
in 1838 – they had cleansed the capital's drains.

There was, however, a hidden cost to this victory. During the 1840s and
1850s, miasma, postulated as the source of disease, became more like a

religious dogma than a scientific hypothesis. When Dr John Snow expertly demonstrated the link between polluted water and cholera in the 1850s, using groundbreaking epidemiological studies of outbreaks in south London and Soho, he was pilloried by the miasmatists ('Has he any facts to show in proof? No!').[1] The ancient belief in the malign power of 'bad air' acquired a stranglehold on the Victorian imagination. Admittedly, not everyone was a devotee. Thomas Carlyle noted privately, 'I do not much believe in that omnipotence of "bad air," which is now so currently accepted as the secret of cholera pestilence. In my native village where the "air" is as pure as at the north-pole, there died just twice the proportion we have lost in London!'[2] William Haywood, likewise, quietly contended that sewer gases were always sufficiently diffused by exposure to the atmosphere, contrary to what he described as 'the current popular dogma'.[3] Nonetheless, the debate between 'contagionists' and 'anti-contagionists', which had raged in 1831, was essentially settled by the 1850s, in favour of the latter – in large part thanks to the sanitarians' tireless promotion of the anti-contagionist, miasmatic message: *foul smell brings disease*. The great sanitary reform of the century – Joseph Bazalgette's sewers – was, therefore, predicated upon a mistaken premise.

Historians of the period have tended to argue that this was ultimately of no importance; that the right decision – improving sanitation – was made for the wrong reasons; and that the gradual acceptance of germ theory, beginning in the late nineteenth century, set matters straight. But much else was ignored and overlooked in the meantime. The mid-century sanitarians were so intent on their campaign against miasmatic cesspools that other forms of urban filth were treated as insignificant; the wider sanitary problems of the metropolis downplayed. Chadwick famously stated that 'All smell is, if it be intense, immediate acute disease,'[4] but his intense, blinkered focus on sewerage alone meant that household refuse, mud and smoke all received comparatively little attention. Some stinks were more equal than others.

Why was Chadwick so obsessed with the particular miasma of failing sewers and clogged cesspools? The stink of drains was certainly not the only stench in town. Visitors found the capital 'smelling of dung like a stable-yard', thanks to its horse traffic.[5] Rotting food in the domestic dustbin produced its own aroma; the great dust heaps where rubbish was recycled were a perennial source of complaint, not to mention other obnoxious trades ('He held in his hand the certificates of five medical gentlemen, that they had examined the premises of Mr. Sinnott, a dust contractor, Mr. Cowan, bone boiler, Mr. Parsons, the proprietor of a laystall, and Mr. Ramsay, a tripedresser and that they contained nuisances prejudicial to the public health').[6]

The crucial difference for Chadwick, when it came to cesspools and sewers, was the drain linking the interior of the house to the fermenting decay below, which turned the home into an 'inverted bell-glass' for noxious fumes. It was this fear which kept many Victorian water closets at the rear of the house, even when connected to the new sewer network. The intrusion into the *home* of the miasmatic phantom created powerful anxieties, which, in turn, powered the nascent sanitary movement. Chadwick, of course, was also immensely impressed with his own plan for a 'venous and arterial system' and the illusory financial returns which might accrue from sewage as manure.

Most of all, though, Chadwick desperately wanted to make a difference. To this end, he needed political power, and freedom from the vexing restraints imposed upon him at the Poor Law Commission. Although he has often been described as doctrinaire, Chadwick was, in many ways, intensely and ruthlessly pragmatic. Sewerage seemed to offer the best opportunity for taking control and effecting widespread sanitary change. The Sewer Commissions were the low-hanging fruit of metropolitan local government, most easily plucked. They had already been the subject of two parliamentary inquiries; they were much disliked by the public; they had no great political supporters; and they had been blamed for the spread of cholera in 1832. Focusing on drains and miasma, Chadwick would systematically denigrate the Commissioners throughout the 1840s, highlighting their failures without recognising their achievements, and happily assume their mantle in the Metropolitan Commission of Sewers. If all this sounds somewhat Machiavellian, such was the nature of the man.

Conversely, Chadwick would carefully avoid the challenges posed by the accumulation of mud and dust precisely because they were the direct responsibility of the metropolitan vestries. The vestries had a collective identity and political influence which the sewer authorities did not. Chadwick knew full well they would fight his centralising agenda tooth and nail. Moreover, in the 1840s the parishes were successfully auctioning off the rights to collect rubbish; money was flooding in from the 'Golden Dustman' Henry Dodd and his fellow entrepreneurs. This made it almost impossible to argue that there was any serious parochial mismanagement of scavenging.

Chadwick's focus on sewerage, therefore, was as much down to his political guile as his dogmatic belief in miasma. The unanticipated result was a hierarchy of filth that prevailed for the remainder of the century. The miasma of sewers and cesspools posed *the* great danger. This made it difficult for later reformers to establish a strong new sanitary agenda. There was a prevailing feeling that the greatest challenge had already been faced down; the greatest battle already won. This would continue until germ theory became firmly established, which allowed reformers and public health officials to conjure up a new type of 'wholesome fear'.

The lingering pall of mud, dust and soot was not, of course, solely Edwin Chadwick's fault. It is hard to contemplate the history of dirt in the nineteenth-century metropolis without laying some blame upon London's vestries. Before the advent of late-Victorian municipal socialism, with some honourable exceptions, these were largely conservative, reactionary bodies, whose greatest wish was to 'keep down the rates'. They were enthusiastic about scavenging whilst receiving payouts from the golden dustmen; less so, when it became clear that rubbish collection and street sweeping would increasingly entail heavy costs. They had little interest in the living conditions of the poor, unless fever despatched too many paupers to the workhouse. They were widely condemned as being too close to their contractors, and were proverbial for their 'trading, jobbery, meanness, and middle-class exclusivism'.[7] These 'grave, mostly elderly men, fathers of families', to quote Bernard Shaw again, could not even contemplate women's toilets without bursts of juvenile laughter and ridicule. They talked much of the virtues of 'local self-government' but the benefits of this vaunted independence were not necessarily extended to the poor, weak and vulnerable.

Vestrydom, however, was not a single homogeneous entity, even if its membership was largely drawn from a narrow social stratum of the middle class. London contained a multiplicity of local authorities with varying degrees of sanitary enthusiasm, and funds. Benjamin Hall would make much of this diversity in his arguments for the reorganisation of local government in 1855, singling out the multitude of hyper-local 'paving boards', responsible for ridiculously small portions of the capital, sometimes mere individual streets or squares:

The case of the Strand was exceedingly singular. There were in the whole of the Strand Union 11 miles of street over which no less than seven different paving boards, each with its establishment of clerks, collectors, surveyors, and other officers, had jurisdiction . . . one of the surveyors was, when appointed, a tailor, and another a law stationer. The cost to the rate payers for maintaining the official staff attached to these boards was 88*l*. a mile.[8]

Hall's speech has been much quoted by historians and undoubtedly accurately represents the chaotic jumble of local jurisdictions, above and beyond the actual parish vestries, that proliferated pre-1855. But it is worth adding an important caveat. Local government in the metropolis was, indeed, diverse. This meant that both incompetent *and* competent authorities, honest and corrupt, large and small, rich and poor, existed cheek by jowl. Whilst many of those involved were unwilling to 'burden the rates' for the sake of sanitary improvement, some went against the grain – not least, the most obvious example, the sanitary-minded City of London. Moreover, the petty officialdom attached to smaller, idiosyncratic districts, by virtue of being responsible for only a small area, *could* actually do a very thorough job. The paving commissioners of the 'Liberty' of the Clink, for instance, a district within Southwark, employed a 'street keeper' from 1810 onwards. He kept a daily notebook, preserved in Southwark's archives – so we know a good deal about his role. This extended to monitoring the lighting of public lamps, the condition of paving and sewers, the activities of scavengers, tackling street encroachments ('The sun blinds in this Liberty much lower than allowed in the bye-laws . . .') and policing the roads for carts blocking pedestrians or traffic.[9] This meticulous officiousness is in stark contrast to the chaotic picture supplied by Hall. Other districts possessed similar petty officials, whether dubbed paving inspectors, street keepers or otherwise, their work little documented. Some were punctilious; others lazy and even dishonest[10] – but their very existence suggests that local authorities were not quite so uniformly dormant and self-interested as their harshest contemporary critics claimed. This is not to deny that metropolitan local government broadly failed in its duty of public cleansing for much of the century; but there is perhaps room for a more nuanced view of 'Bumbledom' than is sometimes allowed.

The general public, in turn, was not simply a struggling mass of humanity, victim of an incompetent ruling class. Many complained, with good cause, about the state of their bins, or the mud on the streets, or their neighbour's cesspool; but the selfsame people might simultaneously deny that *they* should have to pay sewer rates; or that *they* should contribute towards financing the drains of Londoners in the next parish, or even the next street. Furthermore, there were those who simply did not welcome the reforming zeal of Chadwick and his cohorts. The narrow, parochial, penny-pinching 'small government' mindset of the archetypal vestryman existed amongst a large swathe of the middle class, not merely the individuals who took public office. Reformers tried to persuade the reluctant that improved sanitation, public baths, public toilets, model housing etc., would improve the physical and moral well-being of their fellow citizens. For men like Southwood Smith and Lord Shaftesbury, morality was the key: sanitary reforms were as much about preparing the ground for religious improvement as providing physical comforts. But there were many members of the property-owning classes who considered such reform an unnecessary and even undemocratic interference – the residents of Dickens's figurative Cess-cum-Poolton. Others were only swayed by appeals to blatant self-interest. No one, after all, wanted the contagion of the slums to spread to the elegant townhouses of Mayfair, or the leafy suburbs of Highgate or Norwood.

In any case, this book is not about casting blame on the Victorians for their failure to manage the dirt of their great capital, but an attempt to obtain a clearer, more rounded picture of the development of the nineteenth-century metropolis. The rapid growth of London in the nineteenth century presented phenomenal challenges; and the zeal of those who earnestly strived to address them is beyond reproach. Nor is the intent to hint that we have now solved all the problems that so bedevilled our ancestors. The disposal of refuse still relies on the acceptance of 'out of sight, out of mind' but nowadays rubbish travels further. Indeed, in some cases, both legally and illegally, it leaves the country, which hardly seems an improvement,[11] and electronic waste has become the new dustman's gold.[12] The capital's streets are infinitely more clean than those of the nineteenth century; but, below ground, Bazalgette's sewers are full to bursting and a new 'super sewer' is required. Air pollution, meanwhile, has not vanished – *pace* the 1956 Clean Air Act – it has just become less visible, unseen but still deadly, a modern-day miasma.[13] Whether we will address the sanitary challenges of the twenty-first-century metropolis with more or less enthusiasm and ingenuity than our Victorian predecessors remains to be seen.

NOTES

Introduction

1. 'Two Cities: London and Peking', *Fortnightly Review*, June 1899, p. 949.
2. *Punch*, 30 December 1882.
3. 'Where Shall We Go?' *Tinsley's Magazine*, 5 (September 1869), p. 207.
4. Mary H. Krout, *A Looker-On in London*, New York: Dodd, Mead & Co., 1899, p. 37.
5. [George Sala], 'The Great Invasion', *Household Words* (April 1852), p. 73.
6. 'The Casual Observer', 'With a Dirty Boot', *Once a Week*, 11 October 1873, p. 324.
7. [John Wright], *The Dolphin or Grand Junction Nuisance*, London: T. Butcher, 1827.
8. *The Times*, 29 August 1866 p. 4.
9. David W. Bartlett, *London by Day and Night*, [London], 1852.
10. 'London Dirt', *Lloyd's Weekly Newspaper*, 1 August 1875.
11. Lady Harberton was a dress reformer, and we should perhaps take the Piccadilly report, a neat piece of propaganda, as more indicative of the types of Victorian litter than a scientific survey. See Lady F.W. Harberton, 'Symposium on Dress', *Arena*, Vol. VI, New York, 1892, p. 334. For Harberton on 'sputa' on pavements, see *Hearth and Home,* 10 March 1892, p. 531.
12. 'The Face and Complexion', *Weekly Standard and Express*, 2 April 1898.
13. Anon., 'The Empire's Capital', *Review of Reviews*, June 1900, p. 594.
14. *The Times*, 27 May 1885.
15. Edwin Chadwick, cited in David Sunderland, ' "A Monument to defective administration"? The London Commissions of Sewers in the Early Nineteenth Century', *Urban History*, 26 (3) (1999), p. 350.
16. *The Times*, 6 December 1878.
17. *The Times*, 5 March 1845.

1 The Golden Dustman

1. Stage direction from W.T. Moncrieff's *Tom and Jerry*, in Brian Maidment, *Dusty Bob: A Cultural History of Dustmen*, Manchester: Manchester University Press, 2007, p. 91.
2. This was reduced to merely the street cry with the Metropolitan Police Act of 1839 s.14, which forbade the use of any 'noisy instrument'. 'The Dustman was first to forgo his brass clapper; The Muffin-boy speedily followed his shade; And now 'tis the Postman – that

double-tongued rapper – Must give up his Bell for the eve's promenade.' *Illustrated London News*, 27 June 1846.

3. The terms were used interchangeably by the Victorians. Particular arrangements might vary from house to house but the so-called 'dust-hole' or 'ash-pit' was generally not a hole in the ground, but a bunker with a hinged lid. This is clear from various contemporary cartoons and sketches (e.g. *Fun*, 6 November 1878, p. 186) and in a few scattered references in court reports and the press, for example evidence from an 1880 court case: 'I visited the prosecutor's premises and found they had been entered—they had got on the dusthole to the skylight . . .'

4. John Thomson and Adolphe Smith, *Street Life in London*, London: S. Low, Marston, Searle and Rivington, 1877, p. 124.

5. *The Times*, 21 September 1895.

6. LCC, *Minutes*, 13 December 1898.

7. *Morning Chronicle*, 24 April 1855.

8. Whitechapel Board of Works. Dust Committee Minute Book, 1892, No. 1.

9. Charles Booth, *Inquiry into the Life and Labour of the People of London*, Vol. VIII, pt 1, London: Macmillan & Co., 1903, p. 31.

10. Henry Mayhew, *London Labour and the London Poor*, London: Griffin, Bohn & Co., Vol. II, 1861/62, p. 137.

11. 'Dust Ahoy!', *Builder*, 23 September 1871.

12. [Richard H. Horne], 'Dust; or Ugliness Redeemed', *Household Words*, 13 July 1850, p. 380. The decomposing material in the yard, including feline corpses, was euphemistically termed 'soft-core' or 'soft-ware'.

13. *Morning Chronicle*, 18 July 1859; *Standard*, 20 July 1859.

14. 'Interview of Mr Covington with the Chairman and Directors, 5 August 1884', LMA: ACC/2558/SV/1/573.

15. Vestry of St Andrew and St George Holborn Paving, Cleansing and Lighting Committee, P/AH/PA/1/4, 27 May 1793.

16. Clink Paving, Cleansing and Lighting Committee Minutes, 20 June 1810.

17. *Morning Chronicle*, 30 October 1822.

18. Paving board report on Mr Burge's finances, preliminary to legal action, 6 December 1813, Vestry of St Andrew and St George Holborn Paving, Cleansing and Lighting Committee P/AH/PA/1/9.

19. E.g. Minutes of the St James Paving Committee, 1835/1836 STJ/D/1/16/1966.

20. 1 April 1799. Vestry of St Andrew and St George Holborn Paving, Cleansing and Lighting Committee P/AH/PA/1/6.

21. 22 November 1808. Vestry of St Andrew and St George Holborn Paving, Cleansing and Lighting Committee P/AH/PA/1/8.

22. 'The Clerk reported that he had made inquiries as to what has been done by other Parishes and found that in general they shewed a disposition to relieve their Contractors.' 17 May 1813. Vestry of St Andrew and St George Holborn Paving, Cleansing and Lighting Committee P/AH/PA/1/9.

23. Complaints about failure to remove rubbish in the populous parish of St Pancras peaked at 14,534 during 1891, after the parish's contractor all but abandoned his duties. *Report of a Special Committee on the Sanitary Condition of St Pancras*, 10 May 1899.

24. Report on the Sanitary Condition and Vital Statistics of the Parish of St Matthew Bethnal Green, during the year 1885.

25. Board of Works for the St Giles District, Annual Report 25 March 1884 BW/GG/AN/5–8.

26. By the mid-1890s, 14 out of 42 sanitary districts in London still relied upon contractors. LCC. *Report by the Medical Officer submitting summary of Reports by Dr Young on the collection and disposal of house refuse by London Sanitary Authorities.* Public Health Department, No. 207, 22 October 1894.

27. Inaugurated by the Prince of Wales, 'for the purpose of illustrating health in its relation to food, dress, the dwelling, the school, and the workshop'. *The Times,* 9 May 1884.

28. 'It might be suggested, however, that a good curry or stew of a substantial character—and surely there must be such in the Japanese cuisine—could with advantage be added to the present menu . . .' *Morning Post,* 12 September 1884.

29. *Fun,* 13 August 1884.

30. 'We, as Sanitary Inspectors, know only too well, by the number and the nature of the complaints we receive; indeed, there are probably more nuisances arising from foul and offensive dust-bins than from all other causes put together. As a public and widespread nuisance, I consider it has not received from sanitarians the attention it certainly deserves.' Mr D. Richards, *The Removal and Disposal of House Refuse in London,* 1 March 1890 (speech before a meeting of the Association of Sanitary Inspectors of Great Britain).

31. *British Medical Journal,* 13 June 1885, pp. 1207–1208.

32. Shirley Foster Murphy (ed.), *Our Homes and How to Make Them Healthy,* London: Cassell & Co., 1883, p. 364.

33. Board of Works for the St Giles District, Annual Report 25 March 1884 BW/GG/AN/5–8; Fulham Vestry Minutes, 11 January 1888.

34. The Public Health Act of 1875, from which London was exempt, already stipulated a 'moveable receptacle' for homes outside of the metropolis. The *sanitary* house at the International Health Exhibition featured a galvanised movable bin.

35. Whitechapel Board of Works. District Dust Committee Minute Book, 1892, No. 1.

36. Chief Inspector's Report on the Work of the Sanitary Department for year Ending 31 December 1899, Bethnal Green.

37. Board of Works. Whitechapel District Dust Committee Minute Book, 1892, No. 1.

38. Medical Officer of Health report for Hackney, cited in *Public Health* (May 1889–April 1890), p. 118.

39. W. Tagg and L.O. Glenister, *London Laws and Byelaws,* London: Frederick Tarrant, 1908.

40. A survey in the mid-1920s showed the majority of districts with 80–100 per cent of houses having metal bins, but in some the percentage was as low as 20 per cent (Stoke Newington) or even 5 per cent (Poplar). About 6,000 traditional 'ashpits' survived in private houses, 'often in unsatisfactory positions, but they were usually small'. Ministry of Health, *Report of an Investigation into the Public Cleansing Service in the Administrative County of London,* (by J.C. Dawes), London: HMSO, 1929.

41. By-Law No. 7 made by Council under Public Health London Act 91; LCC Minutes, 9 October 1894.

42. LCC Minutes, 18 December 1894

43. *Borrow* v. *Howland,* Queen's Bench, 15 May 1896

44. An 1863 legal case between a south London contractor, Mr Reddin, and the Metropolitan Board of Works, bent on compulsory purchase of some of his property for a new road, reveals the extent of a large establishment, including a 'counting-house, dwelling-house and offices, stables, boiler-house, steam engine-houses, [steam-powered] stampers for pulverising broken crockery into sand, cart-sheds, wheelwright's shop, store-rooms and buildings, dust and manure hills, tot-shop or sorting-room, shoot, and an extensive yard, all communicating and used with each other, and all used by him for purpose of the business'. *Law Reporter,* Vol. 7, Wed. 16 July 1863.

45. *Illustrated London News,* 1 March 1873.

46. The main dust heap in a yard could rise to a considerable height – some 20 feet or more – and collapses and landslides, some fatal, were not unknown; e.g. the *Standard* (1 February 1847) reports a fatality from a mound collapsing beneath a worker, who ended up 'covered by such an immense mass [of dust]' that death was inevitable. Towering dust heaps seem to have been a particular feature of the early 1800s. The great volcano-like dust heap that once dominated the northern end of Gray's Inn Road in the 1820s was approached by 'a road, a quarter of a mile long, on an inclined plane, which continued to wind round it in a spiral direction; and two horses were always requisite to draw a load to the top'. The dust heap

was cleared in 1825 and the contents reputedly sold to Russian brickmakers, to aid in the rebuilding of Moscow.

47. The typical 'hill-woman' was described by one journalist as 'so unsexed that you doubt whether she even be a woman', with a fondness for bare-knuckle fighting to settle disputes ('Dust Ho!' *Good Words*, September 1866, p. 646).

48. Report of the Proceedings of the Vestry of St Matthew Bethnal Green from 25 March 1880 to 25 March 1881.

49. Mile End, for example, had a bill of over £1,000 for 'keep of horses' in 1885, whereas dustmen's wages only came to £645.

50. For example, Mile End still sent 1,380 tons of refuse to brickmakers in 1888 – but this was only 13 per cent of the vestry's total refuse, with the remainder destined for shoots. Vestry of the Hamlet of Mile End Old Town, 32nd Report of the Accounts for the year ending March 25th 1888. See LCC, *Report by the Medical Officer submitting summary of Reports by Dr Young on the collection and disposal of house refuse by London Sanitary Authorities,* Public Health Department, No. 207, 22 October 1894 for a full breakdown of destinations for London's rubbish.

51. 'Poisoning by Vestry', *Saturday Review,* 18 October 1890.

52. Letter from a contractor: 'In consequence of having several complaints about the Dust being brought down here, I must ask you not to send any more in at present, as I have a large heap here now, and look [*sic*] very bad laying about. Later on I may do with some more.' St Giles Camberwell Dust Sub-Committee, Minute Book, April 1889, correspondence with 'James Green, Croxted Lane, Next Dulwich'.

53. By-law no. 10 under Public Health (London) Act 1891 required a distance of 300 yards between shoots and houses, businesses, parks or reservoirs.

54. Vestry of the Hamlet of Mile End Old Town, 29th Report of the Accounts for the year ending March 25th 1885.

55. Mile End, 1892 Annual Report.

56. LCC/CL/PH/1/263 Report on Dust Destructors by the Medical Officer and the Engineer, No.100, 1893.

57. 'The Newington mixture is thus made. A bed of old straw is laid eight inches deep; on this is shot the soft core with all the paper and rags, just as received; then the old straw is heaped up at the edges to form a tank four feet deep. Into this in wet weather the slops are emptied, and dry dust is sprinkled on the top, and it is allowed to stand for [a] week, when the soft core is rotted and the water has drained away. The passengers by the Chatham and Dover Railway can see the mixture in progress any day by the side of the line near Walworth Road Station. The yard communicates with the rail, and the stuff thus made into decent manure is sent away in trucks to the neighbourhood of Meopham, in Kent.' W.J. Gordon, 'The Cleansing of London', *Leisure Hour,* 1889, p. 679.

58. Executive Council of the International Health Exhibition, *The Health Exhibition Literature,* Vol. V, 7 pt 1, London: William Clowes & Sons, 1884, p. 424.

59. Full details can be found in Stephen Beckett-Doyle, *Dirt is Essentially Disorder* (2003), monograph, Southwark Local History Library.

60. Hackney Board of Works, for example, burnt refuse at its Kingsland Basin wharf, 'heaped up in the rudest way possible, so that night and day, week in and week out, a foul fetid odour fills the neighbourhood'. *The Times,* 20 October 1890.

61. Annual report of the Vestry of Mile End Old Town, 1892.

62. 'Out of that dust, the destructor produces steam, and the steam is used to drive a great high-tension engine producing 1,100 volts of electricity from each of three generators, there are, besides, three low tension dynamos, each producing 165 volts', *West Australian,* 8 October 1897.

63. The scheme was, therefore, 'promoted by the unanimous vote of the Vestry to prevent the monopoly of the supply of electricity passing into the hands of a private company'. Metropolitan Borough of Bermondsey, *Souvenir of the Opening of the Electric Lighting and Dust Destructor Works,* 23 January 1902. LMA/4278/01/211.

64. David Owen, *The Government of Victorian London*, Cambridge, MA, and London: Belknap Press, 1982, p. 39.

65. Fabian Society, *The London Vestries: What They Are and What They Do,* Fabian Tract No. 60, 1894.

66. Christopher Derrett, 'More Light, More Power: Electricity Generation and Waste Disposal in Shoreditch, 1897–2009', *Hackney History*, 15 (2009), p. 18.

67. Metropolitan Board of Bermondsey, *Souvenir of the Opening* . . .

68. Fulham, Hackney, Poplar, Shoreditch and Stoke Newington were the only boroughs engaged in electricity generation from incinerators in 1925/26. Ministry of Health, *Report of an Investigation into the Public Cleansing Service in the Administrative County of London*, by J.C. Dawes, 1929, Table XI.

69. [Of Kensington]. 'Three methods are in use: about 49% of the refuse is hauled through Chelsea to a wharf on the river, whence it is sent to a riverside dump on the Essex marshes; 31% is hauled direct to a refuse incinerator, situated on a good spacious site in Hammersmith, and is simply incinerated, there being no outlet for steam; the remaining 20% is loaded into casual barges at the Council's Kensal depot and taken to dumps at Yeading or Harefield in Middlesex.' Ibid., p. 28.

70. Twenty-first Annual Report of the Local Government Board, 1891–92. Supplement containing the report of the Medical Officer for 1891–92, 1893, pp. 108ff.

71. Conference of the Administration of the Public Health (London) Act, 1901, 23 June 1903.

72. William Robson, *The Government and Misgovernment of London*, 1939: 'About twenty [out of 28] of the metropolitan boroughs adopt the discredited practice of employing private contractors to carry out their dust collection and refuse disposal.'

73. Mayor of London, *London's Wasted Resource: The Mayor's Municipal Waste Management Strategy, November 2011*, London: Greater London Authority, 2011.

2 Inglorious Mud

1. *Aberdeen Weekly Journal*, 11 January 1884.

2. *Champion and Weekly Herald*, 20 January 1839.

3. Macadam was widely introduced in the 1820s. By the 1850s, 1,350 miles of streets were macadam, 400 granite 'sets' or 'setts' (blocks), and 5 made of wood. *Daily News,* 7 September 1853.

4. Henry Letheby, 'Chemical Composition of the Mud from the Streets of the City of London', *Supplement to the Chemical News*, 14 June 1867. Granite blocks also created loose stone – the gravel and cement used to fill the interstices came loose over time. See 'Paving and Paving Stones', *Mechanic's Magazine*, 31 May 1861, p. 364.

5. *Aberdeen Weekly Journal*, 11 January 1884.

6. 'It can scarcely be less now, than 1,000 tons [of dung] daily in the metropolis.' *Report on the Application of Science and Art: Street Paving and Street Cleansing of the Metropolis, c.*1875 [Guildhall, Fo. Pam. 505]. Urine was rarely discussed, but one finds occasional mentions: e.g. 'The wood pavement laid down in Regent-street about thirty years ago was removed because it had become so saturated with ammonia that the emanations tarnished the plate in the silversmith's shops.' 'Metropolitan Atmospheric Pollution', *British Architect*, 16 July 1880, p. 25.

7. *Morning Post*, 17 April 1865.

8. *Illustrated London News*, 4 January 1890.

9. A City of London survey by William Haywood found that only a third of falls were 'complete' – which he defined as not merely falling to the knees or haunches, but when the horse had to be freed from its harness. *Report on the Accidents to Horses on Carriageway Pavements,* 1874.

10. W.J. Gordon, *The Horse World of London*, London: Religious Tract Society, 1893, p. 183.

11. 'Slippery Streets', *The Lancet*, 30 December 1883, p. 1132.

12. *Hearth and Home*, 28 February 1895.

13. 'Germans and Frenchmen, indeed, all foreigners, often wonder why Englishmen turn up their trousers at the bottoms even in fine weather; they do so simply by reason of unbroken habit – a habit born of necessity.' 'Impressions of England', *Fortnightly Review*, October 1891, p. 55.

14. *Poor Man's Guardian,* 6 November 1847, p. 7.

15. James Winter, *London's Teeming Streets 1830–1914*, London: Routledge, 1993.

16. *Punch*, 14 December 1861.

17. *Lady's Newspaper*, 16 March 1850.

18. See F.H. Spencer, *Municipal Origins*, London: Constable, 1911, p. 202.

19. 'Accordingly, two or three days after snow has fallen, when there has been abundant time for accidents, a constable goes round to each house, and leaves a printed paper requiring the householder to clear away the snow. If he chooses to disregard the notice, he seldom or never hears any more about it, and as a matter of course very many do choose to disregard it.' *Pall Mall Gazette*, 3 December 1875.

20. *The Times*, 6 January 1894.

21. *The Times*, 4 January 1892.

22. 'Philosophy of Scavenging', *Spectator,* 1 November 1851.

23. Joseph Whitworth, in 1844 *First Report of the Commissioners for inquiring into the State of Large Towns and Populous Districts*, Appendix, p. 204.

24. See the Saint Giles District, Statement and Account 1875/76, Camden Local Studies BW/GG/AN3, for a discussion of how a bad winter created 50 per cent more 'slop' than the previous year.

25. 'Impressions of England', *Fortnightly Review*, October 1891, p. 556.

26. *The Times*, 5 January 1867.

27. Vestry of St Andrew and St George Holborn Paving, Cleansing and Lighting Committee. Annual Statement, 1848.

28. Henry Mayhew, *London Labour and the London Poor,* London: Griffin, Bohn & Co., 1861/62, Vol. II, p. 210. 'Street-sweeping degrades a man, and if a man's poor he hasn't no call to be degraded. Why can't they set the thieves and pickpockets to sweep?'

29. Minutes of Camden Town Paving Board, 10 December 1822. Camden Local Studies P/PN1/PA5/M/1.

30. B.M. Croker, 'A Third Person', *London Society*, March 1893, p. 232.

31. For example, a Mr Calvery asked for permission to lay down a crossing at Brookes Market from the front of his house 'obliquely to the corner of the market'; minuted 27 July 1800, Vestry of St Andrew and St George Holborn Paving, Cleansing and Lighting Committee, P/AH/PA/1/6.

32. The United Services Club, for example, petitioned St James's Paving Committee for a 'granite crossing' to be laid across Pall Mall in 1834 (*The Age*, 19 January 1834).

33. '. . . viewed the east end of Little James Street and are of opinion it will tend to make the way from the said street to the Workhouse more cleanly and safe in the Night time if a Crossing were made from the South East Corner of the Street to the Gateway on the Opposite side of Gray's Inn Lane.' 20 May 1816, Committee for Paving St Andrew Holborn and St George the Martyr P/AH/PA/1/10; 'Your Committee recommend that a new crossing be laid down near the Cedars Hotel, at a cost not exceeding £15 . . .' Fulham Vestry Minutes, 29 September 1886.

34. Minutes, Kensington Paving, Lighting and Cleansing Committee, 20 August 1858.

35. *The Times*, 10 November 1862.

36. According to the *Daily News* (7 September 1853) a sweeper's besom could be obtained 'from any oil shop' (paint sellers) for '2½d to 4d'. A proper broom might be had for 10d. but this would perhaps look too professional to elicit sympathy.

37. '. . . a dog, cat, rabbit or guinea-pig – which suggested good nature and awakened sympathy'. Alfred Rosling Bennett, *London and Londoners in the 1850s and 1860s*, London: T. Fisher Unwin, 1924, p. 58.

38. 'Asiatics in London', *Sunday at Home*, 13 June 1874. For the original story relating to the ambassador, see e.g. *Reynolds's Weekly News*, 23 June 1850.

39. *Morning Chronicle*, 20 April 1859.

40. For the 'street crossing sweeper juvenile club' organised under the patronage of Lord Brougham, see letters from its secretary to the *Morning Post*, 28 December 1865; 11 December 1866.

41. *Morning Post*, 26 October 1883.

42. *Chambers's Edinburgh Journal*, 24 July 1841.

43. *Fraser's Magazine*, 1838, pp. 39–49.

44. 'On Wednesday, each man was properly enrolled and furnished with a blue cloth badge to fasten round the left arm upon which were worked the letters "GPD" (Grosvenor Place District) and a corresponding number to one which is registered at the secretary's office against the wearer's name.' 'The Crossing Sweepers of Belgravia', *Illustrated London News*, 16 September 1854.

45. *The Times*, 16 September 1895.

46. Recalled by Alfred Tennyson Dickens, the author's son, *Nash's Magazine*, September 1911.

47. E.g. *Morning Post*, 5 February 1897; *Standard*, 24 October 1900.

48. 'Job' meaning a corrupt arrangement, as in jobbery. The outright accusation can be found in James Williamson Brooke, *The Democrats of Marylebone*, London: William Jones Cleaver, 1839 p. 124, and oblique hints in the various newspaper reports.

49. The contract was finalised with the Metropolitan Wood Paving Company in early November 1839. *Era*, 3 November 1839.

50. *Builder*, 1843, p. 418.

51. *Builder*, 1845, p. 332.

52. *Poor Man's Guardian*, Issue 7, 18 December 1847, p. 53. James Winter in his detailed study of Cochrane ('The Agitator of the Metropolis', *London Journal*, 14(1), 1989) quotes a lovely example of his rhetoric: 'Won't you put it through, by Jove? Won't you! Then if you don't, mark – we'll keep possession of this place till you do. I tell you that we insist on that being put. You tell us to go to the Poor Law Board. What the devil have we to do with the Poor Law Board? We pay our rates, my good fellow, and this is our proper place.' *The Times*, 29 July 1852.

53. *Lloyd's Weekly London Newspaper*, 14 May 1848.

54. *The Times*, 7 March 1848.

55. Ibid. The 'strolling adventurer' was a reference to his authorship of *Journal of a Tour*, which had become public knowledge the previous year, and fatally damaged Cochrane's ambition to become an MP.

56. *Morning Chronicle*, 16 February 1848.

57. *Morning Chronicle*, 19 April 1848.

58. 'Vice presidents' in 1847 included His Grace the Duke of Grafton; Earl of Devon; Lord Dudley Coutts; Stuart, Earl of Antrim; Sir James Clark, Bart; Sir Wm Magnay; Benjamin Bond Cabbell; Lord John Russell; Lord Rob. Grosvenor; Lord Viscount Ranelagh; the Bishop of Durham; Sir G.T. Staunton, Bart and Thomas Southwood Smith.

59. Sampson Low, *The Charities of London*, 1850, p. 150.

60. Trials took place between 1 December 1845 and 24 January 1846 (*Morning Chronicle*, 20 October 1851); 9 May 1851–29 September 1851 (*Daily News*, 11 October 1851); 1 January 1852–c. 21 June 1852 (Midsummer Day) (*Illustrated London News*, 22 November 1851; *The Times*, 12 May 1852).

61. *The Times*, 14 January 1852.

62. £11,938, versus the contractor's £5,160. *The Times*, 12 May 1852.

63. *The Times*, 19 May 1852.

64. *The Times*, 23 December 1852.

65. Winter, *London's Teeming Streets*, p. 133.

66. During a day's tally in 1881, 29,396 out of 71,983 vehicles entering the City of London fell into this heavy goods category. E.W.J. Richmond Cotton, 'The City of London, its Population and Position', *Contemporary Review* (January 1882), p. 84.

67. *Morning Chronicle*, 20 October 1851, quoting a report by William Haywood.

68. Costs of contractor scavenging rose from £9,126 in 1865 to £22,620 in 1867. Streets Commitee Report Book COL/CC/STS/0101/001, 2 October 1866.

69. 'Mr. Reddin said he had an injunction in Chancery on him as to his yard in South St., at the suit of the Metropolitan Board of Works . . .' COL/CC/STS/0101/001, 8 May 1866.

70. 'The Casual Observer', 'With a Dirty Boot', *Once a Week* (11 October 1873), p. 324.

71. W.J. Gordon, 'The Cleansing of London', *Leisure Hour* (September 1889), p. 602.

72. The irrigation system of Isaac Brown & Co. was trialled in Prince's Street in the mid-1870s. See *The Times,* 30 April 1874.

73. The City's Streets Committee resolved to lay down nothing but asphalt or wood from 1874 onwards. *The Times*, 30 April 1874.

74. '. . . since Threadneedle-street has been asphalted the office of crossing-sweeper has become a sinecure', *Morning Post*, 13 September 1880.

75. 'A Day in the Census of the City', *Saturday Review of Politics, Literature, Science and Art* (December 1881), p. 748.

76. See Annual Reports of St Giles District Board of Works. The board kept the street orderly system for the remainder of the century; but it would replace its team of twenty-eight boys with twelve men in 1898.

77. J.D. Symon, 'A Day in the Life of a Scavenger Boy', *English Illustrated Magazine* (December 1898), pp. 305–307.

78. Thomas Blashill, 'The State of London Streets', *Perspectives in Public Health,* 22 (1) (January 1901), pp. 6–23.

79. *Leisure Hour* (December 1895), p. 129.

80. *Dickens Dictionary of London*, London: E.J. Larby [*c*.1908,] 'Motoring' p. 135.

81. *The Times*, 28 February 1910.

82. 'Since the multiplication of newspapers, opening of stores, and the vast importation of foreign goods wrapped in paper, the litter that accumulated in the streets of London was enormous . . . He had special men in his district to do nothing but pick up paper, the cost being some £300 or £400 a year . . . It was not unusual to see piles of cardboard boxes and paper come out of the houses, the result of a lady having been shopping and making bargains.' Blashill, 'State of London Streets', p. 17.

3 Night Soil

1. 1844. *First Report of the commissioners for inquiring into the state of large towns and populous districts,* pp. 166, 214; Alum., *Sanitary Reform and Sanitary Reformers,* London: Edward Stanford, 1855, p. 24.

2. Metropolitan Commission of Sewers, *Report of The Surveyors on House Drainage,* August 1848, p. 38. See also City of London General Purposes Committee, 13 September 1849, noting 'about three shovels full' of 'cloths, rags and pottery' found at the bottom of a cesspool, once emptied. Other sources also mention a residue of rags, which might well have been sanitary towels or toilet paper.

3. The hours were restricted to between midnight and 5 a.m 'from Lady-day to Michaelmas' and 6 a.m. for the winter months, by the Metropolitan Police Act of 1829 – reflecting similar detailed prohibitions already in local Acts.

4. According to a City of London report from 1849, a third of privies were in cellars, a third 'in passages and other parts of the house' and a third in 'yards and outer premises'. *The Times,* 24 October 1849.

5. 1844 *First report of the Commissioners for inquiring into the State of Large Towns and Populous Districts*, p. 244.

6. See house drainage diagrams in William Eassie, *Sanitary Arrangements for Dwellings*, London: Smith, Elder & Co., 1874.

7. 1847. *Metropolitan Sanitary Commission. First Report.*

8. Eassie, *Sanitary Arrangements for Dwellings*, p. 80.

9. Ibid., p. 81.

10. Minutes, Clink Paving, Cleansing and Lighting Committee, 29 June 1808.

11. There was considerable overlap between the two trades. There were some professional 'master nightmen' but many were dust contractors, master chimney sweeps and bricklayers (members of this profession built cesspools), for whom emptying cesspools was a minor but profitable sideline (householders typically paid one or two pounds for the work). Their employees, likewise, were usually not professionals but a rag-bag of labourers from various trades, dustmen, chimney sweeps and others, supplementing their wages with 'night work'. See tabulations in Mayhew, *London Labour and the London Poor*, Vol. II, pp. 452 ff.

12. *British Patent Reports*, Vol. XIV, No. 1105.

13. I am very grateful to Stephen Astley, Curator of Drawings at the Museum, for these details.

14. 1831 *Second Report from the Select Committee on Windsor Castle and Buckingham Palace.*

15. Source: Stephen Astley, Soane Museum. Mrs Yandall would have been a contractor, owner of the business, rather than doing the work herself.

16. 'The Main Drainage of London', *British Medical Journal*, 23 July 1859.

17. Metropolitan Sanitary Association, *The Public Health: A Public Question, First Report of the Metropolitan Sanitary Association*, London: The Association, 1850, p. 44.

18. William Haywood, *Report . . . on the Ventilation of Sewers*, 1858. CLA/006/AD/07/040.

19. The year 1815 is often given as a crucial date thanks to a passing remark by James Simpson, Vice-President of the Society of Civil Engineers, giving evidence to the Select Committee on the Metropolis Water Bill in 1851; but there was clearly variation in both regulation and practice in different parts of the capital.

20. There were five companies involved in this confederacy and held to account in *The Dolphin*: the ancient New River Company, whose reservoirs at Islington were first filled with water from Hertfordshire in 1613; the Chelsea Water Works Co. (est.1722); West Middlesex (1806); East London (1807); Grand Junction (1810). *Civil Engineer and Architect's Journal*, Vol. 3 (1840), pp. 45–46.

21. John Loude Tabberner, *A Letter to the Right Hon Viscount Morpeth on The Past, The Present and the Probable Future Supply of Water to London*, London: Longman & Co., 1847, p. 10. See also David Sunderland, 'Disgusting to the Imagination and Destructive of Health?' *Urban History*, 30 (3) (2003), pp. 359–380 for a defence of the water companies' actions.

22. *Morning Chronicle* from 21 April 1824 in John Wright Papers, London Metropolitan Archives, CLC/520, Box 172.

23. *The Times*, 15 September 1824. The putative company was part of the stock market bubble of the mid-1820s, and never got off the ground.

24. Ibid., 10 April 1827.

25. 'Appeal for indemnifying Mr Wright', London Metropolitan Archives, CLC/520/MS14872.

26. 1828 *Report from the Select Committee on The Supply of Water to The Metropolis*, p. 45.

27. *The Times*, 19 March 1827, letter from W.M. Coe, Grand Junction Company's secretary.

28. 'Thames Water Question', *Westminster Review*, 23 (1829), pp. 31–42.

29. 1828 *Report from the Select Committee on The Supply of Water to The Metropolis*, p. 71.

30. In a new edition of Paris's *Treatise on Diet*, published in 1828. Noted in 1828 *Report from the Select Committee on The Supply of Water to The Metropolis*, p. 152.

31. *The Times*, 15 November 1831.

32. Pioneering work on intravenous saline injection by Dr Thomas Latta of Leith (the solitary medic who deduced the need for swift rehydration and devised a treatment) was largely ignored by his contemporaries. See R.J. Morris, *Cholera 1832: The Social Response to an*

Epidemic, London: Croom Helm, 1976, pp.166–170; N. MacGillivray, 'Dr Latta of Leith', *Journal of the Royal College of Physicians of Edinburgh,* 36 (2006), pp. 80–85.

33. *The Times,* 16 November 1831.
34. Central Board of Health, *Sanitary Hints Respecting Cholera,* 14 November 1831.
35. *London Medical and Surgical Journal,* 31 (2) (1 September 1832), p. 139.
36. W. Coldwell, *Imperial Magazine,* 13 (January 1832), pp.15–17.
37. Vestry of St Andrew and St George Holborn Paving, Cleansing and Lighting Committee, P/AH/PA/1/13, 7 November 1831.
38. City of London, Report from Portsoken Ward, undated [1832] LMA CLC/W/LA/006/MS09959.
39. 1850 *Report of the General Board of Health on the Supply of Water to the Metropolis.*
40. City of London Parish/Ward Reports [1831/2] COL/CC/HEB/02/001–003.
41. Ibid.
42. *The Times,* 26 October 1831.
43. *The Times,* 5 November 1851 on 'the line [of houses] from Hyde-park-corner to beyond the Knightsbridge Barracks'.
44. Letter from 'A Unitarian Dissenter', *The Times,* 26 March 1832.
45. *The Times,* 21 June 1832.
46. Regulations printed in the *Supplement to the London Gazette,* 20 July 1832.
47. *The Times,* 29 August 1832.
48. 1834 *Report Inquiring into the Administration and Practical Operation of the Poor Laws,* App.(A), p. 107.
49. *Cholera Consultation,* pub. S. Knight, Sweeting's Alley, 27 Feb. 1832. Francis A. Countway Library of Medicine; MMC 46. http://ocp.hul.harvard.edu/dl/contagion/olvwork374474
50. The Metropolitan Sanitary Commission of 1847 estimated 5,275 deaths in London, out of a population of nearly two million in 1847–48. Metropolitan Sanitary Commission, *First Report,* p. 15.
51. 1838 *Second Report from Select Committee on Metropolis Improvements,* p. 63.
52. *The Times,* 12 November 1831.
53. 'On Haverstock-hill, now a populous place, an open ditch, bordering England's lane, remains as it has been for years, collecting the sewage from Hampstead downwards, and emitting in summer a pestiferous reek . . . From Lambeth to Kennington, to Camberwell, to Walworth, to Greenwich, and all through the yet surviving hortulan suburbs, the fields and thoroughfares are redolent of sewage.' *Builder,* 29 October 1853.
54. J.S. Curl, *The Victorian Celebration of Death,* Newton Abbot: David & Charles, 1972, p. 139.
55. The eight divisions of the metropolis were: Westminster; Surrey and Kent; Holborn and Finsbury; Poplar; St Katherine's; Tower Hamlets; Greenwich; and the City of London.
56. These were the same sorts of issues that dogged vestrydom: self-selection (the government simply appointed whomever the existing Commissioners nominated); a lack of transparent accounting; amateurism; cronyism in the awarding of contracts; an unwillingness or inability to co-operate with each other. They had already been raised in an 1823 select committee (1823 *Report from the Select Committee on Sewers in the Metropolis*).
57. Ibid., p. 24.
58. *Burkett* v. *Crozier,* reported in *Morning Chronicle,* 12 December 1827.
59. James G. Hanley, 'The Metropolitan Commissioners of Sewers and the Law, 1812–1847', *Urban History,* 33 (3) (2006), p. 356 on *Masters* v. *Scroggs* (1815).
60. 1840 *Report from the Select Committee on the Health of Towns,* p. 122; see also p. 126 for another example.
61. Ibid., p. 84.
62. Sir John Squire, *Illustrated London News,* 21 February 1948, p. 202.
63. Thomas Balston, *John Martin, 1789–1854. Illustrator and Pamphleteer,* London: The Bibliographical Society, 1934, p. 392.

64. It only receives a bullet-point summary in the final report. The press were kinder. The *Examiner* called it 'the best [solution] that has been offered'; *The Times* liked the idea, but questioned its feasibility.

65. 1834 *Report from Select Committee on Metropolis Water*. The committee was reporting on the survey of alternative water sources that had been commissioned in 1828 and taken six years to complete, under the sluggish guidance of Thomas Telford. The finished plans – suggesting a new canal from Hertfordshire – were the subject of much recrimination between Telford and his amanuensis, James Mills; and the committee, not finishing its work in 1834, was not reconvened in the following year.

66. 1838 *Second Report from Select Committee on Metropolis Improvements*, p. 149.

67. Mary L. Pendered, *John Martin, Painter, His Life and Times,* London: Hurst & Blackett, 1923, p. 21.

68. Ibid., p. 214.

69. Ibid., p. 202. There was always some debate on the topic, even in Martin's lifetime. His published plans were certainly the first containing intercepting sewers to appear so prominently before the public.

70. *Reprint of the Report of the Committee appointed to take into consideration Mr Martin's Plan for Rescuing the River Thames from every species of pollution*, 1836.

71. *Standard*, 27 May 1839.

4 Removable Causes

1. *Westminster Review,* April 1828, p. 416.

2. The cost of administering relief had grown from £1.5 million in 1775 to £7 million in 1832. See S.E. Finer, *The Life and Times of Sir Edwin Chadwick,* London: Methuen, 1952, p. 42.

3. 1834 *Report Inquiring into the Administration and Practical Operation of the Poor Laws*, p. 131.

4. *Blackwood's Magazine,* June 1837, p. 842.

5. *Westminster Review,* April 1828, p. 416.

6. See 'Three Reports of the Sub-Committee, appointed by the Fever Institution, to direct the White-washing with quick Lime of those Dwellings of the Poor, in which Infection has lately subsisted.' *The Reports of the Society for Bettering the Condition and Increasing the Comforts of the Poor,* Vol. III (London, 1802).

7. Christopher Hamlin, *Public Health and Social Justice in the Age of Chadwick, 1800–1854,* Cambridge: Cambridge University Press, 1997, p. 108.

8. 1837–38 *Poor Law Amendment Act*, App. 1, p. 9.

9. Ibid., App. 2, pp. 9–10.

10. *Examiner*, 20 August 1842.

11. 1842 *Report . . . on an inquiry into the Sanitary Condition of the Labouring Population of Great Britain*, p. 38.

12. Finer, *Life and Times, op. cit.,* p. 223.

13. *Architect, Engineer and Surveyor*, February 1843, pp. 52–54.

14. E.g. Joseph Gwilt, respected architect and surveyor to the Surrey and Kent Commission. *Architect, Engineer and Surveyor,* June 1843, pp. 169–172.

15. Richard Kelsey to Edwin Chadwick, 5 September 1842. Box 45, Edwin Chadwick Collection, University College London.

16. *The Times*, 27 July 1844.

17. John Simon, *English Sanitary Institutions*, London: Cassell & Co., 1890, p. 198, footnote.

18. *The Times*, 23 November 1846.

19. *Daily News*, 11 July 1849.

20. 1852 *General Board of Health. Report on the Sanitary Condition of the Epidemic Districts in the United Parishes of St Giles and St George Bloomsbury,* citing a report dated 7 July 1849.

21. *The Times*, 28 January 1848.

22. *The Times,* 3 November 1848.

23. 1848 *Disinfecting fluids and metropolitan sewers. Copies of orders issued by the Commissioners of Sewers of the Metropolis, and of correspondence in relation to experiments on disinfecting fluids.*

24. 'Much of the accumulation in these Sewers is caused by their being made receptacles for the dust and refuse of the houses in their vicinity. The practice is caused in a great measure – First, by the want of dust-bins – Secondly by the refusal of the dustmen to remove the dust and rubbish unless paid for so doing.' *Metropolitan Commission of Sewers, Report on Flushing Sewers*, 10 October 1848.

25. *The Times*, 28 January 1848.

26. 1850 *Metropolitan Commission of Sewers. Account in abstract.*

27. Commissioners for Paving and Improving the Parish of St James, 2 July 1849, STA/A/2/6/2278b.

28. *The Times*, 24 October 1849.

29. 'In London [in 1832], the attacks were 14,144 and the deaths 6,729; the population of London then being 1,681,641 ... In 1848/9 the attacks were about 30,000, and the deaths 14,601; the population at that time being 2,206,076.' *Morning Post*, 21 September 1850.

30. *The Times*, 14 September 1849; *Daily News*, 12 October 1849.

31. *The Times*, 2 July 1849.

32. William Haywood, letter to J. Newlands, 22 October 1850, CLA/006/AD/08/009.

33. 1850 *Report of the General Board of Health on the Supply of Water to the Metropolis*, p. 26.

34. Ibid., p. 306.

35. Dr John Snow had recently printed *On the Mode of Communication of Cholera*, in September 1849 (which would be republished in expanded form in 1855), suggesting polluted water as the delivery mechanism.

36. Finer, *Life and Times, op. cit.*, p. 404.

37. [Richard H. Horne], 'A Time for all Things', *Household Words*, 22 March 1851, p. 617.

38. [Henry Morley], 'Our Last Parochial War', *Household Words*, 21 May 1853, p. 266.

39. *The Times*, 11 July 1854.

40. See *The Times*, 8 May 1847; *Daily News*, 17 February 1852; *The Times*, 16 February 1853.

41. 1837 *Royal Commission on Municipal Corporations*; 1854 *Royal Commission on the Corporation of the City of London.*

42. *Report of the Committee of the Vestry of St Marylebone on the Sanitary Condition of the Parish*, November 1847, p. 8.

43. Hansard, House of Commons, 6 July 1854, cols 1303–1304.

44. Edwin Chadwick, *On the Requisite Attributions of a Minister of Health*, London, 1878, p. 25.

45. *Illustrated London News*, 17 May 1851.

46. Benjamin Ward Richardson, *The Health of Nations*, London: Longmans, 1887, Vol.II, p. 197.

47. 1848 *Metropolitan Commission of Sewers: Report on Tubular House Drains, Laid Down at Peckham, Surrey*, 21 October 1848.

48. 'In my district it is becoming a rare chance to discover one.' Lionel Beale, Medical Officer of Health of St Martin-in-the-Fields, *The Times*, 18 May 1859.

49. Cesspools under houses also had to be built airtight; and privies 'screened and fenced from public view': Metropolitan Buildings Act 1844, Sched. H.

50. 1855 An Act for the better Local Management of the Metropolis, 18 & 19 Victoria, c.120, s.81.

51. 1872 *Return from the Metropolitan Board of Works, of copy of all replies received from the vestries and district boards of the Metropolis to their circular letter of 1st August 1870, asking for information of works of sanitary and street improvements in the several districts since the passing of the Metropolis Local Management Act, 1855.*

52. Anon., *Sanitary Reform and Sanitary Reformers*, London: Edward Stanford, 1855, p. 80.

53. William Haywood, letter to William Tite, 25 October 1850, CLA/006/AD/08/009.

54. Maxwell Fraser, 'Sir Benjamin Hall and the Administration of London', *Transactions of the Honourable Society of Cymmrodorion,* pt 1 (1963), p. 78.

55. *Illustrated London News,* 9 September 1854.

56. 1855 *General Board of Health. Letter of the President of the General Board of Health to the Right Honourable The Viscount Palmerston, Secretary of State for the home Department &c. &c. accompanying a report from Dr Sutherland on Epidemic Cholera in the Metropolis in 1854.*

57. *Illustrated London News,* 9 September 1854.

58. 1855 *General Board of Health. Letter of the President . . .,* p. 15.

59. *The Times,* 26 June 1858.

60. *The Times,* 17 August 1857.

61. 'The Silver Thames', *Saturday Review,* 19 June 1858, p. 631.

62. *Examiner,* 26 June 1858.

63. *Illustrated London News,* 3 July 1858.

64. *The Times,* 21 July 1858.

65. *The Lancet,* 31 March 1860.

66. Bazalgette was largely vindicated, although he agreed to forgo the commission. See Stephen Halliday, *The Great Stink of London,* Stroud: Sutton Publishing, 1999, p. 91.

67. Jasper Rogers, *Facts and Fallacies of the Sewerage System of London and Other Large Towns,* London: Atchley & Co., 1858, p. 13.

68. Halliday, *The Great Stink of London,* p. 93.

69. *The Times,* 5 April 1865.

70. 1867 *Public Health. Ninth report of the Medical Officer of the Privy Council.*

71. Lord Frederick Spencer Hamilton, *My Yesterdays,* London: Hodder & Stoughton, 1930, p.10.

72. David F. Schloss, 'Homes of the London Poor', *Time,* July 1885, p. 22.

73. *Builder,* 23 December 1871.

74. Janet Roebuck, *Urban Development in 19th-Century London,* London: Phillimore, 1979, p. 93.

75. John Hollingshead, *Underground London,* London: Groombridge & Sons, 1862, p. 58.

76. We learn from Mayhew that sewermen, at least in the mid-century, generally disdained the Davy lamp – the safety lamp, used by miners, which would not ignite gas in the atmosphere – as not giving sufficient light.

77. See 1858 *Report from the Select Committee on the River Thames.* I am grateful to Dr D.M. Collins, Parliament's Estates Archivist and Historian, for confirmation of the pipe's survival.

78. *The Times,* 6 September, 1878.

79. *Standard,* 25 November 1878.

80. *Daily News,* 19 August 1881.

81. *The Times,* 13 October 1888.

82. *Daily News,* 10 February 1898.

83. [London County Council], *The London County Council, What it is,* 1895, pp. 13–14 [LSE Pamphlet http://www.jstor.org/stable/60225409].

5 Vile Bodies

1. 1842 *Report from the Select Committee on Improvement of Health of Towns . . . Effect of Interment of Bodies in Towns,* p. 60.

2. 'Nonconformists' and 'Dissenters', catch-all terms for those outside the established Church, i.e. not members of the Church of England.

3. The former situated off Church Street, near Islington Green; the latter off Deverell Street, New Kent Road. See Isabella M. Holmes, *London Burial Grounds,* London: T. Fisher Unwin, 1897.

4. The ground now forms part of the churchyard around Old St Pancras Church, behind St Pancras Station.

5. The decomposing body produces a mix of gases, 'hydrogen sulfide, carbon dioxide, methane, ammonia, sulfur dioxide and hydrogen' (Arpad A. Vass 'Beyond the Grave – Understanding Human Decomposition', *Microbiology Today*, Vol. 28, November 2001), capable of inducing asphyxia in a confined space; not poisoning large populations.

6. John Evelyn, *Silva, or a Discourse of Forest Trees*, London: Todd, 1786, p. 32.

7. Adam Clarke, *Commentary on the New Testament*, Vol. I, London: Butterworth, 1817; Luke 7:12.

8. Carden was born in 1798. According to his letter to Health of Towns Association, quoted in the *Court Magazine and Monthly Critic*, 1 October 1847, p. 16, he first visited Père Lachaise in 1818.

9. 'Cemetery of Père la Chaise', *The Mirror of Literature, Amusement and Instruction*, 8 January 1825.

10. Carden mentions studying under famous medical men in Edinburgh between 1822 and 1824, in an open letter to the people of Stirlingshire written as part of his parliamentary candidacy. *Derby Mercury*, 21 February 1855.

11. 'The General Cemetery Company', *Royal Lady's Magazine*, 1832, p. 100.

12. Quotes from an undertaker's bill, 1836, in Dion Clayton Calthrop, *I Will be Good!* London: Little Brown, 1929.

13. 'Economic Funeral Society', *London Magazine and Review*, June 1825, p. 240.

14. *General Burial Grounds Association Prospectus*, 1825, p. 1.

15. *General Cemetery Company Prospectus*, 1830, p. 12.

16. 'The General Cemetery Company', *Royal Lady's Magazine*, p. 100.

17. Ibid.

18. The small Low Hill Necropolis opened in early 1825; the much larger St James's Cemetery was built in 1825–29.

19. 'The General Cemetery Company', *Royal Lady's Magazine,* p. 103.

20. 'The Life, Death, Burial, and Resurrection Company', in *The Spirit of the Public Journals for the Year M.DCC.XXV*, London: Sherwood, Gilbert and Piper, 1826, p. 108.

21. *John Bull,* 9 May 1825.

22. 'The General Cemetery Company', *Royal Lady's Magazine*, 1832, p. 101.

23. 'The Pyramid' – letter from Willson, *Standard*, 26 November 1829.

24. 'London Churchyards', *Westminster Review*, August 1843, p. 180.

25. 'Libel', *Morning Post,* 20 February 1832.

26. There are scant records for 1825, but some of these men may have been involved in the earlier venture. The 1842 Annual Report of the GCC notes: 'In the year 1824 the Projectors of the GCC found the parochial places of burial in a state most offensive to public decency . . .' implying that there was some continuity between the earlier and the later schemes, above and beyond Carden's involvement.

27. Hansard, House of Commons, 13 May 1830.

28. Reported in the *Standard*, 6 July 1830.

29. R. Richardson and J.S. Curl, 'George Frederick Carden and the Genesis of the General Cemetery Company', in J.S. Curl (ed.), *Kensal Green Cemetery,* Chichester: Phillimore, 2001, p. 33.

30. *The Times*, 13 July 1831.

31. 'An Enemy's Charge', *Household Words*, 20 October 1855, p. 267.

32. *Morning Chronicle*, 28 August 1832 [?].

33. *Morning Post*, 20 February 1832.

34. Radical MP Joseph Hume would briefly moot the idea in the House of Commons in 1833 and 1834 of banning urban burial – but did not take the idea any further. *Morning Chronicle*, 27 February 1834.

35. 'City Board of Health', *Morning Chronicle*, 19 September 1849.

36. J.S. Curl, 'The General Cemetery from 1833 to 1842', in Curl (ed.), *Kensal Green Cemetery,* p. 101.

37. Letter to Health of Towns Association, quoted in the *Court Magazine and Monthly Critic*, 1 October 1847, p. 16.

38. *Court and Lady's Magazine, Monthly Critic and Museum* (March 1842), pp. 261–263. This magazine was owned by Carden and frequently sang his praises. For a reference to Carden's ownership, see 'SINGULAR CASE', *Morning Post*, 27 August 1852.

39. *Lloyd's Weekly London Newspaper*, 9 October 1853.

40. *Daily News*, 1 April 1859. On his death in 1875, Carden also held soon-to-expire leases on eleven properties in Pentonville, Lambeth and Brixton.

41. 'The fees for interment in the suburban burial ground in the Bayswater-road belonging to their own parish were 15s. . . . the fees for interment at the more distant cemetery are 30s. for each burial.' Chadwick, *Supplementary Report on the Results of a Special Inquiry into the Practice of Interment in Towns*, 1843, p. 103. Undertakers also charged more for burials at distant suburban cemeteries due to 'the number of men taken out, whose whole day is occupied'.

42. *Fireside Magazine*, Vol.1 (1819), p. 418.

43. *Morning Post*, 10 March and 9 May 1834.

44. Information on housing generously supplied by Dave Walker, Kensington Archives. The site was previously considered as the location for a county lunatic asylum.

45. The precise date is not clear, but George Walker, speaking in 1847, would note that he had lived 'in the parish . . . in the neighbourhood of Drury Lane' for thirteen years. *Leicester Chronicle*, 25 December 1847.

46. The ancient custom of building cemeteries beyond the city walls led to sites outside the metropolis being dubbed 'extramural' by Walker and others; sites within the city, likewise, whether churchyards or private burial grounds, 'intramural'.

47. G.A. Walker, *Gatherings from Graveyards*, London: Longman, 1839, p. 94.

48. Walker and Carden certainly met on at least one occasion. Carden attended a public meeting organised by Walker in 1847. His self-importance and repeated interruptions intensely riled Walker's supporters. *Standard*, 16 September 1847.

49. Walker, *Gatherings*, p. 8.

50. Ibid., p. 156.

51. G.A. Walker, *Burial Ground Incendiarism*, London: Longman, 1846, p. 3.

52. Malaria, lit. 'bad air', in this period a synonym for miasma.

53. Walker, *Burial Ground*, p. 6.

54. 1842 *Report from the Select Committee on Improvement of Health of Towns . . . Effect of Interment of Bodies in Towns*, p. 71.

55. Ibid., p. 60.

56. 'Marylebone Vestry – The Health of Towns Bill', *Morning Chronicle*, 12 June 1843.

57. '*Health of Towns': An Examination of the Report and Evidence of the Select Committee*, London: John Snow, 1843, p. 111.

58. Hansard, House of Commons, 8 April 1845

59. *Monthly Magazine, or, British Register*, April 1803, p. 213.

60. *Morning Post*, 22 December 1843.

61. *The Times*, 26 February 1845.

62. *The Times*, 5 March 1845.

63. G.A. Walker, *The Second of a Series of Lectures delivered at the Mechanics' Institution, Southampton Buildings, Chancery Lane, Jan. 22 1847, on the actual condition of the Metropolitan Graveyards*, London: Longman, 1847, p. 27.

64. *Standard*, 16 April 1846.

65. 'Poison Gas Works', *Punch*, 25 April 1846.

66. *Lloyd's Weekly London Newspaper*, 5 November 1843.

67. Showing respect was an expensive business. In a bill from 15 January 1835 for St James Clerkenwell preserved at the Museum of London – coming to £2 4s. in total – the tolling of the church bell costs 10s., nearly a quarter of the overall cost of the funeral (ITEM 93.160/19).

68. Edwin Chadwick, *Supplementary Report on the Results of a Special Inquiry into the Practice of Interment in Towns*, 1843, p. 46.

69. *Morning Chronicle*, 24 September 1850, cited in Michael Henderson, et al., *'He Being Dead Yet Speaketh'*, MOLA Monograph 64, Museum of London Archaeology, 2013, p. 58.

70. *Poor Man's Guardian*, No.5, 4 December 1847.

71. *Examiner*, 11 December 1847.

72. *Era*, 5 March 1848.

73. Ibid.

74. 'The Vampyre', *Punch*, 4 October 1847.

75. *Daily News*, 17 October 1849.

76. *The Times*, 28 September 1849.

77. *Daily News*, 28 June 1850.

78. William Cunningham Glen, *The Metropolitan Interments Act, 1858*, London: Shaw, 1850, Introduction, p. 4.

79. The Bishop of London, addressing the Mackinnon inquiry in 1842, noted: 'I consider it improper, perhaps I can say nothing more than it is a matter of feeling.'

80. The initial estimate for buying up 'the magnificent seven' was a quarter of a million pounds. Finer, *Life and Times*, p. 397.

81. J.S. Curl, *The Victorian Celebration of Death*, Newton Abbot: David & Charles, 1972, p. 126.

82. *Morning Chronicle*, 9 June 1855.

83. *Morning Post*, 22 June 1855.

84. *Morning Post*, 16 October 1856.

85. *Morning Chronicle*, 19 November 1858.

86. J. Stevenson Bushnan, *Cholera and its Cures*, London: Orr & Co., 1850, p. 122.

87. *Lloyd's Weekly London Newspaper*, 9 September 1855.

88. Henderson et al., *'He Being Dead Yet Speaketh'*, p. 277. e.g. Sheen's Ground, the Ebenezer Chapel and the Gibraltar Chapel all charged 8s. in 1840. The new cemetery at St Pancras would have first-, second- and third-class graves, prices at £1 11s. 6d.; £1; and 12s. respectively (*Standard*, 4 September 1855).

89. 'An Old Printer,' *A Few Personal Recollections*, London (Printed for Private Circulation), 1896, p. 27.

90. First suggested by Mr J.R. Croft in the *Mechanics' Magazine*, 1837, according to J.C. Loudon, *Gardener's Magazine*, 1843, p. 299.

91. James Greenwood, *The Mysteries of Modern London*, London: Diprose & Bateman, 1883, p. 73.

92. Pam Fisher, 'Houses for the Dead', *London Journal*, 34 (1) (2009), p. 10.

93. *Daily News*, 20 October 1855; *Morning Chronicle*, 19 April 1856.

94. *The Times*, 8 October 1859.

95. A charity, established by Lord Brabazon in 1882.

96. *Birmingham Daily Post*, 26 September 1888.

6 The Great Unwashed

1. The phrase appears in the 'dedicatory epistle' to Edward Bulwer-Lytton's *Paul Clifford* in 1830 and its origin is often ascribed to the author. In fact, it can be found a little earlier elsewhere: 'Departure of London Anglesey', *Morning Post*, 22 January 1829, which reprints a piece from the *Dublin Mail*.

2. 1844 *First Report of the Commissioners for inquiring into the State of Large Towns and Populous Districts*, p. 397.

3. The use of stale urine or 'wash', alluded to by the Bishop of London when advocating public washhouses in 1844. *See* Edward H. Gibson III, 'Baths and Washhouses in the English Public Health Agitation', *Journal of the History of Medicine and Allied Sciences* (1954), p. 398. Soap cost 6s. 8d. per lb. in the early 1800s.

4. 1842 *Report to Her Majesty's Principal Secretary of State for the Home Department from the Poor Law Commissioners on an inquiry into the Sanitary Condition of the Labouring Population of Great Britain,* p. 64.

5. *The Times,* 23 October 1844.

6. 1844 *First Report of the Commissioners for inquiring into the State of Large Towns and Populous Districts,* p. 222.

7. Mayhew, 'Letter III', *Morning Chronicle,* 26 October 1849.

8. *The Times,* 16 December 1853.

9. Letter by E.A. Webb, *City Press,* 29 March 1890.

10. Endorsement within an advertisement for Bradford's Patent Washing Machines, 1879.

11. 'Special Commission on the Spread of Disease through Laundries', *The Lancet,* 18 August 1877, pp. 249–251.

12. 'Income and Management: III', *Cassell's Household Guide,* London: Cassell & Co., *c.* 1879, Vol. I, p. 78.

13. John Fisher Murray, 'Physiology of London Life', *Bentley's Miscellany,* 1 January 1844.

14. *Northern Journal of Medicine,* Vol. 4 (1846), p. 174.

15. There is no fixed date for the advent of the bathroom, but they became increasingly common from the 1870s. For example, the best 'Class 1' houses on the 'Model' Shaftesbury Park Estate, Battersea, built in that decade, contained a first floor with 'three bed-rooms and a little bath-room'. Other grades of house on the estate did not.

16. *Court and Lady's Magazine, Monthly Critic and Museum,* December 1842, p. 96.

17. Thomas Carlyle, Letters: to John A. Carlyle, 22 July 1834; to Jane Welsh Carlyle, 11 July 1843. Carlyle Letters Online http://carlyleletters.dukejournals.org/

18. Letter to Henry Austin, re Tavistock House, 14 October 1851. Jenny Hartley, *The Selected Letters of Charles Dickens,* Oxford: Oxford University Press, 2012, p.238

19. [Richard Carlile], *The Moralist* [*c.*1823], p. 82.

20. 'Personal Cleanliness', *Livesey's Moral Reformer,* May 1838, p. 113.

21. 1848 *Report on the capabilities of the metropolitan workhouses for the reception and treatment of cholera,* p. 52.

22. Thomas Wright, *The Great Unwashed,* London: Tinsley Brothers, 1868, p. 8.

23. *Oldbaileyonline.org* WILLIAM SMITH, Killing > manslaughter, 18th September 1837.

24. William Buchan MD, *Treatise on the Prevention and Cure of Diseases,* 8th edn, London: A. Strahan, T. Cadell, 1784, p. 111.

25. *Literary Register,* 1828, p. 212.

26. 'Anyone who travels by Clapham Junction may witness the use of certain clay pits for the purposes of ablution . . .' 'Metropolitan Swimming Places', *Bell's Life in London,* 8 August 1874, p. 6.

27. Francis Wey, an 1850s' French tourist, describes a memorable incident at Brighton where, 'doing as the Romans do', he took a nude dip in the sea, only to be confronted upon his exit by three disapproving ladies patrolling the beach to discourage Sabbath-breaking: 'I rose slowly, like Venus, from the waves. Striving to adopt a bearing both modest and unconcerned, reminiscent of the lost traditions of innocence of a younger world.' Francis Wey (trans. Valerie Pirie), *A Frenchman Sees the English in the 'Fifties,* London: Sidgwick & Jackson, 1935, p. 297.

28. *Literary Gazette,* 1824, p. 571.

29. 'The poorer class bathe in the canal from Limehouse to Bromley at their peril, being sometimes taken into custody for it.' 1833 *Report from the Select Committee on Public Walks,* p. 19.

30. R.E. Dudgeon, *The Swimming Baths of London,* London: Henry Turner & Co., 1870.

31. Letter to *The Times,* 30 July 1844.

32. Letter to *The Times,* 14 September 1843.

33. *Penny Satirist,* 26 August 1837.

34. 1840 *Report from the Select Committee on the Health of Towns*, pp. 183–185.

35. See 'Kitty Wilkinson – a civic myth?' *http://www.bathsandwashhouses.co.uk/archive/about/kitty-wilkinson*

36. *The Mirror of literature, amusement, and instruction*, 18 July 1840. Unfortunately, I have found no further references to this scheme.

37. 1835 6 Will. IV.–Sess. 1835. A bill to facilitate the formation and establishment of public walks, play grounds, baths and places of healthy recreation and amusement in the open air.

38. *The Times*, 18 October 1844.

39. *The Times*, 21 December 1844.

40. *The Times*, 23 October 1844.

41. Relations between the two organisations are confused, variously described as separate, related or synonymous by contemporary and latter-day sources. See Gibson, 'Baths and Washhouses', p. 402.

42. 'The Free Baths and Wash-houses at East Smithfield', *Chambers's Edinburgh Journal*, 14 August 1847, p. 103.

43. *The Times*, 11 December 1845.

44. Hansard, House of Lords, 29 June 1847.

45. Hansard, House of Commons, 22 July 1846.

46. Hansard, House of Lords, 26 July 1846.

47. Alfred Ebsworth, 1853 *Facts and Inferences Drawn from an Inspection of the Public Baths and Washhouses in the Metropolis* (London: William Brickhill, 1853), pp. 5–6, cited by Joseph R. Skoski, *Public Baths and Washhouses in Victorian Britain, 1842–1914*, Bloomington, IN: Indiana University Press, 2000, p. 95.

48. Committee for Promoting the Establishment of Baths and Washhouses for the Labouring Classes, *Public Baths and Washhouses: Suggestions for Building and Fitting Up Parochial or Borough Establishments*, London: Rivington & Co., 1850, p. 5.

49. Dudgeon, *Swimming Baths*. See Dudgeon's reviews of baths, *passim*.

50. Christopher Love, *A Social History of Swimming in England, 1800–1918*, London: Routledge, 2008, p. 20.

51. *Daily News*, 28 May 1847.

52. *London Quarterly Review*, October 1856, p. 195.

53. Dudgeon, *Swimming Baths*.

54. Posters from the Goulston Square model baths, quoted by Skoski, *Public Baths*.

55. Ebsworth, *Facts and Inferences*, p. 15.

56. Ibid., p. 8.

57. *A Manual Compiled under the Sanction of the London Swimming Club*, London: Leverell, 1861, p. 40.

58. Minutes of the Baths and Washhouses Committee, St George, Hanover Square, Special Report of the Commissioners for Public Baths and Washhouses, 16 June 1887.

59. *Illustrated London News*, 17 July 1875.

60. A similar venture, attempted in the early 1890s, near Somerset House, was outlawed as an 'eyesore' by the London County Council in 1892.

61. *Daily Mail*, 5 August 1898.

62. Mayor's Committee, New York City, 'The Administration of Foreign Baths', *Report on Public Baths and Comfort Stations*, 1897, p. 126.

63. St John Hackney, Minutes of the Commissioners of Baths and Washhouses, Preliminary Report, 23 March 1891.

64. Robert Owen Allsop, *Public Baths and Wash-Houses*, London: E. & F.N. Spon, 1894, p. 84.

65. A. Hessell Tiltman, 'Public Baths and Washhouses.' Paper read before the Royal Institute of Public Health, Blackpool, 26 September 1899, p. 4.

66. Paddington Commissioners of Baths and Washhouses, Minutes, Report of Sub-Committee on St Pancras Baths, read 31 July 1872.

7 The Public Convenience

1. The original structure could contain 64 men and 64 women in separate communal chambers. After the Great Fire, the toilet section was reduced to twelve seats. *See* P.E. Jones, 'Whittington's Longhouse', *London Topographical Record*, 23 (1974), pp. 27–34.

2. *The Times*, 6 May 1844.

3. Vestry of St Andrew and St George Holborn Paving, Cleansing and Lighting Committee, P/AH/PA/1/13, 15 March 1830.

4. Ibid., 5 November 1832.

5. Minutes of the Paving Board of the Brewer's Estate, P/PN1/PA3/M/1, 9 July 1818.

6. Charles Ellerman, *Sanitary Reform and Agricultural Improvement*, London: Peirce & Hyde, 1848, p. 71.

7. 'On Human Exuviae and Soil-Holes', *Farmer's Magazine*, December 1809, pp. 497–501.

8. Report on Public Waiting Rooms, RSA Council Minutes, 27 April 1853.

9. Erika Rappaport, *Shopping for Pleasure*, Princeton, NJ: Princeton University Press, 2000, p. 82.

10. 'To obtain this much-needed accommodation, some ladies go to restaurants and order refreshments which they do not require, and others to milliners' and confectioners' shops.' James Stevenson, *Report on the Necessity of Latrine Accommodation for Women in the Metropolis*, 1879.

11. GLAUCUS, *Farmer's Magazine*, August 1809, pp. 314–331.

12. '[O]ne was experimentally erected about the year 1830 in the Poultry, but I believe that, as communal speculation, as well as in every point of view it proved a failure'. William Haywood, 'Public Urinals', *Report to the Commissioners of Sewers*, 5 March 1850, CLA/006/AD/042.

13. 'Henry Street, the Urinal at the North West Corner of this Street which is of Wood, is very incommodious and a nuisance to the Neighbourhood and should be taken down and a new Urinal of Stone set up in its place and the water carried away by a drain into the sewer.' Vestry of St Andrew and St George Holborn Paving, Cleansing and Lighting Committee P/AH/PA/1/13, 17 May 1830; 'an upright stone on the Northside of the urinal would screen persons using it and that a Stone of this description should be placed there', ibid., 22 August 1831; 'the stone which separates the urinal from Vinegar-yard, is higher than a man', Old Bailey Online, *Robert Patrick Goulding*, 27 November 1854.

14. Haywood, 'Public Urinals'.

15. Petition to Vestry of St George, Hanover Square, 3 November 1857, STG/C/2/9/1020.

16. There were two important court cases that established that, in and of itself, a urinal was not a public nuisance, and that the onus was on complainants to show the nuisance caused in particular locations: *Biddulph* v. *St George's Hanover Square Vestry* (1863); *Vernon* v. *St James, Westminster Vestry* (1879; 1880); with the latter going to the Court of Appeal.

17. *Spectator*, 21 November 1846.

18. [Charles Cochrane], *Sanatory Progress: Being the Fifth Report of the National Philanthropic Association*, London: J. Hatchard & Son, 1850.

19. *Morning Post*, 7 July 1848.

20. [Cochrane], *Sanatory Progress*, p. 93.

21. 1849 *Metropolitan Commission of Sewers. Letter of Mr Bazalgette, C.E., on Establishment of Public Conveniences.*

22. See Finer, *Life and Times*, p. 442.

23. *Sheffield and Rotherham Independent*, 22 February 1851.

24. *The Times*, 6 May 1851.

25. *Official Descriptive and Illustrated Catalogue of the Great Exhibition*, Vol. II, London: Clowes & Sons, 1851, p. 670.

26. *The Times*, 4 and 6 June 1851.

27. *The Times*, 12 July 1851.

28. Intriguingly, an early draft at the RSA also includes 'pastrycooks', but perhaps such establishments were not, on reflection, sufficiently respectable; or perhaps a lady delicately informed the committee that eating-places already tended to offer access to a private WC.

29. *The Times*, 26 May 1851.

30. RSA Council Minutes, 23 June 1852.

31. Henry C. Owen, *Report . . . upon the proceedings of the Waiting-rooms Committee*, RSA Council Minutes, 27 April 1853.

32. *Standard*, 11 December 1855.

33. *Standard*, 15 August 1863.

34. *The Lancet*, 10 May 1856.

35. Report of the Medical Officer of Health, Greenwich, 1898, p. 79.

36. George Bernard Shaw, *Candida*, 1898.

37. William Haywood, in Report of the Works Executed by the Honourable Commissioners of Sewers (1851) pp. 29–33 CLA/006/AD/07/37.

38. The Board of Works for the Saint Giles District, Statement and Account, 1857/1858 BW/GG/AN2.

39. William Haywood, letter to M. Meredith, 5 March 1851, CLA/006/AD/08/009.

40. *The Lancet*, 15 November 1884.

41. *The Times*, 6 November 1867.

42. *Old Bailey Online*, HENRY HARRISON, Theft > extortion, 16th August 1852. http://www.oldbaileyonline.org/browse.jsp?id=t18520816-841&div=t18520816-841

43. William Haywood in Report of the Works Executed by the Honourable Commissioners of Sewers (1851), pp. 29–33, CLA/006/AD/07/37.

44. Medical Officer of Health Annual Report, St James Westminster, 1879, p. 21.

45. *British Medical Journal*, 23 November 1889, p. 1193.

46. Letter to the Sewer Commissioners, 13 December 1858, CLA/006/AD/03/113, pp. 1029–1032.

47. Lawrence Wright, *Clean and Decent*, London: Routledge & Kegan Paul, 1960, p. 200.

48. Ibid., p. 201; see also George B. Davis and Frederick Dye, *A Complete and Practical Treatise upon Plumbing and Sanitation*, London: E. & F. Spon, 1898, pp. 171–172.

49. Jasper W. Rogers, *Facts and Fallacies of the Sewerage System of London and other large towns*, London: Atchley & Co., 1858.

50. Surveyors' Letters 1846–1850, Haywood, 7 May 1850, CLA/006/AD/08/008.

51. Reports of Haywood, 8 May 1855, CLA/006/AD/043.

52. *British Architect*, 8 May 1885, p. 221, quoting report made to Paddington Vestry in May 1885.

53. *Girl's Own Paper*, 14 October 1899.

54. Rose Adams, letter to the Bethnal Green Vestry, 13 December 1878, quoted in *Report on the Sanitary Condition and Vital Statistics of the Parish of Saint Matthew, Bethnal Green, during the year 1878*.

55. A letter suggesting the establishment of public closets was actually put to the MBW in 1874 by the Strand District Board; but nothing came of it.

56. Stevenson, *Report on the Necessity*.

57. City of London Streets Committee Minutes, 22 February 1881, COL/CC/STS/03/004.

58. Minutes of the Commissioners of Sewers, 11 January 1881, p. 8.

59. *Pall Mall Gazette*, 14 May 1884.

60. Letter to Streets Committee, 7 January 1884, COL/CC/STS/03/.

61. Report to the Streets Committee . . . upon the provision of Closet Accommodation for Women, 29 April 1887, COL/CC/STS/03/06.

62. 'The Ladies Lavatory Company', letter in *The Lancet*, 15 November 1884, p. 898.

63. Minutes of the Commissioners of Sewers, 2 August 1883.

64. *British Architect*, 10 July 1885, p. 18.

65. St Margaret and St John, Special and Annual Report, June 1889, p. 255.
66. St James's had already tried to build a 'subterranean latrine' in Great Marlborough Street in 1871. It is not clear whether this included WCs; and whether it failed due to structural problems or local objections. See the *Builder*, 2 December 1871.
67. St James, Westminster, Annual Report, 1889/90, p. 99.
68. *Public Health*, October 1891/September 1892, p. 318.
69. W.T. Stead, *London County Council Election, 1892: the elector's guide, a popular hand-book for the Election 1892*, London: Review of Reviews, 1892, p. 38.
70. *The Times*, 30 August 1892.
71. *The Times*, 24 August 1892.
72. *The Times*, 29 October 1892.
73. '9. Public lavatory accommodation to be provided for both sexes.' London Reform Union, progressive programme for local elections in Tower Hamlets, 'The Vestry Elections,' *Daily News*, 6 May 1898.
74. 'The Unmentionable Case of Women's Suffrage', *The Englishwoman*, February–April 1909, pp. 112–121; I am deeply indebted to Barbara Penner's article of the same name for alerting me to this story (*Journal of Design History*, 14 (1) 2001, pp. 35–51).
75. Davis and Dye, *Complete and Practical Treatise*, pp. 171–172.
76. E.C.S. Moore, *Sanitary Engineering*, London: B.T. Batsford, 1901, p. 430 (with thanks to @CrossnessET Crossness Engines).
77. Barbara Penner, 'Female Urinals: Taking a Stand', *arcade*, room 5, issue 2 (2001), p. 28.

8 Wretched Houses

1. *Poor Man's Guardian*, issue 20, November 1847.
2. George Godwin, *London Shadows*, London: George Routledge & Co., 1854, p. 1.
3. Quoted in J.R. Poynter, *Society and Pauperism*, Toronto: University of Toronto Press, 1969, p. 92.
4. Anne Hardy, 'Urban Famine or Urban Crisis? Typhus in the Victorian City', *Medical History*, 32 (1988), pp. 401–425.
5. 'Indulgence, repletion, satiety, the morbid sensibility and irritability, incident to refinement and luxury, predispose the affluent to infection and a fatal disorder.' C. Stanger, *Remarks on the Necessity and Means of Suppressing Contagious Fever*, London: W. Phillips, 1802, p. 11.
6. *Medical and Physical Journal*, Vol. II, From August to December 1799, p. 411. See also the evidence of Dr Thomas Bateman, physician at the Fever Hospital, 1818 *Report from the Select Committee on Contagious Fever in London*, p. 16.
7. 'So far was infection from spreading about the Manchester fever-house that the adjacent streets, which in eight months previous to its opening, in 1796, furnished two hundred and sixty-seven cases of fever, at the end of the two subsequent months furnished only *twenty-five*; in July 1797 only *five*; in August only *one*; and in September of the same year, *none*.' John Clark, *A Collection of Papers Intended to Promote An Institution for the Cure and Prevention of Infectious Fevers in Newcastle and Other Populous Towns*, Newcastle: S. Hodgson, 1802, p. 46.
8. Stanger, *Remarks*, p. 35.
9. Committee Minutes of the Fever Hospital, 19 April 1801. From the 'Certificate' [statement of intent] drawn up by the 'Physicians of the Hospitals & Dispensaries in London' presented at the inaugural meeting, sponsored by the Society for Bettering the Condition and Increasing the Comforts of the Poor.
10. Ibid., 26 June 1801: 'Resolved that a sub-committee be appointed with authority to direct the white-washing with hot lime those dwellings of the poor in the Metropolis where infection has subsisted that the said Committee do consist of Dr Murray, Mr Bernard and Mr Redit that they be authorized to draw on the Treasurer for a sum not exceeding £20; and that they shall report at every Meeting the number of houses so white-washed and the names of the persons inhabiting them.'

11. The Society for Bettering the Condition and Increasing the Comforts of the Poor, *Three Reports of the Sub-Committee appointed by the Fever Institution, to direct the White-washing with quick Lime of those Dwellings of the Poor, in which Infection has lately subsisted,* Vol. III, London: The Society, 1802.

12. The Fever Hospital would introduce its own covered litter with a washable lining – and be vexed by the habit of curious strangers lifting the covering of the curious 'machine'.

13. But only two landlords. In 1800, according to the rate-collector, Nos 1–16 belonged to a Jonathan Dimsley; Nos 16–20 to a John Duncombe.

14. Committee Minutes of the Fever Hospital, 2 July 1803.

15. Ibid., 24 June 1803.

16. Ibid., 26 April 1805: 'The Inspector to the Fever Institution has had frequent occasion to notice the filthy state of part of Caroline Court and houses adjoining Great Saffron Hill from want of Cleansing, there having been several cases of Fever from thence; these courts are chiefly inhabited by Poor Irish whose Dwellings are generally extremely dirty, besides has had some cases where the offer of lime washing apartments has been refused two lately one in London Lane Smithfield, the other in Monmouth Street.'

17. Minutes of the Paving Committee, St Andrew and St George, Holborn, 4 February 1805.

18. Committee Minutes of the Fever Hospital, 26 September 1806; 22 February 1807.

19. The Society for Bettering the Condition and Increasing the Comforts of the Poor, *Report of the Society,* London: The Society, 1814, p. 220.

20. 1842 *Report from the Select Committee on Improvement of the Health of Towns, together with the minutes of evidence, appendix, and index. Effect of interment of bodies in towns,* p. 35.

21. The Metropolitan Police Courts Act, 1839, s.41.

22. 1842 *Report to Her Majesty's Principal Secretary of State for the Home Department from the Poor Law Commissioners on an inquiry into the Sanitary Condition of the Labouring Population of Great Britain,* pp. 344–346.

23. 1850 *Report of the General Board of Health on the Epidemic Cholera, 1848 & 1849,* p. 86.

24. Geoffrey Finlayson, *The Seventh Earl of Shaftesbury,* London: Methuen, 1981, pp. 281, 284.

25. 1836 *Report from the Select Committee on Metropolis Improvements,* p. 7.

26. George Rogers, *A Letter to Thos. Wakley,* London: J. Pattie, 1837.

27. Geoffrey Tyack, 'James Pennethorne, and London Street Improvements, 1838–1855', *London Journal,* 15 (1990), p. 46.

28. *The Times,* 7 March 1844.

29. *Illustrated London News,* 2 January 1847.

30. *Lady's Newspaper,* 27 November 1847.

31. 'Church Lane, St Giles', *Fraser's Magazine for Town and Country,* March 1848, pp. 257–260.

32. Health of Towns Association, *Abstract of the proceedings of the public meeting held at Exeter Hall, Dec. 11, 1844,* London: C. Knight, 1844.

33. *The Times,* 5 July 1849.

34. *The Times,* 22 October 1849.

35. Ibid.

36. Metropolitan Sanitary Association, *The Public Health: A Public Question, First Report of the Metropolitan Sanitary Association,* London: The Association, p. 21.

37. *Builder,* 17 June 1876.

38. Cottage Improvement Society for North Northumberland, *Second Annual Report of the Committee of the Cottage Improvement Society for North Northumberland,* London: Whittaker, 1843, p. 36ff.

39. *Lloyds Weekly London Newspaper,* 14 July 1844.

40. *Labourer's Friend,* No. 1, New Series (June 1844), pp. 3–4.

41. John Nelson Tarn, *Five Per Cent Philanthropy,* Cambridge: Cambridge University Press, 1973, p. 16.

42. *The Pictorial Handbook of London,* London: Henry G. Bohn, 1854, p. 268.

43. Thomas Southwood Smith, *Results of Sanitary Improvement,* London: Charles Knight and J. Cassell 1854, p. 7.
44. *The Times,* 8 December 1831.
45. *Morning Chronicle,* 26 March 1834.
46. *The Times,* 7 July 1837.
47. *Morning Post,* 26 May 1843.
48. *Morning Chronicle,* 14 September 1849.
49. S.C. Gant, *Notes and Queries on the Public Health Act 1848,* London, 1855, p. vi.
50. *Morning Post,* 1 July 1851.
51. George Godwin, *Town Swamps and Social Bridges,* London: Routledge, 1859, p. 7.
52. Henry Roberts, *The Improvement of the Dwellings of the Labouring Classes,* London: SICLC, 1859, p. 21.
53. *Morning Post,* 30 April 1852.
54. *Builder,* 22 March 1856.
55. *Builder,* 7 February 1857.
56. 'Wild Court, Past and Present', *Ragged School Union Magazine,* Vol. 7 (1855), p. 190.
57. John Hollingshead, *Ragged London in 1861,* London: Smith Elder & Co., 1861, Appendix, p. 273. Statistics show Tyndall's Buildings as the least occupied of SICLC accommodation, with 25 per cent of its family rooms empty.
58. Anthony Wohl, *The Eternal Slum: Housing and Social Policy in Victorian London,* London: Edward Arnold, 1977, p. 147.
59. Ibid., p. 74.
60. John Simon, *Report on the Sanitary Condition of the City of London,* 1850/51, C. Dawson, p. 23.
61. St Giles District Board of Works Annual Statement 1856/57: report, 11 October 1856.
62. St Giles District Board of Works Annual Statement 1856/57: report, 29 March 1856.
63. Over £20 million, in modern money, according to the National Archives currency converter.
64. Thomas Archer, *The Terrible Sights of London,* London: Stanley Rivers & Co., 1870, p. 443.
65. 'Cottage Property in London' in Octavia Hill, *Homes of the London Poor,* London: Macmillan, 1875, p. 1.
66. Rev. Billing to Commissioners for inquiring into the housing of the working classes, in Wohl, *Eternal Slum,* p. 198.
67. Annual Report of the Medical Officer of Health, St Giles, 1870–71 s.65.
68. Wohl, *Eternal Slum,* p. 87.
69. Holborn District Board of Works Board Minutes, 11 April 1870; 18 November 1872; 12 March 1874.
70. Under the 1877 Metropolitan Street Improvements Act.
71. 1882 *Report from the Select Committee on Artizans' and Labourers' Dwellings,* p. 6.
72. David Owen, *The Government of Victorian London,* London: Belknap Press, 1982, p. 113.
73. 1882 *Report from the Select Committee on Artizans' and Labourers' Dwellings,* p. 10.
74. Andrew Mearns, *The Bitter Cry of Outcast London,* London: James Clarke & Co., 1883, pp. 5–8.
75. 1882 *Report from the Select Committee on Artizans' and Labourers' Dwellings,* p. 43.
76. 'Is it not Time?', *Pall Mall Gazette,* 16 October 1883.
77. Sarah Wise, *The Blackest Streets,* London: Vintage, 2009, pp. 263–265.

9 The Veil of Soot

1. *The Times,* 2 January 1855.
2. *The Housemaid, Her Duties and How to Perform Them,* London: Houlston & Sons, 1870, p. 57.
3. *The Times,* 2 January 1855.

4. T. Pridgen Teale, 'How to Keep out the Dust and Let in the Fresh Air', *British Architect*, 1891, p. 256.

5. *Health and healthy homes: how to secure healthy and comfortable houses*, London: Sanitary Engineering and Ventilation Co., 1877, p. 44.

6. *Leicestershire Mercury*, 20 August 1881.

7. 1844 *First report of the Commissioners for inquiring into the State of Large Towns and Populous Districts*, p. 29.

8. 'A Lady', in *Common Sense for Housemaids*, London: Thomas Hatchard, 1853.

9. George Elson, *The Last of the Climbing Boys,* London: J. Long, 1900, p. 50.

10. 'Chimney Sweepers' Climbing Boys', *Literary Panorama,* 1817, p. 635.

11. Contrary to some confused claims earlier in the century, late-Victorian medical studies showed conclusively that the disease only developed in adulthood, not childhood.

12. 1862 *Children's Employment Commission. First Report of the Commissioners*, p. 299.

13. John Hollingshead, *Miscellanies,* London: Tinsley Brothers, 1874, Vol.III, p. 308.

14. J.C. Hudson, 'On Cruelty to Sweeps', *Pamphleteer*, 1822, p. 410.

15. 31 July 1872, Paddington Commissioners of Baths and Washhouses Minutes: Report on Marylebone Baths.

16. *Punch*, 9 January 1858.

17. Lord Frederick Spencer Hamilton, *My Yesterdays*, London: Hodder & Stoughton, 1930, p. 26.

18. Vestry Minutes of St Andrew Holborn and St George the Martyr, 17 December 1817.

19. 4&5 William IV, c.35, An Act for the Better Regulation of Chimney Sweepers and their Apprentices and for the Safer Construction of Chimneys and Flues.

20. 3&4 Vict., c.85, An Act for the Regulation of Chimney Sweepers and Chimneys.

21. Ingesting soot was another hazard in the close confines of a chimney. Henry Mayhew notes in *London Labour and the London Poor* (1851): 'Some sweepers assure me that they have vomited balls of soot.'

22. 38 & 39 Vict., c. 70, Chimney Sweeps Act 1875.

23. *Sunday School Hive*, 1 September 1883.

24. Hansard, House of Commons, 8 June 1819.

25. W. Frend, *Is it Impossible to Free the Atmosphere of London . . . from the Smoke and Deleterious Vapours with which it is hourly impregnated?* London, 1819, p. 1.

26. 1819 [Report of the] *Select Committee on Steam Engines and Furnaces*, p. 10.

27. An Act giving greater facility in the prosecution and abatement of Nuisances arising from furnaces used in the working of steam engines (1821), c.41 ('The Steam Engines Furnaces Act').

28. Hansard, House of Commons, 7 May 1821.

29. 1803 An Act for Paving, Lighting, Watching, and Improving the Town of Bradford; 1806 An Act for Paving, Lighting, Cleansing, and Watching the Burgh of Paisley and Suburbs thereof; 1812 An Act for Better Paving, Lighting, Watching, Cleansing, and otherwise Improving the Town of Birmingham. Similar acts, with anti-smoke clauses, would continue to be passed throughout the 1820s.

30. See Rebecca Jemima Adell, 'Creating Parliamentary Smoke. The Quest for a National Smoke Pollution Law in Nineteenth-Century England', PhD thesis, University of Alberta, Edmonton, 2005, pp. 62 and 65.

31. *Morning Chronicle*, 6 April 1824.

32. H. Heaton, 'Benjamin Gott and the Industrial Revolution in Yorkshire', *Economic History Review,* 3 (1) (January 1931), pp. 45–66.

33. *Leeds Mercury,* 23 October 1824.

34. *John Bull*, 26 September 1825, on south London factories.

35. W. Stanley Jevons, *The Coal Question*, London: Macmillan, 1866, XII.8.

36. J.H. Brazell, *London Weather*, London: HMSO, 1968, p. 102.

37. Max Schlesinger, *Saunterings In and About London*, London: Nathaniel Cooke, 1853, p. 84.

38. *Civil Engineer and Architect's Journal*, November 1841, p. 386.
39. 1842 *Report to Her Majesty's Principal Secretary of State for the Home Department from the Poor Law Commissioners on an inquiry into the Sanitary Condition of the Labouring Population of Great Britain*, pp. 296–297.
40. Molesworth chaired the Manchester Association for the Prevention of Smoke, formed in 1842, and had already petitioned parliament for legislation. He was also Mackinnon's brother-in-law. See E. Ashby and M. Anderson, 'Studies in the Politics of Environmental Protection: The Historical Roots of the British Clean Air Act, 1956', *Interdisciplinary Science Reviews*, 1 (4) (1976), p. 281.
41. Peter Thorsheim, *Inventing Pollution*, Athens, OH: Ohio University Press, 2006, p. 16.
42. 1843 *Report from the Select Committee on Smoke Prevention*, p. 134.
43. *The Times*, 24 July 1845.
44. *The Times*, 2 May 1846.
45. *The Times*, 7 August 1846.
46. *The Times*, 18 September 1846.
47. John Simon, *Report of the Sanitary Condition of the City of London*, 1850, p. 74.
48. *The Times*, 30 April 1852.
49. *The Times*, 9 August 1853.
50. The MP for Southwark, Apsley Pellatt, a glass-maker, secured an initial exemption for glassworks and potteries, on the grounds of the technical difficulties of consuming smoke at the constant high temperatures required for their work; but this was removed by subsequent amending legislation, and the Act's application to steamboats extended along the full length of the Thames.
51. For Broome's letters, see *The Times*, 1 July 1856; 14 July 1856; 25 June 1857.
52. Charles Wye Williams, *Prevention of the Smoke Nuisance*, London: J. Weale, 1856, p. 41.
53. *The Times*, 13 August 1872.
54. 'A Fog in the Streets of London', *Illustrated London News*, 12 January 1867.
55. 'The Royal Academy Exhibition', *Royal Cornwall Gazette*, 27 February 1880.
56. *The Lancet*, 3 January 1874.
57. Walter Noel Hartley, *Air and its relations to Life*, London: Longmans & Co., 1876, p. 69.
58. 'Our London Letter', *Sheffield and Rotherham Independent*, 13 December 1873.
59. *Eastern Post*, 20 December 1873.
60. *Journal of the Society of Arts*, 19 November 1880.
61. 'Retrospect of the Medical Sciences', *Provincial Medical Journal and Retrospect of the Medical Sciences*, 7 (179) (2 March 1844), pp. 439–442.
62. *Spectator*, 2 October 1880.
63. Sir Arthur Helps, *The Claims of Labour: An Essay on the Duties of the Employers to the Employed*, London: William Pickering, 1844, p. 132. Helps was convinced of the gradual 'silent noxiousness' of smoke to growing children.
64.. *The Times*, 13 October 1880.
65. *Punch*, 29 January 1881.
66. 'The Physique of the Boers', *The Lancet*, 10 February 1900.
67. William Delisle Hay, *The Doom of the Great City*, London: Newman & Co., 1880. See also Robert Barr, 'The Doom of London', *Idler*, 1892; Fred Whyte, 'The Four Days' Night', *Pearson's Magazine*, 1903.
68. George Gissing's diary, quoted in Pierre Coustillas, *London and the Life of Literature in Late Victorian England*, Hassocks: Harvester Press, 1978, p. 19.
69. 'Congress of the Sanitary Institute of Great Britain', *The Times*, 27 September 1882.
70. *Mechanics' Magazine, Museum, Register, Journal and Gazette*, 1843, p. 323 [letter from N.N.L.].
71. *The Times*, 13 February 1892.
72. Sara Jeannette Duncan, *An American Girl in London*, London: Chatto & Windus, 1891, p. 30.

73. René Gimpel, *Diary of an Art Dealer*, trans. J. Rosenberg, London: Pimlico, 1992, p. 129, cited in Christine Linda Corton, 'Metaphors of London Fog, Smoke and Mist in Victorian and Edwardian Art and Literature', PhD thesis, University of Kent at Canterbury, 2009, p. 182.
74. Hester Caldwell Oakley, 'Love in a Fog', *McClure's Magazine,* August 1898, p. 332.
75. 'Walter', *My Secret Life,* New York: Grove Press, 1966, Book XI s.2276.

Epilogue

1. Steven Johnson, *The Ghost Map*, London: Penguin, 2006, p. 205, quoting *The Lancet.*
2. Thomas Carlyle, Letters: To Edward Fitzgerald, 19 October 1854 Carlyle Letters Online http://carlyleletters.dukejournals.org/
3. William Haywood, Minute Book. Letter, 22 November 1858. CLA/006/AD/06/044.
4. 1846 *Report from the Select Committee on metropolitan sewage manure,* p.109.
5. 1850 *Report by General Board of Health on Supply of Water to Metropolis*, p. 235.
6. *Morning Post*, 19 November 1846.
7. *Spectator*, 24 March 1855, p. 13.
8. Hansard, House of Commons, 16 March 1855.
9. Clink Street Keeper's Notebook, 3 May 1830. Southwark Archives.
10. 'Old Brown, the streetkeeper, would not see that, and for this reason – when he went in front of that shop, he turned his back whilst the butcher put a rump steak or a couple of mutton chops in his pocket!' *Daily News,* 20 March 1863.
11. '. . . old computers, were among the 450 tonnes of electronics illegally exported to Nigeria, Ghana and Pakistan . . .' Environment Agency Press Release, 6 December 2012.
12. 'UK recycling industry has potential to create 10,000 new jobs, report finds', *Guardian*, 11 June 2013.
13. 'ClientEarth, a group of campaigning lawyers that has brought the case, will say that . . . air pollution from nitrogen dioxide (NO_2) and particulates now kills as many people each year in Britain as obesity and road accidents combined', *Guardian,* 7 March 2013.

BIBLIOGRAPHY

Books, Pamphlets and Journal Articles

'A Lady', *Common Sense for Housemaids*, London: Thomas Hatchard, 1853

Allen, Michelle, *Cleansing the City: Sanitary Geographies in Victorian London*, Athens, OH: Ohio University Press, 2008

'An Old Printer', *A Few Personal Recollections*, London (Printed for Private Circulation), 1896

Anon., 'Ainger's Plan for Preserving the Purity of the Thames', *Mechanics' Magazine* (2 October 1830), pp. 81–85

— *A Manual Compiled under the Sanction of the London Swimming Club*, London: Leverell, 1861

— 'Asphalte', *Journal of the Society of Arts* (17 May 1872), pp. 562–563

— 'Baths and Washhouses', *London Quarterly Review* (October 1856), pp. 182–200

— *Cassell's Household Guide*, London: Cassell & Co., *c.*1879

— 'Church Lane, St Giles', *Fraser's Magazine for Town and Country* (March 1848), pp. 257–260.

— *Dickens' Dictionary of London*, London: E.J. Larby [*c.*1908]

— 'Dust Ho!' *Good Words* (September 1866), pp. 645–648

— 'Economic Funeral Society', *London Magazine and Review* (June 1825), pp. 239–240

— *Engineers and Officials*, London: Edward Stanford, 1856

— 'Gatherings from Grave-Yards', *Westminster Review* (January 1842), pp. 201–216

— 'Growth of a Hospital', *All the Year Round* (10 August 1861), pp. 475–480

— 'Health of Towns': *An examination of the report and evidence of the Select Committee; of Mr Mackinnon's Bill; and of the acts for establishing cemeteries around the metropolis*, London: John Snow, 1843

— 'Improved Sewers or Water-Courses', *Kaleidoscope, or, Literary and Scientific Mirror* (6 September 1825), pp. 76–77

— *International Health Exhibition, London 1884, Guide to the Sanitary and Insanitary Houses*, London: Executive Council of the International Health Exhibition, 1884

— 'London Churchyards', *Westminster Review* (August 1843), pp. 149–182

— 'Metropolitan Atmospheric Pollution', *British Architect* (16 July 1880), p. 25

— 'Metropolitan Improvements', *Westminster Review* (October 1841), pp. 404–435

— 'New Cemetery Project and Cemeteries', *London Magazine and Review* (July 1825), pp. 363–370

— 'On Human Exuviae and Soil-Holes', *Farmer's Magazine* (December 1809), pp. 497–501

— 'Public Baths and Washhouses', *British Architect* (10 February 1899), pp. 102–103

— 'Public Baths and Washhouses', *Sharpe's London Magazine* (19 September 1846), pp. 321–323

— *Reprint of the Report of the Committee appointed to take into consideration Mr Martin's Plan for Rescuing the River Thames from every species of pollution*, 1836

— 'Reports of the Society for bettering the Condition and increasing the Comforts of the Poor', *Monthly Review, or, Literary Journal* (December 1804), pp. 422–425

— 'Reports of the Society for bettering the Condition and increasing the Comforts of the Poor', *New London Review, or, Monthly Report of Authors and Books* (June 1799), pp. 545–553

— 'Results of Poor Laws Commission', *Westminster Review* (April 1833), pp. 427–471

— *Sanitary Reform and Sanitary Reformers*, London: Edward Stanford, 1855

— 'Society for Bettering the Condition of the Poor', *European Magazine and London Review* (March 1805) pp. 203–204

— 'Specification of the Patent granted to Henry Phillips of Penhoe, in the County of Devon, Chemist, and James Bannehr, of Exeter, in the same county, for improvements in the manufacture of manure. Dated October 27, 1859', *Repertory of Patent Inventions* (1 August 1860), pp. 110–111

— 'Sweeping and Dusting', *Bow Bells*, 6 September 1889, p. 224

— 'Thames Water', *Polar Star of Entertainment and Popular Science*, 3 (1830), pp. 49–52

— 'Thames Water Question', *Westminster Review*, 23 (1829), pp. 31–42

— 'The Dirt of London', *Chambers Edinburgh Journal* (24 July 1841), pp. 209–210

— 'The Empire's Capital', *Review of Reviews* (June 1900), p. 594

— 'The Free Baths and Wash-houses at East Smithfield', *Chambers's Edinburgh Journal* (14 August 1847), pp.102–104

— 'The General Cemetery Company', *Royal Lady's Magazine* (1832), pp. 98–103

— *The Housemaid, Her Duties and How to Perform Them*, London: Houlston & Sons, 1870

— 'The Life, Death, Burial, and Resurrection Company', *The Spirit of the Public Journals for the Year M.DCC.XXV*, London: Sherwood, Gilbert and Piper, 1826

— 'The Main Drainage of London', *British Medical Journal*, 23 July 1859

— *The Pictorial Handbook of London*, London: Henry G. Bohn, 1854

— 'The Virtues of Dirt', *Examiner* (13 May 1848), p. 306

— 'To Paul D'Angely, of Paris, in the Republic of France, Gent., for certain improvements in the construction of privies and urinals', *London Journal of Arts, Sciences and Manufactures and Repertory of Patent Inventions* (Vol. 38, 1851), pp. 88–89

— 'Two Cities: London and Peking', *Fortnightly Review* (June 1899), p. 949

— 'Where shall we go?' *Tinsley's Magazine*, 5 (September 1869), p. 207

— 'Wild Court, Past and Present', *Ragged School Union Magazine*, 7 (1855), pp. 190–192

Archer, Thomas, *The Terrible Sights of London*, London: Stanley Rivers & Co., 1870

Ashby, E. and Anderson, M., 'Studies in the Politics of Environmental Protection: The Historical Roots of the British Clean Air Act, 1956', *Interdisciplinary Science Reviews*, 1 (4) (1976), pp. 279–290

Asphitel, Arthur, and Whichcord, John Jr., *Observations on Baths and Wash-Houses*, 3rd edn, London: John Weale, 1852

Bailey, James Blake, *The Diary of a Resurrectionist*, London: Swan Sonnenschein & Co., 1896

Balston, Thomas, *John Martin, 1789–1854. Illustrator and Pamphleteer*, London: The Bibliographical Society, 1934

Bartlett, David W., *London by Day and Night* [London], 1852

Bazalgette, Joseph, *On the Main Drainage of London*, London: William Clowes & Sons, 1865

Beckett-Doyle, Stephen, *Dirt is Essentially Disorder*, 2003 [monograph, Southwark Local History Library]

Bellhouse, E.T., *On Baths and Wash-Houses for the People*, Manchester: Cave and Sever, 1854

Bennett, Alfred Rosling, *London and Londoners in the 1850s and 1860s*, London: T. Fisher Unwin, 1924

Blackie, Alex B., *Wood Pavement: its origins and progress*, London: Sherwood, Gilbert and Piper, 1843

Blashill, T., 'The State of London Streets', *Journal of the Royal Society for the Promotion of Health*, 22 (6) (1901), pp. 6–23

Booth, Charles, *Inquiry into the Life and Labour of the People of London*, Vol. VIII, pt 1, London: Macmillan & Co., 1903

Brazell, John Harold, *London Weather*, London: HMSO, 1968

Brooke, James Williamson, *The Democrats of Marylebone*, London: William Jones Cleaver, 1839

Brown, Glenn, *Water-Closets. A Historical, Mechanical and Sanitary Treatise*, New York: The Industrial Publication Company, 1884

Buchan, William, MD, *Treatise on the Prevention and Cure of Diseases*, 8th edn, London: A. Strahan and T. Cadell, 1784.

Bushnan, J. Stevenson, *Cholera and its Cures*, London: Orr & Co., 1850

Bynum, W.F., 'Hospital, Disease and Community: The London Fever Hospital, 1801–1850', in *Healing and History*, ed. Charles E. Rosenberg, New York: Science History, 1979, pp. 97–113

Calthrop, Dion Clayton, *I Will be Good!* London: Little Brown, 1929

Camden, Charles, 'Filthy Lucre', *Good Words* (January 1879), pp. 738–742

Cape, George A., *Baths and Wash Houses,* London: Simpkin, Marshall & Co., 1854

[Chadwick, Edwin], 'Life Assurances', *Westminster Review* (April 1828), pp. 384–421

Chadwick, Edwin, *On the Requisite Attributions of a Minister of Health*, London, 1878

Cholera Consultation, S. Knight, Sweeting's Alley, 27 Feb. 1832 (Francis A. Countway Library of Medicine; MMC 46) [broadside]

Clark, John, *A Collection of Papers Intended to Promote An Institution for the Cure and Prevention of Infectious Fevers in Newcastle and Other Populous Towns*, Newcastle: S. Hodgson, 1802, p. 46

Clarke, Adam, *Commentary on the New Testament*, Vol. I, London: Butterworth, 1817

Cochrane, Charles, *How to Improve the Homes of the People!*, London: W.S. Johnson,1849

[Cochrane, Charles], *Sanatory Progress: Being the Fifth Report of the National Philanthropic Assocation*, London: J Hatchard & Son, 1850

Coldwell, W., *Imperial Magazine,* 13 (January 1832), pp. 15–17

Committee for Promoting the Establishment of Baths and Wash-Houses for the Labouring Classes, *Public Baths and Wash-Houses. Suggestions for building and fitting up parochial establishments*, London: Rivington & Co., 1850

Committee of Baths and Wash-Houses for the Labouring Classes, *The First General Report of the Committee of Baths and Wash-Houses for the Labouring Classes in the North-West District of the Metropolis,* London: Henry Mitchener, 1848

Committee of Management, *A Plea for the Very Poor, being the First General Report by the Committee of Management of the Leicester-Square Soup-Kitchen, and Mount St Bernard Hospice,* London: James Nisbet, 1850

Cottage Improvement Society for North Northumberland, *Second Annual Report of the Committee of the Cottage Improvement Society for North Northumberland*, London: Whittaker, 1843

Council of the Statistical Society of London, *Report of a Committee of the Council of the Statistical Society of London, consisting of Lieut.-Colonel W.H. Sykes, V.P.R.S., Dr Guy, and F.G.P. Neison, Esq., To Investigate the State of the Inhabitants and their dwellings in Church Lane, St Giles's,* 1848

Curl, James Stevens, 'John Claudius Loudon and the Garden Cemetery Movement', *Garden History*, 11 (2) (Autumn 1983), pp. 133–156

— *Kensal Green Cemetery,* Chichester: Phillimore, 2001

— *The Victorian Celebration of Death*, Newton Abbot: David & Charles, 1972

Davis, George B. and Dye, Frederick, *A Complete and Practical Treatise upon Plumbing and Sanitation*, London: E. & F. Spon, 1898

Derrett, Christopher, 'More Light, More Power: Electricity Generation and Waste Disposal in Shoreditch, 1897–2009', *Hackney History*, 15 (2009), pp. 12–22

Dudgeon, R.E., *The Swimming Baths of London,* London: Henry Turner & Co., 1870

Duncan, Sara Jeannette, *An American Girl in London,* London: Chatto & Windus, 1891

Eassie, William, *Sanitary Arrangements for Dwellings,* London: Smith, Elder & Co., 1874

— 'The Sanitation of Houses, especially in the Matter of Drainage', *British Architect,* (1 October 1875), pp. 180–182

Ellerman, Charles, *Sanitary Reform and Agricultural Improvement,* London: Peirce and Hyde, 1848

Elson, George, *The Last of the Climbing Boys,* London: J. Long, 1900

Este, M.L., *Remarks on Baths, Water, Swimming, Shampooing, heat, hot, cold and vapor baths,* London: Gale Curtis and Fenner, 1812

Evelyn, John, *Silva, or a Discourse of Forest Trees,* London: Todd, 1786

Executive Council of the International Health Exhibition, *The Health Exhibition Literature,* Vol. VII, pt 1, London: William Clowes & Sons, 1884

'Ex-Vestryman', 'The Problem of London', *Chambers's Edinburgh Journal* (March 1899), pp. 225–230

Fabian Society, *The London Vestries: What they are and What they do,* Fabian Tract No. 60, London, 1894

Fardon, Richard, 'Citations Out of Place', *Anthropology Today,* 29 (1) (February 2013), pp. 25–26

Finer, S.E., *The Life and Times of Sir Edwin Chadwick,* London: Methuen, 1952

Finlayson, Geoffrey, *The Seventh Earl of Shaftesbury,* London: Methuen, 1981

Fisher, Pam, 'Houses for the Dead: The Provision of Mortuaries in London, 1843–1889', *London Journal,* 34 (1) (March 2009), pp. 1–15

Flick, Carlos, 'The Movement for Smoke Abatement in 19th-Century Britain', *Technology and Culture,* 21 (1) (January 1980), pp. 29–50

Fraser, Maxwell, 'Sir Benjamin Hall and the Administration of London', *Transactions of the Honourable Society of Cymmrodorion,* pt1 (1963), pp. 70–81

Frend, W., *Is it Impossible to Free the Atmosphere of London . . . from the Smoke and Deleterious Vapours with which it is hourly impregnated?* London, 1819

Galton, Douglas, 'The Exhibition of Smoke Abatement Appliances', *Art Journal* (April 1882), pp. 104–105

Gant, S.C., *Notes and Queries on the Public Health Act 1848,* London, 1855

Gauldie, Enid, *Cruel Habitations: A History of Working-Class Housing, 1780–1918,* London: George Allen & Unwin, 1974

George, Rose, *The Big Necessity,* London: Portobello Books, 2009

Gibson, Edward H. III, 'Baths and Washhouses in the English Public Health Agitation', *Journal of the History of Medicine and Allied Sciences* (1954), pp. 391–406

GLAUCUS, *Farmer's Magazine* (August 1809), pp. 314–331

Glen, William Cunningham, *The Metropolitan Interments Act, 1858,* London: Shaw, 1850

Godwin, George, *London Shadows,* London: George Routledge & Co., 1854

— *Town Swamps and Social Bridges,* London: Routledge, Warne & Routledge, 1859

Gordon, W.J., 'The Cleansing of London', *Leisure Hour* (1889), pp. 601–604; 676–680

— *The Horse World of London,* London: Religious Tract Society, 1893

Green, Hugh, 'How London is Governed', *Public Administration,* 9 (1) (January 1931), pp. 41–48

Greenwood, James, *The Mysteries of Modern London,* London: Diprose and Bateman, 1883

Halliday, Stephen, *The Great Stink of London,* Stroud: Sutton Publishing, 1999

Hamilton, Lord Frederick Spencer, *My Yesterdays,* London: Hodder & Stoughton, 1930

Hamlin, Christopher, 'Edwin Chadwick, "Mutton Medicine," and the Fever Question', *Bulletin of the History of Medicine,* 70 (2) (1996), pp. 233–265

— 'Predisposing Causes and Public Health in Early Nineteenth-Century Medical Thought', *Social History of Medicine,* 5 (1) (1992), pp. 43–70

— 'Providence and Putrefaction: Victorian Sanitarians and the Natural Theology of Health and Disease', *Victorian Studies,* 28 (3) (Spring 1985), pp. 381–411

— *Public Health and Social Justice in the Age of Chadwick, 1800–1854,* Cambridge: Cambridge University Press, 1997

— *A Science of Impurity: Water Analysis in Nineteenth-Century Britain,* Berkeley, CA: University of California Press, 1990

— Christopher and Sheard, Sally, 'Revolutions in Public Health: 1848, and 1998?' *British Medical Journal* (29 August 1998), pp. 587–591

Hanley, James G., 'The Metropolitan Commissioners of Sewers and the Law, 1812–1847', *Urban History,* 33 (3) (2006), pp. 350–368

Hardy, Anne, 'Water and the Search for Public Health in London in the Eighteenth and Nineteenth Centuries', *Medical History,* 28 (1984), pp. 250–282

— 'Urban Famine or Urban Crisis? Typhus in the Victorian City', *Medical History,* 32 (1988), pp. 401–425

Hartley, Walter Noel, *Air and its Relations to Life,* London: Longmans & Co., 1876

Hay, William Delisle, *The Doom of the Great City,* London: Newman & Co., 1880

Health of London Association, *Report of the Health of London Association on the Sanitary Condition of the Metropolis,* London: Chapman, Elcoate & Co., 1847

Health of Towns Association, *Abstract of the proceedings of the public meeting held at Exeter Hall, Dec. 11, 1844,* London: C. Knight, 1844

Heaton, H., 'Benjamin Gott and the Industrial Revolution in Yorkshire', *Economic History Review,* 3 (1) (January 1931), pp. 45–66

Henderson, Michael, et al., *'He Being Dead Yet Speaketh',* MOLA Monograph 64, Museum of London Archaeology, 2013, p. 58

Hessell Tiltman, A., 'Public Baths and Washhouses.' Paper read before the Royal Institute of Public Health, Blackpool, 26 September 1899

Hill, Octavia, *Homes of the London Poor,* London: Macmillan, 1875

Hollingshead, John, *Ragged London in 1861,* London: Smith Elder & Co., 1861

— *Miscellanies,* London: Tinsley Brothers, 1874

— *Underground London,* London: Groombridge & Sons, 1862

Holmes, Isabella M., *London Burial Grounds,* London: T. Fisher Unwin, 1897

[Horne, Richard H.], 'Dust; or Ugliness Redeemed', *Household Words* (13 July 1850), pp. 379–384

— 'A Time for all Things', *Household Words* (22 March 1851), pp. 615–617

Hounsell, Peter, *London's Rubbish: Two Centuries of Dirt, Dust and Disease in the Metropolis,* Stroud: Amberley Publishing, 2013

Jeffries, Nigel, 'The Metropolis Local Management Act and the Archaeology of Sanitary Reform in the London Borough of Lambeth, 1856–86', *Post-Medieval Archaeology,* 40 (1) (2006), pp. 272–290

Jephson, Henry, *The Sanitary Evolution of London,* London: T. Fisher Unwin, 1907

Jevons, W. Stanley, *The Coal Question,* London: Macmillan, 1866

Johnson, Steven, *The Ghost Map,* London: Penguin, 2006

Jones, P. E., 'Whittington's Longhouse', *London Topographical Record,* 23 (1974), pp. 27–34

Knight, Charles, *The Popular History of England,* London: Bradbury and Evans, 1862

Krout, Mary H., *A Looker-On in London,* New York: Dodd, Mead & Co., 1899

Leapman, Michael, *The World for a Shilling: How the Great Exhibition Shaped a Nation,* London: Headline, 2001

Leigh, John Graham, *London's Water Wars: The Competition for London's Water Supply in the Nineteenth Century,* London: Francis Boutle, 2000

Letheby, Henry, 'Chemical Composition of the Mud from the Streets of the City of London', *Supplement to the Chemical News,* 14 June 1867

Lobb, Harry W.M., *Hygiene or the Handbook of Health,* London: Simpkin Marshall & Co., 1855

[London County Council], *The London County Council: What it is,* 1895

Love, Christopher, *A Social History of Swimming in England, 1800–1918,* London: Routledge, 2008

Low, Sampson, *The Charities of London*, London: Sampson Low, 1850

Luckin, Bill, ' "The heart and home of horror": The Great London Fogs of the Late Nineteenth Century', *Social History,* 28 (1) (January 2003), pp. 31–48

MacGillivray, N., 'Dr Latta of Leith', *Journal of the Royal College of Physicians of Edinburgh* (36) 2006, pp. 80–85

Maidment, Brian, *Dusty Bob: A Cultural History of Dustmen*, Manchester: Manchester University Press, 2007

Malcolmson, Patricia E., 'Laundresses and the Laundry Trade in Victorian England', *Victorian Studies*, 24 (4) (Summer 1981), pp. 439–462

Mayhew, Henry, *London Labour and the London Poor,* Vol. II, London: Griffin, Bohn & Co., 1861/62

Mayor of London, *London's Wasted Resource: The Mayor's Municipal Waste Management Strategy, November 2011*, London: Greater London Authority, 2011

Mayor's Committee, New York City, 'The Administration of Foreign Baths', *Report on Public Baths and Comfort Stations*, 1897

Mearns, Andrew, *The Bitter Cry of Outcast London*, London: James Clarke & Co, 1883

Metropolitan Sanitary Association, *The Public Health: A Public Question, First Report of the Metropolitan Sanitary Association,* London: The Association, 1850

Moore, E.C.S., *Sanitary Engineering*, London: B.T. Batsford, 1901

[Morley, Henry], 'An Enemy's Charge', *Household Words* (20 October 1855), pp. 265–270

— 'Our Last Parochial War', *Household Words* (21 May 1853), pp. 265–270

Morley, John, *Death, Heaven and the Victorians,* London: Studio Vista, 1971

Morris, R.J., *Cholera 1832: The Social Response to an Epidemic,* London: Croom Helm, 1976

Murphy, Shirley Foster (ed.), *Our Homes and How to Make Them Healthy,* London: Cassell & Co., 1883

Murray, Hugh, *Where to Go in York: The History of Public Conveniences in the City of York,* York: Voyager, 2000

Newlands, James, *Report on the Establishment and Present Condition of the Public Baths and Wash-Houses in Liverpool,* Liverpool: Hewson and Procter, 1857

Owen, David, *The Government of Victorian London*, Cambridge, MA, and London: Belknap Press, 1982

Paneth, Nigel et al., 'A Rivalry of Foulness: Official and Unofficial Investigations of the London Cholera Epidemic of 1854', *American Journal of Public Health,* 88 (10) (1998), pp. 1545–1553

Parsons, H. and Franklin M.D., *Half a Century of Sanitary Progress, and its Results*, London: Bedford Press, 1899

Pendered, Mary L., *John Martin, Painter, His Life and Times,* London: Hurst and Blackett, 1923

Penner, Barbara, 'Female Urinals: Taking a Stand', *arcade,* room 5 issue 2 (2001), pp. 24–37

— 'A World of Unmentionable Suffering: Women's Public Conveniences in Victorian London', *Journal of Design History,* 14 (1) (2001), pp. 35–51

Pickstone, John V., 'Dearth, Dirt and Fever Epidemics: Rewriting the History of British "Public Health", 1780–1850', in *Epidemics and Ideas: Essays on the Historical Perception of Pestilence,* ed. Terence Ranger and Paul Slack, Cambridge: Cambridge University Press, 1992, pp.125–148

Poynter, J.R., *Society and Pauperism,* Toronto: University of Toronto Press, 1969

Rappaport, Erika Diane, *Shopping for Pleasure: Women in the Making of London's West End,* Princeton, NJ: Princeton University Press, 2000

Rendle, W., *London Vestries and their Sanitary Work,* London: John Churchill & Sons, 1865

Richards, Paul, 'R.A. Slaney, the Industrial Town, and Early Victorian Social Policy', *Social History*, 4 (1) (January 1979), pp. 85–101

Richardson, Benjamin Ward, *The Health of Nations*, London: Longmans, 1887

Richardson, Ruth, *Death, Dissection and the Destitute,* London: Phoenix Press, 2001

Richmond Cotton, W.J., 'The City of London, its Population and Position', *Contemporary Review* (January 1882), pp. 72–87

Rob Roy [pseud.], *Ten Thousand Street Folk and What to do with them*, London: London Reformatory and Refuge Union, 1872

Roberts, Henry, *The Improvement of the Dwellings of the Labouring Classes*, London: SICLC, 1859

Robson, William, *The Government and Misgovernment of London*, London: George Allen & Unwin, 1939

Roebuck, Janet, *Urban Development in 19th-Century London*, London: Phillimore, 1979

Rogers, George, *A Letter to Thos. Wakley*, London: J. Pattie, 1837

Rogers, Jasper W., *Facts and Fallacies of the Sewerage System of London and Other Large Towns*, London: Atchley & Co., 1858

Rooney, David, 'Visualization, Decentralization and Metropolitan Improvement: "light-and-air" and London County Council Photographs, 1899–1908', *Urban History*, 40 (3) (August 2013), pp. 462–482

Russell, Rollo, 'The Reduction of Town Fogs', *Nineteenth Century and After: A Monthly Review* (January 1902), pp. 131–143

[Sala, George], 'The Great Invasion', *Household Words* (April 1852), pp. 69–73

Salus Populi Suprema Lex, S. Knight, London, 1832 [broadside]

Sandwith, Humphry, 'Public Health', *Fortnightly Review* (February 1875), pp. 254–270

Sanitary Engineering and Ventilation Company, *Health and Healthy Homes: How to secure healthy and comfortable houses*, London: The Company, 1877

Schlesinger, Max, *Saunterings In and About London*, London: Nathaniel Cooke, 1853

Schloss, David F., 'Homes of the London Poor', *Time* (July 1885), pp. 18–28

Schneer, Jonathan, *The Thames: England's River*, London: Abacus, 2005

Shaw, George Bernard, 'The Unmentionable Case for Women's Suffrage', *Englishwoman* (February–April 1909), pp. 112–121

Sheard, Sally, 'Profit is a Dirty Word: The Development of Public Baths and Wash-houses in Britain, 1847–1915', *Social History of Medicine*, 13 (1) (2000), pp. 63–68

Simon, John, *English Sanitary Institutions*, London: Cassell & Co., 1890

Sinclair, Sir John, *The Code of Health and Longevity*, 3rd edn, London: B. McMillan, 1816

Skoski, Joseph R., *Public Baths and Washhouses in Victorian Britain, 1842–1914*, Bloomington, IN: Indiana University Press, 2000

Snow, John, *On the Mode of Communication of Cholera*, 2nd edn, London: Churchill, 1855

Society for Bettering the Condition and Increasing the Comforts of the Poor, *Report of the Society*, London: The Society, 1814

— *Reports of the Society*, Vol. III, London: The Society, 1802

— *The Twenty-Fifth Report of the Society*, London: The Society, 1805

— *Three Reports of the Sub-Committee appointed by the Fever Institution, to direct the White-washing with quick Lime of those Dwellings of the Poor, in which Infection has lately subsisted*, Vol. III, London: The Society, 1802

Southwood Smith, Thomas, *Results of Sanitary Improvement*, London: Charles Knight and J. Cassell, 1854

— 'Use of the Dead to the Living', *Westminster Review* (July 1824), pp. 59–97

Spencer, F.H., *Municipal Origins*, London: Constable & Co., 1911

Stanger, C., *Remarks on the Necessity and Means of Suppressing Contagious Fever*, London: W. Phillips, 1802

Stead, W.T., *London County Council Election, 1892: the elector's guide, a popular hand-book for the Election 1892*, London: Review of Reviews, 1892, p. 38

Stevenson, James, *Report on the Necessity of Latrine Accommodation for Women in the Metropolis*, 1879

Stradling, David and Thorsheim, Peter, 'The Smoke of Great Cities: British and American Efforts to Control Air Pollution, 1860–1914', *Environmental History*, 4 (1) (1999), pp. 6–31

Sunderland, David, ' "Disgusting to the imagination and destructive of health"? The Metropolitan Supply of Water, 1820–1852', *Urban History*, 30 (3) (2003), pp. 359–380

— ' "A Monument to defective administration"? The London Commissions of Sewers in the Early Nineteenth Century', *Urban History,* 26 (3) (1999), pp. 349–372

Symon, J.D., 'A Day in the Life of a Scavenger Boy', *English Illustrated Magazine,* (December 1898), pp. 305–307

Tabberner, John Loude, *A Letter to the Right Hon Viscount Morpeth on The Past, The Present and the Probable Future Supply of Water to London,* London: Longman & Co., 1847

Tagg, W. and Glenister, L.O., *London Laws and Byelaws,* London: Frederick Tarrant, 1908

Tanner, Andrea, 'Dust-O! Rubbish in Victorian London, 1860–1900', *London Journal,* 31 (2) (November 2006), pp. 157–178

Tarn, John Nelson, *Five Per Cent Philanthropy: An Account of Housing in Urban Areas between 1840 and 1914,* Cambridge: Cambridge University Press, 1973

'The Casual Observer', 'With a Dirty Boot', *Once a Week* (11 October 1873), pp. 323–326

Thomson, F.M.L., 'Nineteenth-Century Horse Sense', *Economic History Review,* 29 (1) (February 1976), pp. 60–81

Thomson, John, and Smith, Adolphe, *Street Life in London,* London: S. Low, Marston, Searle and Rivington, 1877

Thorsheim, Peter, *Inventing Pollution: Coal, Smoke and Culture in Britain since 1800,* Athens, OH: Ohio University Press, 2006

Trench, Colonel, *A Collection of Papers relating to the Thames Quay,* London: Carpenter & Son, 1827

Trentmann, Frank and Taylor, Vanessa, 'From Users to Consumers: Water Politics in Nineteenth-Century London', in *The Making of the Consumer: Knowledge, Power and Identity in the Modern World,* ed. Frank Trentmann, Oxford: Berg, 2005, pp. 53–79

Turvey, Ralph, 'Horse Traction in Victorian London', *Journal of Transport History,* 26 (2) (September 2005), pp. 38–59

— 'Street Mud, Dust and Noise', *London Journal,* 21 (2) 1996, pp.131–148

Tyack, Geoffrey, 'James Pennethorne, and London Street Improvements, 1838–1855', *London Journal,* 15 (1990), pp. 38–56

Walker, George Alfred, *Gatherings from Graveyards,* London: Longman, 1839

— *Burial Ground Incendiarism,* London: Longman, 1846

— *Interment and Disinterment, or, A further exposition of the practices pursued in the metropolitan places of sepulture,* London: Longman, 1843

— *On the Past and Present State of the Intramural Burying Places,* London: Longman, 1852

— *The Second of a Series of Lectures delivered at the Mechanics' Institution, Southampton Buildings, Chancery Lane, Jan 22 1847, on the actual condition of the Metropolitan Graveyards,* London: Longman, 1847

'Walter', *My Secret Life,* New York: Grove Press, 1966

Ward Richardson, Benjamin, *The Health of Nations,* London: Longmans, Green & Co., 1887

Wey, Francis (trans. Valerie Pirie), *A Frenchman Sees the English in the 'Fifties,* London: Sidgwick & Jackson, 1935

Whitworth, Joseph, *On the Advantages and Economy of Maintaining a High Degree of Cleanliness in Roads and Streets; with an account of the construction and operation of the Street-Sweeping Machine,* London: William Clowes & Sons, 1847

Williams, Charles Wye, *Prevention of the Smoke Nuisance,* London: J. Weale, 1856

Wilson, H.W., 'Will London be Suffocated', *National Review* (June 1901), pp. 598–609

Winter, James, *London's Teeming Streets 1830–1914,* London: Routledge, 1993

Wise, Sarah, *The Blackest Streets,* London: Vintage, 2009

Wohl, Anthony, *Endangered Lives: Public Health in Victorian Britain,* London: Methuen, 1984

— *The Eternal Slum: Housing and Social Policy in Victorian London,* London: Edward Arnold, 1977

[Wright, John], *The Dolphin or Grand Junction Nuisance,* London: T. Butcher, 1827

Wright, Lawrence, *Clean and Decent,* London: Routledge & Kegan Paul, 1960

Young, Ken, 'The Politics of London Government: 1880–1899', *Public Administration,* 51 (1) (March 1973), pp. 91–108

Government Reports

Hansard

1802: *Report from the committee on Dr C. Smyth's petition, respecting his discovery of nitrous fumigation.*

1818 *Report from the Select Committee on Contagious Fever in London*

1819 *Select Committee on Steam Engines and Furnaces*

1823 *Report from the Select Committee on Sewers in the Metropolis.*

1828 *Report from the Select Committee on Anatomy*

1828 *Report of the Commissioners Appointed by His Majesty to inquire into the State of the Supply of Water in the Metropolis*

1828 *Report from the Select Committee on The Supply of Water to The Metropolis*

1830 *Report from the Select Committee appointed to inquire into the general operation and effect of the laws and usages under which select and other vestries are constituted in England and Wales*

1831 *Central Board of Health. Sanitary Hints Respecting Cholera*

1831 *Second Report from the Select Committee on Windsor Castle and Buckingham Palace*

1833 *Report from the Select Committee on Public Walks*

1834 *Report Inquiring into the Administration and Practical Operation of the Poor Laws*

1834 *Report from Select Committee on Metropolis Sewers*

1834 *Report from Select Committee on Metropolis Water*

1836 *Report from the Select Committee on Metropolis Improvements*

1838 *Second Report from Select Committee on Metropolis Improvements*

1838 *Poor Law Amendment Act. Copy of the Report of the Poor Law Commissioners relative to certain charges which have been disallowed by the auditors of unions in England and Wales*

1839 *Fifth Annual Report of the Poor Law Commissioners: with appendices*

1840 *Report from the Select Committee on the Health of Towns*

1840 *Report from the Select Committee of the House of Lords appointed to inquire into the supply of water to the metropolis*

1842 *Report to Her Majesty's Principal Secretary of State for the Home Department from the Poor Law Commissioners on an inquiry into the Sanitary Condition of the Labouring Population of Great Britain*

1842 *Report from the Select Committee on Improvement of the Health of Towns, together with the minutes of evidence, appendix, and index. Effect of interment of bodies in towns*

1843 *Report from the Select Committee on Smoke Prevention*

1843 *Report on the sanitary condition of the labouring population of Great Britain. A supplementary report on the results of a special inquiry into the practice of interment in towns*

1844 *First report of the Commissioners for inquiring into the State of Large Towns and Populous Districts*

1845 *The Second Report of the Commissioners for Inquiring into the State of Large Towns and Populous Districts*

1846 *Smoke Prohibition. Report addressed to Viscount Canning*

1846 *Report from the Select Committee on metropolitan sewage manure*

1847 *Metropolitan Sanitary Commission: First Report*

1847 *Metropolitan Sanitary Commission: Second Report*

1848 *Metropolitan Commission of Sewers: Disinfecting fluids and metropolitan sewers. Copies of orders issued by the Commissioners of Sewers of the Metropolis, and of correspondence in relation to experiments on disinfecting fluids*

1848 *Metropolitan Commission of Sewers: Report of The Surveyors on House Drainage*

1848 *Metropolitan Commission of Sewers: Report on Flushing Sewers*

1848 *Metropolitan Commission of Sewers: Report on Tubular House Drains, Laid Down at Peckham, Surrey*

1848 *Metropolitan Sanitary Commission: Third Report*

1848 *Report on the capabilities of the metropolitan workhouses for the reception and treatment of cholera cases*

1849 *Metropolitan Commission of Sewers. Letter of Mr Bazalgette, C.E., on Establishment of Public Conveniences*

1850 *Report by the General Board of Health on the supply of water to the metropolis*

1850 *Report of the General Board of Health on the Epidemic Cholera, 1848 & 1849*

1850 *Report on a general scheme for extramural sepulture*

1850 *Metropolitan Commission of Sewers: Account in Abstract of Receipt and Expenditure*

1852 *First report of the Commissioners for the Exhibition of 1851, to the Right Hon. Spencer Horatio Walpole, &c. &c. one of Her Majesty's principal secretaries of state*

1852 *General Board of Health. Report on the Sanitary Condition of the Epidemic Districts in the United Parishes of St Giles and St George Bloomsbury*

1855 *General Board of Health. Letter of the President of the General Board of Health to the Right Honourable The Viscount Palmerston, Secretary of State for the Home Department &c. &c. accompanying a report from Dr Sutherland on Epidemic Cholera in the Metropolis in 1854*

1855 *Metropolitan districts paving, &c. Returns relating to the paving, cleansing, and lighting*

1857 *Metropolitan drainage. Return to an order of the Honourable the House of Commons, dated 31 July*

1858 *Report from the Select Committee on the River Thames*

1862 *Children's Employment Commission. First Report of the Commissioners*

1867 *Public health. Ninth report of the Medical Officer of the Privy Council*

1872 *Return from the Metropolitan Board of Works, of copy of all replies received from the vestries and district boards of the Metropolis to their circular letter of 1st August 1870, asking for information of works of sanitary and street improvements in the several districts since the passing of the Metropolis Local Management Act, 1855*

1882 *Report from the Select Committee on Artizans' and Labourers' Dwellings*

1887 *Report from the Select Committee of the House of Lords on the Smoke Nuisance Abatement (Metropolis) Bill*

1893 *Twenty-first annual report of the Local Government Board, 1891–92. Supplement containing the report of the Medical Officer for 1891–92*

1929 *Ministry of Health. Report of an Investigation into the Public Cleansing Service in the Administrative County of London, by J.C. Dawes*

Manuscripts, Archival Material
Camden Local Studies and Archives

— Brewer's Estate. Minutes of the Paving Board. P/PN1/PA3/M/1
— Camden Town. Minutes of the Paving Board. P/PN1/PA5/M/1
— Holborn District Board of Works. Minutes
— St Giles District Board of Works. Annual Reports. BW/GG/AN/1–8
— St Andrew and St George Holborn. Paving, Cleansing and Lighting Committee. Minutes. P/AH/PA/1/1–13
— St Pancras Vestry. Report of a Special Committee on the Sanitary Condition of St Pancras. 10 May 1899

Guildhall Library

[Foster, P. Le Neve], 'Report on the application of science and art to street-paving and street-cleaning of the metropolis', [1873], Guildhall, Fo. Pam. 505

Hackney Archives & Local History

— St John Hackney. Minutes of the Commissioners of Baths and Washhouses

Hammersmith and Fulham Archives and Local History Centre

— Fulham Vestry, Minutes

Institute of Civil Engineers

— Minutes

London Metropolitan Archives

— Bermondsey. Metropolitan Borough of Bermondsey. Souvenir of the Opening of the Electric Lighting and Dust Destructor Works, January 23rd 1902. LMA/4278/01/211
— City of London. William Haywood. Letters CLA/006/AD/08/009
— City of London. William Haywood. Minute Books. CLA/006/AD/06/044
— City of London. William Haywood. Minute Books. 'Public Urinals', *Report to the Commissioners of Sewers*, 5 March 1850. CLA/006/AD/042
— City of London. William Haywood. Report . . . upon the Ventilation of Sewers, 1858. CLA/006/AD/07/040
— City of London. William Haywood. Report on the Accidents to Horses on Carriageway Pavements, 1874. COL/PHD/AD/07/517
— City of London. William Haywood. Report to the Streets Committee . . . upon the provision of Closet Accommodation for Women, 29th April 1887 COL/CC/STS/03/06
— City of London. William Haywood. Surveyor's Letters. CLA/006/AD/08/008
— City of London Board of Health returns. COL/CC/HEB/02/001
— City of London Parish/Ward Reports [1831/32] COL/CC/HEB/02/001-003
— City of London Report from Portsoken Ward, undated [1832] LMA CLC/W/LA/006/MS09959
— City of London. Report of the Works Executed by the Honourable Commissioners of Sewers (1851). CLA/006/AD/07/37
— City of London. Commissioners of Sewers. CLA/006/AD/03/113
— City of London. Streets Committee. Minutes. COL/CC/STS/0101/001-04
— 'Interview of Mr Covington with the Chairman and Directors, 5 August 1884'. ACC/2558/SV/1/573
— John Wright Papers. CLC/520
— London County Council. Minutes
— London County Council. Report on Dust Destructors by the Medical Officer and the Engineer No.100 1893. LCC/CL/PH/1/263
— St Marylebone. Report of the Committee of the Vestry of St Marylebone on the Sanitary Condition of the Parish, 13th November 1847. P89/MRY1/685

Royal Free Hospital Archives

— Committee Minutes of the Fever Hospital

Royal Society of Arts

— Council Minutes

Southwark Local History Library

— Clink Paving, Cleansing and Lighting Committee, Minutes
— Clink Street Keeper's Notebook
— St Giles Camberwell Dust Sub-Committee, Minute Book

Tower Hamlets Local History & Archives

— Mile End Old Town. Annual Reports
— St Matthew Bethnal Green. Annual Reports
— Whitechapel Board of Works. Dust Committee Minute Book, 1892

Thomas Carlyle Letters

— *see* http://carlyleletters.dukejournals.org

University College London

— Edwin Chadwick Collection

Westminster Archives

— Kensington. Paving Lighting and Cleansing Committee. Minutes
— Paddington Commissioners of Baths and Washhouses. Minutes
— St George Hanover Square. Petition to Vestry of St George, Hanover Square, November 3rd 1857. STG/C/2/9/1020
— St George Hanover Square. Minutes of the Baths and Washhouses Committee, St George, Hanover Square. Special Report of the Commissioners for Public Baths and Washhouses 16th June 1887
— St James Westminster. Commissioners for Paving and Improving the Parish of St James. STA/A/2/6/2278b
— St James Westminster. Paving Committee. Minutes. STJ/D/1/16/1966
— St Margaret and St John, Special and Annual Report, June 1889

Medical Officer of Health Reports
Annual reports from:

City of London
Greenwich
Holborn
Mile End Old Town
Paddington
St George Hanover Square
St Giles's
St James Westminster
St Matthew, Bethnal Green
also
London County Council, *Report by the Medical Officer submitting summary of Reports by Dr Young on the collection and disposal of house refuse by London Sanitary Authorities.* Public Health Department, No. 207, 22 October 1894

Periodicals

Aberdeen Weekly Journal
Architect, Engineer and Surveyor
Athenaeum
Bell's Life in London
Bentley's Miscellany

Birmingham Daily Post
Blackwood's Magazine
British Architect
British Medical Journal
Builder
Chambers's Edinburgh Journal
Champion and Weekly Herald
City Press
Civil Engineer and Architect's Journal
Court Magazine and Monthly Critic
Daily Mail
Daily News
Eastern Post
Englishwoman
Era
Examiner
Fireside Magazine
Fortnightly Review
Fraser's Magazine
Fun
Gardener's Magazine
Girl's Own Paper
Graphic
Hearth and Home
Illustrated London News
John Bull
Journal of the Society of Arts
Labourer's Friend
Lady's Newspaper
Lancet
Law Reporter
Leeds Mercury
Leicester Chronicle
Leisure Hour
Literary Panorama
Literary Register
Livesey's Moral Reformer
Lloyd's Weekly London Newspaper
London Gazette
London Medical and Surgical Journal
London Quarterly Review
Mechanic's Magazine
Mirror of Literature, Amusement, and Instruction
Monthly Magazine, or, British Register
Moralist
Morning Chronicle
Morning Post
Northern Journal of Medicine
Pall Mall Gazette
Pamphleteer
Poor Man's Guardian
Provincial Medical Journal and Retrospect of the Medical Sciences
Public Health
Punch

Reynolds's Newspaper
Reynolds's Weekly News
Royal Cornwall Gazette
Saturday Review
Sheffield and Rotherham Independent
Spectator
Standard
Sunday at Home
The Times
Weekly Standard and Express
West Australian
York Herald

Theses

Adell, Rebecca Jemima, 'Creating Parliamentary Smoke: The Quest for a National Smoke Pollution Law in Nineteenth-Century England', PhD, University of Alberta, 2005

Cambridge, Nicholas Anthony, 'The Life and Times of Dr Alfred Carpenter 1825–92', MD, University of London, 2002

Corton, Christine Linda, 'Metaphors of London Fog, Smoke and Mist in Victorian and Edwardian Art and Literature', PhD, University of Kent at Canterbury, 2009

Hepplewhite, Anne, ' "The Public Vocation of Women": Lectures to Ladies on Sanitary Reform in England, 1855–1870', MA, Simon Fraser University, 1996

Hounsell, Peter, 'Brickmaking in West Middlesex from 180', PhD, Thames Valley University, 2000

McCabe, Sarah, 'The Provision of Underground Public Conveniences in London with Reference to Gender Differentials, 1850s–1980s', MA, Institute of Historical Research, University of London, 2012

Smith, Virginia Sarah, 'Cleanliness: Idea and Practice in Britain, 1770–1850', PhD, University of London, 1985

Websites and Databases of Primary Sources

19th Century British Newspapers (Gale Cengage)
19th Century UK Periodicals (Gale Cengage)
British Periodicals (Proquest)
Google Books
House of Commons Parliamentary Papers (Proquest)
Illustrated London News (Gale Cengage)
JSTOR
Lancet (Science Direct)
Old Bailey Online
Periodicals Archive Online (Proquest)
The Making of the Modern World (Gale Cengage)
Times Digital Archive 1785–2007 (Gale Cengage)
Westlaw

ILLUSTRATION ACKNOWLEDGEMENTS

ACKNOWLEDGEMENTS

M Y THANKS TO Heather McCallum at Yale University Press for taking an interest in this project when it was barely a glint in my eye and for her canny editorial wisdom throughout; also, Matthew Wright for making a connection. Much of the research for this book has been carried out via an astonishing range of historical databases, provided by my part-time employer, the London School of Economics. I am very grateful that UK universities provide such facilities for all their staff, whether in teaching or (as in my case) support roles; likewise, for access to LSE Library. I would also like to thank Westminster Archives and the Wellcome Institute for access to their online resources; and acknowledge the generosity of Niall Boyce at *The Lancet*. The print sources for this book have often been particularly obscure, preserved by the hard work and dedication of staff in London's local studies libraries and archives. I would like to thank all at Camden Local Studies and Archives, and the London Metropolitan Archives, where I have engaged in many days' study, as well as the archivists at Tower Hamlets Local History and Archives, and Southwark Local History Library. More particularly, I am grateful for the individual assistance of Stephen Astley at the John Soane Museum; Stefan Dickers at the Bishopsgate Institute; Phoebe Harkins at the Wellcome Institute; Jane Harrison at the Royal Institute; Tabitha Wood at the Science Museum Archives; Victoria Rea, archivist of the Royal Free Hospital; Carol Morgan at the Institute of Civil Engineers; Evelyn Watson at the Royal Society of Arts; Sally England, Hackney Archives; Dave Walker of the Royal Borough of Kensington and Chelsea; and Mark Collins at the Parliamentary Estates Directorate. Writers and scholars have been very generous with access to their published and unpublished research, including Peter Hounsell, Sarah McCabe, Clare Horrocks, Alastair Owens and Nigel Jeffries – with particular thanks to Alastair and Nigel for their abiding interest in cesspools. I would also like to acknowledge the gracious advice of Steve Maughan on Victorian religion, and Nigel Tyrell on rubbish collection in modern London. Friends have been very supportive – not least, the magnificent Paul Elbourne, and the marvellous historians Sarah Wise and Lucy Inglis. I am also grateful to all the people who have taken time to chat with me on Twitter, covering everything from Victorian urine deflectors to the perils of a London fog. A comprehensive list is impossible, but special thanks to Caroline Shenton, Emily Brand, Jane Young, Peter Watts, Judith Flanders, Carlton Reid and Patrick Baty, who provided various invaluable leads for my research (and the anonymous but appreciated staff on the @BL_Ref_Services account). Also, I am much indebted to Julia Lee and Andy Stone for their urinal quest in darkest south-west London, going far beyond the call of duty, or nature.

Finally, as ever, thanks to my Mum and Dad for buying me so many books when I was little; and Joanne and Clara, for living with the unfortunate consequences.

INDEX